A Long, Deep Furrow

A Long, Deep Furrow

THREE CENTURIES OF FARMING IN NEW ENGLAND

Howard S. Russell

ABRIDGED AND WITH A FOREWORD BY
Mark Lapping

 UNIVERSITY PRESS OF NEW ENGLAND
Hanover and London, 1982

HD
1773
.A 2
R 872
1982

Library of Congress Catalogue Card Number 81-51605
International Standard Book Number 0-87451-214-x
Printed in the United States of America

To the farm people of
New England, past and present

Contents

viii   Contents

Illustrations

Foreword

AT THE TIME of its publication in 1976, Howard Russell's *A Long, Deep Furrow* seemed to be something of a long obituary for New England agriculture. The number of farms had declined to less than twenty-five thousand and fewer than six million acres were under active cultivation. Eighty percent of the foodstuffs consumed in New England were imported from other regions and nations. The U.S. Department of Agriculture predicted that further decline was inevitable. But something else was happening in New England, and Russell's volume figured to be right in the middle of things. Spurred on by an awareness of New England's food supply vulnerability (highlighted by the independent trucker's strike of 1978), the need to maintain the region's "working rural landscape," and not a little nostalgia, urban and rural New Englanders renewed their interest in and commitment to agricultural concerns. Without exception the state governments of the region took steps to protect and retain their farmland bases. Policies to enhance the economic viability of agriculture were introduced in the areas of marketing, credit for farmers, transportation of commodities, and research and education. The state agricultural departments were transformed from almost purely regulatory bodies to become aggressive boosters of Yankee farming. Many small and part-time producers moved into the marketplace. And a new generation of agricultural spokespersons—commissioners of agriculture, farmers, teachers, consumers, and others—emerged to lead what future regional historians will record as the farming renaissance in New England.

All of this activity was occasioned and prompted by numerous public forums, assemblies, publications, and debates. Throughout these discussions Russell's book occupied a central role as a storehouse of New England's agricultural tradition. If a spiritual malaise had overcome the region's farming, then Howard Russell was there showing all that a rich and varied past was ours. Many caught his enthusiasm and commitment and thought that New England's farming tradition could be renewed.

A Long, Deep Furrow was immediately seized upon by students and critics alike as nothing short of a masterpiece of regional history. It is a work of erudition and sensitivity, one that rivals the outstanding agricultural histories of Bidwell, Day, and Woodward, other great chroniclers of New England farming. Howard Russell was far too modest a man to include himself in this group. He belongs.

This abridgment of A Long, Deep Furrow will enable new audiences to read and enjoy this classic. This edition retains most of the text, though nearly every chapter has been edited somewhat; the extensive bibliography has been eliminated. The notes remain to provide a guide to further reading.

A Long, Deep Furrow will be of interest to readers and students of New England history and life, agriculture, environmental studies, and rural affairs and development. I know of few books which so successfully integrate the elements of biogeography with socioeconomic and cultural patterns within the context of agriculture as a way of life and livelihood. Most of all, the book is a testament to the Yankees who farm the sides of mountains, take gambles on weather and markets like a pack of riverboat cardsharps, and who consistently fly in the face of the "conventional wisdom" which says there is no New England agriculture!

I wish to personally acknowledge and thank Tom McFarland, Director of the University Press of New England, and David Horne, Director Emeritus of the Press, who encouraged this project. Long before I, they came to love the book and to recognize its singular value. Mrs. Russell's support must also be acknowledged for her permission to allow the abridgment. I hope that she will not be disappointed with the results. My deep appreciation is extended to my wife Joyce and our children who have lived with Howard Russell's words for these past several years. Finally, I note with pleasure and affection a debt that cannot be repaid to my former colleague and "incredible" friend, Carl H. Reidel of the University of Vermont. Carl made us believe that all things were possible.

Jericho, Vermont and   MARK LAPPING
Guelph, Ontario
May 1981

Acknowledgments

I T WOULD BE a delight to thank here by name all who have contributed to the preparation of this book. Their number is legion, for it has been a half-century in the making. Visits to unnumbered farms, markets, and county and state agricultural offices have enriched and broadened personal farming experience. At least two-score reference librarians, of every New England state and elsewhere, have helped; so have numerous correspondents, official and lay, from the most diverse places. Farm people and agricultural officers beyond computation, including the older generations of my own family, have provided information, wit, and wisdom; hired men, and knowledgeable chauffeurs encountered on trips through the English countryside where New England farming had its roots, have had their part, along with published writers and historians, some of whom are recognized by specific citation.

Clearly, an attempt from memory or inadequate files to thank certain individuals by name would be unjust to a host of others, living and departed, whose assistance might chance to be overlooked. This, therefore, is my comprehensive expression of appreciation and gratitude to all who have in any way helped.

Aside from persons, a book of this scope would have been impossible without the resources of Boston's great libraries. The riches of the Athenaeum year after year have generously been made available to me, as has the assistance of its competent staff. Across the street the enormous collections of local and governmental history at the Massachusetts State Library with its helpful corps of workers have been an invaluable resource. Harvard's stacks were used for several years. The specialized collections of the Massachusetts Historical Society, the Massachusetts and the Worcester Horticultural societies, the American Antiquarian Society, Old Sturbridge Village Library, the Essex Institute, and Peabody Museum have all contributed, together with at least twenty state, college, and local libraries and museums, including Boston's great Public Library. My local Wayland library has with cheerful courtesy obtained scarce volumes by interlibrary loan. To all of these, my gratitude.

As with libraries, so with scholars and friends. Especial appreciation, however, goes to Dr. Wayne D. Rasmussen, Executive Secretary of the Agricultural History Society for advice and encouragement; to his associate, David Brewster; to Henry Bailey Stevens, retired Editor and Extension Director Emeritus of the University of New Hampshire; and to Clarence S. Day, historian of Maine's agriculture (whose works, as a dependable resource, have made a more extended Maine bibliography superfluous). All these have read the manuscript and made valuable suggestions. Nor should encouragement from friends now deceased be forgotten, especially that of the late George L. Moore, for thirty years creator of that sparkling, history-rich house organ *Food Marketing in New England*, and James Watson, for some decades editor of the century-old *New England Homestead*.

Beyond all these, if this history is readable, may I pay tribute to the suggestions, patient proofreading, and indexing of Mrs. Russell, Radcliffe honor graduate and former English teacher; to our daughter Constance S. Russell, long in publishing; to my editor, David Horne, for his contributions of wisdom and experience; and to my typist, Mrs. Kathryn Maher, for patient struggles with bad handwriting and frequent revisions.

Finally, may I acknowledge the encouragement of the numberless friends who along the way have helped make of a long, demanding task its own reward.

Wayland, Massachusetts   HOWARD S. RUSSELL
March 1975

Note: Although great care has been taken to verify the many dates that appear in the text and the words "first" and "earliest" have been applied with discretion to invention, discoveries, and new procedures; I make no guaranty, explicit or implied, that such dates and statements are not subject to correction.

I. THE ROOTS

1. New England's First Farmers

L ONG BEFORE any white settler brought the first plow, tillage of New England soil for food was an old story. Archaeological evidence leads to the conclusion that its beginning may well date back a millennium: others place the advent of flint corn, at any rate, as recently as A.D. 1400. Before agriculture was developed, men are believed to have inhabited parts of the New England area perhaps ten thousand years earlier still.[1]

When Roger Williams talked farming with his Indian friends in Rhode Island, they told him that in the beginning the crow brought their ancestors "a graine of corne in one Eare, and an Indian or French Beane in another from the great God Kantantowit's field in the Southwest, from whence come all their Corne and Beanes."[2] Recent plant research confirms this tradition, at least as to the origin of maize.

However crude these agricultural beginnings may have been, by the time white explorers were able to observe and record their agriculture, New England natives were growing for food not only corn and beans in substantial quantities, but also squashes, pumpkins, watermelons, and Jerusalem artichoke roots, as well as tobacco for smoking and gourds for utensils. Some tribes at least appear to have encouraged desirable grapevines, nut- and acorn-bearing trees, and berries, and developed deer pasture as a source of meat.

Indian tools were crude but effective. For breaking ground, a pointed three-sided stone hoe or the shoulder blade of deer or moose bound to a long handle served as a mattock. A hoe made from a large clamshell on a wood handle or some similar light sharp instrument did the weeding. In a new field the natural fertility might be sufficient. In an old field herring rotted in the hill would bring the crops to successful maturity. Conveniently close to spring planting time, these herring and other fish rushed up the rivers and brooks to spawn at their headwaters and were taken in weirs. In the fall the harvest was stored near the cabins in spacious underground barns dug in dry banks or knolls, for the Indians were a long way from being improvident.

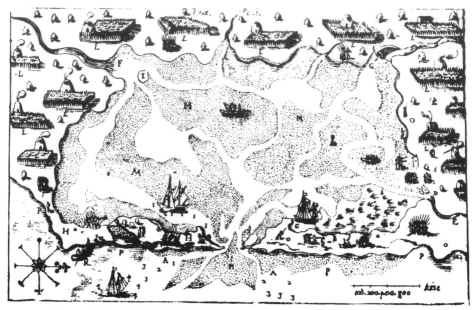

1. Nauset, Cape Cod.
In 1605 Champlain found this Indian village on Cape Cod's east shore well peopled, surrounded by cabins and cornfields—the corn, in late July, 5½ feet tall. "L" on his map, he states, denotes "dwellingplaces of the savages that till the land." *Champlain*, Voyages *(1878), courtesy of Boston Athenaeum.*

So far as is known, the local type of corn was the hard northern flint, often white but grown in many separate strains and colors.[3] Beans were of the climbing type, also well varied. Seeds of all these and of the other vegetables were carefully selected and the strains kept pure. Indian crops were often sizable. Both Pilgrims and Puritans sought and followed native advice on cultivation practices and for some years were happy to add to their own meager food supplies by repeated purchases of native corn, in more than one case like Winthrop's and Pynchon's to the extent of hundreds of bushels.[4]

These crops—corn, beans, squash, pumpkins, and artichokes—furnished a substantial part of the native food. The rest of the vegetable portion of their diet and much of their pharmacopoeia came from nuts, acorns, roots, berries, and wild plants. To some of these, even though not domesticated, they gave calculated attention and help, as they did also to hunting grounds, so that they would be attractive to deer and game. Fish of many kinds and meat from hunting balanced their menu. The skins from wild animals provided clothing, materials for snowshoes, and many other necessities.[5]

Such was the condition of New England agriculture when the first farmers from Europe reached its coasts.

Persons lacking agricultural experience who think farming a simple operation little realize the vast differences in soils, climate, and types of crops and animals; nor can they readily appreciate the importance of accumulated knowledge inherited locally from previous generations of husbandmen, lack of which can make farming an especially hazardous and unfruitful operation. Each of these factors is important as it relates to the enterprise of the passengers of the *Mayflower*, which on December 21, 1620, dropped anchor in Plymouth Harbor to open the agricultural annals of New England.

First, the terrain. If any single factor proved the key to the eventual success of the Pilgrim enterprise, it was that their exploring party found at Plymouth not merely a sheltered harbor but a tract of tree-cleared hillside, long farmed, but whose numerous former cultivators had been completely swept away by a recent pestilence. Had the newcomers been forced to chop their way to their first few acres of cropland and harvest or to fight the original occupants for possession, it is hard to see how they could have survived.

Plymouth soil was and is poor; but on the other hand it was what farmers call "old land" and of a character unusually easy to work. This proved another most fortunate circumstance; for the *Mayflower* lading included not a single plow—everything had to be done with clumsy hand tools, and years were to pass before this soil would feel the tread of an ox.

Second, the climate, which at the beginning was also favorable. The mild winter of 1620–21 was succeeded by an early spring; and the summer season proved normally productive, untroubled by the long weeks of drought that in some succeeding seasons were to plague the cultivators, accustomed as they were to the frequent showers of England and the cool, gray skies of Holland. Moreover, New England's was in the main a healthy climate, without the deadly chills and fever of the lowland colonies of Virginia and Guiana.

But it was in the knowledge of local crops and practices, essential to agricultural success in any part of the world, that the newcomers were most handicapped. Just how much farming experience did the Pilgrims bring with them to the New World, and how valuable was it to their survival?[6] The background of those who were to become their leaders—

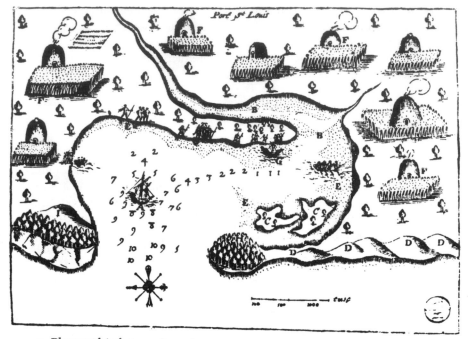

2. Plymouth's future site, 1605.
A deadly pestilence, sweeping away the Indian inhabitants, had left open for the Pilgrims this long-tilled site, which they named Plimoth. When Champlain mapped it fifteen years earlier, only the two points were forested. "F" on the map refers to "Cabins where the savages till the ground." *Voyages (1878), courtesy of Boston Athenaeum.*

Bradford, Brewster, Carver, Winslow, and Standish—may throw some light on that question.

William Bradford's grandfather and the uncles who brought him up were substantial farmers at Austerfield, on the border between Yorkshire and Nottingham. As a lad they had "devoted him like his ancestors unto the affairs of husbandry," though the youth's health was frail. However, at about the age of seventeen he came under the influence of Reverend John Robinson and the congregation of Separatists in the neighboring village of Scrooby. When these were soon forced by government persecution to flee to Holland, young Bradford went with them, ending any agricultural training.

William Brewster, considerably older than Bradford and a leader in the Scrooby congregation, was the village postmaster and bailiff (or superintendent) of the manor there. Since a major route of travel passed through Scrooby, the postmastership was of some importance; but the manor area was chiefly fenland and wash, a district of very limited, poor farms.

John Carver, who backed the Pilgrim enterprise financially and became the colony's first governor, had always been a businessman. Such were the original leaders. So far as records show, none of them nor any others from the Leyden group were in any way connected with agriculture while they were exiled in Holland.

At Southampton, among the seventeen persons from London who there joined the Pilgrim party, was Edward Winslow, destined eventually to become a governor of the colony. He was a printer, though in station describing himself as a yeoman. Myles Standish was and remained a professional soldier. So much for the persons of prominence. Some of the passengers who joined the Pilgrim company at Southampton came from Kent and rural areas of southern England. All in all, however, though Bradford says that many of the Pilgrims came originally from a plain country life,[7] actual agricultural experience among the 102 people who embarked in the *Mayflower* was apparently not great.

In any case farming in the mild, showery climate of southeast England or beneath the overcast skies of Holland could have scarcely prepared the voyagers to grow crops in the burning drought and heat of New England's summer, with neither plow nor ox. Nor would experience in livestock-raising among lush English meadows be of much value in a country where the chief meat source for some time was to be wild deer. As Roland Usher has truly said, the Pilgrims lacked everything but virtue.[8]

So it was incredible good fortune when, with a "Welcome, Englishmen," out of the woods stepped an English-speaking Indian, Hobomok (or Samoset), who had learned a smattering of English from fishermen frequenting Monhegan Island off the Maine coast, and when on March 22 he returned with Squanto, a native born on this very soil. Captured by an English ship captain and forcibly removed to Europe, Squanto had been spared from the sickness that took off every other inhabitant of Plymouth's Indian village. In England he had learned to speak the Pilgrims' tongue.

Wise in the ways of New World agriculture, Squanto has properly been called the first of America's "agricultural advisers." He showed the Pilgrims how to burn the four or five years' accumulation of weeds, poverty grass, and hardhack from the old fields; and how with mattocks and grubhoes to break up the soil on as much as twenty-six acres. Next, following the Indian custom, they manured twenty with the herring (or shad) that almost filled the Town Brook at the time of their spring migration, and then planted this twenty with the confiscated maize seed, a grain which they confessed they had never before known. On the other six acres they broadcast English barley and pease, which they must have "hacked in" with pickaxes or heavy hoes.

For only twenty-one men and six grown boys, as Usher points out, to loosen and prepare twenty-six acres; to seine the fish, carry them up from the stream, and distribute two or three to each of the thousands of corn-hills; then to draw up earth over them, drop the seed and cover it—all without a vehicle and with only hand tools—was a tremendous job.[9]

The twenty acres of corn brought a considerable harvest; a little barley and no pease at all was the result from the six acres of European grain. Altogether, the crop was sufficient, nevertheless, to enable the Pilgrims, Squanto, and other Indian friends whom the settlers by this time had made from Massasoit's village on Narragansett Bay thirty miles away, to celebrate with a bounteous Thanksgiving feast, complete with games and merriment. Moreover, each man, woman, and child who had survived the winter's deadly fevers could thereafter be rationed a peck of cornmeal a week. With shellfish and wild fowl this would keep all alive and in health. This first harvest had not been gained without tragedy, however. Unaccustomed to field work or physical toil and under an unseasonably hot April sun, Governor John Carver collapsed and died of a stroke, the first casualty of New England agriculture that history records.

The planting of the first two years was done on a joint or communal basis, and so was the trading that the group soon began with Indian tribes along the shore. This communal farming had its origin in the type of joint-stock business organization which had been necessary to secure capital for the voyage. The harvests secured might have sufficed, had not the arrival of two additional groups sent by the London backers of the colony doubled the mouths to be fed; for the newcomers brought no provisions with them. Once landed, some of the new arrivals were not even willing to work for the common good. A starving time ensued. The supply of food, no more than enough even for the original group, had to be rationed very closely, and general discontent and privation followed. Hungry persons even stole green corn from the stalks before it could mature.

A change in method was clearly necessary. With the spring of 1623, after a petition from the planters, the colony's General Court dropped the communal system and assigned each family its own parcel of tillable land, one acre for each person, to cultivate for its sole benefit. The new plan brought prompt improvement: it "made all hands very industrious, so as much more corne was planted than other waise would have bene. . . . The women now went willingly into ye feild, and tooke their little-on(e)s to set corne . . . whom to have compelled would have been thoughte great tiranie and oppression."

Though there were still no oxen to plow with, that season's harvest was so much better that all had enough to eat, and things began to look up. By 1625 the colony could even load a small vessel with corn and send it eastward to be traded with the Kennebec Indians for furs to be sold in Europe to pay debts. This date is one to be remembered. It marks the first instance of commercial agriculture in New England, and the first agricultural export by its people.

By 1627 the colony had been successful enough in trade with the Indians for furs so that a deal could be made to buy out its complaining English backers. Outstanding obligations were compromised for a fixed amount, and eight of the leading men, acting on behalf of all, assumed the debt remaining.

Relieved thus of uncertainties, these leaders called the colonists together and outlined a new plan for the farming on which everything depended. They proposed a division by families of the available arable or planting land, and of the livestock. It was to be on a share basis; both types of property were to become individual possessions. Each man was to be allotted one share of land. If married, he was to be entitled to an extra share for each member of his family. Each share was to be good for twenty acres, so that a whole family might readily receive as much as a hundred acres. The entire area of "settable or tillable" land was to be laid out fairly by a committee, and evened as to quality. Each tract would have some frontage on the shore or a stream. Then the tracts were to be distributed by lot. It was even arranged that people might exchange land so as to be with congenial neighbors. By 1638, Usher calculates, Plymouth had 356 fields covering five square miles between the Jones River on the north (now in Kingston) and the Eel River to the south.

The livestock was divided also. One cow and two goats were allotted for each six shares, so that every family could have its own milk, butter, or cheese. In addition the hogs, now increased to 146, were proportionately divided. With a considerable herd of cattle it seemed best to hold all meadowland in common ownership and assign areas for mowing to each householder annually according to his need, an old English custom. All woodland and unallotted land remained in direct control of the colony.

The plan, which was not far from the traditional arrangements of an English village, was hailed as fair by all, and for some time content reigned. As one result, by 1629 Plymouth was not only profitably trading surplus corn for furs with Maine Indians but exchanging corn and tobacco for needed commodities with the Hollanders who had now begun the colony of New Netherland at the mouth of the Hudson.

Thus at the end of its first decade of struggle, New England's earliest colony, though still poor, was settling successfully into a new way of life. No plow had yet turned a furrow. The hoe remained the chief agricultural tool. No power mill had yet sawed a board or ground a grist. All was done by hand. Not a sheep had been shorn, if indeed any had yet arrived. An order of the General Court in 1633 implies that sheep were still scarce. Yet the Pilgrims had plenty to eat and a surplus to exchange for clothing and indispensable supplies. In this single decade they had learned from the natives the essential lessons of practical food production and by costly trial and error some features of agricultural trade as well. Each family had been settled in possession of what is today known as a family farm and had been provided foundation livestock. The arrangements reflected to some extent customs remembered from English village life; yet to a substantial degree they foreshadowed something quite different: the course that farming, in New England and later in the United States, was destined to follow for the next three centuries.

Meanwhile a few scattered homesteaders had filtered in at inviting spots along the shore to the north, while on a harbor fifty miles northeast the seed was already sown for a vigorous new colony, far better financed, and equipped with substantial agricultural experience.

2. Massachusetts Bay

CAPTAIN JOHN SMITH'S MAP and published book and similar descriptions of the world beyond the Atlantic influenced others besides the Leyden exiles who settled Plymouth. More fishermen continued to appear seasonally on the northern New England coast where cod were so plentiful. More adventurers began to attempt other settlements. Thomas Weston tried a colony at Weymouth on the shore north of Plymouth in 1622, but it lasted less than a year. The next year Robert Gorges took over in the same general location. This group broke up, yet from an agricultural viewpoint it proved not altogether in vain, for Reverend William Blaxton, probably from Gorges' company originally, in 1625 or 1626 put down roots on open and empty Shawmut Peninsula in what was to become Boston Harbor and soon had an orchard and garden started on the southwest slope of the Trimountain. Across the harbor, Samuel Maverick, from Weston's or Gorges' group, sat down on Noddle's Island and later was found farming there. In a separate enterprise a Captain Wollaston with thirty or forty others made a beginning on the open hillsides of what was to become Quincy.

Meanwhile, hoping for profits in the waters toward Maine, where fish were extraordinarily abundant, merchants and fishermen had started small settlements to replace their former seasonal fishing stages. By 1623 a Scot, David Thomson, had begun a stay at the mouth of the Piscataqua in what is now Portsmouth, New Hampshire, which lasted three years. Edward Hilton and companions landed that year also and founded a permanent settlement beside the river at Dover Point. On Maine shores, a few people had moved in at York and at the Saco River and Pemaquid areas. In 1623 a mercantile company from Dorchester, England, landed fourteen men on Cape Ann to pass the winter there, and increased the group by thirty-two the next year. Roger Conant, formerly at Plymouth, next at Nantasket in Boston Harbor, was called to become manager of this Cape Ann enterprise. In 1626 he transferred its operations to Naumkeag, now Salem.

Who of these various groups may have been first to break up the soil, or what they planted, no record states; but by 1632 the settlement on the Piscataqua had a sufficient start in planting to sail sixteen hogsheads of grain, apparently Indian corn, by boat to Watertown on the Charles River to be ground at a new mill there.

Evidence as to livestock beginnings is more exact. The merchants from southern England who financed the Cape Ann project must have realized that families a long way from home (for Conant's wife was with him and other wives began to arrive) could scarcely survive contentedly on fishing alone. Reverend John White's "Brief Relation" of the enterprise of the Dorchester Company of Adventurers mentions a small vessel bearing "kine" sent to Conant at Cape Ann in 1625. Part of the men stationed there returned to England that fall, but Conant and some conscientious ones stayed to look after the cattle. After removal of the experiment to Naumkeag in 1628, twelve more cattle arrived, bulls among them.[1]

Conant was by occupation a salter or ship chandler; among his group only one, Thomas Gardner, was listed as "agriculturist." Before long, however, they were trying tobacco as well as corn, apparently in old Indian fields. To grow these they must have observed the methods of Indian neighbors and obtained Indian seed. Though agriculture was not their primary interest, a few of them persevered as farmers for the rest of their lives.

The Naumkeag project took on a much more ambitious aspect in 1628 when Master John Endecott arrived to act as governor under commission from six gentlemen who with others had recently acquired the rights to the area from the earlier Council for New England and taken over the interests of the Dorchester Adventurers, for whom Roger Conant had been superintendent. He and the other "Old Planters," as they came to be called, already experienced on the soil, were scarcely pleased to be superseded, but Conant fortunately was a mild man and his objections moderated as Endecott assigned each of them 200 acres of good land. The name Salem, given the new settlement, signified peace.[2]

Wealthy capitalists from London and the east part of England were now behind the Naumkeag venture: merchants, clothiers, leather dealers. They began to ship over substantial supplies of cattle, horses, tools, and seeds, in addition to fishing gear. They also sent additional colonists. Governor Endecott and his neighbors could soon count at least forty dairy cattle besides young stock, forty milch goats, a dozen mares—with John Woodbery, a horse fancier, to watch over their foaling. There were also increasing numbers of rabbits. There may have been poultry, too, for tame turkeys are listed in the items the Massachusetts Bay Company ordered to be sent to Endecott.[3]

With all this livestock, plus hogsheads of oats and dried pea seed, farming now began in earnest; so that when the next season Reverend Francis Higginson arrived in a shipload of settlers, he could write home enthusiastically of the "Abundance of corne planted by them, very good and well liking." This language sounds as though he meant Indian corn, for he mentions it elsewhere with admiration. He rejoiced also to see green peas growing, as good as ever he ate in England. Endecott soon started a vineyard and began to try out berries, fruits, and nuts, both native and imported.[4] It was only four years until, at his 300-acre Orchard Farm in Danvers, he set out his famous pear tree. For three centuries it bore fruit; eventually it was but a stone's throw from Boston's roaring circumferential highway, Route 128. Judging from the English records, potatoes may have been sent Endecott to try, also, though so far as is known without practical result. As "The Governor and Company of Massachusetts Bay," the English sponsors of the infant settlement in 1629 secured from King Charles a charter authorizing them to establish and administer a colony occupying territory stretching from Charles River on the south to three miles beyond the Merrimack River to the north. Now began on the shores of Massachusetts Bay a colonization project of a size and character unparalleled in the modern world. It was painstakingly geared to the possibilities of the newly settled countryside. Twenty thousand English, men, women, and children, flooded in during the decade 1630 to 1640. These had all to be provided with food.

Success in such an undertaking depended in the main on three factors: a soil that could provide sustenance for both livestock and crops; an adequate supply of livestock, tools, and equipment; and, beyond all, an experience and competence in farming that would enable the settlers to supply the needs of both human immigrants and the beasts that accompanied them. It will be the purpose here to discover how these requirements were satisfied and both man and beast fed.

First as to the land. Like the Plymouth colonists of the previous decade, the Puritan migration had the enormous good fortune to enter upon an inviting shore, formerly well inhabited by native Indians but in 1630 almost empty. The Bay coast had the advantage of affording several excellent harbors, a number of small rivers for access to the interior, and a wealth of forest within reach. Besides all these, the site awaiting the colony included thousands of acres of natural grass, of types reasonably adequate for the needs of cattle, and substantial areas of open, tillable land. Parts of this land had been in comparatively recent Indian cultivation: beyond that, much had been kept open purposely by seasonal Indian fires. In general the soil was of considerably better quality than that

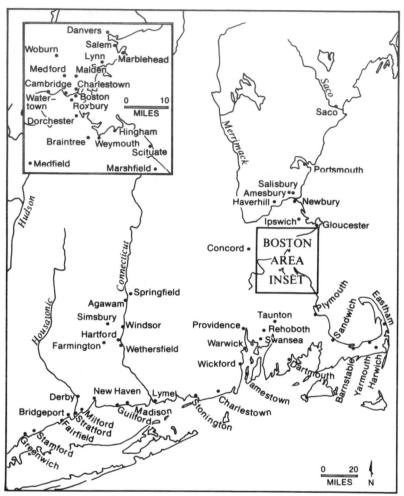

Danvers
Woburn Salem Marblehead
Lynn
Medford Malden
Cambridge Charlestown
Water-town Boston
Roxbury
Dorchester
Hingham
Braintree Weymouth
Scituate
Medfield
Marshfield

0 10
MILES

Hudson

Saco
Saco

Merrimack

Salisbury
Amesbury
Haverhill Newbury
Portsmouth

Ipswich Gloucester

Connecticut

Concord BOSTON
AREA
INSET

Springfield
Agawam
Simsbury
Windsor
Hartford
Farmington Wethersfield

Housatonic

Taunton
Providence Rehoboth
Warwick Swansea
Wickford
Jamestown

Plymouth
Sandwich
Eastham
Dartmouth
Barnstable
Yarmouth
Harwich

Derby New Haven Lyme
Bridgeport Madison
Milford Guilford
Stratford Charlestown
Fairfield Stonington
Stamford
Greenwich

0 20
MILES N

CUCL

3. Apart from access by water, two factors appear to have governed the
choice by New England's colonizers of sites for their towns. This map
illustrates one: the availability of an open area already cultivated or at
least cleared by the native Indians. Such clearings offered the settlers a
ready-made site for home lots (dwelling, outbuildings, garden, orchard,
night pasture) together with nearby land cultivable for grain. According
to credible evidence, every town named on this map (all settled by 1650)
had such a precleared area as a nucleus. Some early settled towns—for
example, Newport and Middletown, R.I., and Sudbury, Mass.—are not
included. Despite circumstantial evidence, diligent inquiry has turned
up no adequate proof. *Cartography Laboratory, Clark University.*

found by the Pilgrims at Plymouth. Yet the same strange circumstance prevailed as at Plymouth—considered by the colonists to be providential: the scourge of illness that had wiped out Plymouth's Indians had likewise left only three or four small and weak Indian villages anywhere about Boston Bay, well populated as it must formerly have been.

A second advantage for the Massachusetts Bay Colony was in adequate leadership, capital, and preparation. Much was by this time known of the possibilities of the new land, and the directors of the enterprise planned carefully. The financial backing of the sponsoring company was sufficient; the most important needs of the venture could be adequately met. The tools, seeds, plants, and animals that were thought most necessary were provided in liberal quantities almost from the beginning.

From the records it becomes clear at once that the Bay company management expected farming in the new colony to be carried on as far as possible after the English manner. Livestock and grain were to be its main props; supplemented by fruits, vegetables, and cultivated fibers. There was no intention to let the colonists be dependent on Indian practices alone, helpful as those had been to the impoverished Pilgrims at Plymouth. Livestock in quantity came with the first ships, and continued coming. So did European seeds and plants.

All such supplies might have been thrown away, however, had the Bay Colony immigration not included a substantial proportion of persons of seasoned agricultural experience. Because the farm-trained portion among the newcomers proved so important in shaping not only the agricultural but the commercial and political future of Massachusetts Bay and every one of the colonies that eventually fanned out from it, the English origins of these farm people deserve particular attention, together with the agricultural traditions and practices in which they had been trained.

To begin with, the new governor of the Massachusetts Bay Colony, John Winthrop, besides being able in the field of law, was a countryman and had been lord of the manor of Groton in Suffolk. In New England he from the first became a farm proprietor, acquired an orchard (perhaps previously set by Conant) on Governor's Island in Boston Harbor, and promptly stocked his Ten Hills farm beside the Mystic just north of Boston with cattle and tools brought from England.

Among the long list of passengers who filled the Winthrop fleet arriving with him in 1630 or who landed during the next decade, the occupations of over 300 males (other than servants), chiefly heads of families, have been determined as a result of the painstaking research of Charles E. Banks.[5] Among these immigrants, but seventy-five, fewer than one fourth, are listed as yeomen (who were not necessarily farmers) or as husbandmen. One in six was from London and unlikely to have had farm experience, though of these some may originally have been from the country. Aside from these city dwellers, the immigrants listed included numerous merchants, armourers, bakers, carpenters, shoemakers, smiths, tanners, weavers, and other tradesmen, as well as the large number of servants and laborers. Of these, weavers and tanners were most likely to have been rural dwellers, and as tenants on some manor to have at least possessed a garden, a cow, and a few sheep or poultry. Yet useful as the industrial skills of all such craftsmen might prove for the success of the Bay Colony, any important contribution from them to the settlement's agricultural success could scarcely be expected.

It appears a tribute, then, to the modest number of husbandmen, in particular to the livestockmen among them, as well as to the careful preparations by the Company for provisioning the colony from England, that only the first two or three years of the venture were seasons of real want for the newcomers. Once these years were over, the colony seldom failed to be adequately fed and eventually in part clothed by the production of its professional farmers, with such supplements as the rest might be able to provide. Indeed, hardly had the first decade ended before merchants would find it possible to accumulate surplus grain and provisions to be shipped abroad in order to obtain in return needed salt, apparel, and manufactured goods.

Consider what was involved in so momentous a change as this resettlement. Each countryman had to sell or lease his land, or if a tenant abandon his copyhold, renouncing cherished ancestral or acquired rights and privileges. He had then to provide himself with tools and equipment for his new enterprise; and pay the heavy cost of transporting household, goods, and livestock three thousand miles to a new and uncertain world. Beyond this, he had to provide in advance supplies for the subsistence of his family, servants if he had them, and stock, for many months at least after arrival.

To these financial considerations must be added a farmer's inborn conservatism, and the uncertainties connected with the practice of agriculture anywhere, any time, but especially in an unknown land and climate. This may well explain why, in the passenger lists, the number of farmers appears proportionately small.

Yet leave they did; and many of them were destined to serve in their new townships as in their old ones, as mainstays of community life. When, during anxious discussions between husband and wife across the trestle table and by the fire in a hundred East Anglian farmhouses, descriptions of the faraway new land were read and proposals for emigration pondered, it must, at least sometimes, have been listening to a higher voice than man's which overweighed the powerful ties of home and kin, and brought the decision to leave behind so much for what might prove to be so little.[6]

3. Stirring the Soil

LATE IN JUNE 1630, the eleven vessels of Governor Winthrop's fleet dropped anchor in Boston Harbor and began setting ashore their 700 passengers, with livestock and supplies, on the peninsula of Mishawum, soon to become Charlestown. On hand to greet them were blacksmith Thomas Walford, its original settler, snug "in a palisadoed and thatched house," and ten families who had been sent over from Salem in 1629 by Governor Endecott. Each of these ten had been provided a two-acre home lot, with instructions to fence in common.[1]

In an enterprise such as starting a New England colony, many things had to be done all at once. What would now be called farm work formed only a small proportion of the essential tasks. The first need was shelter. Carpenters and servants had come in the ships, and the wealthier planters hired them for building. Others who lacked wealth had to put together makeshift shelters, until such time as each family could provide squared timbers, split clapboards or weatherboarding, and build properly. Then the house would be perhaps a two-room peaked-roof dwelling of the type long used in England. Roofs were of thatch at first, chimneys often of plank.

While this and similar essential work went on, someone had to look after the stock. Old English custom set the example. Each town hired its cowherd. In 1635 Newe-Towne employed a goatherd also, and Salem needed two such. These herdsmen picked up the animals of a whole village in the morning, drove them to pasture, and delivered each to its owner's lot at evening, when the householder or some of his family could milk ewe goats and cows.

Weatherboard shelters for such milking cattle began to appear, similar to those of Old England's eastern counties. Dry stock and young cattle, however, still had to grow long coats and shift largely for themselves even after several years. To secure the weaker animals from wild beasts, wealthy Cambridge proprietors had their servants surround hundreds of acres of ground with one general fence a mile and a half long. William Wood records that at Master Matthew Cradock's plantation on the Mystic in Medford, "he hath impaled a park where he keeps his cattle till he can store it with deer."[2] With much stock by necessity grazing at large, fencing was as necessary to keep them out of tilled land as the wild

4. Pounds for stray livestock. *Howard S. Russell collection.*

beasts. One or more common fields were usually completely enclosed as soon as possible by the whole village. Thereafter, under the eyes of the town's fence viewers, each landholder was required to keep up his share of the common fence. In addition each family had also to protect its individual garden and orchard. With so much fencing done in haste and of rough materials, and so many animals grazing and rooting, fencing complaints and damage suits for animal trespass for years constantly harassed town officials and courts.

Wealthy homesteaders on the cramped Boston peninsula, lacking space and meadow to keep stock properly, were granted grazing land across the Back Bay in Muddy River (now Brookline) or got permission to pasture their animals on islands safe from wolves.

Hungering for vegetables, villagers had early begun gardens. Newe-Towne in 1634 granted a garden plot near the meeting house to "Mr. Stone"; and the Proprietors' Records of 1635 describe several more. Alvan Ervington and others were allowed timber from the common for fencing theirs. Roxbury and Dorchester settlers planted vegetable gardens near their dwellings. Amongst the puddingstone on their hillsides, apple and pear seeds and cherry stones were soon sprouting from the soil. In each of the dozen new villages that before long ringed Boston Bay and dotted the North Shore, colonists were trying out fruit. They planted the Indian's corn, bean, and pumpkin as well as their own carrots, parsnips and turnips, all of them roots that do well in spaded ground. To protect these, Cambridge in 1636 ordered fines levied whenever cocks, hens, and turkeys damaged gardens. Some settlers wished to grow tobacco, but the General Court frowned. A special dispensation allowed the "Old Planters" such as Roger Conant, who had grown it all along, to have "tobacco yeards."

Altogether, agriculture was looking up. Boston decreed a market for every Thursday, indicating that produce and animals were for sale. For several years after 1635 farmers did very well, and when Stephen Daye set up his Cambridge printing press, the first booklet printed (1639) was that useful agricultural item, an almanac. New colonists came in every ship. Before starting across, many had sold out in England and had money in their pockets. From the planters already established at the Bay and in Plymouth they bought stock at high prices. Plymouth stockmen took in newly arrived English cattle and bred and fed them, in consideration of a share of their offspring.

Each year the General Court laid out fresh townships and arranged for them to be peopled. In the older towns at the Bay good herbage was already at a premium; people left, saying that the plowable plains were too dry and sandy. In some towns, Cambridge for example, religion and politics bred disagreements, and the discontented and the unsuccessful were already looking toward fresh horizons. Such property as they left behind was readily salable to new arrivals from the ships. So soon after the beginning, emigration had started.

Livestock, desirable as it was, met the food needs of the colonists only in part. If the newcomers were to have bread, land must be broken up at once, and in the beginning nearly all the work had to be done by hand. Except on fields that the Indians had quite recently cultivated, this was no easy task, even where, as Edward Johnson later put it, "The Lord [had] mitigated their labors by the Indians' frequent firing of the woods." Yet, in his words, "Standing stoutly to their labours [they] tare up the roots and bushes which the first yeare bears them a very thin crop till the soard of the earth be rotten, and therefore they have been forced to cut their bread very thin for a long season."[3]

During these earliest years of scarcity only a small beginning could be made toward preparing ground properly for European grain. Later, as the colony developed, a plowman might be engaged with his team of four or six oxen to break up the land, but for a considerable time plows, plowmen, and oxen were very few. Regardless of this lack, to most of the newcomers producing grain appeared a necessity, and almost as much for beer as for bread. At Plymouth the Pilgrims had sown English grain the very first season, as has already appeared; but lacking animal manure and the plow they had to learn that the lean sandy soil of their Indian fields was too poor for wheat and barley. Grain enough they did secure, however, even without plowing, by following Squanto's directions and fertilizing Indian corn with fish directly in the hill. At the Cape Ann settle-

5. A tight pale fence with split pickets driven deep kept hungry animals out of gardens and orchards. *Perley*, History of Salem *(1924)*.

ment later in the 1620 decade, native Indian corn seems also to have been the chief cereal.

Individual householders tried wheat in their gardens, the only spots safe from hogs and larger animals, but Salem's order passed in 1639 that fences be kept up "forasmuch as divers of our town are resolved to sow English grain this spring," shows that progress was slow, for a dozen years had passed since Salem's founding. Wheat seldom took kindly to soils along the coast, nor did barley become of importance in early times except in a few areas. Opinions differed as to quality. "Wheat and barley are not thought to be as good as these grains in England," wrote a Bay colonist to an English friend, "but Rye and Pease are as good as the English. Beans also there are very good." Captain John Underhill was of a different mind. In 1638 he reported "in the Bay as good English grain as can grow in any part of the world."[4]

Regardless of ill success, farmers continued to experiment with wheat as soon as land could be got into fit condition, for that was the grain for which English stomachs hankered. Wheat had a second merit. As soon as necessity drove the colony to exporting, it became a staple that traders could readily sell: so it was made receivable for taxes. As a result, even Salem farmers eventually began to harvest some wheat. On Cape Cod also wheat was sown: the better fields there might yield 15 to 20 bushels to the acre. Nevertheless conditions on the coast were seldom fully congenial for it. In 1646 caterpillars attacked both wheat and barley; deer trespassed upon the fields; and after a few years black stem rust appeared. By mid-century it had become clear that for the great part of the colonies the combination of "rye and Injun" must become New England's main reliance for bread. It was a combination that proved satisfactory and remained popular into the twentieth century.

Before the end of the first decade the towns earliest settled had encouraged millers to construct wind and water mills. Town meetings offered special inducements in land grants and tax exemption, for millers and millwrights were never plentiful. Yet a century and a half would have to pass before the quern or Indian mortar in which grain was pounded by hand, as well as the hand sieve to sift out the flour, could be completely given up in frontier settlements.

At least one belt of soil did prove well fitted for European grains, however: the many miles of alluvial terraces bordering the Connecticut River from Middletown north. As this rich valley began increasingly to draw settlement, the dream of the colonies' governing bodies of wheat as an exportable staple, to be sold for silver and gold or imported commodities, became more fully a practical reality. The Pynchons, traders of Springfield, might sometimes ship as much as 2,000 bushels to Boston, a large amount when reaped with a sickle and threshed by hand. The Connecticut Valley, therefore, has been called the continent's first wheat belt. As time passed, the Valley's wheat area was to shift steadily northward. In 1644 "the blast took hold of Connecticut and New Haven" and wheat spoiled, but Indian corn, barley, pease, and rye were spared. Since the disease spread slowly, new land up river continued for several decades to grow wheat to be shipped to Boston and elsewhere. Hadley, Massachusetts, for example, raised wheat: scarcely sowed rye at all until 1685.[5]

Next to wheat, barley was the desired crop. Englishmen felt that they must have beer, though after a generation or two in New England the settlers decided that cider would do as well. Barley was also good for bread and broth. Oats did only fairly; less adaptable than rye, it filled out poorly.

Despite success here and there, it took only a few years of disappointment with European cereals, during which the native maize provided regular harvests, to prove without question that Indian corn was to be king in New England. Englishmen might not take to it with enthusiasm, but from necessity all the settlements learned to grow and eat it. Their hogs and poultry, less finicky, enjoyed it whenever they could get at it. Not only was maize a reliable yielder of grain, excellent food for man and a superior ration for poultry and animals, but its stalks if cut at the proper time could furnish palatable winter fodder for the cattle that were so important to New England farming.

A special advantage to corn growing was that alewives to fertilize it found their way naturally far inland, up every stream with a pond at its head; while at the shore it would thrive on either fish or king crabs. Wherever animal manure was available, this likewise grew good corn.[6] In new settlements the ability of corn to do well on unplowed fields under hoe culture alone was especially valuable. "The chiefest Corne they planted before they had Plowes was Indian Graine," said Johnson; but, he added, at first anything beyond four or five acres was rare.

Corn did have disadvantages. Dogs played havoc with fish in the fields and had to be hobbled for three or four weeks till the fish rotted. The fence around the common cornfield must be kept tight or cattle would spread ruin. Important officers in each town, therefore, were the haywards (hedge wards) or fence viewers, already mentioned, who saw to it that each villager kept his section of fence in sound condition. Birds did such damage that town authorities required each householder to kill a dozen blackbirds and three crows annually.

Yet corn was not hard to raise. Like their Indian tutors, the settlers waited till the white oak leaves reached the size of a mouse's ear before planting. After it was up, cultivation was the next step, to control the inevitable weeds. At first, and in primitive settlements for a long time, tillage was by hoe alone; but by 1637 the Bay Colony could count up to thirty-seven plows, each able to turn over an acre or more a day of tilled land, and oxen had been trained to draw them. After the corn was up, where plows were available, two successive light plowings, the furrow thrown toward the row, would cover the weeds.[7] Harvesting was simple: ears were left on the stalk till well ripened, picked at a convenient time and drawn to the farm yard for husking, and the stock then turned into the field to clean up all that was left.

Growing grains and planting gardens and orchards were by no means the only pressing early duties. Another immediate need was fuel. Since most villages were laid out as far as possible on or adjoining land left open by the Indians, the nearest firewood might well be at a distance, an eighth of a mile, for example, at Plymouth's beginning. Thus getting fuel for daily cooking and enough for the winter fireplace was in itself no small task. A second essential was water for household needs, often from a common spring. The cutting and curing of salt and fresh meadow hay for winter feed for stock was another absolutely necessary labor, and still no place to store it when secured except in stacks in the open. Truly the burdens of existence must have appeared endless.

To carry out such tasks some of the better-off colonists had brought along young relatives, or indentured servants who had bound themselves to work for seven years for board, lodging, and a modest reward at the end. Others bought from shipmasters the terms of service of persons who had indentured themselves to the captain to pay their passage. Some free laborers had come also; but wages were high, and it was chiefly wealthy planters such as those at Cambridge and New Haven who could afford to hire them. At both Plymouth and the Bay some proved too lazy to work voluntarily and had to be forced to do so.[8]

Getting in the harvest was of such vital public importance that the authorities were obliged to step in, as they had on occasion done in Old England, and order mechanics and artisans to assist. The Bay General Court notified local constables in 1646 that because the harvest times of hay, corn, flax, and hemp usually came so close together, they were authorized to impress labor. In every town where the request was made to them, artificers and handicraftsmen could be required to work by the day for neighbors needing them, to mow, reap, and get the crops (for wages, however,) on penalty of a fine equal to two days' pay.[9]

Most farmers, nevertheless, depended on their own labor and that of their boys and girls, and on the help of neighbors. Governor Winthrop set the example at the Bay, as had the Plymouth leaders. Says one of his friends, the governor "was a discreet and sober man . . . putting his hand to any ordinary labor with his servants." Roger Williams at Providence tells of his own work at planting.[10] Leading men in Connecticut likewise worked in their own fields, and so did many ministers.

Ordinary farmers shared with neighbors in the heavier tasks also, although this had disadvantages, one of which was offered by John Josselyn: "Many hands make light work . . . But many mouths eat up all."[11]

One sufferer in such a situation might well be the farm wife. The custom of English yeomanry was that she should not be called on to help in the field.[12] Her hands were already full with kitchen, dairy, perhaps poultry, and the vegetable garden. As wool-growing gradually increased and the colony authorities called for a flax patch in every household, the spinning wheel and weaving frame were added to her domain. Without running water, sometimes at first without even a fireplace chimney for cooking, and working largely with only wooden utensils, woman's lot was hard indeed.

Thus early New England began the habit of industry on the part of all—a force that was to become a transcendent regional characteristic. By the end of the first decade the need for shelter was being met more satisfactorily. There were still temporary hovels in Bay Colony towns, dug into the sides of banks or hills and roofed over; and there were "wigwams," perhaps round, dome-roofed cabins like those of the Indians. Many families, however, had built framed houses, often of but one or two rooms yet with chimneys of plank or stone. Roofs at first were of thatch, till frequent fires caused authorities to ban them. Some householders, already established in larger dwellings and with wide acres and numerous cattle, were called rich.

Here and there mechanics were at their tasks. Smiths shaped iron tools on forges, tanners conditioned hides, cobblers tapped shoes, coopers hooped buckets and barrels. Village life was well begun.

4. Distance Beckons the Uneasy

A LL ALONG the winding Massachusetts Bay shore, wherever salt grass caught the eye, exploring stockmen were petitioning the General Court to be allowed to set up new townships. The adjoining upland might be only moderately fertile, even chiefly ledges and woods, yet cattlemen brought up amid England's grassy vales and tidal marshes coveted the salt hay in the lowlands. At Weymouth and Braintree on Massachusetts Bay's south shore and at Ipswich, Newbury, and Salisbury to the north, a list of applicants was assembled—heads of families of known good character and standing, who would agree to live there and support a town and minister—and the General Court had its commissioners mark out towns. Some of the planters of a new township were from older settlements, some newly arrived by ship. All had to be well vouched for. After the site had been examined by a trusted committee, the General Court formally authorized the town grant. Squatting and haphazard settlement were not permitted.[1]

Fresh-water marshes exhibited drawing power also. In addition to Concord, founded in 1635, and Sudbury on the Musketahquid in 1638, the alluvial grasses of the Charles brought Dedham into being in 1636, and later Medfield, further up river. Charlestown farmers followed the fertile Mystic Valley north to begin Medford and Woburn. The Nashua River meadows soon enticed settlers inland to Lancaster.

In Plymouth Colony the same magnet drew ambitious men toward new locations. Reluctantly the Plymouth authorities permitted their neighbors to leave the close-knit mother town and its scant fertility and set up new and distant farmsteads beside inviting hay lands. Duxbury, Green Harbor (Marshfield), and Hingham, their tidal marshes rich in salt hay, drew planters northward. The miles of green salt meadow on the Cape Cod shore and Indian fields there open for tillage beckoned still others to plant Sandwich, Barnstable, and Yarmouth, and to move inland to Taunton at the head of Mt. Hope Bay.[2]

It has already been recorded how, before the Massachusetts Bay migration, the trade in fish had caused commercial interests to locate agents and employees at the outlet of the Piscataqua River at what were to become Portsmouth and Dover, New Hampshire, and the nearby Maine coast. Speculative eyes soon turned to the neighboring forests also. In the early 1630's sawmills were set up and a start made in turning the splendid pine and oak of the Piscataqua watershed into merchantable lumber and spars.

Agriculture came as a natural development from all this. A London fish merchant, David Hilton, and his brother William had sat down at Dover Point beside the Piscataqua under a patent from the Council for New England. They raised grain on both the Maine and New Hampshire sides, and by 1632 had hogs also. That year two Piscataqua men, Thomas Commack and Edward Godfrey, freighted sixteen hogsheads of corn to Watertown in the Bay Colony for grinding.[3] In 1631 Mason and Gorges, as the Laconia Company, after vainly trying to develop Indian trade in the interior, received a patent in the same area. Eventually twenty-two women were numbered among the settlers. A company agent wisely wrote home that the capitalists could hardly expect good returns unless they furnished cattle as well as hired hands.[4]

In the course of three years the company landed several score of large yellow cattle at Cow Cove. A Virginian captain also arrived at Boston in 1633 with a load of 100 young cattle from St. Christopher, some of which he sold at Piscataqua, some at York, Maine. Unfortunately the chief mover of the Laconia enterprise, Captain John Mason, died. When his estate came to be settled, a hundred of the big yellow cattle were herded over the paths to Boston for sale by the manager of Mason's property (a fraudulent act on the part of Mason's agents, Sanborn's *History of New Hampshire* claims). There they brought twenty-five pounds sterling each, a price above the ordinary. A 1635 inventory of the Mason assets included, besides cattle, 40 horses, almost 200 sheep, and 54 goats. More cattle from Bristol reached this northeastern coast in 1636 and 1638. A deposition of a somewhat later period was to the effect that most of the cattle then found in Maine inherited some of the Mason cattle's blood.[5]

In 1638 the pleasant lands on the river entering Great Bay from the south attracted thirty-six families from Boston, among them at least two husbandmen. With their dissident pastor John Wheelwright, they founded Exeter, (New Hampshire). About the same time cattlemen newly arrived from England took over the immense salt marshes and inviting upland of what was to become Hampton, New Hampshire. In 1641 Dover and Portsmouth, till then self-governed, placed themselves under Massachusetts' jurisdiction.[6]

Further east, the Saco Valley soon counted 150 people. Near what is now Portland, Maine, Richmond Island and Cape Elizabeth had for a decade been harboring white inhabitants who raised Indian corn and pumpkins. They also tried vegetables and English grain—all cultivated by hand behind high, tight fences to keep out wild animals. Pigs multiplied, fed largely on fish waste. John Winter had seventy on Richmond Island in 1634 in connection with his fishing and farming enterprise and had provided shelter for them. But wolves and Indians made swine-keeping difficult except on islands offshore. Two years later Winter claimed that between them they had cost him two hundred porkers. Maine's earliest local court decreed death for either wolf or Indian if discovered and convicted. Though considerable farming went on, fish and timber were to remain for many years the chief props for people of the New Hampshire and Maine coasts.[7]

Estimable and high-principled as were the Massachusetts Bay leaders, they ruled with so stiff a hand that not all could bear it, and the Puritan hive around Boston and the Bay began early to swarm south to Rhode Island and inland to the Connecticut Valley. The first to leave had been the gentleman who bid Winthrop welcome, peace-loving Reverend William Blaxton, planter of New England's original orchard on the Shawmut peninsula that was to become Boston. In 1634 he sold his property on Trimountain's southwest slope to the newcomers, and, buying "a stock of cows" with the money, and taking with him apple seeds and little trees, found a new haven to the southward under the Plymouth Colony's patent.[8] On a hillside in what is now Cumberland, Rhode Island, at the foot of which flowed the river that today honors his name, Blaxton planted his second orchard. Sprouts from certain trees that he set out were still bearing Rhode Island Sweetings two centuries later. As time went on and he occasionally went in to Providence to preach, this good man would fill his saddlebag with apples to delight the children of that primitive settlement who had never before tasted them.[9]

Blaxton left Massachusetts Bay voluntarily, but others were pushed out. The year after he departed, the magistrates banished Roger Williams, teacher beloved by his Salem church. He headed southwest, first to Seekonk, where he did planting on Plymouth Colony soil. Then, following a friendly warning from Plymouth, he abandoned his venture there and with five companions in a canoe paddled west to found the town of Providence, not far from Blaxton's seat. A Londoner, Williams may never previously have farmed; but his friends the Indians must have taught him the necessary skills. Many a time, he wrote, "was my time spent at the hoe . . . for bread."[10] It is recorded that he planted with his own hands two former Indian fields, one in today's Roger Williams Park at Providence. Other malcontents joined him. Soon they had cattle, corn, and tobacco. Governor Winthrop remained his friend, and within a few years he and Williams had a joint herd of hogs rooting and clamming on Prudence Island in Narragansett Bay.[11]

On the excellent soil of the large island of Aquidneck on the Bay's east side, Mrs. Anne Hutchinson of Salem, likewise banished with her followers, sat down; they founded the prosperous farming villages of Portsmouth, Middletown, and Newport. Like the others they had cattle and hogs. For pasture they turned also to Conanicut Island, which the Indians had cleared. Hogs soon grew so numerous and troublesome that they had to be banished to uninhabited islands.[12]

The removal of dissidents to Rhode Island was to prove less important agriculturally, however, than the emigration of other uneasy colonists to the wide and fertile intervales of the Connecticut Valley. The Plymouth authorities and the New Amsterdam Hollanders had both been eyeing the river as an opening for settlement, agriculture, and the fur trade. Learning from the visiting sachem Wahquimmacut of the attractions of the broad valley with its open meadows, in the fall of 1632 Plymouth sent Edward Winslow to take a look. In June of the next year the Hollanders from New Amsterdam appeared and built a fort at what was to become Hartford.

Ignoring their threats, a Plymouth expedition sailed by and started a trading post and settlement of their own upriver on land that they bought from the Indians at the confluence of the Farmington River. In the fall of 1634 appeared John Oldham with ten followers from Watertown at Massachusetts Bay and sat down at Wethersfield, below the Dutch. Oldham's group, so far as records show, appear to have been the first Europeans to stir the soil in Connecticut; they sowed rye, presumably "hacking it in" with hand tools, on one of the untenanted Indian fields. The next year brought several small groups from the Bay with cattle and swine, one sitting down close to the Plymouth people at Windsor. Besides these, others claiming the land under a patent came up from Saybrook at the river's mouth. Winter drove most of the adventurers from the Bay back to their old homes. "Otherwise," explains Winthrop in his history, "they had all perished as some did." With the help of the Plymouth people and the local Indians a few hardy ones stuck the winter out. Some of the cattle, roaming the meadows on the east side, lived well all winter without human care. Altogether, however, so much stock perished that the financial loss was heavy.[13]

The first duty of the newcomers before winter was to throw up palisades and temporary shelter for their families. Man and beast both found the new life hard going. "Things went not well at Connecticut," wrote

Governor Winthrop at the autumn's end. Some cattle died and many cast their young, as had the cattle of the year before. Apparently the new arrivals planted some rye that fall.

Undaunted, these determined colonizers stuck the next winter out, and so did their wives and the stock. Building shelters and caring for families and livestock left little chance that season for tillage. Women had to be cautioned against feeding seed grain to poultry and hogs. But it all paid off. By 1638 Pastor Hooker could write back to the Bay that his own eight cattle never did better than last year. So things improved. A Hartford farmer who died in 1640 had 13 cattle, 3 horses, 13 goats, and 13 swine, 160 bushels of Indian corn, 30 bushels of summer wheat, and 12 of pease. Another (called "average"), dying in 1641, left 4 cows, 3 goats, 8 hogs, 5 acres of Indian corn, an acre each of wheat, oats, and meslin, and some pease and barley.[14]

More western settlements began. At the mouth of the Quinnipiac River on Long Island Sound wealthy London merchants were attracted by the harbor and the possibilities of trade. Though lacking any patent, in 1638 they built themselves large dwellings, started a mercantile town, New Haven, and set up an independent government. Near them a few Yorkshire farmers established homesteads. West of New Haven, at the mouth of the Housatonic, Hertfordshire families chose tillable fields to begin Milford. To the east, a group of farmers from Kent and Surrey in 1639 sat down beside the shore at Guilford. Both Milford and Guilford were for a time self-governed. A group of restless families from Concord found Fairfield. This town and adjoining Stratford acknowledged the authority of Connecticut, as the three valley towns, now organized as a government, were called. Not until 1662 did Connecticut get a royal charter and annex New Haven and the rest—at which time some dissidents left for New Jersey! Again and again the newcomers began with the benefit of fields long used and fertilized by Indian predecessors, or settled beside natural meadows.[15]

Up the Connecticut at Hartford the earliest settlers, hankering for cider, started apple trees. Among these was an English Pearmain tree that in 1853, two centuries later, still bore fruit. Bent also on improving its neat stock, Hartford soon appointed a committee to pick out promising calves to be saved for breeding. In another important initiative, Hartford, Windsor, and Wethersfield drew up and adopted the famous "Fundamental Orders" that were to protect the political rights of Connecticut citizens for generations.

Further north on the same Connecticut River one of Massachusetts Bay Colony's enterprising leaders, William Pynchon, with a dozen fam-

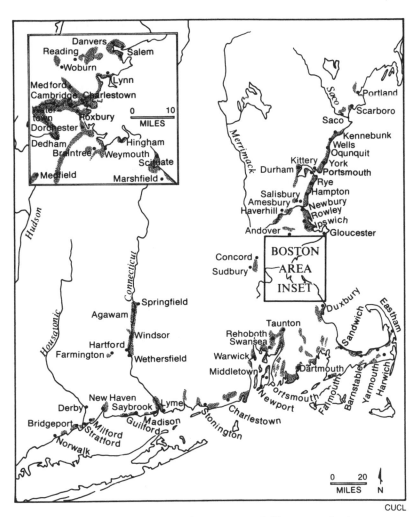

CUCL

6. This map (based on U.S. Geodetic surveys) illustrates the importance to the English colonists of available feed for their cattle. The site of every town named (all settled by 1650) adjoined natural salt or fresh hay marsh. The marsh offered the prospect that by breeding livestock the village could live and prosper (as all did). *Cartography Laboratory, Clark University.*

ilies, made a bold start on the silt terraces of Agawam. They had driven stock from Roxbury by Indian trails the hundred-odd miles across Massachusetts. Almost at once the cattle and hogs made trouble by feeding on the unfenced cornfields of the local Indians, and the settlement had to be moved across the river to the less attractive meadows of the east bank at what was to become Springfield.

As the 1630 decade ended, villages dotted southern New England's coasts and its principal river valleys. Most of them were small; but with Boston they housed perhaps 20,000 or more people of English origin. The farmers among them were well stocked with cattle, hogs, and goats, all increasing by geometrical progression. They also could count many horses, some sheep, considerable poultry. Bees were on hand at least by 1639, and spread through the woods often in advance of the colonists. At Rowley, on the North Shore of Massachusetts Bay, from wool of local sheep, Yorkshire weavers in 1638 wove America's first bolt of woolen cloth.[16]

So with grain from the fields, and beef, pork, milk, butter, and cheese from the pastures and marshes, besides a little cultivated fruit and the most essential vegetables from the garden, the end of the first decade found the bulk of New England country people with food enough. They had shelter for themselves and the more valuable or delicate of their stock. A few, like Lady Fenwick at Saybrook by the mouth of the Connecticut, could soon even enjoy gardens of flowers and herbs. The New England town had also taken root, both as a body politic and as a social and agricultural community.

Up to 1640, the economic life of the colonies had been influenced chiefly by immigration and supplies from the mother country. It was soon to undergo a drastic change of direction, and farming with it.

5. To Market, to Market

ABOUT 1640, with the calling of the Long Parliament in England, followed by civil war, immigration of new planters and inflow of their cash capital to New England dropped to a trickle. A speculative market for livestock and commodities created by the sale of these necessaries to newcomers arriving with money to spend had been to the first comers a harvest, to quote William Bradford's words. Now this prosperity collapsed. It became difficult to dispose of goods, cattle, and improved land and buildings. The sale value of animals dropped to a quarter of what they had brought during the great migration, and the General Court had to set a price on corn and make it legal tender. Even at low prices, stock was hard to sell. Plymouth Colony farmers who had prospered by supplying Bay newcomers with stock lost their outlet. Butter and cheese had for some time been cheaper than in England, but now grain that settlers had begun to find profitable fell in price. Merchants could no longer move imported goods. Everywhere trade languished.[1]

Yet in real assets—available timber, fish, livestock, and agricultural produce which, rather than currency, constituted true wealth—the country still abounded. Moreover, as always, low prices opened possibilities. Though England itself offered a poor market, due in part to political troubles, the wars in Europe which disrupted business for merchants of that continent opened opportunities to New World traders. The eyes of the leaders of the Bay Colony turned southward. Virginia, first settled in 1607, had begun to raise tobacco by 1612 and to export it a few years later. It soon became that colony's almost sole crop. The rapid increase of plantations in the West Indies concentrating on sugar offered ambitious New England traders a market for surplus meat, grain, and livestock. Ships were needed to develop such a commerce; but New England was favored with a wealth of shipbuilding resources, as well as with a great number of safe, deep, and accessible harbors.

Its colonists, not only merchants by profession but farmers and tradesmen, had come to the New World experienced in buying, selling, and trading grain, wool, horses, stock, poultry, dairy products, and other produce at the 800 fairs and markets held regularly in every part of the English realm. Many a New England settlement was named after such a market town. In eastern England, at places where marsh hay was abundant, stockmen had made a business of buying in cattle from a distance to fatten, then selling them to drovers and butchers for the London market. In England's eastern and southern counties, a constant trade in wool and cloth for export had gone on for generations. Buyers regularly came to Kent and the Severn Valley for fruit.[2]

So trade in stock and produce was an old story to many a New Englander. Already a lively commerce had grown up between the well-established planters of Plymouth Colony and the new arrivals at the Bay, and both had carried on frequent transactions with New Amsterdam. Thus when the local economy languished, nothing could be more natural than to look abroad for markets, as well as to consider what imports could be dispensed with.

Governor Winthrop's journal recites the measures adopted. "These straits set our people on work to provide fish, clapboards, plank, etc. and to sow hemp and flax (which prospered very well) and to look out to the West Indies for a trade for cotton. The general court also made orders about payment of debts, setting corn at the wonted prices, and payable for all debts which should arise after a time prefixed."[3] With matters at home thus stabilized, the colony looked abroad for new income.

Nature gave assistance to budding trade. A drought in the West Indies brought demands for foods that New England was happy to supply. As Winthrop put it in his *History* in 1647: "It pleased the Lord to open to us a trade with Barbados and other islands . . ." That year Boston sent Barbados a deckload of horses; the next year one of cattle; in the same year New Netherland came to New Haven for beef. Meanwhile, in 1645, 20,000 bushels of grain had gone out, and export of grain grew so vigorous that in the spring of 1648 Massachusetts had temporarily to forbid its shipment to the West Indies, Portugal, and the Spanish islands in order not to go short herself. The ban was soon lifted, but the next year the colony had to stop export of mares, lest its reservoir of horseflesh dry up. Through the 1650's trade in commodities of many sorts grew fast. Providence merchants, for example, sent tobacco to Boston, which reshipped it to London. A whole ton went to Newfoundland, the settlers there finding it more advantageous to fish than to farm in the island's brief summer.

The result of all this enterprise soon showed in work for all and a market for every type of farm produce. Carpenters and mechanics were fully employed on dwellings, barns, shipping. "Now it is wonderfull," exclaimed Maverick in 1660 (he had preceded the Puritans to Boston Harbor), "to see the many Vessels belonging to the Country of all sorts and seizes from Shipps of some reasonable burthen to Skiffes and Cannoes, many other great Shipps of Burthen from 350 Tunns to 150 have been built there, and many more in time may be." Merchants were taking in European coined money and Spanish bar silver. They bought lumber for sale. They collected flour, meat, and vegetables from the country to provide food for the crews, whether engaged in distant foreign trade, or manning the hundreds of smaller vessels that were soon taking fish off Cape Sable. Bakers set up shop not only to bake bread from the farmers' grain for townspeople, but to bake hard "bisquits" to feed sailors and residents of tropic islands a thousand miles away.[4] For the sale of animals and farm produce towns like Hartford, Charlestown, Salem, Lynn, and others authorized local market days weekly or oftener. In 1652 Massachusetts even set up its own mint. The early days of scarcity were over.

The effect of this burgeoning trade is described by Samuel Maverick from his farm on Noddle's Island, as he looks across at Boston: "The Towne is full of good shopps well furnished with all kind of merchandize and many Artificers and Trad'smen of all sorts." The influence of improved trade, he notes, has spread into the smaller towns. A dozen miles to the north, at "Wooburne" "They live by furnishing the Sea townes with Provisions as Corne and Flesh and also furnish the Merchants with such goods to be exported." To the southwest: "in Dedham live many Bisquett makers and Butchers and have vent enough for their Commodities in Boston."

In the Connecticut Valley grain abounded. Some stockmen had embarked on the profitable English custom of finishing the hogs of others for market. Western Rhode Island by 1661 had horses as a staple exportable to the West Indies, often through Boston, the chief horse mart. In June 1669 Thomas Minor of Stonington recorded in his diary, how he set forth for Boston on a Monday, sold his string of horses and got home Saturday. Such horses for the West Indies were intended not to draw plows but to transport people and goods on their backs or to power treadmills for crushing sugar cane.[5]

Massachusetts, Plymouth Colony, Rhode Island, and Connecticut all raised horses for export. In Massachusetts two farmers out of three had horses, at least a mare. Horses at first were small, perhaps such as today's visitor to England finds grazing wild in the New Forest near Southampton, but better blood was introduced. Grown often cheaply by running more or less wild in pasture, they had to be identified by the owner's brand, required by law. A considerable number could be packed on the deck of a moderate-sized "horse jockey," as the export vessels came to be called. The animals sold so well in the tropics that it became profitable to steal and drive them to some sequestered landing for export.

So agricultural trade built up. Small packets plied from inland estuaries and every little harbor along the coast to Boston, Charlestown, Newport, and Manhattan, where larger ones assembled cargoes for distant markets. Almost every day two packets sailed between Scituate and Boston. New London, New Haven, and Milford, Connecticut, traders sent vessels to both Boston and Manhattan. New London gathered hides, furs, and the skins of wild animals, and ordinary farm produce. Wethersfield's chief product so far was pipestaves. Warehouse Point at the Connecticut River falls received the produce of the upper valley. Boston and Plymouth merchants complained that Connecticut Valley grain flooded their markets, and in 1650 New Netherland's Secretary reported to Holland that the Dutch colonists could buy all kinds of livestock from New England more cheaply than from overseas. Little coasting boats carried almost everything. A Martha's Vineyard vessel wrecked among the Elizabeth Islands in 1667 had aboard, according to William Weeks, its commander, "48 bu. Indian corne, fower barrels of pork, 4 hydes, 1 firkin of buter, 1 small casks of suett about 40ᵉ, on(e) barrel of tobacco, about 34 or 35 cotton wool; 26 bushells meale; 8 bushells of it wheate meale, the rest Rye or Indian meale; 1 bushell wheate, 1 bushell of Rye, 2 bushells turnepps, one bushell of Inions."[6]

All this active trade had wide ramifications, with eventual results not then to be imagined. While Boston and Salem built their trade in beef and pork for the West Indies, the wealth of hides and skins accumulated by slaughterhouses close by led readily, as it had in Old England, to tanning, the making of shoes, and their export, so that it was natural that Massachusetts should become shoemaker to the new continent.

Export of pipestaves became inextricably tied to imports of molasses, and its distillation into rum; which became the staple of the African slave trade. Thus do the patterns of history become woven and interwoven.

Besides the animals and crops that farmers grew, the third crop, wood and lumber, deserves further discussion. The forest was especially helpful because it furnished winter employment. Timber was sometimes the product of individual properties but was often cut legally by permission or illegally without it, from undivided town commons, even from highways. Its first use, naturally, was at home for building materials, fencing, and farm tools, and for the needs of local artisans—the bark, for example, was used by tanners. Immense quantities of wood were burned in fireplaces for heating and cooking.

Shipbuilders of Portsmouth, Medford, and New London required the best of oak and pine for their vessels. As time went on, newly built vessels replaced wrecked and wornout ships; others were sold abroad. As New England's trade expanded, shipbuilding offered a growing market for forest products.

Lumber went as cargo also: barrels in which salt fish, beef, pork, and many other goods were exported; shooks and hoops for hogsheads, in which to bring back molasses; or pipestaves for Madeira wine. Entire cargoes were of clapboards. With other cargo in the hold, a deckload of sawn boards and plank—even the frame and siding of an entire house—might be added. Long spars were cut not merely to rig the ship itself but for sale to foreign riggers. Maverick tells, for example, how the town of Hingham in 1660 was supplying Boston with not only wood, timber, and boards but masts as well, from its pine plains.

With the straight, tall pine of southern Maine and New Hampshire to draw on (Maine's first sawmill is said to date from 1633 or 1634), Portsmouth became a great lumber port. An incoming vessel might leave its imported cargo at Boston, then at Portsmouth take on a new lading of lumber and perhaps cattle, together with furs, salt meat, and salt fish. England's timber was becoming scarce. The war with Holland in 1652, which cut off her Baltic Sea sources of wood, gave an extra fillip to New England's lumber trade. Merchants began to buy into sawmills. The less valuable cordwood went to Boston and Salem to keep town dwellings warm and their bread baked. Firewood might come direct from nearby towns by oxcart, or from all along the shore in little wood boats that sailed for fish in summer.[7]

A further source of forest income was the preparation of charcoal for the furnaces of the iron bloomeries that soon developed at Saugus, Taunton, and other locations where bog iron ore was found. These furnaces bought enormous amounts of wood, to be turned into charcoal by professional colliers.[8] As early as 1643 another industry had opened: tapping evergreen forests for naval stores: pitch and tar.

Yet such wholesale use of wood already caused misgivings. The notion that in colonial New England the forest was wantonly destroyed is completely contradicted by the public records of the time. On the contrary, measures were taken almost from the beginning to conserve the woodlands. Many settlers had come from areas of England where wood was scarce and furze and faggots had to be used to cook the meals. Fifteen English counties were practically destitute of timber by the time of New England's settlement, and forest laws were strict and penalties severe.[12] By English standards, the woodland of New England's shore was truly plentiful. Yet the settlers deliberately chose for their early towns sites such as Plymouth, Boston, Cambridge, Concord, Hartford, Milford, Fairfield, Springfield, and Newport, to name but a few where the Indians had cultivated or at least partially deforested. The newcomers therefore acted almost at once to preserve a resource the value of which for farming, shipbuilding, and commerce they well knew from experience.

6. Patterns from Home

N EW ENGLAND SETTLEMENT, except for the earliest founded communities and Rhode Island, went on according to well-defined plans derived, in large part, from early English practices. In all the territory under control of the Massachusetts Bay and the Connecticut colonies, once the original landings were over, the pattern was set by the colony's General Court. Plymouth Colony also did its best to keep a tight rein on where its people lived and farmed, though its land system tended at an early date more to individual than to community management. In no colony were would-be settlers expected or for long permitted to squat in spots of their own choosing.

The underlying principle was that title to the whole country, both land and water, rested in the king. Out of his bounty he made grants, not always carefully defined as to extent, to certain corporations and individuals, the latter generally highly placed. These persons or corporations in turn were to provide capital and inhabitants to develop their territories, and decide terms of settlement not specified in the charter. Charter terms varied from one colony to another, being quite different in the southern colonies from those of New England.

Absence of one customary provision from its charter made the Massachusetts Bay Company decisively different from earlier colonization enterprises. The location for the conduct of the company's affairs was not specified. The colony was therefore doubly fortunate. Not only were the leaders of the migration persons of superior character and experience, but they brought their charter, the document itself, with them to the New World. Citing its authority as they interpreted it, they at once established the colony's governing body on the new soil, instead of attempting, as had other grantees, to control its operations from England. The effects were immediate.[1]

From Boston, the capital of the actual territory to be administered, the Company's General Court authorized and directed the establishment of each new town; specified its limits; decided who the proprietors of its lands should be; and set forth the powers and duties of its inhabitants and local magistrates. The Court's control was extended at first even to the towns that the Court authorized in Connecticut, later to New Hampshire and Maine, and the attempt was made to include Rhode Island.

Concord, first town to be established inland on fresh water, may serve as an example of how the Court proceeded with the settlement and organization of a township. An adventurous trader, Simon Willard, had followed an Indian trail northward in the quest for furs. He returned to Boston with the tale of an extensive tract of open Indian fields, beside a wide stretch of grassy river meadow that looked good as a locality for cattle. The explorer and others, including friends newly arrived in the colony, petitioned the General Court to grant them this site for settlement. The Court appointed a committee of trusted persons to investigate. They reported favorably. The Court then directed them to lay out a village and to allot lands to prospective settlers who agreed to inhabit. The result was the town of Concord.[2]

In carrying out such a mission in a virgin, unsettled countryside, the planners would naturally follow the familiar pattern of an English village.[3] In most English villages the houses with their garden plots and stables stood close together, facing one or more highways, within easy reach of the church and not far from the manor with its green or park. So for their New World town, the committee or its surveyor would first trace on a suitable location the outline of "The Street," as it was often designated, with perhaps another joining it at an angle. Facing this highway, sometimes on one side only, perhaps on both, they marked out a series of contiguous home- or house-lots, usually of similar proportions. One purpose was to establish a congenial community, each household with neighbors, friends, and church close by; another was to provide for close supervision by authority; a third was mutual protection.

In the new colony of Massachusetts Bay, in Plymouth Colony, and in Connecticut, the General Courts insisted that a bargain agreeable to both sides be made with any Indians who inhabited or claimed title; and Rhode Island colonists made similar bargains. Having compensated them for the land, a deed of the land of the new township was formally signed and recorded.

A closely settled village was almost uniformly the pattern. To a majority of the newcomers, the idea of scattered farmsteads on outlying disconnected sites would have been strange and repugnant. In most districts of England the villagers had been used to living sociably alongside one another, the byres (barns or sheds) for their stock adjoining each dwelling; a croft or nightpasture and their gardens and fruit trees in the rear. From these home lots they were accustomed to go out to the fields to cultivate their crops. These crops were usually planted under an agreed-on pattern in individual strips in large common fields. A common herdsman led or drove the stock of all to pasture in the common "waste" or woods.

In Massachusetts Bay, therefore, the public commission, acting under authority of the colony's General Court, arranged the preliminaries for the new township after a similar model, and reported to the Court as to its investigation and recommendations. Next, the heads of families who proposed to become the proprietors of the new settlement each certified to that intention. If their number was sufficient (usually at least forty were required) and they satisfied the Court that they were responsible persons, intending to occupy, they were assigned a specific tract and accorded the powers of a body politic, and the Court gave the new town a name. The General Court ordinarily endowed such a town with at least thirty-six square miles of territory and often much more. The intending settlers then chose their homesteads according to the plan already prepared, often by drawing lots.

From that point on, those whose names had been included could and did elect their local officers, pass bylaws, and handle the town's affairs more or less after the fashion of the English town or parish they had known at home; except that in their new situation, with no bishop to appoint a rector, they chose their minister. They were now proprietors of their home lots and any meadow or plowland assigned them individually, and from that time forward they had power over all the rest of the common and undivided land within the township limits.

In early days the townsite chosen was likely to be on or adjoining a tract left clear by the Indians. In Concord and in neighboring Sudbury alike, it ran along the south or west side of a protecting hill; near a river ford and a small entering stream, at a spot where the intersection of Indian paths or a ford offered logical choices for proposed highways.

In a few towns a home lot was as small as an acre or even less, at the beginning. Ordinarily, however, its size was four or five acres, and it might be as much as ten, even twenty acres. In any case it would be enough, as in Old England, for a dwelling, garden, fruit orchard, and buildings for the family's stock, plus an exercise ground or small night-pasture for the animals. The house lots were frequently all of the same size but sometimes varied according to investment and social order, and were set up side by side in one unified plan. At the start of the division one suitably located lot was reserved for the meetinghouse, one or more "glebe" lots for the ministry, and, as time went on, other lots for education and a burying ground.

To every occupying family went also title to certain "rights," including a share in the village's most important asset, meadows, which were to furnish hay for its cattle; a share in its arable or plow land for growing "corn" or grain for food; and a share in its woodland and waste, to provide necessary pasture, building materials, fencing, and fuel to cook with and to keep the family warm.

Whether the prospective settler were farmer, sailor, tailor, or tanner, each head of a family who was to become a proprietor in the new community was entitled to such a home lot and the rights that appertained to it. No one paid for his lot, but in return for the privileges granted him, the General Court expected each to become a partner in the town and a builder of its communal life.

Economic equality was by no means intended or expected. Aside from the home lot, some persons received much more than the minimum allotment of meadow and "arable." This might be in recognition of the larger capital or estate that they were prepared to invest in the new community. Thus, if a "planter" brought with him a dozen cattle rather than a single cow, naturally he would need more meadow or mowing to carry them through the winter, plus other things in proportion. In the division, therefore, he was accorded extra rights. If the new proprietor had a wife, or if an additional asset was several sons, he would require extra land to feed and support them. On the other hand, it was clear that with such a number of helpers, a head of household should be able to handle more land to advantage. A large family, therefore, as a rule got proportionately extra rights.

This was the general pattern for Massachusetts Bay and Connecticut, with certain variations in Plymouth Colony after its first decade. It was familiar to everyone, for the roots of the township and agricultural systems ran back in Britain across medieval times into Scandinavian, Saxon, Roman, and Celtic customs through at least two thousand years.

One basic difference in the terms of settlement compared to common Old World practice was that once a settler was received as a member of the group under the required conditions of character and residence, all land and rights allotted were ordinarily held in fee simple: no rents to pay, no lord or bailiff to placate. Every proprietor became a freeholder, and could sell or bequeath his property, subject only to the customary requirement that it be first offered to the town, unless disposed of to a new owner approved by the community as suitable to become one of its members. The latter provision was to discourage absentee ownership.

Other customs brought from the homeland prevailed. Allotments of plow land (called arable) were usually portions in one or more large town fields, often former Indian-cleared tracts, the planting of which was according to a single pattern determined seasonally by the town. Town meeting or town selectmen set the date by which fence was to be mended alongside and proportionate to each man's cultivated section. When the crop was grown, the town determined how soon harvest should be finished, so that the town's cattle could be turned in to feed off the straw, stalks, and weeds. Town authority decided the number or "stint" of animals each was entitled to pasture, according to his agreed-on "rights."

Often the town provided one or more town bulls, and employed one or more herdsmen to gather at each man's gate his stinted number of cattle, goats, or sheep, drive them as a single herd or flock to pasture, and return them. Each morning the cowherd blew his horn for the householders to bring their creatures to their gates. He watched the animals through the day in the woods and meadows, and returned them at sundown to their owners. Horses, hogs, turkeys, geese, and fowl were in most places allowed to run at large, but the town set the beginning and duration of periods during which they must be yoked or hobbled to prevent their damaging gardens and cornfields.

As the generations passed and more and more of the town's common lands came to be divided and assigned to individuals, this ancient system was gradually modified and eventually outgrown. Crops were thereafter planted according to each man's pleasure, and stints of all sorts were done away with. Yet because of the convenience of the system, common herding and pasturage persisted in some towns even to the twentieth century. In these later times, and quite soon in Plymouth Colony, houses began to go up on outlying land; and a system of scattered and individually owned and operated farms at length took over. Even so, the close-knit village remained and in hundreds of towns exists today, its highways and lots little altered.

One factor that modified the general rule of land proprietorship in all the colonies was the occasional grant of a large acreage as compensation or as an honorarium to some public official or prominent personage. Moreover, as time went on, fiscal necessities, land speculation, and political pressures brought about changes in the original pattern.

The town meeting ran the town, under the statutes of the General Court. Following ancient English usage, after warning by a constable, the heads of families gathered at the hour appointed, at first in some central tavern or dwelling, or even outdoors under a tree. As soon as time and increase of wealth permitted, the town would vote to erect a meeting-house to be used both for this local assembly and for worship. "All triv-eall things e. c. shall be ordered in the towns," the General Court of Massachusetts Bay decided in 1635. In time it became burdensome for the citizens to leave their work for the frequent decisions required to handle ordinary business of the community. Hence they came to elect three, five, seven, sometimes more, "chosen men" or "townsmen," who eventually received the title of selectmen. Not seldom it was hard to find persons willing to accept such offices, almost all unpaid and time-consuming, and penalties were set for refusing.[4]

In disposing of common lands and common property, only proprietors could vote. In other town matters eventually all male inhabitants possessing a certain modest amount of personal property or land, the "inhabitants," came to receive the privilege. At first only the "freemen," persons selected and named by the General Court of the Commonwealth as worthy, members all of them of the established Congregational Church, might vote on the election of magistrates and representatives to the General Court. This also was liberalized. However, in the Body of Liberties adopted by the Massachusetts General Court in 1641, an essential ancient English right was reaffirmed. "Every man whether Inhabitant or fforreiner, free or not free" is entitled "to come to any publique Court, Council or Towne meeting and either by speech or writing to move any lawful, seasonable, and materiall question, or to present any necessary motion, complaint, Bill or information," though he had to do it in an orderly manner.[5]

The general pattern of the origin of New England town government has been set forth. Suffice it to say that as population increased and as ownership of land and other wealth came to be dispersed among many persons, the right to vote, first in town affairs and later in colony affairs, was eventually acquired by almost all male inhabitants who had property worth recording. Sometimes this occurred only after bitter local struggles, especially over land distribution. The village is a small commonwealth, says Maitland, "with an old self-adjusted scheme of common rights and duties,"[7] but this ideal often did not evolve in local practice without ferment and strain.

Each town appointed its committees to lay out highways, saw to their repair, contracted for cartbridges, engaged the town minister, provided his firewood, seated the meetinghouse, paid bounties for destroying predators, collected taxes, and arranged countless other details. Before the fish ran upstream in the spring, the town set the dates for seining them, or let out the privilege of taking them, and appointed fish wardens to supervise the whole.

Certain of the town's duties were prescribed by the General Court. In Massachusetts Bay this included collecting colony taxes, seeing that children received moral training and education, looking after the poor, sealing weights and measures. All the colonies required inspection of export commodities such as staves, bread, salt, meat, fish, and tobacco, packed in kegs. The brands of large animals had to be recorded in a town book before they were permitted to be at large, shipped, or sold. The selectmen received also the duty of setting a fair value on staple commodities for purposes of exchange or barter, and for paying taxes and debts.

About much of these and similar procedures little was new. Most found English precedents in the customs of the manor or parish, and the statutes of the several King Henrys, King John, even back through William the Conqueror to Celtic, Saxon, and Danish customs.

Two duties were building fences and roads. Every man was bound to improve the road against his "tenement," and keep up his portion (often several portions) of the town hedge, wall, or fencing. This had been the rule in England for at least four centuries. In the colonies, fencing was required not only to keep animals in but, more importantly, to keep them outside cultivated fields and gardens. The painted and sometimes artistically ornamental white picket fences with gates that line old New England village streets are reminders that once cattle and hogs were frequent passersby, unwelcome in gardens.

The colonies' first roads were poor but laid out by town committees wide enough for the passage of cattle and so that riders might as far as possible avoid boulders and sloughs. Before long they had to be improved for the passage of oxcarts and hayricks. Periodically all able-bodied men were called out to labor on them, on pain of a fine.

Each town elected one, later two, representatives to the General Court or assembly of the colony. With the magistrates, these formed its governing body, under the Crown. However, a town entitled to two frequently sent but one. Many times, pleading poverty, towns asked to be excused altogether.

7. Settling In

DWELLINGS and other farm buildings followed traditional dimensions. They were of one or more "bays" measuring a rod of 16 or 16½ feet, or of some proportion of this ancient English farm dimension. Thomas Lechford describes an early Massachusetts Bay house 16 × 14 feet, with chimney outside. In Concord, Elisha Jones' house of two rooms, one above the other, built in 1640, had a 12 × 8 foot fireplace. In a fairly large house built at Sandwich on Cape Cod in 1642, the front room measured 16 feet square. Edmund Rice's house at Sudbury, put up in 1647, was planned 30 × 16; and the "Peak House," still standing at Medfield, was laid out 24 × 14½, and 10 feet to the eaves, with four very small windows. At Sudbury Edmund Rice's barn was 50 feet long with a 12-foot stud. Cambridge Records of the 1670's mention barn lengths of 17, 18, and 30 feet; a lean-to (1683) was to be 30 × 10 feet with a 4-foot stud. As to the outhouses and hovels where young stock, goats, and poultry must have found shelter, very little is recorded, though tax lists often mention them.

As part of the home lot each household soon had its "pleasant gardens with kitchin gardens," to borrow Wood's words. In Cambridge in 1635 house after house is listed as having a garden and "backside," though lots there were small compared to those in most towns. Manured with fish at first, gardens had to be well enclosed by pales (closely spaced vertical stakes driven into the ground, or slats fastened to two rails), to prevent dogs from making a meal of the fertilizer. For his fence, the householder got permission of the selectmen or timber warden to cut posts and pales from the common woodland. (On Cambridge's "Tory Row" fences of pales today still enclose a few front yards.)[1]

Until fruit trees had time to reach bearing, "instead of Apples and Pears they had Pomkins and Squashes of divers kinds," Johnson records. One visitor likewise wrote that pumpkins and squash were the chief fruit that supported the English when they first settled; in fact, pumpkins were all this man saw in the market at Salem. More than one colonist was enthusiastic about the way vegetables grew, especially the roots. "Our turnips, parsnips, and carrots are here both bigger and sweeter than is ordinary to be found in England," boasted Pastor Higginson of Salem: "Pease of all sorts and the best in the World." In his *New England's Rarities Dis-*

covered, Josselyn declares, "I never heard of, nor did see in eight year's time one worm eaten pea."

Old customs endured. A Medford gardener notes in 1648: "Sown one peck of pease, the moon in the full." The muskmelons and watermelons were especially juicy, Josselyn thought, and cabbages grew "exceeding well." At Plymouth, besides the usual roots, Bradford's poem tells of cucumbers, radishes, coleworts, and cabbages.[2]

As to fruit, John Endecott's seeding of apples was so successful that in 1648 he traded 500 three-year apple whips with William Trask for 200 acres of land, not a bad bargain either way. The age of the saplings is notable, because four years earlier Endecott had suffered a catastrophe. "My children," he wrote Governor Winthrop, "burnt mee at least 500 trees this spring by setting the ground on fire neere them."[3]

Governor Winthrop too was strong for fruit. From trees on Governor's Island in Boston Harbor, perhaps started by Roger Conant before Winthrop's advent, he was delighted eight years after his arrival to be brought ten very fair pippins; and he planted more at his "Ten Hills Farm" on the Mystic.[4]

Householders everywhere were soon planting seeds of apples, pears, cherries, and other fruits about their dwellings. By 1646–47 Reverend Mr. Danforth of Roxbury could record: "Aug. 1. The great pears ripe." "Aug. 3, The long apples gathered." "Aug. 12 Blackstone's apples gathered." "Aug. 15 Tankerd apples gathered." "Aug. 18, Kretoin pippins and long red apples gatherd." and by 1649, on July 20 he had "apricocks ripe."[5]

In the fall of 1646 Reverend John Eliot, at Nonantum (now Newton), rewarded each Indian child in his catechism class with an apple. The famous Roxbury Russet, still the best apple for cider and one of the longest winter keepers, is thought to have originated about 1647 in the town for which it was named. Fruit added to property values. In 1648 the will of John Balch of Beverly left to his widow one-half of "thc great fruit trees," the other half to his oldest son, and to his younger sons the younger trees.[6] An orchard is mentioned at Amesbury in the Merrimack Valley in 1649.

Though much of Plymouth Colony's soil was less well adapted to fruit than that of Massachusetts Bay, Governor Thomas Prence, elected in 1634, set pear trees in Eastham on Cape Cod about 1640, one of which was still capable of yielding 15 bushels of fruit 200 years later. A pear tree set at Yarmouth and another at Truro were likewise fruiting bountifully at ages well beyond two centuries. Kentish cherries and plums did well in Plymouth Colony, also.

In what is now Rhode Island some of the Reverend Mr. Blaxton's original Yellow Sweetings at his Study Hill home in Cumberland, then under the Plymouth patent, were called the richest and most delicious apples of the whole kind. They were reported thrifty still in 1765, and at least two trees of his orchard were fruiting in 1830, almost two centuries after he started them. At Newport in 1639 six acres were granted to William Coddington for an orchard, the second recorded in what was to become Rhode Island.[7]

Connecticut's first comers from The Bay had scarcely sat down before they were starting apples. One tree at Hartford, said to date from 1638, was still bearing in 1853. Hedrick credits George Fenwick of Saybrook with the first New England nursery, well started by 1641. He had cherry and peach trees as well as apples. Henry Wolcott of Windsor, a magistrate there, had 32 orders for trees from 25 customers in 1641; and a decade later sold 500 apple trees in one lot, to be paid for half in wheat, half in pease. In the Connecticut Valley, however, Hollanders seem to have been ahead of their rivals, the English. When de Vries in 1639 visited their fort near Hartford, he saw forty or fifty cherry trees near the redoubt full of fruit (but possibly native rum cherries). After the English settled the Connecticut shore, Thomas Minor at Stonington recorded grafting 100 trees in 1663, and the next year gathered in all 120 bushels of apples and "pounded 6 barrels of sider."

A desire for cider and vinegar was the chief reason for the planting of apples that went on everywhere. The English found that barley for their customary beer grew poorly, but that apples for cider, which had been a beverage only in the fruit-growing counties at home, would thrive almost universally. Henry Wolcott of Connecticut in 1671 boasted to John Josselyn that in one year he made 500 hogsheads. A hogshead of cider ordinarily sold at 10 shillings. Some pears went into another alcoholic drink, perry. Josselyn made cherry wine, and so, he said, did many others.

By 1643 Johnson claimed that there were as many as 1,000 acres of orchards and gardens in the Bay Colony, and in 1660 Maverick commented: "The great abundance of English Fruite, as Apples, Pears, Apricocks, Cherries, Muskmellons, Watermellons &c is not to be believed but by those that have seene it."[8] He might have added gooseberries and barberries, both brought from England.

For most families the orchard, like the vegetable garden, was one of the features of the home lot, where the apple yard was companion to the turnip yard and tobacco yard, each fenced against wandering stock. If Johnson is to be believed, on village home lots it was not long before the flower garden became companion to the vegetable garden. When the lilac appeared beside the front door no diarist records.

8. The Farm Family

How, in general, was the farm family getting along at the end of the first half century?

As to food, it was eating heartily and wholesomely by the standards of that century, though not always daintily. Gone were the early days of dependence on biscuits and beer out of English ships, corn bought of Indians, and clams dug on the shore. Indian corn was indeed still a mainstay of the colonists' diet, but it was corn of their own raising, and in the older settlements corn ground by a water mill rather than pounded in a quern or mortar to be mixed with water into cakes called bannock.

A second food soon adopted from the native Indians was beans. No Boston baked beans for a considerable time, but beans or peas cooked soft in pork or beef pot liquor (as in the famous pease porridge of the children's rhyming chant) and eaten hot or allowed to jell. In winter it might be frozen and a section cut off as needed. Beans boiled with corn kernels into Indian succotash made a popular combination.[1]

Added to corn and beans, two other Indian vegetables, squash and pumpkin, became a great resource. "Pumpkin Porridge being as much in esteem with New England Saints as Jelly broth with Old English sinners," as jocular Ned Ward put it. In 1674 Benjamin Tompson looked back on the time "When Cimnels [summer squashes] were accounted noble bloud among the tribes of common herbage Food." For pottage and pudding and custards and pies our pumpkins and parsnips are common supplies," as the popular Forefathers' Song put the situation in rhyme.[2] Even more common than the parsnip among vegetables of English origin were the turnip, the onion, and in time the cabbage.

As has been noted, for meat no animal furnished so much so quickly and cheaply as the porker. Hunting his own acorns, groundnuts, Jerusalem artichokes, and other roots, with shellfish to eke out in winter near the shore, the hog grew with little expense except perhaps for some grain at the end. A fat little pig made a good roast, as John Dunton recorded in his journal. Hog weights at killing time in the fall ran low by modern standards, seldom up to two hundred pounds. Nevertheless the animal provided hams, bacon, lard, and barreled salt pork. Salt meat had been the winter dish most relished in the old country. Salt pork became for two centuries in all seasons the chief reliance of the farm wife in the new.[3]

Getting a supply of beef involved much more time and trouble than one of pork, since good hay was as yet scarce. Yet practically every farmer, and even the village mechanic, tried to keep a few cows. The cow furnished milk, in summer at least, to eat with his gruel, plus butter and cheese for his family. Before long there might even be a surplus for sale. A calf could be killed for veal, or occasionally an older animal to supply the corned beef barrel.

Sheep were scarce at first and provender suitable for them lacking; but immigrants from English sheep counties began rearing them on dis forested islands or in niches safe from wolves. Well before the end of the half century Reverend Edmund Browne could report for Massachusetts that mutton as well as pork was usually eaten there.[4] Yet even in Essex County, despite its plentiful meadow hay, midcentury inventories list sheep in considerably fewer than half the farm estates.

Hunting might help to vary the farm family's diet, though as early as 1646 Portsmouth and Newport on Aquidneck Island (now Rhode Island) were limiting the deer-hunting season to winter. A thief who entered a house at Truro on Cape Cod in 1647 made away with venison, along with such usual products of the farm as beef, bread, butter, cheese, and tobacco. At Oxford in central Massachusetts, at a date much later, a farmer claimed that it was as easy to bring in a fawn from the woods as to get a lamb from his sheepfold. Migrating fowl, especially wild pigeons, were a common table delicacy in spring and fall. Fish, too, were good food in the short period in spring when they pushed up the streams to spawn in their headwaters.

The wild berries and grapes that do so well over most of New England helped satisfy the newcomers' taste for fruit. In June wild strawberries were common. Josselyn called the numerous "Skyecoloured" or blueberries "a most excellent summer dish." "They usually eat of them put into a Bason, with Milk and sweeted a little more with Sugar and Spice." Dried berries were mixed into puddings. Bees from across the seas were soon on hand to fertilize the blossoms of fruit trees. As bees began to provide honey, tarts made from apple, pear, and quince were added to the diet. Pumpkins, eaten at first as vegetables, eventually went into pies also.[5]

By the end of the half-century sugar was being imported in such quantity that ordinary people could afford it. One Essex County farmer in 1651 sold a Salem merchant 12 bushels of rye and took home sugar;

along with it went a doll and a bird-whistle. (This incident is to be recalled when it is argued that all Puritans were hardhearted and severe.)

Farm people ate from wooden trenchers or bowls, sitting at a wood trestleboard according to English custom. Everybody used knives, wooden spoons, and their fingers. Crockery, glassware, and pewter began to come in, but for the ordinary family these for the most part were still in the future.

For clothing farm people were likely to go short. Imported cloth was expensive. The spinning wheel and the loom would not for a considerable time become part of every household's furnishings. "The Farmers," says Johnson, "deemed it better for their profit to put away [sell] their cattel and corn for cloathing, than to set upon making of cloth . . ." So they were likely to sell a cow or two for something to wear. At first all clothing was worn to shreds. Then as hides and skins were tanned and cured right on the farm or by the village tanner, these became raw material for leather coats, breeches, and aprons for the men. Shirts and women's wear were apt to be of coarse gray cloth, sometimes cotton, sometimes woolen. The first American center for cloth manufacture was Rowley, in Massachusetts Bay, settled by experienced Yorkshire textile workers. Here in 1638, from the wool of local sheep, they wove the first bolt of woolen cloth in America, 83½ yards long. Except for the men, the members of the family would spend most of the summer barefoot. Soon, however, the village cobbler made them boots or shoes from the hides of their stock for Sabbath and winter wear.[6]

Within a decade or two the English were settling in, their most pressing needs met, and many achieved a fair degree of comfort. Their dwellings were small and not infrequently crowded, but at least they afforded shelter. The more valuable stock was housed also. Towns had put up small, plain meetinghouses to which all went for worship, and the men for town meetings. They had begun to lay out highways and had long since been collecting taxes. Already the general level of welfare was such that the Colony's magistrates were worried about the idleness of some who along with the "saints" had been attracted to the new land.

Johnson's *Wonder Working Providence* summed up the situation in 1654: "There are not many towns in this country, but the poorest person in them hath a house and land of his own, and bread of his own growing if not some cattel; besides flesh is now no rare food, beef, pork and mutton being frequent in many houses . . ."[7] Johnson was overoptimistic, but in the main his description was justified.

In thinking of the seventeenth century farm it is essential largely to discard the picture of the modern, self-contained farmstead. Except in the very smallest operations, as towns over the years divided their reserves of common land among the proprietors, the farmer's holdings would come to include, besides the home lot, several separate pieces of meadow or salt marsh from which he got his winter hay, plus upland scattered among various locations, often at a considerable distance from his dwelling. All this would be in addition to his one or several pieces or "gates" in the common or cultivated fields. There he grew his grain, and had pasturage rights to follow.

The harvest from his cultivation was ordinarily of small proportions by modern standards. Although a large percentage of early inventories contain items of Indian corn, very seldom does the total count run as high as 50 or 60 bushels; or, if standing in the field, five or six acres is a notably high figure. The majority of inventories are much smaller. Not over half the inventories mention the English bread grains: wheat, rye, or barley, except perhaps for a little in the house for cooking. Anything over five or ten bushels of such grain is highly unusual, though an occasional large farm with several yoke of oxen and presumably hired labor may have as high as 200 bushels. Generally the harvest is on a small scale.

Moreover carts and wains are few on farms for the first forty years and plows even less common. Such heavy work as was essential would seem to have been arranged for with professional plowmen and teamsters who did such operations for many others, perhaps plowing the entire common arable with some equivalent manual labor by the individual farmers in return.

Livestock numbers for a whole town might be impressive, as Johnson and others added them up, but from today's point of view the numbers per individual farm were far from weighty. A dozen cowkind, even when it included not only mature animals but younger ones from one, to three years old, was a large herd for the first fifty years of the New England colonies. With sheep the situation was similar. In Newbury at the mouth of the Merrimack by 1660, John Cutting's total of 47 sheep in all, or John Dowlett's flock of 76 plus 10 lambs at Rumney Marsh in 1681, were enormous compared to the usual flock of from three to a dozen. Hog numbers on individual farms ran from a single sow to a total of perhaps a dozen swine in all, in some cases including young pigs. Once more Dowlett at Rumney Marsh heads the list of those surveyed, with 29. Livestock numbers in Connecticut appear similar.[8]

Such statistics do not imply incompetence, lack of ambition, or idleness, nor do they suggest any lack of good food for the farm family or preclude the possibility of a salable surplus to be traded to some merchant. They merely illustrate the immense expenditure of labor and time involved in farming before the advent of modern machinery and chemical fertilizers. To support a family of five to a dozen with only the hoe, scythe, sickle, axe, and spinning wheel for tools required not only knowledge of farming but continuous labor for the whole family through all daylight hours, which often provided no more than the simple necessities of shelter, food, fuel, and clothing that modern Americans are apt to regard as their rightful minimum.

So with unending labor the first dwellings had been built, and makeshift shelters for the stock arranged. Gardens had been laid out, manured, and planted, and apple and pear trees set. Indian corn, rye, and wheat had been grown, harvested, and ground for the family's food. At winter's beginnings hogs and beef were ready to be slaughtered, portions exchanged with neighbors or sold, and the balance salted. Trees had been cut, fuel hauled, highways laid out, meetinghouses provided.

By the end of the colonies' first half century, the old folks had mostly died, and the next generation had taken over the farms. Persistent; intelligent application had brought to farm families adequate food, shelter, and means not only of existence but of a considerable degree of comfort. In some few cases wealth had begun to accumulate.

How then are the accomplishments of the farmers of New England's first half century and their agriculture to be assessed?

First and most essential, the new colonies were fed. There was no starvation such as plagued Virginia's earliest years. It was done at the beginning by breeding livestock in plenty; and not long afterward sufficient harvests of grain, fruits, and vegetables were added.

In part this achievement resulted from adequate planning by the sponsors of the Massachusetts Bay Colony across the seas. In part it rested on the preparation of much of the landscape by the colony's vanished Indian predecessors. In part the outcome was the fruit of the settlers' own heavy toil and struggle. Yet the success of these first New England farm people went beyond essentials. Before even the second decade was complete, they were helping to provide masts and plank for shipbuilding and lumber and livestock to accompany the fisherman's contribution to the cargo. Thus they supplied a foundation for the foreign trade that helped the colonies to achieve an economically sound life.

This, however, was not the whole achievement. Following principles ingrained from a millennium and more of English rural experience, they bore the strain of transplanting and adapting an ancient system of local village self-government to rough new circumstances in a rough new land. They did this with success so complete that the pattern then established was to prove not only adequate but adaptable enough to serve with only minor changes for three and a half centuries to come. Indeed eventually in essence it would spread half way across the continent, to govern much of the rural heart of a nation then undreamed of.

Now, at the end of their first half century, the first generation had completed the foundation. A second generation, no longer transplanted Englishmen but native to the soil, had begun to build thereon. The work of both was to be tried by the fire of Indian warfare. On these country-born farm people the brunt of the death and destruction of King Philip's War was about to fall.

II.
WAR AND TRADE,
1675-1775

9. A Surplus to Sell

A PHRASE THAT HISTORIANS have frequently used to describe the agriculture of New England's early generations is "subsistence farming." The words imply that the early farmer, once he had chopped out a spot in the forest, spent the rest of his life and energies barely keeping himself and his family in food—planting just sufficient grain and raising only enough animals to furnish milk for their porridge, wool for their backs, and shoes for their feet. There were many such, but a more accurate description even for this type of agriculture is "self-sufficient farming," as some historians have more precisely described it.

Self-sufficiency certainly was the first objective of nearly all early farmers. Because of inadequate capital, distance from markets, or poor land, some never got beyond it. Included in this category of farming might be the tradesmen, fishermen, and sailors who on their village lot had a cow and a sow, who grew a little corn or wheat, set a dozen fruit trees, and perhaps dug a kitchen garden while for the most part pursuing their primary occupations. Yet the phrase "self-sufficient farming" affords only a partial picture of what in numerous instances actually went on almost from the beginning, and especially after the first decade when it became clear that if they were to survive economically, the Bay Colony and its neighbors had to find products that could be sold outside New England. As decades passed, to grow and dispose of at least some farm produce beyond the family's requirements became more and more the goal of New England farm people. As Governor Thomas Hutchinson later put it, they gradually fell into the trade most natural to the country.

In the very year 1676 when King Philip and his allies were harassing the outlying towns of Massachusetts and Rhode Island, Edward Randolph, the English customs collector sent out by Charles II, made a detailed report, perhaps a trifle inflated, to the Committee For Trade and Plantations across the sea regarding New England's economic situation, in particular its exports. In addition to the cod, mackerel, large fat herring, furs, and bar iron, all of which he mentions, he gives a list of other exportable commodities, the fruits of agriculture and lumbering.

Among those he counted: all things necessary for shipping and naval furniture; pines for masts the best in the world, pitch, tar, and hemp; clapboards, pipestaves, planks and dealboards; horses, beefs, sheep, hogs,

and goats; great plenty of wheat, rye, barley, oats, and pease. Of agricultural products, he states, salt beef and pork, pease, flour, biscuit, and
malt had long been going to Virginia, Maryland, Jamaica, and the West
Indies; together with horses, dealboards, pipestaves, and houses ready
framed. Ship's masts, timber, and wood products were exported to England, Spain, Portugal, their islands, and Gibraltar; and to other parts of
Europe were sent "such commodities as are vendible." Some New England ships, he says, have recently sailed as far as Guinea, Madagascar,
and those coasts. Thirty master-builders put together ships from the native lumber and sell several yearly in England and other parts, for they
build them well and at low cost.[1]

This trade affected individual areas in differing ways. New Hampshire,
which until well into the eighteenth century was settled chiefly along
the coast with its great salt marshes, abounded in cattle. Along Great Bay
and the Piscataqua River its towns had also developed an important lumber trade; as much as 20,000 tons of boards and pipestaves a year was
claimed.[2] Cattle, hogs, and horses were driven over the road from coastal
points and the interior to Boston; salted beef went by coaster.

From Bristol and Newport, Rhode Island, onions locally grown started
for Guiana with a load of horses and lumber. Rhode Island's fat sheep
went overland to market in Boston. New London and Milford, Connecticut, shipped horses, cattle, and salt meats to Boston, Newfoundland, and
the West Indies, and soon added wool, hemp, flax, cider, boards and
staves, tar, and pitch.[3]

At the head of the Connecticut River estuary, Wethersfield exported
wheat and other grains grown on alluvial valley soils, and after 1700 was
a famous source of onions. Upriver in Massachusetts John Pynchon and
others did a thriving business growing pork and beef to send down the
great river to salt water, whence it went packed in barrels either to Boston or directly abroad. When New Jersey suffered a drought in 1687 New
England supplied Indian corn. Wool crossed the sea to France, Spain, and
Portugal; New England soap helped keep Virginians clean.[4] Some merchant families raised cattle and horses for export on farms of their own.
The variety and volume of exports from the score of New England ports
is amazing.

Johnson in an earlier decade had exclaimed, "Nor could it be imagined
that this Wilderness should turn a mart for Merchants in so short a space.
Holland, France, Spain and Portugal coming hither for trade . . ."[5] All the
commerce mentioned was developed before the 1600's were over, while
the first generation of colonists were little more than in their graves.

7. Principal eighteenth-century farm productions, by area. *Cartography Laboratory, Clark University.*

With the coming of the eighteenth century, agricultural exports increased. Country produce flowed to the merchants of Boston, Salem, Newport, New London and New Haven by coaster and oxteam and on the hoof, to be sent wherever it might bring a good return. For example, a daily packet sailed between the South Shore town of Scituate and Boston. On one June day in 1724 six separate "horse jockeys" sailed out of New London for the West Indies, each ship loaded, in addition to other cargo, with a score or more of the animals that traders had collected. The horses were destined for sugar mills or for saddle and pack animals. An ordinary freighter might carry up to 45 horses, in addition to its main cargo of hoops and staves below deck. A large ship with built-in pens might accommodate 150 to 200.[6]

Other livestock went also. On December 5, 1730, a neighborhood cargo from Warwick on the west shore of Narragansett Bay was ready to sail on *The Little Mary*, Captain Stuckley Stafford, master, for Antigua and the Leeward Islands. Besides five horses, the bill of lading included "56 hogs, 84 gees, 190 hens, Boards 4460 ftt. Staves 1900, Shingles 5500, 11 bbls. fish, 7 BB apples, 1700 lb. Cheese."[7]

To Virginia, which concentrated on tobacco, its single money crop, Boston in 1711 sent in one vessel 5½ tons of pork, 690 bushels of corn, and 207 bushels of wheat, very possibly originating in the Connecticut Valley and brought around Cape Cod.[8]

The lading of the New London sloop *Fox* for St. Thomas, in November 1759, illustrates the diversity of cargo that Thomas Allen, New London merchant, could collect from the farms of Connecticut and central Massachusetts. It included "10 bbls. Pork, 8 bbls. Beef, 14 bbls. Fish, 14 casks Bread, 800 Staves, 6500 ropes Onions, 55 Cheeses, 16 kegs Briskets, 50 bu. Potatoes, 10 boxes Sope, 50 Shoats, 32 Gees, 7 Duz ½ of Fowls, 1 Duz Ducks, 47 Turkeys, 13 bbls. Apples."[9]

How such a cargo could be brought together is hinted by intermittent entries from the diary of Joshua Hempstead, farmer-trader of New London. Here are a few samples: "June 18, 1714 I shipped a bl of Tallow on bord Capt. Boss, weight 159 lbs"; "July 16 I shipped 82 lbs. candles—a Ram, 6 lb. Shoe Thread for Barbados." On one Madeira voyage he sent 10 pounds of tobacco and 28½ pounds of beeswax; on another 41½ pounds of bayberry tallow that his son had gotten of a neighbor. Small items like these might be entrusted for sale to friendly captains. On the last day of December 1718, Hempstead wrote in his diary: "I sent 2 Geese 82 ganders by Jonathan Bailey to St. Citts" (St. Christopher). On June 3, 1719, he records the result: "Jonat Bailey hath been over & brought Some Cotton ye Effects of ye Geese I sent by him Last Winter. Still due 2 to 3." Just what was still due is lost to us! At times shipments might even be the result of an order from abroad. William B. Weeden tells of a Surinam planter in 1763 ordering beef, pork, flour, mackerel, fish, tobacco, a bull, two cows and two heifers, and also peacocks, six tame geese, and one dozen ducks.[10]

Trade to the north was of a slightly different character. On Oct. 20, 1764, after the end of the French war, the Massachusetts sloop *Fannie and Jennie*, loaded with 38 tons of brick and tile, also carried 2 chaises, 20 boxes of candles, 40 dozen cabbages, 22 cattle, and 70 sheep. On the

31st the schooner *St. Elizabeth*, in the same brick trade, had on board 5 barrels of apples, 12 dozen cabbages, 44 oxen, 40 sheep, and 5 hundred weight cheese.[11]

As the eighteenth century advanced, additional products from the country found a market. Ships and ship timber went to England, to the other American colonies and the West Indies. Stands of forest too far from coast or river to be sold as timber were now being burned and turned into potash and pearlash, chemical products which were light, easily transported, and in demand in Great Britain. Salt hay went to the South along with beef, pork, dairy products, and apples. Rhode Island had long been exporting its tobacco, and tobacco-growing in Connecticut must also have been considerable.[12] In 1742 Providence cargoes for the West Indies listed up to 5 tons per ship.

Flax was becoming important. The Scotch-Irish, settled in New Hampshire in 1718, began at once to grow it and make it into very good thread and linen. More valuable for trade than the fiber was the seed, which was shipped in bulk from the Connecticut Valley to Ireland, to be sown in that linen center where seed did not mature well. By the middle of the eighteenth century Connecticut was shipping out flaxseed to a value of 80,000 pounds a year, much of it to Ireland, as Victor Clark notes.[13] In more modest amounts seed went to market from small country towns such as Chatham on Cape Cod, Hingham in the Massachusetts Bay Colony, and Peacedale, Rhode Island. It passed as currency in country stores. The local product was not always received with enthusiasm. In 1774 a Philadelphia merchant wrote to Newport complaining that from experience they had found the seed from New England and Rhode Island to run short.

Active commerce bred thriving markets for farm produce, not merely to lade the ships but to provision them. The hundreds of fishing vessels from Marblehead, Gloucester, and Cape Cod towns consumed quantities of salt pork, beef, biscuit, and other food both when fishing in the summer and when carrying cargo in winter. Another modest type of traffic easy to overlook is the great number of boats supplying wood fuel to the port towns, the crew of each of which required provisions.

Whaling, by the middle of the eighteenth century, was also thriving and by the 1770's Massachusetts alone counted over 300 vessels which had to be provisioned for considerable voyages. For example, the sloop *Susannah*, out of Martha's Vineyard, Captain Pease master, heading for whales in the West Indies, in 1763 took on board "7 bbls. beef, 4 bbls. pork, 3 bbls. flour, ½ firkin butter, 1 side good leather, 1100 lbs. bread, 50 lbs. cheese, 4 bu. beans, 3 bu. meal, 4 bu. turnips, 2 bu. potatoes, 16 bu. corn, 14 lbs. candles." The Vineyard and Nantucket between them had 60 whalers out that year; 101, two years later; and 125, in 1768. In 1767 the sloop *Betsey* was fitted for a short whaling voyage at Dartmouth, Massachusetts. Her supplies included "4 bbls. pork, 60 lbs. tallow, 60 lbs. butter, 45 bu. corn, three hundred weight of bread, 66 gr. of flour, 1 cheese, 2 bu. beans, and 166 lbs. beef."[14]

The live freight carried on merchant vessels consumed farm produce. For each horse, cow, ox, or sheep bound for the West Indies, a vessel had to take aboard 200 to 500 pounds of hay according to destination; for each horse, 10 to 15 bushels of oats also. A ship loading 50 horses might need as much as 10 to 12 tons of pressed hay and 500 or more bushels of oats, in addition to food for the crew. Hogs and poultry, to arrive at market in good condition, required grain. In 1768 the New London sloop *Sally* stocked 23 bushels of corn, presumably for its 73 turkeys.[15]

The recurring eighteenth-century wars with the French and Indians swelled demands for market produce. The garrisons of forts had to be provisioned. The colonies outfitted thousands of men for land campaigns and hundreds of ships for the expeditions against Port Royal, Louisburg, and Quebec which dominate the history of this century. The Louisburg troops, for example, numbered over 4000, sent in small vessels; both soldiers and crews had to be fed.[16]

Even though New England early in the eighteenth century was importing flour and other supplies from colonies further south, it becomes clear that the salable surplus its farm people produced beyond subsistence requirements played an important part in the region's foreign commerce and in its income from abroad.[17]

Without entering into the economics of the rise and fall of prices, inflation from paper money, harassing difficulties of exchange and credit, or the limiting acts of Great Britain and the colonists' evasions of them, it becomes apparent how intertwined agricultural production and commerce were. Despite the newness of the country, despite wars that so frequently impinged on orderly progress, all through this century of 1675–1775 New England farmers to a considerable degree enjoyed that essential of a successful agriculture, substantial markets, and they produced the commodities to meet the demands.[18]

Two forces influenced the farmer's choice of what to grow for sale. One was his estimate of what the drover or the merchant shipping to southern or foreign trade would buy for resale at some river port or West Indies island or in Europe. The other was the needs of the people of his market town nearby. From the beginning the colony governments had tried to encourage trade of both kinds by providing local market places and making regulations to ensure fair trade.

For Boston, back in 1633 the Court of Assistants had made Thursday the weekly market day, and in 1635 they designated a market site at the head of what is now State Street. They ordered the land cleared and the pits that pockmarked it, formerly used by sawyers producing plank and boards, to be filled.[19]

In 1656 the will of Captain Robert Keayne, a wealthy Boston merchant, left 300 pounds for a market house and conduit, the latter to serve as a safeguard against fire. Up to that time both market facilities and fire protection must have been poor, for the will read: "I having long thought and considered of the want of some necessary things of public concernment which may not be only commodious, but very profitable and usefull for the Town of Boston, as a market place and cundit, the one a good help in danger of fyre, . . . the other usefull for the country people who come with their provisions for the supply of the towne, that they may have a place to sett dry in and warme, and . . . leave their corne or other things safe that they cannot sell, till they come again, which would be both an encouragement to come in and a great means to increase trading in the Towne also."

A visitor to Boston in 1709 offers this picture of how the town was eating: it was "plentifully supplied with good and wholesome provisions of all sorts . . . Though the town is large and populous they could never be brought to establish a market in it . . . the country people always oppose it. Their reason is, if market days were appointed all the country people coming in at the same time would glut it."

At length Peter Faneuil, a rich merchant, thought to make marketing more effective for both buyers and sellers by offering the gift of a new market building. Whether to accept it or not brought on a battle at town meeting. The crowd was so great that the session had to adjourn to the town's largest church, and the margin for acceptance was only seven votes out of 747. A site was picked on town-owned land close to the dock.

Faneuil's offer to add to his gift a second story for use as a town hall turned the tide of sentiment; and when the building was opened two years later on September 16, 1742, he received the thanks of the town, and the hall was named for him. Provision dealers rented a few market stalls on the street level, but public acceptance was lacking and the market was closed in 1747. It opened again the next spring, closed in 1752, then opened once more. In 1761 fire burned all but the outer walls. With funds from a lottery it was rebuilt two years later, stood through the lean days of the Boston Port Bill and the War for Independence, and today Seth Drowne's grasshopper vane still looks down from the cupola on visitors from every part of the continent.[20]

When demand was good, merchants sent their own buyers direct to the farm districts. These dealt with the country stores that began to appear and act as collection centers. A merchant might set up a branch of his own to exchange imported household needs, rum, and molasses for meat, grain, and cheese. Toward the middle of the eighteenth century agents of the Browns, Providence merchants, rode north into interior Massachusetts picking up meat, grain, and other country produce to turn over at a profit. The Allens of New London had a store at Shrewsbury, near Worcester, Massachusetts; the Trumbulls one at Lebanon, Connecticut. Agents for merchants shipping horses scoured Rhode Island and Connecticut bargaining for strings of nags for the West Indies.

After the end of the French wars, as demand for butter and eggs increased, itinerant collectors began to travel the back towns assembling dairy and poultry products for sale in Boston and other markets. Drovers brought cattle over the road to the slaughterhouses in Essex County, Massachusetts, and elsewhere, at which both hides and meat were salable. Cow traders visited the farms in the Connecticut Valley and other interior points and picked up cheap animals to fatten where provender was plentiful; the meat, after slaughter, was barreled for the export trade.

Concentration of agricultural products gave birth to what today might be termed infant industrial complexes. Did the introduction of shoemaking at Lynn fill Danvers, next door, with tanneries? Or did the plentiful hides from the cattle of the Merrimack Valley, New Hampshire, and Maine, brought to Topsfield and Danvers for slaughter, make practical Lynn's commercial shoe industry? At any rate at least by 1739 Danvers was tanning large numbers of hides, while at Lynn cordwainers were busy fashioning shoes of textiles and leather for sale in quantity and for export, a marriage of supply and demand that was to continue there for over two centuries. Roxbury, whither cattle converged from south and west, was another tanning center.

The presence near the rivers to the eastward of an immense supply of forest products especially of oak and pine, much of it the fruit of the winter labor and ox teams of farmers, made possible expansion in shipbuilding, at as little as three fifths of English costs. Not only did this become a great industry itself, but the ships furnished the vehicles for both the fisheries and the export trade that were for so long mainstays of the New England economy. Conversely, the return lading of molasses supplied the New England distilleries. Hogsheads and barrels in which fish, molasses, rum, and tobacco were handled were also products of winter employment for local farmers.

Important relationships such as these between farming and trade were foundation stones for the prosperity of the area which are too often ignored altogether or taken for granted. More than one similar close interconnection of local agriculture with manufacturing and commercial enterprise, frequently overlooked, appeared in the period of industrialization that followed the Revolution.

10. Growth of the Land: Grass and Grain

SOIL QUALITY varied greatly from one colony to another, and even more between areas within each colony. Reverend William Hubbard in his *General History of New England*, written about 1680, summed it up: "For the generality of the soyle, it is of a lighter sort of earth, whose fruitfulness is more beholding to the influence of the heavens, advantages of the seasonable skill and industry of the husbandmen, than the strength of its own temper."[1]

Perhaps careless soil mining, scarcely to be called agriculture, was to be expected in newly opened frontier towns where, at first, crops could feed on centuries of accumulated fertility in forest soil or river silt; yet the painstaking habits of English farming and soil enrichment and lessons in fertilizing derived from Indian tutelage were continued in the settlements, especially where markets were available.

The supply of manure was often inadequate, but the need for hauling and spreading it was recognized early. As far back as 1641 at Marblehead, Archibald Thomson drowned when his boat sank while he was moving dung. This circumstance was a matter of particular note, because it was a Sabbath. In 1676 Samuel Richardson of Woburn and his little son were carting manure to a field and returned to find that the Indians had murdered his wife and daughter. Entry after entry in Joshua Hempstead's early eighteenth-century diary notes how this Stonington farmer carted dung and spread it, as much as fifteen loads in a single day, and seaweed also. In Hingham in the Bay Colony, on March 13, 1757, Joseph Andrews recorded that he began to sled dung. Reverend Timothy Walker, first minister of Concord, New Hampshire, began to sled dung early each March. Zaccheus Collins of Lynn was hauling dung all the first week of May 1762, his diary states. After it had been dumped on the fields, it had to be beaten up. As it had been in England sheep manure was especially prized where available. In an accounting that apparently included other farmers besides the diarist, Hempstead paid "ye Shepard . . . wt was due for ye Dung."

In Connecticut shore towns the early settlers also dug peat out of swamps, carted it to their fields and piled it to crumble under the weather.

At Narragansett, Rhode Island, Rev. Jared Eliot saw swamp mud carted into a cow yard to increase the dung, and was told it served the purpose very well. On his own place he had success with what he called "shell sand," and with seaweed. Cape Cod farmers and others on the southeast shore fertilized with herring; but apparently with time the runs decreased, for in 1718 Sandwich ordered its herring reserved for food. On the Bay side of the Cape farmers chopped up horseshoe crabs to fertilize corn hills.

Despite such additions it can scarcely be doubted that by the middle of the eighteenth century much land, of only moderate original fertility, particularly in areas distant from the shore and herring rivers, had been cropped and pastured until yields were small, or it was left for pasture alone. This may have been a reason why some farmers, or at least their younger sons, were anxious to find new land, and awaited only the end of Indian warfare to venture into the wilderness to secure it.

Although the farmers among the English settlers of New England appear in the main to have been livestock men, they and others experienced in different branches of agriculture had come expecting to grow wheat, rye, barley, and other grains, at least for their own use. As soon as plows and oxen were available they set about it. Massachusetts exported wheat in bulk even in the 1640's, largely to Europe. Within a half century, however, the spread of smut or mildew, particularly in spring-sown wheat, had discouraged many, especially those near the sea. "We Reapt ye yard of wheat: it is blasted," laments a farm diarist. A manuscript diary of 1663 quoted by C. L. Flint states that the best wheat and some other grain was so blasted in many places that whole acres were not worth reaping.[2]

Yet at Stonington, Connecticut, beside Long Island Sound, on August 16, 1663, Thomas Minor wrote: "We had 700 sheaves of wheate, 13 score without the Barne," which appears to spell abundance. A decade later on January 2 he noted: "I had threshed Two Ackers of winter wheate wee had in all 38 bushells," not a bad yield for any farm. In other coast towns some farmers continued to raise the crop. In that fateful year 1676 when Philip's Indians were abroad, John Jacob of Hingham, south of Boston, went to his wheat field on Glad Tidings Plain to try to shoot a trespassing deer, and was himself shot by Indians.[3] This was the very period when Josselyn was recording mildew and blasting.

As natural fertility decreased and disease increased, farmers seeded rye and wheat together. The resulting harvest and the bread made from it, an accustomed combination in England, was called maslin or meslin. Eventually the hardier rye took over for the most part in the older sections of the colonies, although on April 19, 1775, when the British troops marched through the Lexington countryside, the tradition is that spring was so far advanced that the young wheat ruffled in the breeze.

The Connecticut Valley became the breadbasket of New England: first the area about Hartford, then the middle section, and finally the intervales in Vermont and New Hampshire. A woman who grew up in Hatfield, Massachusetts, but had removed in 1767, recalled in her old age that the fields of grain there were immense, without fences. Northfield, Massachusetts, on the New Hampshire line, had a good wheat crop in that year 1767 when the province was offering a bounty for wheat. Meslin, then rye, took over here also, and the wheat center moved still further north. In the years before the Revolution the Coos meadows at the oxbow of the Connecticut, to quote their historian Reverend Grant Powers, "became to other infant settlements, north and south of them what the granaries of Egypt were to Canaan . . . in the . . . seven years of famine." An aged man later recalled the time when those in necessity carried up their silver shoe buckles to the Coos and exchanged them with farmers there for wheat.[4]

It took about two generations for farmers in the older towns to decide what caused the blight of their wheat crop. They noticed that the rust was most destructive in the neighborhood of barberry bushes, a fruit introduced from England. In 1726 Connecticut ordered the bushes destroyed. In 1758 Massachusetts followed, though Salem had been ahead with a local bylaw in 1747. At least one Salem grain grower was pulling up the bushes the year before that. Doubters remained until scientists showed in the nineteenth century that the farmers' observations had been correct.

Barley was scarcely the common crop that it had been in England, but some farmers grew it for barley "fire-cake" and to brew beer. An occasional inventory records fifty to a hundred bushels. On April 13, 1708, the Reverend Joseph Green of Salem, a considerable farmer, recorded brewing three barrels of beer. During the siege of Boston in 1775, a lady entered in her journal for July 21: "Major Vose having returned from an expedition to Nantasket reports that they took off about a thousand bushels of barley . . . besides the hay," indicating heavier production than has been ordinarily suspected.[5]

In Connecticut, Hempstead grew oats alone or with barley from time to time through thirty years from 1711. So did others. But Doctor William Douglass called New England barley a hungry, lean grain that made no good malt liquor. The oats too were lean, chaffy, and dark in color, he said. Peas were sometimes a companion crop to oats, sometimes separate. Lord Adam Gordon commented on the country about Boston: the soil, he said, was kindly, producing every European grain and root in plenty and perfection besides Indian corn.

For barley to become beer, hops were necessary. Woburn, north of Boston, made these a specialty. Judge Samuel Sewall visited the noted hopyards there in 1702. A Massachusetts cargo for Newfoundland in 1718 included hops. Joshua Hempstead in Connecticut was fencing his hopyard and poling his hops between 1735 and 1743; Birket saw hops growing near New Haven in 1750; on February 26, 1763, the schooner *Bernard* took 3,000 pounds of hops and 400 bushels of barley from Massachusetts to New York. Yet, judging from the evidence of estate inventories, neither hops nor barley appear to have been widely grown in New England before the Revolution. Lord Gordon remarked one cause: "although they grow good barley, and . . . hops grow there everywhere, with little trouble or culture, more large and high than any I remember in Surrey," they were little valued. "Cyder is their common drink."[6]

Yet, however much European grain some farms and certain areas might grow, and even export, it was not enough. Long before the Revolution the port towns were importing breadstuffs from the Middle Colonies for their growing populations.

"Besides Indian Corn." That phrase of Lord Gordon's points to the mainstay of New England's cereal production all through the sixteen and seventeen hundreds. Maize was thoroughly at home in New England. It was immune to wheat blast and most diseases. Even on poor land it yielded some grain and fodder. Most farm inventories include it, either harvested or by the acre.

One of corn's virtues is that the grain is equally nourishing and healthful for man and beast. For livestock, Thomas Anburey, a British army officer in the Revolution sized it up: "Indian corn is certainly the heartiest and most strengthening food for cattle and poultry, and gives their meat firmness and excellent flavor."[7]

On old land the best culture practice was to plow, crossplow, harrow smooth; then furrow and crossfurrow at intervals of from 3 to 4-½ feet according to the quality of soil, and plant at the intersections. After the corn plants came up, light furrows plowed lengthwise between the rows threw the earth toward the hill, followed by hoeing to kill or cover weeds. After these first cultivations the hoe was used once, sometimes twice, according to need. Bean vines twined up the cornstalks, and pumpkin seeds planted at intervals provided foliage to cover the ground for the final few weeks, smother weeds, and produce welcome additional food.

A much less elaborate method developed as new settlements in the eighteenth century reverted to an Indian practice: planting, with a hoe only, in the fresh soil between tree trunks and burnt logs—rough culture but successful. In August cornstalks might be lopped early to cause the ears to mature, or left on the field after harvest for stock to browse on.

When the harvest was ready and the ears had been drawn in from the field, it was husking time. Joshua Hempstead of New London, Connecticut, and his boys in the fall of 1711 husked corn at night till 10 o'clock, his diary records. On another October day he picked more for the boys to carry to the garret for storage. A week later, he turned all the corn in the chamber garret. As the years went by he changed his method, spent some days cutting poles, and made a "Cribb" the last week in October. On November 4 his diary records: "I finished Cribbing the Corn." One year, with a neighbor's oxen, his sons carted in "1 Load of Corn and 1 of pumpkins."

Connecticut liked its corn yellow, Rhode Island liked it white. It was, in any color, New England's most valuable grain.[8]

11. Growth of the Land: Vegetables and Fruits

O F ALL PLANT immigrants to arrive in New England after the early 1600's, none was more welcome or proved more important to its economy than that which accompanied the influx of Scotch-Irish settlers toward the end of the second decade of the 1700's. The potato, a Peruvian vegetable sent back to Spain by de la Vega or some other conquistador in the previous century, had been shipped to Virginia in 1622 and included among a list of plants and seeds ordered shipped to Governor Endecott in 1628; but if the tubers arrived and he planted them, nothing seems to have come of it. He may have preferred the other roots: parsnips, carrots, and turnips, all of which promptly took hold in their new surroundings. It was not long, however, before potatoes were imported for food, 15 tons from Bermuda in one shipment in 1636, "which were a great relief to our people," said Winthrop. But like the oranges and lemons that came with them, they must all have been eaten; no planting is mentioned. In Pennsylvania a rich merchant is said to have tried potatoes in his garden in or about 1685. At a Harvard Commencement in 1707 potatoes appeared on the menu, perhaps also from Bermuda.[1]

The first potatoes of any historic consequence to arrive in the English colonies, however, came with five shiploads of families of Scottish blood from Londonderry, Ireland, immigrants from the colony of that race domiciled in northern Ireland during the previous century. Some of these immigrants spent the winter in Portland. A few settled permanently at nearby Cape Elizabeth and about Casco Bay. Sixteen families were granted land in the Merrimack Valley in southern New Hampshire, and on April 11, 1719, began settlement there, naming their town Londonderry for their Irish home. Others dispersed into central and western Massachusetts. The next year, 1720, more came to settle on the Maine coast and plant potatoes at Wells, while others sat down about the mouth of the Kennebec.

Whether the New Hampshire group of immigrants in the spring of 1719 grew the first Irish tubers in North America, as the potato monument at Derry states, or whether the first seed planted was in Nathaniel Walker's garden at Andover, Massachusetts, or that put in the ground by the Youngs who journeyed west to Worcester, is a matter of debate. There is credit enough for all.[2] Potatoes are said to have been introduced in Connecticut the following year and by 1735 were being sold in Rhode Island. It seems to have been 1750 before the Connecticut Valley took up the new crop.

What is clear is that within two decades New England farmers were harvesting the tubers not only in those areas but in places as scattered as Norwich, Connecticut; Warwick, Rhode Island; Arundel (Kennebunk), Maine; Lynn, on the coast; and Westborough in central Massachusetts. Moreover, by 1745, at least, New England had begun to export potatoes. Following the middle of the century its potatoes were being shipped south to Virginia in vessels from New Hampshire, Salem, and Boston; and from New York as well. In 1759 the cargo of the New London sloop *Fox*, for St. Thomas, included fifty bushels. Not long after that a Martha's Vineyard whaler listed two bushels for its crew. In Connecticut the new crop proved so satisfactory that in 1767 Reverend John Devotion, writing from Westbrook on Long Island Sound, was enthusiastic: "We improve in Potatoes in this Colony exceedingly. Many farmers raise 500 bushels pr. An. I don't think myself stored without 150 Bush per. An."[3] Apparently several varieties were tried, for Douglass in 1755 writes: "Irish potatoes . . . is much planted in New England, thrives well and is of good use; varieties here are the rough coat, red coat, flat white and long white: my taste prefers the rough coat."

Difficulties similar to the ones that were to plague potato growers in the next century appeared early. One was price fluctuation. In Weeden's "Table of Prices," printed in the supplement to his *Economic and Social History of New England*, potato values vary widely from year to year. The second hazard is mentioned in a local history. Just before the Revolution a potato disease prevailed extensively in eastern Massachusetts which the author judged to have been similar to the blight that was to prove so devastating in the middle of the next century.

All in all it is not too much to say that the arrival of the Scotch-Irish with their potatoes proved one of the most important events of New England's whole agricultural history, with an influence that was to spread much farther still. Yet that was only one of their contributions. Almost from the beginning, colonial governments considered cultivation of flax important to provide linen. In 1640 Connecticut directed its inhabitants to plant either flax or hemp and tend and husband both. Attempts must have been made to grow it further up river, for in 1646 Springfield forbade washing flax in a brook used for dressing meat. The Valley soils proved adaptable and flax became a staple commodity in trade there. Clark estimates that by the middle of the century Connecticut's export trade in the seed alone was worth 80,000 pounds sterling a year. It was three fourths of a century later when in 1718 a mill to press out linseed oil, a flaxseed derivative important for paint, medical, and industrial uses was opened at New Haven. Others followed, one at Hatfield, Massachusetts, another at Derby, Connecticut, at the confluence of the Housatonic and Naugatuck rivers, which prospered for a considerable time. Silas Deane of Connecticut told John Adams in 1774 that 35,000 bushels of flaxseed went to New York yearly in exchange for salt. In eastern Massachusetts flax is occasionally included in inventories in Essex, Middlesex, and Suffolk counties. Hingham on the South Shore grew 1735 pounds in 1773; Cape Cod also grew considerable just before the Revolution, as did the Germans who in 1748 had colonized Broad Bay in Maine. In Rhode Island, South County raised it in great quantity.

It appears to have been the settlers who came to New Hampshire from the north of Ireland, however, expert in textile experience, who opened the full possibilities of growing flax, twisting its fibers into thread, and producing fine linens, as Yorkshire weavers had been doing with woolens at Rowley in Massachusetts since the previous century. To grow and harvest the crop, "ret" or rot the stems, separate the fibers, and comb them out were matters of skill as well as long, smelly, hard, and dirty work. Spinning the thread and turning it into fine linens or even coarse tow cloth for rough work required more skill and more labor. James Birket in 1750–51 had this to say of the New Hampshire colonists' success at it: "This province also produces . . . exceeding good flax of which the Irish settled at Londonderry make very good Cloth & fine Ounce thread . . . and I'm informed this little town increases very much."[4]

New England flax growing, however, was mostly on a small scale. For example, Reverend Timothy Walker of Concord, New Hampshire, in general quite a large farmer, on May 5, 1764, sowed a bushel of seed and harrowed it in. Matthew Patten of Bedford, also in that province's moderately fertile Merrimack Valley on September 7 and 9, 1765, cleaned his harvest of 64 pounds of flax seed. Joseph Andrews of Hingham, Massachusetts, took only a day or two each fall to thresh out his flax seed. Traders took flax in barter, had machines to beat out seed, and assembled many small amounts at export points.

Colonial authorities also tried by bounties to encourage hemp growing, since cordage was so important for the rigging of ships. Whether soils were not well adapted for it, manure scarce, experience lacking, or the cost of labor too high, its cultivation made little headway. Both large and small farmers tried the crop, however. On May 13, 1767: "Between the

8a and b. Breaking and swingling flax. From flax harvest to linen thread there were twenty hard, dirty steps. *Chase*, History of Old Chester *(1889)*.

(8a)

house and barn I sowed about 3 quarts of hemp seed in all," Patten records. By contrast, in 1764, Stiles states in his "Itineraries," Captain Stevens of Boston, with 6,000 acres of new land in the hills of Ashford, Connecticut, seeded thirty acres, tended by a man and a boy who cultivated by plowing between rows. It took thirty hands to pull the crop. He expected to harvest twenty tons of hemp worth 60 pounds sterling, besides 200 bushels of seed worth 20 shillings per bushel: its total value was 1,400 pounds, Dr. Stiles estimated.[5] Clearly agricultural speculation is of ancient origin! Yet so far as any record shows, despite bounties, hemp growing remained a very minor practice.

Tobacco growing, forbidden at first in both Massachusetts and Connecticut, got a slow start, though Plymouth was selling some to the Hol-

(8b)

landers by 1628. By 1657, however, Milford, Connecticut, town meeting was granting liberty to Charles Deal to purchase Milford Island with its buildings for a tobacco plantation, and three years later the colony's governor, John Winthrop the younger, wrote that tobacco had brought some good crops. Soon items of tobacco were appearing in Rhode Island inventories. By 1682 Ipswich records indicate that tobacco "yards," fenced for protection, were common in Essex County, Massachusetts. In 1694 it was being grown in Deerfield, for a daughter of the Belding family escaped the Indians by hiding among tobacco hanging in the garret. By the end of the century Connecticut was exporting it.[6]

Windsor and the other Connecticut Valley towns around Hartford became the center of cultivation. Wethersfield in 1704 had to forbid encroachment on public land by persons wishing to grow it. After the French wars eastern Connecticut also got into tobacco growing. The product went abroad packed in barrels and tierces as well as in hogsheads, 400 pounds to the cask. Some went to the West Indies to be made into cigars, some to England, some to Europe. Shipments varied all the way from a lot of 31 pounds that Joshua Hempstead in 1712 sent, along with 7½ pounds of beeswax, by his friend Captain Mainwaring to "Madara" (the Captain brought him a cask of wine when he returned), or the four tierces that Thomas Allen shipped in the schooner *Triumph* from New London to the West Indies in 1759, to cargoes of 12,000 to 21,000 pounds that Elizabeth Ramsey records.[7]

The trade became so important that in 1753 the Connecticut General Court made it mandatory for each town to choose at least two surveyors and packers to make sure that no tobacco went out unless well ripened, sufficiently cured, and in every way good and merchantable. Massachusetts in 1724 made tobacco a commodity in which taxes could be paid, and tobacco growing crept up the Connecticut Valley (Ramsey estimates fifteen acres in Hatfield, Massachusetts, by 1771); but the crop was not yet of commercial importance in that colony.

Rhode Island was in the business early. By 1727 James Brown was shipping tobacco from Providence to Martinique; Obadiah Brown in 1734 sold a shipment of 8 hogsheads at St. Eustatia, but a lot sent to France in 1764 received a cold reception because its variety was unsuitable. Eventually the Rhode Island province is said to have produced 200,000 pounds a year, though dark colored and not of the best quality. In 1766, with tobacco in over supply, by a secret agreement the Browns and other Rhode Island firms formed what today would be called a cartel to allocate quotas and maintain export prices in the West Indies. Rhode Island tobacco is said to have been packed in empty molasses barrels, often returning to the area from which the molasses had been imported.[8]

Growing this crop had all the present-day hazards. In August 1731, Hempstead noted "a very great Hail" at Norwich, severe enough to break windows and ruin the delicate leaves of the tobacco in the fields. In the middle of September 1764, frost took much of the Rhode Island crop. However, from small beginnings, for some parts of New England the future of tobacco was to prove bright indeed.

The first vegetables to become of importance in the new colonies appear to have been the roots. Parsnips were a popular garden vegetable from the beginning. Turnips, at first grown in gardens or from seed scattered among squash hills, were sometimes sown with wheat in new ground. They were useful also to fill spots in fields where corn had failed to germinate. They came to be very abundant. In July 1722 Hempstead was plowing for them as a field crop, but had to fence them. Along with potatoes they were among supplies furnished at public expense to Acadian refugees in 1757. Douglass wrote that the best New England turnips were from new lands northeast of Boston. Numerous cargo lists include "roots."

Onions, a garden crop at the beginning in the Bay Colony, were grown also at Plymouth, and by John Winter in 1634 on Richmond Island, Maine. They had been a commercial crop in Lincolnshire, England, before the Puritan settlement and they did not wait long to be produced for market in New England, for the cargo list of a coaster on Long Island Sound in 1667 included a bushel of them. By 1686, a decade after the death of King Philip, Colonel Byfield, one of the purchasers of this chief's fertile Mt. Hope lands in what is now Rhode Island, was exporting them from Bristol. Deacon Bosworth of the same town in 1691 sent off 540 ropes grown on his farm. (Onions had been woven together into "ropes" in England.) By 1707 a Boston-built vessel listed 25 barrels in its cargo for Surinam. In the summer and fall of 1718 Boston vessels carried onions to Surinam, Barbados, Newfoundland, and South Carolina. At Wethersfield, Connecticut, which was soon to become a very large producer, Benjamin Adams sold 71 bushels in 1710. By the middle decades of the eighteenth century vessel after vessel from this port, New London, and Boston, bound for the West Indies, carried shipments of from 1,000 to 6,500 ropes of commercial-sized onions. The largest onions went loose in barrels. In 1760 Connecticut recognized the importance of the crop by setting standards for bunched onions.[9]

The Indian vegetables—squashes, pumpkins, and beans—continued popular among the colonists. Paul Dudley of Massachusetts tells how in 1699 a single pumpkin dropped by accident in a small pasture where cattle had been fed produced 260 fruits as big as a half-peck measure, which helps explain their general cultivation. "The inhabitants plant great quantities of squashes," observed the British officer Thomas Anburey in 1777. "The seed [is] cultivated with assiduity." Even in rural Rhode Island where vegetables were few, summer squashes were often on the table.

Besides the roots commonly found in gardens, gentlemen, ministers, and farmers near the port towns, perhaps with an eye on the market, were raising certain green vegetables, peas, cauliflower, and melons, and trying out asparagus and others. In Connecticut a 1655 hog-damage complaint had included cabbages. Thomas Minor was setting plants three years later. Hempstead raised them in an enclosure in 1713. Benoni Waterman, storekeeper of Warwick, Rhode Island, sold cabbages in 1735; and the Germans at Waldoboro, Maine, grew them from the first.

Seed merchants appeared. By 1719 Evan Davies, a Boston importer, was advertising in the *Boston Gazette* all sorts of fresh garden seeds as well as "English Sparrow-grass Roots." In 1768 William Davidson, a gardener on Seven Star Lane, one of several Boston dealers previous to the Revolution, offered 56 varieties of vegetable and herb seeds. Nathaniel Bird, a Newport bookseller, dealt in garden seed in 1763, Charles Dunbar in 1764, and in the same town Gideon Welles had Connecticut onion seed for sale. Field and garden seed advertisements appeared in the *New Hampshire Gazette* in 1766 and 1770.[10]

These dealers must have found customers, for on April 23, 1742, Dr. Holyoke's Salem diary tells of planting mushrooms, and in other springs appear such items as peas, beans, and onions. On February 19, 1753, he sowed gourds, cucumbers, and lettuce under glass in his "hotbed," and in June 1763 he was cutting asparagus, "1836 heads in all." Hotbeds must have caught on, for in 1762 windows suitable for them were advertised in Boston. Andrew Faneuil, Peter's uncle, is credited with New England's earliest greenhouse. When he died in 1737, his nephew Peter continued to grow fruits and other rarities in it. A royal official named Hulton put up another in Brooklin in 1768. Hulton's sister, who wanted to try out such things as artichokes and broccoli, wrote a friend in England of putting 500 heads of the finest celery into it in the fall. But she added: "It is strange what little improvements are made in gardening here." Marked improvement was to wait largely till after the Revolution, though at Saybrook, Connecticut, Jared Eliot was already trying a new garden plant, rhubarb, started from seed that Benjamin Franklin sent from London in 1760. Green peas, at least, were plentiful in the early market: in the warm spring of 1775 by June 17.[11]

Among vegetable enemies the pea weevil appeared, spreading north from Philadelphia to infest field peas and cut down their production in the Connecticut Valley; and Jared Eliot at Killingworth in the Connecticut province in order to anticipate losses from the turnip fly felt obliged to sow turnip seed at three-inch intervals.

If there was one European crop to which New England soil and climate proved especially adapted, it was the apple. The ease of its production, the generous crops, and the juiciness of the fruit not only caused it to fill a need in the diet but within a generation or two from the first landing made cider the common beverage in place of the beer the colonists had at first considered almost indispensable.

How readily the apple took to its new environment is revealed by an observation from the Berkshire Hills just before the Revolution. By 1770 the whole length of the Indian path between the settlement of the Stockbridge tribe at Great Barrington, Massachusetts, and the Scaticoke village at Kent, Connecticut, nearly 40 miles along the Housatonic, was said to be lined with apple trees. They stood at irregular intervals, sprung from apple cores thrown away by traveling natives who had promptly learned to enjoy the Englishman's fruit.[12]

Parson Joseph Green of Salem grafted 59 "cyons" onto 24 of his trees on an April day in 1701, his diary tells us. On April 11, 1709, Nehuman Hinsdale was driving a cartload of apple whips from Northampton to the newer town of Deerfield. Most such activities went unrecorded. In 1730 the century-old trees started by Boston's original settler, William Blaxton, were still bearing. Diarist Joshua Hempstead set out over sixty Sweetings as a nursery behind his stable at Norwich, Connecticut, on April 17, 1742. Perhaps this number was more or less a standard planting, for on April 24, 1764, Reverend Timothy Walker of Concord, New Hampshire, entered in his diary this notation: "Set about 60 young apple trees in ye house lot." The next day he "Made log fence around my young orchard," an essential precaution in a new area where cattle and deer

9. At a cider mill: tuns of cider, New England's favorite drink. *Howard S. Russell collection.*

roamed free. Lord Adam Gordon, just before the Revolution, exclaims that every road is lined with apples and pears: even the poorest farmer has at least one orchard.[13]

Some of the fruit went into pies, dried apples, and apple molasses, an excellent source of sweetening, which may explain why Sweeting trees were especially popular. Some were fed to fatten hogs. Most were crushed and turned into cider and vinegar. One village of forty families near Boston made 3000 barrels in 1721. Judge Joseph Wilder of Lancaster is said to have made 616 barrels in 1728. As part of the normal yearly supplies to be furnished his widow, a Worcester County farmer in the Bay Colony about 1750, included three barrels of cider. How the totals could mount may be gathered from an estimate taken from the valuation lists for Middlesex County, Massachusetts Bay, for 1764. The county's total is 33,436 barrels of cider, or seven per family, well over a barrel for every man, woman, and child.[14]

Export of apples, even of cider apples, was not uncommon; but most of the cider and the vinegar made from it must have been consumed in New England, for at this period neither appears often in cargo lists. Some was distilled into brandy or applejack. Torrington, Connecticut, for example, had four cider mills and one brandy still in 1774. Cider appears also as an accepted medium of exchange. In 1762 Ruel Baldwin of Woburn, in Massachusetts Bay, picked up a load of earthenware at the Charlestown port of entry, paying for it in cider.

Pears, too, were planted plentifully—along roads, in gentlemen's orchards, and in backyards; peaches also. The Bartlett pear is said to have been propagated in Roxbury in 1770. Judge Paul Dudley of Roxbury, who was fond of tall stories, claimed to have picked 800 peaches from a single tree, as well as pears eight inches across.

Josselyn back in the seventeenth century had rejoiced in all the wealth of fruit. "The Quinces, Cherries, Damsons set the Dames at work. Marmalade and preserved Damsons is to be met with in every house . . . I made Cherry wine, and so many others for there is good store of them both red and black." Maverick, scarcely less enthusiastic, added "Apricocks, Musk Mellons and Water Mellons" to his fruit list. John Hancock's famous garden included nectarines, quinces, limes, and mulberries, as well as peaches.[15] Among bush fruits barberries and currants, both brought over from Europe for cultivation, were the most widely grown— the former so numerous that near Dover, New Hampshire, a Mrs. Heard escaped the Indians in 1689 by hiding in a barberry thicket.

Caterpillars were already a nuisance. Miss Hulton described how at the beginning of the season they ate so much of the foliage that the trees had "a most dreary aspect in the summer." Hempstead's diary tells of his staying home in April 1712 to pick caterpillars off his trees. Whether these were tent caterpillars or canker worms is not clear; probably they were both. The year 1771 is said to have been an exceptionally bad cankerworm year, and in Westfield, Massachusetts, the next spring, Reverend John Ballantine's diary tells how a multitude of caterpillars stripped the orchards. On May 29, 1750, Hempstead found the wild pigeons feasting on canker worms in his bare trees. A "peach worm," perhaps the borer, had already put in an appearance.

12. Growth of the Land: Livestock

WRITERS ON COLONIAL NEW ENGLAND, if they pay more than cursory attention to its agriculture, have often treated farming as though it were a single comprehensive occupation, carried on practically everywhere according to a uniform pattern. Yet almost from the beginning the types of agriculture varied in response to natural conditions of soil and surroundings, available markets, and the experience an individual farm family brought or inherited from England.

At least by the end of the first half century, farming was dividing into two major categories: crop production and livestock and its products. Important as were the field, vegetable, and fruit crops in the century of 1675–1775, livestock production in its several branches, and the products and industries connected with it, were in this period of at least equal historical consequence. Not only did crops and livestock vary in importance from one district to another, however, but the livestock industry itself became concentrated in certain areas.

The one animal raised nearly everywhere, though not most important in numbers or value, was the hog. How important swine were in the New England economy is illustrated by the well-known story of Reverend Eleazar Wheelock, who in 1770 removed his Indian school from Lebanon, Connecticut, to Hanover, New Hampshire, there to found Dartmouth College. The cavalcade consisted of seventy persons: family, students, and neighbors; but ahead of it was driven the herd of Connecticut hogs that was to help put the enterprise on a practical basis in its new home.[1]

In early settled towns hogs ranged the woods, according to the custom of forested districts in England (though by contrast with Old England, in New England their number was usually unstinted). They lived on acorns, nuts, and roots; and in the fall the family would gather additional bushels of nuts and acorns for their winter feed. Wolves and bears took toll, but an old boar, if allowed to grow tusks, was a match for almost any wild marauders. Moreover when winter storms arrived, he would lead the herd back to the shed, where he knew that corn and slops would be waiting.

Hog growers in colonial times, as ever since, faced losses not easy to explain. Matthew Patten of Bedford, New Hampshire, on October 10, 1767, sorrowfully recorded: "The boys found our barrow hog dead who had been missing . . . and we missed our grown sow this morning, what the distemper I know not." Sometimes it might have proved better not to find them. On a May day in 1635 a farmer named Clough, at Kingston in the east part of the New Hampshire colony, found a hog dead and examined a swelling on its throat. Within three weeks he was dead and three children of the neighborhood likewise from what was thought to be a similar throat distemper.[2]

Hogs might be driven over the road to market or, if their number was small, be killed at home. Home slaughter was most likely after cold weather began—often in early January, with some neighbor to help in return for a share in the pork. Cut into merchantable pieces and salted, barreled pork was a local medium of exchange as well as an export commodity. A Milford, Connecticut, receipt dated December 26, 1723, records payment by John Holbrook of Derby of 136 pounds of pork at three cents a pound "upon the account of the Bridge Logs of Derby," presumably a tax payment. A Rehoboth, Massachusetts, merchant's account in 1719 charges for killing one hog a shilling sixpence: equivalent in the account to 40 pumpkins or 2 pounds of butter. Merchant Jonathan Trumbull, later Connecticut's governor, packed pork at Lebanon. He bought hogs in the fall and shipped the barreled pork to several ports.[3]

Sheep raising is a specialized calling. Sheep require good pasturage free from thickets and briers likely to catch and tear their wool coats, protection from predatory animals, and careful, knowledgeable attention on the part of man. Much of New England's surface, even in the 1700's, was still too untamed for their somewhat fastidious appetites. Most of Maine and New Hampshire was not yet sheep country. After three fourths of a century many towns held yearly wolf hunts and offered rewards for wolf heads. Dedham, only 10 miles south of Boston, began to keep sheep in 1667. The town put its bounties high, but it took three decades before every wolf was gone.

Despite such drawbacks, as time passed, the number of sheep in the colonies showed substantial increase. Partly this was due to inducements offered by colony and town governments, their economies short on cash and overdependent on woolen imports. To improve and add to the sheep pasture available, and to prevent damage to the fleece of the sheep, Connecticut required every adult male to work a day each year at clearing brush from the commons. Northampton, Massachusetts, followed Connecticut's example. Springfield in 1654 gave John Pynchon ownership of Round Hill for bringing in forty sheep for sale, and in 1680 decreed that every inhabitant keep at least three sheep. Weymouth, also in the Bay Colony, in 1673 limited the number of horses allowed on its commons to afford better grazing for its sheep. New Hampshire offered tax benefits for sheep raising.

A dog that killed sheep was treated as a murderer and hanged. Northampton fined owners of "Large Doggs Going at Large." By contrast, one Buzzards Bay town kept four dogs especially trained to protect its flocks from foxes.

Well into the decades preceding the Revolution, sheep towns followed Old England custom and as in East Anglia employed municipal shepherds to take charge of town flocks. Newbury, at the outlet of the Merrimack River, with 5,635 sheep, toward the end of the seventeenth century gathered most of them into four flocks. Ipswich on Massachusetts Bay's North Shore had nine such in 1702. Branford, Connecticut, in 1770, had two. Its shepherds took each flock to its own sheepwalk on the common undivided lands of the town. Every commoner was permitted to pasture the number of sheep to which his rights of common entitled him. At night, according to old English custom, the shepherd brought the flock back from its own course to the arable common field. There movable fencing was changed each day so that each commoner's cropland eventually had the benefit of a night's manuring, one of the traditional objects of sheep raising. This enriched plot was often sowed to turnips, sometimes planted to potatoes. At Deerfield a particular part of the arable thus fertilized was known long after as "The Turnip Field." In the fall, if the field was cultivated in common, as at Deerfield, the crop of roots was divided in proportion to each commoner's stint of sheep. (In Essex County a bushel of turnips was worth a cord of wood.) So that a stockman might know his animals, and also to prevent theft, each sheep was marked with pitch on its wool, its ear, or both, with the earmark of its owner, registered with the town clerk.

Although sheep raising had at first been largely confined to islands and points safe from wolves and stray dogs, as more pasture was cleared, wolves decreased, and the demand for wool kept growing, sheep men were led to increase their flocks. Of the 86 Massachusetts inventories mentioned in connection with swine, 28 had sheep, six of them with over 50 mature animals each. Besides the large flocks of such towns as Newbury and Ipswich in the Bay Colony, by 1678 Rumney Marsh (Chelsea) and the Boston Harbor islands sheltered 1,544. Across the harbor by

1773 Hingham's sheep numbered 3,162. At Reading, north of Boston, the commons were thick enough with sheep to remind Daniel Neal of Devon's fields in England.

Dartmouth on Mt. Hope Bay in 1768 counted 7,108 sheep and goats (probably few of the latter). When Governor William Brenton of Rhode Island died, he left 1,500 sheep, according to his estate inventory; but on his Rocky Farm at Newport he is said to have had at one time 11,000.[4] South Kingstown on the westerly shore of Narragansett Bay, Rhode Island, first entered sheep marks on its records in 1696, but long before the Revolution the great South County landowners counted individual flocks in thousands.

In Connecticut Ezra Stiles, preaching here and there, found in 1770 in Branford a flock of 3,000, and one of the town's shepherds thought the entire township's total to be 10,000. In New Haven a flock numbered 1,300 out of an estimated 4,000 in the First Parish—and there were two other parishes.

Yet the numbers in such towns were less than those on the grassy islands off the coasts: Nantucket with 15,000 in 1773; Martha's Vineyard with 20,000 is called a vast sheep pasture. All sent their surplus wool to the mainland for sale. Such totals were often the sum of many farm flocks. As an example of a small flock, on June 30, 1756, Joshua Hempstead brought back from shearing at Stonington "2 Baggs of wool my 9 fleeces & 12 lb & 7 fleeces of Christophers 13 lb ¾." Where the sheep ran in town flocks, as in Nantucket, the number allowed each owner was likely to be strictly stinted, and at intervals the excess was slaughtered and sent to market as mutton.

From the localities mentioned it is clear that in this century up to 1775 sheep raising on a large scale more or less followed the coast and the offshore islands, all with wide marshes or grasslands. It also extended up rivers where towns such as Deerfield in the Connecticut Valley, Dedham on the Charles, and Reading on the Ipswich River provided broad grassy intervales.

The sheep business appears to have been influenced considerably by economic conditions and the bounties offered by the colonies. Clark, in his *History of Manufactures,* states that prices of wool fell by half in the depression years following the end of the French Wars.

"Wool . . . is pretty plenty where I live," wrote Reverend James McSparran, of Rhode Island about 1753, "yet if you throw the English America into one Point of View there is not half enough to make Stockings for the inhabitants."[5]

Two types of animal are said to have composed the sheep population. One was a breed with dark or spotted faces and legs, from England's south coast; the other, a larger and longer type with white faces, originating in Holland, from which numerous purchases were made in the early years of the colonies.

An occasional cargo for the West Indies from Boston or New London included sheep, often designated as "fat sheep," apparently to be sold live for food, since unlike beef and pork, mutton was not satisfactory either salted or smoked. Birket liked the mutton for eating. Visiting New Hampshire in 1750, he said: "Their Sheep are Small but the meat very Sweet, fat & well tasted."

Unlike sheep, cattle were to be found in every town and in nine out of ten farm inventories. Nearly every farm, even those of village tradesmen, had at least a family cow for milk and perhaps butter or cheese. Seldom were herds large, often four to eight plus young stock—except in Rhode Island's southerly towns, where they might number 50 to 100 on great estates. The size of herds was kept modest not solely from absence of a large local market for milk and cheese but, for a long time, by the lack in all but a few localities of sufficient hay to carry dairy stock productively through the winters. In old, settled, eastern Massachusetts there were, in 1767, about two cows for each five persons.

Oxen had a special place and value. They moved heavily loaded drays in port towns. On the farm they pulled the plow, hauled grain to the mill, delivered ship timber and logs, jockeyed boulders out of the grain field, and drew in hay, apples, and firewood. Equally important, after a few years of such labor, at the end of some season's toil the ox would be put in a yard or stall, offered several weeks of rest and princely feed, then slaughtered in cold weather, for the family's winter meat or to go as barreled salt beef to the West Indies. For such reasons, in a new town like Ashfield in the Berkshires, in 1766 settled only two decades, oxen outnumbered milch cows: 35 oxen to 31 milkers. Long-settled Haverhill, on the other hand, had 716 cows to 252 oxen, and in the three eastern Massachusetts counties as a whole the ratio was nearly three cows to one ox.

What little breeding or selection of cattle there was in most of New England tended to produce a modest-sized, hardy, willing type of animal better designed for pulling loads and fattening into beef quarters than for strictly dairy purposes. Birket commented in New Hampshire in 1750: "Their Cattle [meaning oxen] are small but seemingly very strong, having Short thick bodies and Short Limbs."[6]

Great improvement in breeding could scarcely be expected while cows were served by common town bulls running with the town herds, though it was an immemorial custom brought from England. Braintree, in the Bay Colony, in 1710 appropriated six pounds "for keeping bulls to run at large" at not over 20 shillings per bull, each "to be a good sufficient bull of 2 years old." The town operated on a similar basis for the next forty years. Durham, Connecticut, selectmen were directed in 1716 to provide good bulls, three years old, for only 15 shillings each. In 1728 Springfield paid from 10 to 40 shillings each to twenty citizens for use of their bulls to breed the town's cattle. With over 52,000 cows three years old in the Bay province alone in 1735, to say nothing of those younger, how many cheap bulls must have fathered how many nondescript young stock in the whole of New England![7] One advantage New England did have: it seems to have escaped the enormous losses of cattle from disease that plagued Europe in the eighteenth century.

Cattle had to be hardy to survive. It was not till November 11 that Reverend Ebenezer Parkman, pastor at Westborough in the Bay Colony, in 1737 recorded: "We first tyed up our Cattle in ye Barn." Life for cattle was even more rugged in new settlements. Like many another, the earliest settler at Marlboro in southern Vermont, named Whitmore, carried his cow through the first winters on wild grass and hay from a beaver meadow helped out with "browse," the tender foliage of evergreen trees. At Cornwall in Connecticut's northwest hills, settled 1738 to 1740, early comers kept their cows alive at times with venison broth. In even older communities where hay land was limited, cattle might get little but corn husks and corn fodder in winter. No wonder an outside observer wrote in a book published in 1775 that in the management of cattle, New England farmers had the worst imaginable notions. It was true of some, though writers in parts of England were making similar complaints of the farmers of that country at the same time.[8]

As to the dairy side of livestock farming, welcome as milk was for making palatable the common breakfast of corn mush and the evening meal of bread and milk, as well as for butter and cheese, little was expected from a milch cow except during the warm months. Butter and cheese of the best quality were for a long time imported from England for the well-to-do. The only true dairy section was southern Rhode Island, where in 1750 J. Birket reported that they had excellent grass and fine cattle. Burnaby a decade later concurred: the whole province, he said, was laid out in pasture or grazing ground, the oxen were the largest in America, the butter and cheese excellent. Really good cheese from any part of New England, when exported to the Middle Colonies or the

South, was likely to be called Rhode Island cheese. Writing from Charleston, South Carolina, in 1766, Israel Brayton told his Newport shippers that cheese sold well there.

Most New England cattle farming, however, was on a very different scale, with a few kine to each farm. In the back towns beef for the farm family's eating was a thing to be looked forward to as a treat. All the local milch cows were assembled in one or more town herds, the young animals and dry cows put in another. Milkers got the best pasture. The rest might not even have a herdsman but be branded and left to range wherever they could find feed. In the Connecticut Valley near Northampton, this meant the woods and burned-over areas that stretched east for twenty to thirty miles to the Ware River Valley.

In towns where the arable was in common, each owner of cow rights was required to keep his proportionate share of the fence in repair or be presented to the court and fined for any damage arising from his neglect. After the crops had been harvested from the enclosed and tilled area, on a date set in October the beasts were permitted to enter and for six weeks pick up the herbage inside the fence, at the end of which they were housed: all according to Old English custom. In late fall many animals were turned over to merchants to help balance farmers' store accounts. The merchants in turn would herd them to Boston or some other port for slaughter, to pay their own bills.

Poultry keeping seems never to have reached large proportions before the Revolution or to have become of marked economic importance, although domesticated turkeys, and dunghill fowl, as hens were still termed, had come to New England with both Pilgrims and Puritans.

Judge Samuel Sewall, for one, discovered the value of Indian corn as poultry feed. On January 13, 1676/7, he writes: "Giving my chickens meat, it came to my mind that I gave them nothing save Indian corn and water, and yet they eat it and thrive very well."[9] If the well-to-do judge kept hens, many ordinary people must have done so, and for the same purpose: to have eggs to eat, at least in spring and fall. Benoni Waterman's account-book at Warwick, Rhode Island, in 1739 put the price of a dozen eggs at a shilling (perhaps in Rhode Island paper); of a fowl at a shilling and a half. At Amherst, inland in the Bay Colony, eggs sold about the year 1700 for threepence a dozen. Ezekiel Read at Rehoboth in 1719 charged two and sixpence for killing three fowls (size and type not noted), close to the equivalent of three pounds of butter.

The word "fowl" was sometimes used to include turkeys or geese. Geese were not plentiful at first, but on December 31, 1718, that ver-

satile Connecticut farmer and trader, Joshua Hempstead, "sent 2 Geese
& 2 ganders by Jonathan Bayly to St. Cits." On the following March 20th
his diary shows that the "Goose Sett 11 Eggs"; April 28, "Goose hatched
9 goslings." As the century advanced, the number of geese apparently increased. When James Birket visited Bristol, Rhode Island, in the middle
of the century, he commented that the only remarkable things there, according to a local saying, were the town's women and its geese. In New
Hampshire he found poultry plentiful: geese, turkeys, ducks, and dunghill fowl, besides wild turkeys in the woods. William Douglass about the
same time added to this list fatted wild pigeons that country people
caught with nets, fed on Indian corn, and brought to market: "delicate
good eating," he considered them.[10]

Live turkeys appear in many West Indies cargoes out of New London in
the years preceding the Revolution, in numbers running from 10 to 60 or
more per shipment, occasionally with geese (32 in one 1759 shipment),
ducks, and other fowl. Turkeys sold at a higher price than geese. Tame
turkeys were to be found even in Maine, where Falmouth parson Samuel
Deane wrote on the 24th of October 1775: "I had seven turkies stole out
of the yard." A Doctor Honyman, in Boston that year, three weeks before
the fateful April 19th, found turkeys priced upward of a dollar each, at
least four times the price of a pullet.[11]

Numerous enemies preyed on crops and stock. The Indians for centuries had grown field crops but had kept no domestic animals except the
dog. When the Europeans appeared with their cattle, sheep, and hogs, the
flesh of all these new animals at once appealed to the taste of wild predators. Chief among them were wolves and bears. As domestic animals increased, this new source of food seems to have caused their enemies to
concentrate and multiply. For the next two centuries the settlers had a
continual struggle to destroy them. Records seldom if ever tell of wolves
attacking humans, though bears, especially those with cubs, sometimes
did so. Loss and damage to sheep and calves never ceased, however. Every
forested town in every New England colony offered bounties for wolves'
heads. The struggle continued for a century even in old seacoast towns,
and inland till after the Revolution. Wildcats and foxes were also pests
for generations. During the quarter century of 1698–1722 the town of
Lynn paid bounties on most of the 428 foxes killed in its woods. In Harvard, Massachusetts, a hunter collected bounties in 1732 on 16 wildcats
and 10 wolves. Hadley, beginning in 1727, in seven years paid bounties
on 2,275 wildcats.

Reverend Henry White tells of the ingenuity of a Connecticut bear in

1766. With a taste for calf, the bear tried to tunnel into the byre, dug out two or three bushels of earth, but struck boulders. He then went at the door, drew the tenpenny nails from its wooden hinges, got his paws underneath the door, pried it open, and made off with the "best of 2 calves." Three times this same bear was driven from a flock of sheep. He enjoyed the honey from a beehive. With a taste for dairy products also, he took bars from the window of the milk room, drank a tray of milk, ate three quarts of solid cream from a punchbowl and carried the bowl five yards. When his career was ended, he weighed out at 162 pounds.[12] In the new community of Thetford, Vermont, Joel Strong, who came in 1768, killed two bears in his cornfield in a single night. Local histories abound in such tales.

Gray squirrels, racoons, crows, and blackbirds found Englishmen's corn as attractive as they had that of Indians, and there was much more of it. Birds enjoyed the new grains: wheat, barley, and rye. Neither rewards for destroying these pests nor penalties for not destroying them seemed to reduce their numbers more than temporarily. Reverend Joseph Green in his Salem diary in 1711 despaired of the squirrels: "They have eaten one-quarter of my corn. It is said that there are millions of them in this village." John Ballantine's Westfield, Massachusetts, diary in the summer of 1758 complained of woodchucks as superabundant, along with squirrels and bears.[13]

To add to the natural destroyers, ships that brought settlers and supplies brought also rats. They spread inland to reach Pomfret, Connecticut, in 1740. They were borne from Providence to Wilbraham, Massachusetts, in the Connecticut Valley in a sack of wool. The black rat is said to have come early, the gray rat not till later, about 1800.

Domestic animals brought their own diseases and pests from Europe. Hog cholera was recorded by the middle of the seventeenth century. In 1708 an imported infectious disease of sheep called scab caused Massachusetts Bay to notify all towns to be on the lookout. In the third quarter of the century a fatal disease of the nose and throat, doubtless glanders or farcy, spread among horses in the Bay Colony. Bot flies also did their deadly work on horses. Just before the Revolution an unidentified distemper visited neat cattle. Rabies appeared for the first time about 1760, killing dogs and swine. A letter to Ezra Stiles in 1761 declared that up to that time New England had known angry dogs and sad dogs but never mad dogs. What seems to have been cat distemper occasioned orders to bury bodies of those afflicted, both dogs and cats. Josselyn in 1660 mentioned roup, brought over with domestic poultry. The extent of such imported diseases and their virulence are subjects that need fuller exploration.

Crops had enemies, too. Among them were insects, both native and imported. Canker worms have already been described. Other enemies that did great damage and caused privation were the army worm and the seventeen-year locust, destroyers that never failed to cause amazement among the colonists. These and forest caterpillars made enough havoc to cause the years 1646, 1649, 1665, and 1666 in the seventeenth century to be especially remembered.

In 1735 worms ate clean thousands of acres of the woods of Essex County, Massachusetts, and reached into New Hampshire. They were smooth on the back with a black streak with white spots. Locusts and grasshoppers caused havoc in Essex County, in Maine, and elsewhere in the years 1734–35, 1743, 1749, 1754, 1756, and 1764, doing their worst in drought seasons.[14]

The year 1770 and the following year saw a species of army worm sweep bare both crops and trees in the upper Connecticut Valley from Massachusetts to the Coos country, and also eastern New Hampshire. Edwin D. Sanborn, a New Hampshire historian, offers a graphic description of the "Northern Army," as it was named. Brown, with a yellow stripe on each side, and the size of a finger, "they marched from the north and northwest . . . to the east and south." So numerous were the worms that they hid the ground completely. They "crawled over houses and barns, covering every inch of the boards and shingles. Every stalk of corn and wheat was doomed. The inhabitants dug trenches, but they soon filled them . . . and the remaining army marched over . . ." They "devoured most of the standing crops and reduced the people nearly to starvation." Timothy Dwight, Yale President, offers his remembrance of this season.[15] The palmer worm, as he calls it, acted largely as Sanborn described it, but to Dwight it was brown and white striped, about two inches long, and marched west to east. In the Oxbow or Coos country wheat and corn were ruined, but peas, potatoes, and pumpkins were not to the worms' liking. Where pumpkins had been planted among the corn a tremendous crop of these matured to provide winter supplies. Great flights of wild pigeons, returning south in September, arrived to gorge on the worms, and the settlers caught and dried the pigeons for winter food to replace meat from hogs and cattle that died for lack of fodder. One family captured 500 of these birds. In older areas, where canker worms were enemies of fruit trees, wild pigeons were likewise welcome.

All through this period weeds spread and increased. Connecticut wheat was full of cockle, Douglass noticed. Near port towns weed plants accidentally imported from Europe had become a great nuisance. He saw the buttercup, white daisy, and fall dandelion thirty miles inland from Boston. The many weeds that Josselyn had earlier listed were the advance guard of a thousand unneeded visitors still arriving in the twentieth century.

13. Wealth from Forests

THOUGH NEW ENGLAND'S SOIL was in general of only fair quality and its climate rigorous, a splendid growth of forest covered its western and northern mountains and valleys, and such parts of its south and east, especially Maine, as had not been cultivated, cleared, or fired by the Indians for their own purposes.

By the colonies' second half-century, harvesting the forest riches had become a mainstay of agricultural and commercial economy in many settlements. Without sturdy natural "knees" for the frame and stout plank for siding harvested from wide-branched white oaks, the vessels that carried New England's booming commerce could scarcely have been launched. Its pines wept pitch to make tight the seams of ships and to render their rigging weatherproof. White pines were perfect for tall, erect masts to bear the sails: "The Treasure and glory of the woods," the eighteenth-century historian Daniel Neal called such trees. The fish, beef, and pork that filled the vessels' holds were barreled in native staves, and packaged staves and hoops accompanied them as exports. A deckload of spars and lumber often completed the cargo.

In frontier towns, the laborious up-and-down whipsaws were still slicing the boles of trees in the middle of the eighteenth century. Elsewhere they had given way to water mills. Sometimes a town obtained a mill by offering inducements in land and tax exemptions. The sawyer was likely to take half the lumber as his toll.

With ship timber, lumber, and staves thus valuable, towns protected their common woodlands. The permission of selectmen or forest warden was necessary to cut timber for a dwelling, barn, or farm implement, just as had been a custom of Old England. Outside speculators as well as thieves got stern warning. Thought for the future was evident. Malden in the Bay Colony in 1689 forbade felling for firewood any trees of less than one foot girth. Hadley forbade cutting young oak and walnut, and selling timber out of town. Watertown in 1649 appointed two citizens to mark trees to be left in the highway "that shall continue for shade." Groton in 1665, only thirty years from founding, had officials designate shade trees to be protected along its ways; Ipswich did the same the next year. On December 16, 1735, Guilford, Connecticut, with few exceptions required liberty from the selectmen to fell or destroy "any Tree or Trees that are now standing or that shall be set out on the . . . Highways of this Town-ship."[1] In 1685 Job Pilsbury petitioned Newbury's selectmen to forbid anyone's cutting a white oak standing on the highway near his father's barn and asked that he might have liberty to preserve it. In 1716–17 the town appointed officers to prosecute any who cut or defaced trees in any highway.[2] Thus early was New England valuing its street trees. Salem, short on shade for cattle, went further. In 1747 the commoners voted bounties for anyone who would set locust trees on its highlands.

Massachusetts had already forbidden tree-cutting on the Province Lands near the tip of Cape Cod, where drifting sand was silting up Cape Cod Harbor at Provincetown, probably a result of burning wood as fuel in the process of making lime from Indian shell heaps. Plymouth Town in 1702 made it illegal to cut pines at its beach, presumably in order to pre-vent the sand from blowing.

Protective measures were needed also to regulate burning over wood-land. In neighborhoods where grazing was of special importance, the En-glish took over the practice of burning large areas, as the Indians had done earlier to furnish deer pasture. In the Connecticut Valley, for exam-ple, Hadley burned miles of woods stretching east of the river; on the river's opposite side Northampton burned westward. In 1713 Waterbury, Connecticut, had to forbid burning for seven years, to let young trees get a start. Not long afterward, Block Island, lacking trees, was forced to dig peat to fuel fireplaces. Massachusetts Bay in 1743 passed a general law to regulate woods burning and prevent the destruction that sometimes ensued. Sandwich on Cape Cod in March 1754 selected forty-two citi-zens to supervise the burning of its woods, the job to be completed by April 16. Public supervision in Plymouth Colony, of which Sandwich had been a part, goes back at least to 1633, when firing after mid-March was banned.

How essential control was appears from the record of destructive forest fires. One started near Lebanon, New Hampshire, in the dry summer of 1761, crossed into Maine, and reached salt water at New Casco after a whole month. Such fires destroyed not only standing trees but labori-ously erected fencing. In a similar Cape Cod fire of 1772 great numbers of sheep were lost.[3]

Fires could do especial damage where evergreen trees were tapped for pitch, turpentine, and resin, activities encouraged in the early eighteenth century by an act of Parliament. Towns containing pine forests were tempted to let out the privilege of bleeding or boxing evergreen groves to obtain income. Whether because of their wealth of pines, ease of trans-portation, or both, the large river valleys and Plymouth County were the focus of this trade. A turpentine distillery was set up in Boston. The business must have begun early in Plymouth Colony, for that colony levied an export tax on tar in 1661,[4] and in 1668 limited its citizens, those who qualified as proprietors, to ten barrels a year. In 1702 the town of Plymouth gave Major John Bradford liberty to "milk" its pines on its commons from Duxbury bounds on the north to Jones River. Sandwich at the head of the Cape in 1707 granted for two years the right to "box" 2000 pines in return for two pounds income, and turpentine rights were valuable along Buzzards Bay in Plymouth Colony.

As to Connecticut, Noah Phelps's history of Simsbury, in the Farmington River Valley, says that pitch and tar began to be made there in 1643. Large amounts came from the valley of the Quinebaug in northeastern Connecticut about 1700. In 1728 Parson Timothy Woodbridge, Jr. shipped five tons of turpentine to New York. In the Connecticut River Valley the practice was forbidden by Windsor by 1696, Glastonbury by 1700, and Hartford in 1709. Enfield, however, permitted it. Upriver in Massachusetts, Westfield granted the right by 1675; Hadley by 1685. Deerfield acted favorably in 1686 but after 1715 forbade tapping. In the Merrimack Valley, Amesbury forbade gathering pitch, tar, and resin for out-of-town sale, but, like many towns, Chelmsford and Dunstable found the grants too profitable to forego.

By an English law of 1685, as modified five years later, the tallest and straightest pines, unless they stood inside a township and had been in private ownership before 1690, were reserved for the Royal Navy, which needed them as masts and spars for warships. No one was to cut a pine of a diameter of two feet or beyond. Some New England pines were of truly magnificent proportions, without a branch below a hundred feet and according to contemporary accounts reaching even as high as 300 feet into the sky. In 1689 Judge Sewall watched a mast start for England from Salmon Falls, New Hampshire. "Two and thirty oxen before, four yoke beside the mast between fore and hind wheels . . . The forty animals drag the massive load to the shore, where it is set afloat in a home-built vessel."[5] Just before the Revolution, Andrew Burnaby likewise was amazed by the tremendous mast trees: "These are of white pine and are, I believe, the finest in the world, many of them being forty yards long and as many inches in diameter. They never cut these down but in times of deep snow . . . when the trees are fallen they yoke seventy or eighty pair of oxen, and drag them along the snow. It is exceedingly difficult to put them first in motion . . . and . . . they never stop upon any account whatsoever till they arrive at the waterside." If an ox is taken ill, he is cut out of the harness and destroyed, he states. Sometimes the mast was felled into a nest of smaller trees to soften the fall. A straight path had to be cut through the woods to the riverbank or head of tide.[6]

The river valleys of New Hampshire and southern Maine furnished most of the royal mast trees at first, and cutting and hauling them gave farm people work and income in winter. Masts were floated down the Merrimack even from Concord, New Hampshire, and from Wolfeboro on Lake Winnepesaukee, both areas noted for splendid pine forests; likewise down the Connecticut.

Difficulty arose when the English government appointed officials to scout and mark all such two-foot trees with the broad arrow that reserved them for the king's use, then tried to enforce the law through vice-admiralty courts. Officers marked trees throughout southern New Hampshire and across into the Connecticut Valley, but the law was continually violated, as it was with regard to oaks in England itself, by lumbermen and landholders interested in sawing timber into salable boards. In New Hampshire 70 sawmills lined the Piscataqua River in 1720, their annual product six million feet. The king's officers received rough treatment in that colony, as did any who tried to obey the law of the arrow in the northern Connecticut Valley. At Northampton, in the Bay Colony, of 363 trees bearing the king's broad arrow, all but 37 disappeared. At Hadley in 1774 a mob prevented execution of the law. With the Revolution and independence the problem disappeared. A present-day reminder is the rarity in eighteenth century dwellings of any boards over 23 inches wide, a dimension adhered to in order to avoid incriminating evidence. By contrast, in houses of the previous century, boards and wainscot may be found running to 40 inches in width.

Besides lumber and spars, among forest products that enjoyed a good market in England previous to the Revolution were potash and its more refined form, pearlash. To make them, a pile of several cords of wood was burned to ashes. These were shoveled into tubs partly filled with brush and straw, and water was filtered through. The lye that resulted was then boiled in iron kettles til the water evaporated, leaving a hard brown residue. An acre of woods might produce up to two tons of potash. By heating this brown cake redhot in a cast iron kettle, the impurities remaining were largely consumed, and what had been yellow potash became creamy white pearlash.[7] Once the peace of Utrecht, in 1713, had ended Queen Anne's War and opened an interval of comparative peace, traders who specialized in potash took advantage by setting up production in interior towns and building shelters to hold their leaching tubs and kettles. The product, broken into small pieces and put up in casks, was sold by the bushel. In comparison to its value, its bulk was small. It was easy to transport long distances and readily salable in the ports, for it was useful for soap and glass making as well as valuable as a component of medicines.

Another outlet for forest products was the tanneries, many of them local but eventually concentrated at cattle markets in the eastern Bay Colony. Tanners needed bark for processing hides and skins. Sumac and the bark of chestnut oak were especially desirable. By the second century local craftsmen were using native woods, cherry a favorite, to make fine furniture, some of it for export.

Tremendous quantities of wood went into fuel. An ordinary dwelling needed twenty cords a year. The minister and the wealthier families with several fireplaces might each need forty or more. Boston, Salem, and other commercial centers were great consumers of firewood, some from nearby farms, much brought by coastwise wood boats from New Hampshire. In the snowy winter of 1726 hundreds of loads are said to have been sledded daily into Boston.

Biscuit and bread bakers had to heat their ovens. The numerous pig-iron foundries and forges also needed great quantities of fuel, largely charcoal. Ironworks were set up wherever bog iron was to be found. The neighborhood of Taunton in southeastern Massachusetts was one center, but by the time of the Revolution they were found even in Vermont. An iron maker required 130–50 bushels of charcoal, the product of five cords of wood, oak and hickory preferred, for every ton smelted. Once the ore in the iron mountain at Salisbury, Connecticut, began to be worked in 1734, the bloomeries there offered a continuous market for charcoal for the next century. One Salisbury iron product was potash kettles. Other consumers of cordwood were the brickmaker and the lime-burner who turned shell mounds left on the shores by unnumbered generations of Indians into building lime.

Farmers themselves used wood in a great variety of ways besides in the fireplace. It furnished frames, plank, and boards for farm buildings, and furniture for the dwelling. Long fences for fields and pickets for the home lot came from light "staddle" or saplings. Because split chestnut logs or red cedar trunks were resistant to decay, they furnished posts. The ox-cart, with its solid wheels, and the plow, harrow, sled, drag, hay rake and fork, flail, shovel, and most other tools were universally of wood, often hardened by charring at the points of wear, or shod with bits of iron. Table dishes, bowls, and spoons were wood at first; cheese vats, firkins to hold butter, milkpans, buckets—all were wood, gouged and whittled out or put together during bad weather by the farmer and his sons.

Local needs for wood and the commercial value of its products made townspeople highly jealous of intrusions on their common woodlands.

After these were divided, the woodlots that resulted became valuable personal possessions.

Among the pioneers who, following the French wars began to settle the scores of new towns laid out by New Hampshire, Connecticut, and Massachusetts in the heavily wooded hills and valleys of western New England and inland Maine, a widely different point of view arose. If the settlers and their families were to survive and prosper in such locations, trees had to be destroyed, the land opened to the sun, and crops planted. That would create problems at a later date.

14. The Ways and the Means

WITH THE RISE of second and third generations, increase in population, and alterations in economic conditions and in farming, the pattern of settlement in New England changed. The original plan of home lots in close-built villages where all lived as a community gave way. In new towns home lots were likely to be larger, of as much as fifty acres or even one hundred acres in some cases. In older towns as the years passed, the outlying common land was distributed in successive allotments. A good deal of buying, selling, and division of property went on. New owners sometimes built homesteads on lots far from the parent village. Moreover the original concept of allotting land without requiring financial payment, and of forming a communal village based to some extent on theocratic principles, yielded to a more materialistic pattern as land gained in value and commerce increased.

Economics caused other changes. In winning the French wars, the New England colonies had made extraordinary efforts and suffered severe losses. These brought on inflation and debts for both colonies and towns, and entailed heavy taxation. Thousands of soldiers had to be paid or otherwise rewarded, and colony treasuries were empty. Debts had to be met, but financial resources were exhausted. The single important available asset of the colonies was unallotted land.

To compensate the soldiers the colonies made grants of land to them or their heirs in new townships laid out especially for this purpose. Massachusetts Bay began this practice in 1725. Two years later it granted seven townships in Maine, which since the middle of the seventeenth century had been under its jurisdiction, to the soldiers surviving from King Philip's War, or the heirs of those deceased. To pay off war debts the colonies laid out more townships in the wilderness and auctioned them off to the highest bidders. The merchants and speculators who were successful bidders then sought settlers to inhabit them. Several factors— population increase, economic necessity, and outright speculation in land—caused Massachusetts Bay to charter 140 towns during the first half of the eighteenth century. Connecticut doubled the number of its towns. Governor Wentworth of New Hampshire carved out tiers of townships in the Connecticut Valley, on both sides of the river, some in territory where Massachusetts also made grants.[1]

These decades now saw the first large-scale emigration from the earlier settled parts of New England. Massachusetts people spilled over into southern New Hampshire's Monadnock mountain region. Valleys and even some of the hills in the Taconics and Berkshires filled with emigrants from lower Connecticut and eastern Massachusetts. In Connecticut settlers pushed into northern Litchfield County; in Massachusetts, into hill towns like Blandford, Tyringham, New Marlboro, Sheffield, and Great Barrington. Further north they pushed west up the Deerfield Valley to Charlemont and Colrain. About 1764 a group of families from Guilford, Connecticut, started a Guilford in what was to become Vermont; others joined them to form the nucleus of Vermont's Chittenden County. Neighbors in Pomfret and Salisbury, Connecticut, remained neighbors in Pomfret and Salisbury, Vermont. People from Hardwick in the Bay Colony began Bennington. Lancaster, beyond the White Mountains in New Hampshire, was settled from Lancaster, Massachusetts. Londonderry, New Hampshire, though itself not long settled, saw ten different swarms of people leave it before the Revolution.

In Portland, Maine, in 1726 Reverend Thomas Smith wrote: "People constantly flocking down here to petition for lots." Again in 1750, after a quarter-century, he wrote: "There is news of a brig full of people gone to Penobscot to settle there." Many of these coastal Maine settlers are said to have come from inland towns of the Bay Colony and New Hampshire. Such emigrants did not depopulate the old-settled towns. Rather, they were overspill from increasing population. If they had held land, it sold readily. The spill went southward also, emigrants settling in New Jersey, North Carolina, Georgia, even in what was later to become Mississippi. It streamed into the Wyoming Valley of the Susquehanna area and into westen New York. It flowed eastward as far as New Brunswick and Nova Scotia, where New England people organized numerous towns on New England models.[2]

The character of the settlers who took up land in the new towns seems often to have differed somewhat from that of people who remained in the home towns. They were apt to be the young and adventurous, ready to take the risk of leaving a comfortable established community with school, church, and neighbors in order to acquire farms of their own in new situations, rough though life there might be. Sometimes, however, a group of neighbors in the home town acquired the rights to a whole new township, sent a committee to spy out the land, plotted the house lots, and in the old town organized a complete town government for the new a year or more before anyone cleared an acre in it. Others arranged for new homesteads with some speculative proprietor who had acquired a large tract and who offered inducements to get settlers to start in a spot where there was not even a road, let alone any society.

These pioneers had an object, and many of them attained it. To quote Samuel Williams, who toward the end of the century wrote of the Vermont settlers: "Amidst the hard living and hard labor that attends the forming of a new settlement the settler has the most flattering prospects and encouragements. One hundred acres in a new town does not generally cost him more than he can spare from the wages of one or two years . . . When he comes to apply his labor to his own land, the produce of it becomes extremely profitable. The first crop of wheat will fully pay for all the expense he has been at in clearing up, sowing and fencing his land, and at the same time increase the value of the land eight or ten times."[3] Such good fortune, however, applied only to the best situations. For most pioneer farmers and their wives the struggle at first was desperate. If they succeeded to some degree, as most of them did, in establishing productive farms and enduring towns, they deserved their modest success.

In country cleared only in parts before the arrival of the English, and without available buildings or livestock, the tools they first needed had been axes, adzes, saws, and carpenter's tools to provide shelter; and mattocks or pickaxes, spades, and hoes to stir the soil and plant and cultivate crops. The Pilgrims had brought such hand tools with them in their small and crowded ship. With them they put up their first buildings, and when spring came planted their hills of Indian corn and a small field of European grain. Having no cattle, there could be no plowing even if they had brought a plow. They needed no dairy utensils, nor fences except pales to keep wild animals from their gardens.

The Puritan colony a decade later was much more adequately equipped, having brought a considerable variety of tools. The passenger lists had included carpenters, wheelwrights, and other tradesmen experienced in their use. The numerous cattle soon made it possible to use plows; but while farm inventories often include plow chains, few farmers owned plows, a situation not unusual in Old England at the time. Even after a half century plows were not plentiful.[4]

As time went on and additional and more varied equipment, especially for transportation, became necessary, carts, wains, and tumbrils with racks for hay could be built completely of local oak and ash, their wheels often cross-sections of some large tough-grained tree with a hole bored through the center of each to receive the wooden axles. This practice continued for generations. Joshua Hempstead, for example, in his diary on March 22, 1742/3, records that he sawed off a pair of pepperage or ironwood wheels for his stone cart. He rounded them properly and, taking advantage of a hole in the center, shaped each to receive the axle. If a simpler vehicle would do, without a wheelwright's help the farmer could put together a sled useful for both winter and summer with round saplings for runners; or make a flat drag or dray. Both continued for a long time to be used to transport dung to the field, bring home corn or rye, or deliver a load of stone for a wall. On November 5, 1719, Hempstead took his plow to Stonington on such a dray or drag. For bringing in hay, a series of branches bound together horizontally would serve to bear the load.[5]

With iron now more plentiful and some farmers more prosperous, a wheelwright could combine hub, spokes, and felloes, and bind the rims with iron tires to make more elaborate wheels for the cart; or he could shoe the sledge or sled with iron runners. According to Abigail Adams, the useful tipcart, too, was known by the time of the Revolution. By 1762 Amesbury farmers were voting in town meeting that sleds should have a uniform width of 4 feet 2 inches. By that date nearly every farm in Suffolk County, Massachusetts, owned at least one cart.[6]

For the entire first two centuries the plow, if a farmer was fortunate enough to own one (and some well-to-do farmers apparently did not), continued to be of ash or other clear-grained wood, although the coulter might be iron and the share protected by narrow flat iron sheets. A good plow-maker gained a reputation. A single ox or cow might pull a small plow, but plowing ordinarily took at least two. Large farmers kept two yokes or more. The most unsatisfactory feature of the wooden plow was the way damp soil stuck to its mouldboard, requiring continuous cleaning. At least one early inventory mentions separately a "breaking-up

10. Early plows were of wood. Added metal patches sometimes protected the mouldboard. *Mapes*, Illustrated Catalogue (*1861*).

plow," among several. The heavy "A" harrow or the square harrow, sometimes double, might be equipped with imported iron teeth although
more likely they were of native wood. The smoothing harrow that covered grass and grain seed lightly, and did the job well, was merely birch
brush bound to a crosspiece. Yet it was so efficient a tool that it persisted
into the twentieth century.

Some of these poor wilderness farmers, however, lacking cattle, as late
as the end of the eighteenth century still had only wooden hand tools to
stir the earth. Their shovels were likely to be fashioned from a thick
plank, suitably hollowed at one end and cut away at the other so as to
leave a center handle. It was a disadvantage in a frontier settlement
to own a shovel shod with iron, because of the temptation for neighbors
to borrow it![7]

Axe, hoe, scythe, and sickle continued to be the most important tools
made of metal. The axe, forged and given an edge by the local blacksmith, or possibly imported, had a straight handle. Neither broad axe nor
felling axe could compare in drive or ease of handling with the modern
axe. Hoes, also made by the smith, were of at least three kinds; the grub
hoe for breaking the ground, the broad hoe, and the narrow hoe for weeding. These were of iron, the two last much heavier than similer modern
hoes.

Saws included the long up-and-down two-man blade already mentioned which continued in use even after sawmills spread widely. The
whipsaw and the crosscut saw are also listed in numerous inventories.
Matthew Patten's diary at Bedford, New Hampshire, as late as 1784 tells
of tribulations caused by the brittle metal of that era, and the hazard of
loaning tools: "I brought home my crosscut saw. Robert Gilchrist broke
above three inches off one end of her and a tooth out toward the middle."

Wedges used for splitting fence rails, clapboards, and shingles are often
mentioned in farm accounts. The larger farmers had grindstones, wheelbarrows, and maybe a vise. The common small hand and dairy tools
mentioned in current inventories have already been listed.

Though not customarily included in the category of tools, among the
necessities as means of production during this first century and a half
were adequate fences, walls, and ditches to keep wandering livestock out
of dooryards, gardens, orchards, and cultivated lands, and to fold sheep at
night. This was a subject of continuous legislation in every town record
generation after generation. With no time in the early years for walls or
ditching, farmers turned to wooden fences. At first, and for a long time
after in new towns, these might be merely rough-piled stumps or brush;

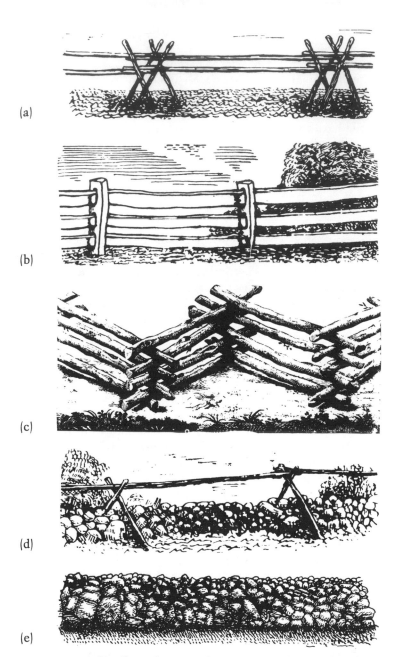

(a)

(b)

(c)

(d)

(e)

11. Fences and walls, to keep stock in—or out: (a) pole; (b) split-rail; (c) Virginia; (d) half-high wall, with rail; (e) stone wall. Source for a–b, d–e: *Perley*, History of Salem *(1924)*. For c: *Luigi Castiglioni*, Viaggio Negli Stati Uniti *(1790)*.

12. Rhode Island wall in the Portsmouth area on Aquidneck (Rhode) Island, noted for superior wall building. *Courtenay P. Worthington photo. Collection of Howard S. Russell.*

but as one generation succeeded another, four types of fence became common. To protect garden plots and dooryards pales were split and driven into the ground, held together at the top by a rail to which each pale could be fastened. Once sawn lumber became common, the picket fence evolved; later it was painted white. Especially where forest was being cleared, a fence of logs laid one atop the other would serve to protect crop land.

Most common, however, once farming was well established, was the rail fence. It was of two types. Over the greater part of New England a rail fence was built after the following fashion. For posts, the farmer felled foot-thick straight-grained trees (chestnut or red cedar preferred because of their resistance to decay). These he cut to six-foot lengths and split in half; next with auger and chisel he mortised the upper portion every four to six inches. He set them in holes dug 9 to 10 feet apart. For rails he took much larger oak or ash trees, cut their boles into 11-foot lengths, and split each length so as to make eight to sixteen rails. Their ends were

13. Gundalow of salt hay, waiting for the tide. *Society for the Preserva-tion of New England Antiquities, Boston.*

then slipped into the mortises of one post after another, the post holes filled, and made solid. If properly done, the fence that resulted discouraged even a hog, provided he had been yoked to prevent digging.

Town meetings or selectmen regulated the height and maintenance of fences. Every town chose fence-viewers to see that they were of the required height and strength and to settle disputes as to their upkeep. At Watertown, Massachusetts, in 1647 a fence was required to have four rails; in 1653, to be 3½ feet high. At first, in Guilford, Connecticut, the height was set at 4 feet, but by 1653 a "sufficient fence" there had to be 4½ feet tall. At Salem the requirement at first was 3–4 feet; at Portsmouth, Rhode Island, in 1671, 4½ feet. By that date experience had taught many towns to insist on 5 feet and at least five rails for all cornfields, gardens, and orchards. Before long, however, the need became clear for barriers more permanent than wood fences.

In New England's glacial terrain, where boulders and fieldstone abound, nothing could match the stone wall for permanence. Building walls served a second purpose—to clear fields and make cultivation easier. Moreover, the job was ideal to fill slack time at almost any season. So in 1677 Watertown had to legislate as to how long stones dug from highways, but not removed, might remain the property of the digger. In 1718 we find Joshua Hempstead digging stones in his orchard meadow. That winter in February he was sledding stones "to make wall by the pear tree." The work went on even in hot weather: on July 28, 1721, he was at home all day stacking hay and making a stone wall. Back in 1714 he had built 201 feet, but almost thirty years later he was still at it: "Mar. 26, 1742: Made Six Rod of Stone wall . . . had 3 hands besides my own."

To build an enduring wall was not only laborious but a work of skill. First the loam was dug out down to the top of the subsoil or the frost line. A bed of small stones, sand, or gravel would replace it where needed. Large boulders, hauled on a stone boat, were next rolled in to serve as a foundation and allowed to settle. Last, field stones of smaller size selected for contour and proportion carried the wall to its intended height of three, four, or five feet. The half-high wall must be topped with a crotch fence and rail. If clearing fields was a main object, the farmer laid up parallel walls a few feet apart, and the interval thus formed provided an excellent dump for still more surplus rocks.

Poorly built walls eventually fell from frost action. The many earthquakes of the colonial period also, as one contemporary writer expressed it, threw down "a vast deal of stone wall." Yet thousands of miles of wall first laid up in the seventeenth and eighteenth centuries still survive two and three centuries later.

15. Life on the Farm

O N MOST NEW ENGLAND FARMS in the century preceding the Revolution, the farmer and his sons did the field work and cared for the livestock, sometimes with the help of a neighbor's son bound out to learn the art of agriculture. For heavy jobs he exchanged work with other farmers nearby.

Large farmers, merchants, and capitalists employed hired labor regularly, and some of them used slaves. The great plantations of southern Rhode Island and adjacent Connecticut, however, were the only areas where agriculture placed large dependence on slave labor.

Little overseas immigration occurred during this century. With fisheries and foreign commerce profitable and frequent calls for men for military service, ordinary labor was not plentiful and wages generally high. Moreover, land, especially in a new town, was cheap and easy to secure. Why, then, should an able-bodied man work for wages for another except long enough to get capital to secure a homestead of his own?

No permanent class of agricultural laborers like those to be found on an English manor existed. Governor Wentworth of New Hampshire in a report to England commented on the fluidity of labor in general: "Scarcely a shoemaker, a joiner, or a silversmith but quits his trade as soon as he can get able to buy a little tract of land."[1] Even though the mechanic did not turn into a full-time farmer, with such a little tract the former apprentice could plant a garden, set an orchard, get hold of a cow, and exchange his skill with the neighborhood for whatever else he and his family needed. To become a landowner was not difficult. The Governor had land to sell, for in each of the dozens of new towns that he chartered, he reserved for himself a tract of 500 acres. On the other hand, land ownership did not create a leisure class. The dignity of the Governor's station did not render him above severe labor on his own farm at Wolfeboro on Lake Winnepesaukee. General John Stark of Revolutionary fame, who operated mills, like many other leading men was also a practical farmer.

How the work of the ordinary farm got done could scarcely be better illustrated than by excerpts from the journal of Joseph Andrews, a sheep man and general farmer of Hingham, twenty miles south of Boston. Besides all the work he did alone, Andrews gave and received assistance:

Sept. 7, 1753	"Helped Uncle And[rew] about carting some dung"
Oct. 30 "	"Finisht Giting Up my Potatoes & Helpt Uncle take up his Flax"
Nov. 2 "	"Helpt Uncle Sat fence . . . and Git Up Some Potatoes"
Nov. 19 "	"Killing my Beef. Simon Stoddard Helpt me killed three"
Jan. 3 "	"Killed my Pigs today, Knight Sprage Helpt me"
Jan. 15 "	"Threshing my Barly: Uncle And helpt me"
Jan. 30 "	"Spent the day in Reckoning with Uncle And"
April 3, 1754	"Down at Plan hills Picking Up Stones All Day, seven of us in all"
May 3 "	"Helpt Uncle And Plowing & Spreading Rockweed"

The 1726–27 Journal of Zaccheus Collins, a farmer and maltster of Lynn, tells a similar but different tale.

5th month	9 "3 men mowing in feald"
	29 "At Marblehead ye boys got in Barly"
6th month	12 "John Fairn a thrashing my barly"
	16 "Allen Freed faned my barly"
8th month	18 "a killing a pr of Oxen Nathaniel & Jonathan Collins and I had between us & my part of it. Beef weighed 363"
1725 5th month	"Ezekiel Collins mowed my barly I cleaned out my rye" [This farmer also did many jobs alone.]

On the other hand Reverend Timothy Walker, the minister-farmer of Concord, New Hampshire, had a slave, "Prince," who worked on his farms regularly. In haying time as many as six men did his mowing, and in March 1746 he speaks of "my men" swingling (beating and cleaning) flax. He, too, got help from neighbors, however. In April 1764 Deacon Hall sowed his hayseed. In November Timothy Chandler helped him cart dung.

At one time Joshua Hempstead at Stonington, Connecticut, was busy with a big job, breaking up land. On May 17, 1715, he records: "I was all day with all ye boys & benja[min] Fox & Peter Latimer breaking up & planting at Jo Lesters I had Mr. Latimers 6 oxen and uncle foxes 2 oxen & Daniel Lesters Plow." The job took all that day and the next. When he brought home the oxen on the third day, he notes that he had plowed one acre plus 70 rods (160 rods to an acre).[2]

Another type of labor found not infrequently in this period was the bound-out or indentured servant. Many early immigrants, it will be recalled, bound themselves by indentures, ordinarily for seven years, to pay for their passage. That particular bargain was by then usually a thing of the past in New England, but it was not unusual even into the nineteenth century for a boy to be bound out to some neighbor who was a good farmer "to learn the art and mystery of husbandry." Such a boy was likely to be well treated, educated much like a son, and at twenty-one given a good start in life by his employer.

A young farmer starting out on his own got lots of help from others. A young Rhode Islander starting in the Berkshires made a pair of shoes for a neighbor. He was aided with a man and horse for a day on his own lot. John May, Jr., an early comer to Woodstock, Connecticut, planned to build a house. In December 1710 he helped a neighbor named Child at logging and dressing flax. On December 30 Child helped him dig his cellar. The next day Joseph Lyon, Jr., "fetched a load of stone for the walls." In January 1711 May helped Child fell trees, helped his landlord make a sled, and helped Ichabod Holmes with his rye. Then on the 16th and again on March 22 three neighbors helped May draw timber for his house. In April two helped hew it. More assistance both ways followed. May bought boards and shingles for his dwelling. On September 12 he finished his frame; next day the neighborhood raised it. One neighbor helped with foundation and chimney, another laid floors. Finally the house was done. May next made a bedstead, and bought a mare. On December 18 he recorded "A Great day's work" (he had got married). He loaded his bride's furniture on a cart at Boston. On New Year's Day 1712 the couple reached Woodstock, both bride and groom on the mare. The household goods came with them the seventy-five miles by oxcart, and only a single chair was damaged.[3]

Sometimes a big job enlisted the whole town. Rev. Ebenezer Parkman, minister-farmer at Westboro, Worcester County, Massachusetts, did not need to worry about getting his harvest home. This is his diary entry for October 11, in the Revolutionary year of 1779: "This day we cut up, carted home and husked out our Indian Corn. Ephraim Tucker went with my Team and Deacon Wood with his, about nine dined here. There were forty or more Men and Boys at Eve[ning] and several neighbors were so generous as to contribute to ye Entertainment. Squire Baker above 50 lbs. of Meat; Mr. Eb[eneze]r. Forbes Beef and 3 cabbages; Lt. Bond, Pork; Mr. Barnabas Newton, a Cheese; Breck [the parson's son] sufficient Rum. Through ye Goodness of God we had a good crop of Sound Corn and ye Joy of Harvest . . . We sang latter part of Ps. 65" (certainly an appropriate harvest ode).[4]

Many other ministers farmed. A parson was occasionally to be found in the ranks of the larger farmers, as had been the case in Old England. Reverend Joseph Green of Danvers on June 23, 1712, had ten men at work, eight "about the house" and two mowing. Reverend Timothy Walker of Concord, New Hampshire—to harvest the native grass on his intervale meadow—in August 1746 had six hands to mow for him. Among the large operators were sometimes merchants like John Hull of Boston, who managed livestock ventures in Rhode Island and farms elsewhere in addition to his Boston occupations.

New England farms with the most numerous labor forces were the great estates of Narragansett planters in southern Rhode Island and nearby Connecticut. These produced livestock and dairy products, and did it with the labor of slaves. Rhode Island ships trading with Africa had brought back enough slaves so that in 1708 the number of "black servants" in that colony is said to have been 426.

By 1748, with prosperity derived from dairying, sheep, and horses, the number had increased to over 3,000; by the end of the next decade, to 4,700. South Kingstown had one negro to each three whites. In Connecticut the number of negroes is said to have reached 6,464 in all, part of them free; and, in Massachusetts Bay, 5,235 by 1746.[5]

A Newport planter, Colonel Godfrey Malbone, bought 3,000 acres at Pomfret, Connecticut, in 1766 to be worked by slaves, and they were there during the Revolution, to the worriment of the countryside, which feared them. One historian puts the largest number on any single estate at forty. Edgar Bacon in his *History of Narragansett Bay* calls slave labor in this period as much a part of Rhode Island life as of Virginia's. Since in all four colonies a considerable number were household servants, it is not clear just how large a number were farm workers; still, the proportion must have been considerable.

As time went on, moral scruples caused a number of Rhode Island planters, largely Quakers, to free their slaves. "College Tom" Hazard, from one of the leading families, has been called one of the first American abolitionists. In 1774 the Assembly voted that all blacks imported into the colony thereafter should be free. Connecticut banned the slave trade the same year. Massachusetts in its Revolutionary constitution in 1781 declared all men free. Connecticut at the Revolution's end made free persons of all negro children born after 1784 and eventually abolished slavery. New Hampshire, where slaves were never numerous, took similar action.

All types of labor considered—hired, indentured, and forced—it was nevertheless on family exertions that the vast majority of farms depended, both for the family's own sustenance and for any produce grown for sale.

Yet life on the farm was by no means unrelieved labor. Diaries of the time tell of such recreations as visiting, quilting parties, husking parties, strawberrying—even "watermeloning"—and fishing.

The health of the colonists during the first few generations appears to have been good.[6] Scurvy and dietary illnesses were rampant during the long ocean voyage and the months of inadequate food and shelter that immediately followed their arrival, causing the death of scores. Of the first settlers of Salem, one in four died the first winter. Of Governor Winthrop's company, arriving in summer, two hundred died like falling leaves before the autumn was over. Such losses must have weeded out the weakest; thereafter the record is favorable. One fortunate circumstance, to which Nathaniel Shaler has called attention was that no new diseases resulted from contact of the English with the native Indians.

Of ailments that the newcomers brought with them, influenza, called in old records "fever and ague" or "epidemical cold with fever," appears again and again. Another complaint common to this age before refrigeration was "malignant dysentery" or "bloody flux." Epidemic "throat distemper" (diphtheria), was often fatal for young people. At Weymouth, Massachusetts, in 1751, the "Throat Distemper Year," 150 died, mostly children. By contrast, for several generations tuberculosis was rare, among the young at least. As one elderly chronicler in a Plymouth Colony town recalled: "In the year 1764 a young man fell into a consumption between twenty and thirty years of age and it passed for a wonder." Michael Wigglesworth's verse seems to bear this out: "New England, where for many years you scarcely heard a cough . . ." A thoughtful local historian suggests that the wide-throated chimneys which so readily ventilated every dwelling may have been a favorable factor in respect to this disease. Helpful also was the practice (though not much considered in the earliest settlements) of choosing elevated locations, airy, with good water drainage and near clear flowing springs, for village sites, in consequence of which, as Worcester County's earliest historian, Peter Whitney, put it, being "to a great degree exempted from fogs, deleterious vapours and exhalations, the inhabitants [of Lunenburg] are remarkably healthy . . ."

Doctors were few, and most of those few ill trained. For seventy-six years, from 1654 to 1730, no surgeon was to be found in the considerable Connecticut Valley town of Northampton. Across the river, neighboring Hadley for thirty-two years had no physician. Ministers' diaries record numerous illnesses and deaths from disease, causes often ill defined, as well as from what today would be termed industrial accidents.

Every provident country family kept herbs, dry roots, and Indian remedies on hand, and tradition attests to their value. Wild strawberries were a remedy for kidney stone and gout. On October 12, 1715, Joshua Hempstead, his diary tells us, was out on the hills getting wintergreen for his daughter, troubled with what is now termed phlebitis, following childbirth. In 1723, on Cape Cod, a youngster in the Bourne family (missionaries to the Indians), was so ill that the physicians gave her up. An Indian medicine man cured her.

In 1679, Guilford, Connecticut, held a special town meeting "to consider whether the inhabitants would buy Mrs. Corster's Physic and Physical drugs." The vote in favor was unanimous, and the next spring, with only a single person objecting, the town voted a special tax to pay for them.

If professional physicians were few, to the courage of one and the scientific mind of a Boston minister goes the credit for control of one of the scourges of the age, smallpox. New England's wide-spreading ocean commerce brought recurring waves of this disease. It devastated the ports and at times swept inland, local quarantine and isolation in pesthouses the only remedy. The inquiring mind of Reverend Increase Mather happened on a report from the eastern Mediterranean of the value of inoculation as a preventive, and he advocated the practice. Against fierce opposition, political, medical, and physical, Dr. Zabdiel Boylston of Boston on June 26, 1721, successfully inoculated, with live vaccine, first his own six-year-old son, Thomas, and later the rest of his household; then 246 others. Of the 246 inoculated, according to Dr. Boylston's account, but 6 died, compared to approximately one in seven of the 5,759 uninoculated who came down with the disease in Boston in the course of two years. Though smallpox was less prevalent away from the ports (Northfield, Massachusetts, had but one case in almost a half-century), a few country physicians near Boston took up the practice successfully. It was to be 1796, however, before Edward Jenner in England learned what dairy people there had long known, that cowpox immunized against smallpox. In the United States Dr. Benjamin Waterhouse, young Harvard professor of physic, was first to begin the practice of cowpox vaccination, again on a young son, and the conquest of the disease followed.

New England's climate made unusual the malaria that plagued the southern colonies, but it found its way occasionally into a port. New Haven, especially in 1658 and 1659, was visited by severe epidemics displaying malarial symptoms.

Before the end of the first century a new minor ailment appeared. It was not unusual to see girls of only twenty "pitifully tooth shaken," as John Josselyn phrased it. Tea and hot bread got the blame that today is visited more accurately on sugar. A local rhymester came near to the truth: "From western isles now fruits and delicacies/Do rot maid's teeth and spoil their handsome faces." Joshua Hempstead of Connecticut on September 14, 1718, sent five shillings by John Adams "to buy Some Tooth powder in Boston." Among products of Paul Revere's foundry were false teeth.

Despite lack of professional medical care, and especially in sharp contrast with southern colonization, New England's health record, for the times, is coming to be considered surprisingly good. Two recent studies of rural areas, those of John Demos, of Plymouth Colony, and of Philip Greven, of Andover, offer evidence of the "salubriousness" so often claimed by local town historians. In the Plymouth records but one birth in thirty appears to have been fatal to the mother. In early Andover, up to 1700, only a little over one in five children died before age 20. Half the females and three fifths of the males lived to be fifty; three in ten men and almost as many women survived to age seventy. Nathaniel Shaler assures us that the size, weight, and beauty of the colonists showed no deterioration from those of Old England, nor did their fecundity. On this important subject much further careful statistical work needs to be done; not only with regard to physical ailments but in the matter of mental illness, for which evidence appears inadequate indeed.

It would be a neat conclusion to this consideration of New England agriculture during the century that ended with the outbreak of the Revolution to offer, as some writers have done, a picture of the "typical farmer" and his family existing on their typical "subsistence" farm. Yet if any judgment were to be drawn from the evidence offered in these pages, it would certainly be that no single, universal, category of farmer and farm existed.

The South County horse breeder, sheep herder and dairyman, exporting Pacers and cheeses to the West Indies, his stock pastured on a thousand acres or more and cared for by slaves and Indians, was one type. A second was the ambitious young man setting out with a wife and all their belongings in a single oxcart, heading for a hundred acres offered by a township speculator on time payment in the backwoods of Vermont or Maine. The well-fixed grandson of the original owner of a long-tilled and well-manured corn and fat-stock farm, or one near an alewife run and a port market, was a third. Still another was the poor Scotch-Irishman or German with not even an ox or plow, who turned over the southern New Hampshire or Maine soil by hand to start his potato crop.

Besides these there were the Connecticut and Rhode Island farmers who in addition to common crops and animals grew onions, potatoes, tobacco, or flax for export; the Nantucket or Martha's Vineyard flockmaster with a thousand sheep; the innkeeper, grist or saw miller, storekeeper, drover, distiller, or tanner with a farm on the side. (For example, a miller on Cape Cod, dying in 1729, among his assets left a pair of oxen, 22 cattle, 2 horses, and a colt. He was one of many.) The shoemaker, blacksmith, or fisherman who ordinarily worked at his trade, usually farmed a little also to help out.[7]

Variations of other sorts existed. Many farmers enjoyed rights of common in towns where methods of agriculture were still governed by town meeting. Others lacked such rights or set up farming on their own separate tracts, newly divided, or in towns late chartered to which such controls never extended. The historian of Keene, New Hampshire, for example, tells how a settler there might obtain as much as 400 acres of fertile but forested land for $25. Such new farms sometimes made their owners wealthy on wheat alone.

The great majority of farmers kept some cows, often a family horse, an ox or a pair, a pig or two, in some areas sheep or goats. To feed this stock they cut a few tons of English (cultivated) hay and double or triple the weight in meadow or salt hay. In one town they might raise perhaps 30 or 40 bushels of grain per farm for family and stock; in another eight or ten times as much. If the farm was in apple country, the cider could run from 10 barrels up: on Cape Cod it would be very little. For many families a cow and a sow, perhaps a few roots and pumpkins, was as far as farming went; with others, agriculture was merely a side issue to commerce or a foundation on which to build a large estate.

Farm families in some areas, where a storekeeper or merchant offered an outlet, increased their income by making woolens, linens, stockings, caps, mittens, and similar items for market in the New York colony or more distant trade centers. A Northampton merchant in 1762 had a stock of 761 locally made brooms. Along the shore many families gathered wild bayberries and from their wax made candles for export; others hammered out nails or made shoes; still others got extra income from beeswax and honey. These and other sources of family income were to be greatly expanded when the Revolution restricted importation; but even in this early period they added to the wide variety that was to be for so long characteristic of New England agriculture and rural life.

The financial condition of New England's farmers was likewise various. Few were really wealthy, though many were comfortable: yet, except on the fringe of the frontier, scarcely any were poor in the sense of lacking essential food, clothing, or shelter. This was not necessarily the consequence of any virtue of the soil even where it was virgin. Rather, as

Robert Honyman phrased the matter in 1775, it was due "to the incomparable industry of the inhabitants," and not least to the severe and exacting labor of farm women and children, though ordinarily they did not do hard field work.

It should always be kept in mind that in the century preceding the Revolution wealth in the form of currency, especially "hard money," was the exception and confined largely to merchants and port towns. In most towns wealth would be measured in land, livestock, and tangible assets together with a balance between a variety of items of all sorts receivable or owed. At any particular date both of the last two, as estate inventories show, were likely to be considerable for with cash scarce, an even settlement between two persons might not be reached readily for years, and no hard feelings either way.

To make up for the shortage of currency the various colonies from time to time made farm products and other commodities legal tender and authorized specific values for them. Wheat, rye, barley, oats, and corn; barreled beef, pork, and fish; flax, hemp, butter in firkins, tobacco, beeswax, boards, and other common items—all appeared on lists of this sort. Such produce was receivable for taxes, for the minister's salary, and similar purposes. As time passed, great variations in values occurred: at New Milford, Connecticut, for instance, between 1715 and 1760, the legal price for wheat went from 4 shillings to 22, and Indian corn from 2½ shillings to 7 in 30 years.[8] This method of placing arbitrary values on commodities not infrequently resulted in disputes over quality. In business transactions such a system made necessary a series of running scores between farmer and farmer, drover and farmer, and merchant and farmer. At infrequent reckonings the balance was often struck by giving orders or notes which, passed from hand to hand, served as a kind of supplementary currency. The problem of exchange was complicated by the issuance of paper money of the various colonies. Fluctuations in value and gains or losses that ensued made barter of one tangible object or product for another likely to be fairer to both parties than the use of the paper script.

A few typical entries in farm and store accounts make this method clear.

From New Hampshire: "I let William Kurr have 3 bushell of potatoes to be paid for in shad or money."

"Amos Gardner got 4 bushels of potatoes for which he is to give me three thousand of shingle nails."

"I got a [plow] shear mould from Thomas McLaughlin . . . toward what he owes me on the fly nets."

Southport, Connecticut, records, as reported by the town's historian Charlotte Lacey, contain this item: "Dec. 16, 1682. Ebenezer Smith hath by way of exchange with Samuel Drake a parcel of fence in quantity five rods, it is made with stones."

From Bristol County, Massachusetts, "Reseeved of Samuel Mason one cheese which waid 7 pounds," balanced by sugar, a whip, and other items.

From Buzzards Bay: "Reckoned with Ebenezer Luce and accounts balanced from the beginning of the world to the date hereof"[9] (a phrase frequently used as a disclaimer of further liability).

Whether agriculture was a vocation or merely a side issue to help feed the household, most farm families lived in decent houses; frame in the villages, of squared logs on the frontier. Almost invariably, except in squatter areas on the fringes in Maine, New Hampshire, and Vermont, they held title to their property in fee simple, and had the right to vote, at least in town affairs. "Everybody has property and everybody knows it," Robert E. Brown quotes a British officer as saying.[10]

All males and many females had some education. Massachusetts Bay had long required public schools in every town, and since 1647 Latin schools in the larger ones. Governor Dummer Academy, a private school at Newbury, Massachusetts, dates from 1726; that same year one was founded at Windham, New Hampshire. In 1771 Braintree was voting tax money for "Women schools."[11] Not infrequently country towns were "presented" to colony governments for not carrying out the law, usually pleading poverty or Indian depredations.

Spelling was often bad, but at the end of the colonial period nearly all the men could read, and write at least their names, an unusual distinction for a whole population at that era in history. Books were to be found in a substantial number of farmhouses, though perhaps only a Bible and almanac (in three-fourths of two hundred farm inventories of a Worcester County compilation).[12] The country town of Woburn produced a distinguished scientist, Benjamin Thompson, later Count Rumford, who discovered that heat was a form of motion.

Community libraries were appearing here and there through the countryside. Citizens of Durham in central Connecticut organized a book company in 1733. Nearby Guilford, Saybrook, Killingworth, and Lyme had begun library associations by 1737; in Connecticut's northeast corner Pomfret, Woodstock, then Killingly and Lebanon followed within two years; Milford got under way in 1745 and West Hartford in 1753. At the westerly end of the colony, Danbury had a public library in 1771, and interior Brooklyn began one in 1775. In the District of Maine, Falmouth, now Portland, in 1763 led the library movement. Hingham in the Bay Colony formed a Social Library in 1771, and a second one in 1773. Newport, Rhode Island, one of New England's principal ports and a fertile farm area, in 1747 built its still famous Redwood Library from the donations of a Quaker of that name, and of others. By 1727 Boston had seen three newspapers started and at Newport one was begun five years later. Others followed. As to periodicals, by 1775 New England was the best served area of the American colonies. They carried mostly news of public affairs and commercial information. Editions were not large, but each copy was likely to have numerous readers.[13]

In 1725 Dr. Nathaniel Ames of Dedham began to offer his popular *Astronomical Diary and Almanac* (other almanacs had been printed still earlier) and farmers were eager purchasers. One Connecticut farm-bred boy, born during the Revolution, tells of a file of these going back to 1720 as "sources of delight and instruction." Strictly agricultural books of local origin seem to have had their inception with the printing in Boston in 1710 by John Allen of the *Husbandman's Guide*.[14]

The first volume to attain influence, however, and to attack soil fertility and cultivation problems, was Jared Eliot's *Essays upon Field Husbandry*. Originally published serially, 1747–59, the essays were printed in 1760 in Boston as a single volume. Eliot, pastor and farmer at Killingworth, Connecticut, had experimented for years on his farm, had traveled in Europe, and had observed farming methods there. His advice was respected.[15]

The emphasis by modern sociology-conscious historians on class distinctions in eighteenth-century New England tends toward misjudgment of a fundamental characteristic of the New England farming town. When the house lots were originally assigned, it was often by lot, always under basic agreement. The result was that on "The Street," up to the time of the Revolution, the larger house of the wealthy and prosperous was as likely as not to be neighbor to a modest cottage. The children of the two grew up together, worshiped together, studied together, and often intermarried. Charles Grant has well stated in his thoughtful study of Kent, Connecticut, that "in many communities leadership and executive authority go with the man rather than the office," true then in country towns, and still true. Governor Hutchinson complained that the vote of a poor man "will go as far in popular elections as one of the most opulent." Everyone worked, for it was sinful not to, and for the first century and a half nothing that could be called a leisure class existed except in a few port towns.[16]

The whole community had a common descent and a single historical tradition. Church membership was open to the poorest, and skin color was no barrier. Franchise requirements were so modest that almost any self-respecting mechanic or small farmer could meet them. All male inhabitants had their share in providing necessary roads, bridges, and town pounds. In New England as in Old England local public office usually carried no salary, entailed plenty of trouble, and was likely to be regarded less as an honor than as a burden. As such it might be more easily borne by the affluent than by the poorer man, but evidence is lacking that election to town office or continuance in it ordinarily caused either envy or discontent among other inhabitants. On the contrary, town by-laws not infrequently prescribed penalties for refusal of an elective office. In 1682 Amesbury, for example, fined Richard Currier for refusing. Plymouth Colony fined selectmen who declined to serve. Michael Zuckerman shows that persons elected to the post of selectman usually had already filled bothersome and undistinguished minor posts.[17]

The wrangles that eventually arose were occasioned far less by pretensions to social superiority by any group than by differing views of old and new comers, "proprietors," and "inhabitants," as to the ownership and allotment of the town's undivided lands; by disagreements over the site of the meetinghouse; and, as settlement spread to outlying sections, by the determination of proprietors in the new villages to have them made separate parishes, if not separate towns, with their own meetinghouses, pastors, officers, and tax rolls. Each of these involved property, money, or public appropriations and taxation. To most New Englanders, these matters—then as now—loomed as of far greater consequence than such a minor question as the order of seating in the meetinghouse for Sabbath worship.

The century 1675–1775 had again and again brought destruction, misery, and death to New England's farms, especially to those on its northern and western fringes. It had taken thousands of men far from home on expeditions of war and, as captives, women and children also; many of both were never to return.

On the other hand, the accidents of geography plus a powerful commercial instinct had sent exports sea-borne to the West Indies and southern markets: pork, cattle, horses, onions, boards, staves, pitch, and other farm cargo. All this became a basis for economic health at home.

The century had added to New England's list of crops a valuable food and salable commodity, the potato. The vegetable arrived in company with the Scotch-Irish, the first immigrants of consequence to enter since 1640. Though at first shown a cold shoulder, these newcomers, with their Irish potato, as it came to be called, and their art of flax cultivation and linen spinning, all proved valuable additions indeed.

Along with potatoes, dairying and horse breeding found markets; and tobacco, a crop inherited from the Indians, began to have commercial importance. Nonetheless, because of their adaptability to soil and climate, the hay crop together with pasturage for livestock, corn cultivation, and the apple tree all remained of prime importance to farm well-being. Small grain and certain English vegetables and fruits did well in favorable locations. Meanwhile, New England built ships and loaded them with cargo, including livestock, produce, and wood products of numerous sorts.

Once the French and Indian wars had ended, a burst of emigration headed west and north. On primeval soil the adventurers would build the world anew, creating from the forest new farms, new towns. By 1776 Maine's three organized counties alone reported 47,279 whites.

Back in the old towns the first wealth of fertility was long gone. The soil's heart had to be laboriously renewed each year from any source of fertility at hand. Yet housing for both man and beast improved, and stone walls and new roads crept across the landscape. Continuing concern for the education of all, unique in the world of that day, meant that nearly every man and many women could read and write at least a little. All received continuous moral and political training. Their century and a half of practice in self-government was now to be consummated in a break with the English mother country and establishment of a new nation.

III. THE REVOLUTION AND
ITS AFTERMATH, 1775-1825

16. Patriotic Fervor

THE EVENTS of Lexington and Concord and the deeds of the farmers of Middlesex and neighboring counties on the fateful morning of April 19, 1775, are the province of the political rather than the agricultural historian.[1] Yet certain observations deserve a place here.

Much has been written of the merchants and politicians whose commercial interests and political ambitions are said to have brought on the conflict, and of the Boston mobs whose actions culminated in the Tea Party. Yet the men who first stood their ground and took the bullets in their bodies at Lexington and Concord and Bunker Hill were neither political nor commercial, nor yet a mob. They were mainly sober, responsible farmers and freeholders. Among them were members of the General Court or its temporary provincial successor. They were the product of a century and a half of a vigorous, self-supporting agriculture on this continent, and descendants largely of the independent-spirited yeomanry and countrymen of England.

The Revolution they began would take some of them to their graves, impoverish others, perhaps improve the condition of a few. It was their free choice and sense of duty, however, which brought these farmers swarming down country roads in the unseasonable heat of that April morning to stake their lives and fortunes on the issues of liberty and self-government.

New England farms were a reservoir not only of men for the Revolutionary armies, but of food and clothing. Here is the ration that the Massachusetts Provincial Congress voted for the first war year: "Each Soldier in the Massachusetts Army shall have . . . per day: 1 lb. bread, ½ lb. beef and ½ lb. pork [in lieu of pork 1¼ lbs. beef, or on one day in seven, 1¼ lbs. of salt fish instead]; 1 pint milk; if milk cannot be had 1 gill of rice; 1 qt. of good spruce or malt beer; a jill of Pease or Beans or other Sauce equivalent"; plus 6 ounces of good butter and half a pint of vinegar weekly, and for each six men one pound of good common soap.[2]

After the Continental Congress took over the system of supply, state governments were assigned quotas periodically, but they continued to rely on the towns for provisions and clothing to fill them. At first it was not difficult to meet the requisitions. Before the long war ended, however, towns were at their wits' end to find the necessary supplies. The little central Massachusetts town of Oxford in 1778 voted to raise its quota of 5,760 pounds of beef for the army. When only 2½ months later another requisition of 11,062 pounds came, the town meeting declined.

In 1780 the Massachusetts General Court levied on its towns a requisition of 2,400,440 pounds of beef. Amesbury, on the Merrimack River, met the call with 33 oxen weighing 900 pounds each. The requisition for Barnstable County (Cape Cod) on September 25 was for almost 36 tons of beef (as well as 156 men) from its nine towns. Harwich, asked to furnish 8,350 pounds but suffering from drought, said that more than one fourth of its families had no meat of any kind during the year. By contrast, in 1781 the Merrimack Valley town of Haverhill, to quote its historian, "raised the enormous quantity of 32,256 pounds of beef for the Continental Army," in addition to sending 28 soldiers for whom the town paid the charges.[3] Greenfield in the Connecticut Valley cut its own expenses so as not to fail to meet the quotas laid upon it. Wells in Maine bought 20,000 pounds of beef to fill one requisition; Windham, Maine, voted cash instead. Vermont had its own garrisons to supply. Pomfret, for example, at the end of 1780 collected 1,600 pounds of flour, 532 of beef, 266 of pork, and 67 bushels of grain for this purpose.

Connecticut early adopted an adequate ration for its troops and promptly appointed a Commissary-General to see that they were supplied. During the terrible Valley Forge winter of 1777–78 Connecticut sent drovers with herds of cattle clear to Pennsylvania. Again in early 1780 Washington at Morristown was desperate. He appealed to Governor Jonathan Trumbull. After an exhausting struggle through the snow of that dreadful winter, the Governor's leaders of the supply train got a drove of cattle and 200 barrels of flour, 100 barrels of beef, and 100 barrels of pork across the ice of the Hudson and delivered them at Newburgh on the promised day. Gen. Washington's comment is said to have been: "No other man than Governor Trumbull could have procured them, and no other state than Connecticut would have furnished them."[4]

In June 1777 Litchfield, Connecticut, supplied butter and cheese enough to provide three tons of iron, presumably from the Salisbury mines. Windsor in 1781 met its clothing quota, also by barter. The town voted to send a thousand bushels of corn or rye flour to Rhode Island as an "equivalent for . . . procuring Linen Cloth for frocks shirts and overalls . . . for this town's quota of clothing for the army agreeable to the acts of the General Assembly."[5] At that very time loyalists in southwestern Connecticut were trading with the British!

The attempts by the Continental Congress and the constituent states to pay the costs of the struggle for independence caused endless economic dislocations, some of which fell heavily on the farms. Since the Congress was without power to tax, the province governments had to take up the burden. The New England provinces relied on poll taxes (one third of Massachusetts' revenue was from this source), property taxes, and borrowing. To meet their quotas of food, clothing, and supplies, and the bounties to secure recruits, the towns collected local rates and often borrowed heavily besides. Long-settled, well-to-do farming towns were best off. Recently settled frontier towns suffered. Town after town in Maine and western Massachusetts had to petition the General Court for tax relief. Newly settled northwest Connecticut was in general poor also.

The summer of 1778 was very dry and crops scant. With grain needed for food, Connecticut forbade its distillation into liquor; and Massachusetts for a time in 1779 embargoed export of food and essential commodities. New Hampshire had already put controls on food exports. The severe winters of 1779–80 and 1780–81 and the summer droughts that succeeded in 1780 and again in 1782, made difficulties greater. Corn was extremely scarce and reached $4.00 a bushel in hard money at Boston. Massachusetts had to send supplies to the Maine coast, where the war had prostrated the lumber and spar trade.

Aside from loans arranged with European powers and its requisitions of supplies from the states, the chief reliance of the Congress was on issuance of paper money. Since no adequate resources backed this Continental currency, it fell rapidly in value, in 1781 depreciating to a rate of 1,000 to 1.

Continually rising prices for food and all commodities resulted. To protect persons on wages and to hold down the cost of the war, state legislatures tried setting prices, and towns set values for exchange on all common commodities. These measures, difficult or impossible to enforce, proved futile. The legal price of wheat at Greenfield in the Connecticut Valley rose from 6 shillings 8 pence a bushel in 1776 to 8 pounds 2 shillings (legal) in 1779. At Pittsfield wheat worth $12.00 a bushel in 1779 was valued a year later at nine times as much. Country barter transactions were less affected, however.[6]

For the first few years of the war, shortages and inflated prices often worked to the benefit of a farmer with stock or produce to sell. Taxes were light then, but later became enormous. He received more in shillings or dollars and was thus able to settle old accounts advantageously. In the market towns wages advanced less rapidly than prices, and with many sailors, fishermen, and mechanics out of work, antagonisms arose. People in the ports accused farmers and traders of being cruel profiteers, for, as Reverend Samuel Lane of Stratham, New Hampshire, noted, "people have Such a poor Esteem of paper Money, that they will not carry in their provisions (tho plenty) for it . . . and people were almost in a Starving Condition in the lower Towns: so that they soon broke over the Stated prices." Ministers preached against the farmers for not accepting the legal prices. Even the army is said to have suffered from profiteering by country people. Occasionally a farmer got rough handling. The result was that farmers refused to bring in supplies, or sought other markets. At Salem at least one farmer was posted in a newspaper for selling above legal prices; but the regulations proved unworkable.[7]

In the later years of the war the situation changed. The French alliance brought their fleet and army to Narragansett Bay in the summer of 1780, with headquarters at Newport. These allies required provisions, and repairs to ships, and they paid in hard money. Merchants received contracts to supply them with flour, beef, and beans, opening an important outlet for the farms of southern Massachusetts, Rhode Island, and eastern Connecticut. New England oxen did much of the hauling. (Also in the Yorktown campaign later in the war.) At the same time the American army was still drawing supplies from Connecticut and western Massachusetts. In the winter of 1781, for example, the Connecticut legislature sent 1,000 barrels of beef and pork to the forces.[8]

A second factor aided the market for farm produce, especially along the seaboard. As the war moved south and the blockade relaxed, privateering increased. Scores of ships received authorization as privateers, mounted guns, and set off after British merchantmen. Though it was a dangerous trade, rewards were high. By 1780, American privateers, largely manned by fishermen, had captured prizes totaling 200,000 tons. Ships and their cargoes condemned by United States admiralty courts and sold at auction helped bring once more to port towns a certain prosperity. Over 600 Massachusetts vessels alone sailed under Continental letters of marque, and the newly independent states issued hundreds more letters of their own. New London, Connecticut, in one month saw eighteen prizes brought in.

Samuel Morison calls attention to how the rush for privateers revived shipbuilding, and how emphasis on speed caused ship design to improve, a factor of great importance to postwar New England. From a farm point of view, provisioning the vessels and their builders must have improved the market for produce. Perhaps this may offer a clue to why at Westborough, forty miles inland, Reverend Ebenezer Parkman, a farmer-parson, on December 21, 1778, wrote in his diary: "Mrs. P. kills 5 geese, 26 dunghill Fowls for market with ye Pork. For it appears necessary to make some money of what we raise that we may be able to purchase what is wanting in other respects." Two days later: "Mr. Joseph Harrington goes with his team for Marblehead, and takes my Pork, Geese and Fowls for marketing."[9] As the war went on, however, and the blockade tightened again, privateering became less profitable and resulted in retaliation on the privateers' home ports, such as New London.

Though little is said about this in general histories, it must have been on farm women and children that the war's effects fell hardest. Calls for men came in hoeing time. With men absent, not only had the women to do unaccustomed field work, but much of the burden of providing requisitions for clothing and other supplies for soldiers and for the needs of the people at home fell on them. Spinning wheels whirred, and weaving looms clacked longer than usual. The women of Gloucester, Rhode Island, made hundreds of yards of linen tow cloth. One town in Connecticut furnished 3,000 yards of woolens. Food supplies had to be stretched. Salt for cooking and meat pickling was often almost unobtainable. Severe want sometimes appeared. Parson Parkman's Westborough diary on March 24, 1779, speaks of "ye Straits and Difficulties to which many of ye people of Bolton are reduced, for want of Bread and how scarce Meat is there," as reported by a relative from that town who dined with him. Adding to the housewife's burdens, smallpox and dysentery were epidemic in 1777 and 1778. Worst of all, many a husband and father gone to the army never returned to his farm.

The soil, too, suffered. With labor scarce, proper manuring, cultivation, and fencing were bound to be neglected, while repairs to buildings and tools were postponed. Weeds and brush could take over pastures. The incessant drain of the war depleted the soils and resources of the countryside. Depreciation of the currency and increased taxes impoverished many of its people.

The exhausting struggle was not, however, without plus items for farm people. Of profound importance, though not appearing momentous at the time, was the decline or total prohibition of human slavery in the New England states. Again, the war gave a great impetus to the metal industries, hitherto kept in leash by British restrictions. At Salisbury, Connecticut, for instance, an iron mountain furnished cannon for the Revolutionary armies. Southeastern Massachusetts, long used to working bog iron, before the century's end had 20 blast and air furnaces, 20 forges and slitting mills, and several trip hammers, and was on its way to becoming a center of nail manufacture. Iron works operated all the way from Plymouth County to Vermont, increased the market for charcoal, and laid the foundation for the farm tool and machine manufacture that was to become so important for the economy of New England and the nation in the next century. The cutoff of imports stimulated enterprise and invention.

It was not an enticing prospect that the soldiers of the Revolution faced when the army disbanded on June 13, 1783. Their pay, if they received it, was in Continental currency and nearly worthless. Even so, "the five years' pay granted to the Continental officers is unjust and ought not to be paid them," according to the Plymouth town of Wareham on February 11, 1784. It "was obtained by undue influence & . . . notwithstanding all their good services we shall esteem them Public Nuisances . . ."[10]

Massachusetts, borne down by a tremendous war debt, had learned from French War experience that patriotic service could be paid for in land. As a result, many a Revolutionary soldier headed for the District of Maine, still a part of Massachusetts, where a hundred acres or more were to be had free or for a promise to pay a modest sum. By 1790 twenty-six new towns were incorporated there. Connecticut ex-soldiers moved north into Vermont or went west to the Wyoming Valley, a rich area claimed by Connecticut in what was to become western Pennsylvania. New Hampshire's grant towns in the western part of that state filled up.

Soldiers who returned to their farms were apt to find buildings in disrepair, fields unproductive, and pasturage scant. A series of especially severe winters from 1783 to 1785 killed fall-sown grain. Great freshets in the river valleys added to rural distress. One historian believes that rural New England suffered an actual decline in real wealth in this period.[11]

17. A New Century Approaches

THE LAST YEARS of the eighteenth century saw a stirring, as of yeast rising, among farm people. In the country towns a multitude of developments, often small in themselves, gave promise of what the next few decades were to bring.

The post-Revolution period is sometimes considered a low point in popular education. If this was true, measures to improve the state of things were already at work. Massachusetts in 1792 offered grants of Maine lands to towns for its encouragement. In 1783 Noah Webster, farmer's son and Connecticut country schoolteacher, published his famous *Spelling-Book*; its circulation would eventually reach twenty million. Next came his *Reader* and two years later his *Grammar for Schools*. Then he went to work on what was to become his greatest achievement, the dictionary. In 1792, nine years after the *Speller*, Jedediah Morse of Woodstock brought out the nation's first geography. This and Webster's three schoolbooks became the foundation of education for the children of all New England. Morse declared: "In New England learning is more generally diffused among all ranks of people than in any other part of the globe, due to the excellent establishment of schools in every township."[1]

Books were becoming common in country towns and among farm people. An analysis of over a hundred inventories of estates of eastern Massachusetts farm operators for the century immediately preceding the Revolution, assembled for other purposes, reveals an item of books in two out of three estates; in some cases apparently little beyond a Bible; in others called a library.[2]

Social library groups which raised funds among members for the purchase of books had been multiplying in country towns for a half century, often under the guidance of the minister. Jeremy Belknap, in his *History of New Hampshire* in 1792, had called village libraries the cheapest and most effective mode of diffusing learning among the people. Even in the war year of 1776, Scituate, Rhode Island, formed one, and within a year of the Revolution's end Wethersfield, Connecticut, had organized its Union Library Association. Late-settled towns like Sutton in central New Hampshire and Brookfield and Peacham in Vermont offered their citizens subscription libraries before the century closed,[3] and battered Castine in Maine organized one in the new century's first year.

More colleges appeared. Brown University began in 1764; Eleazar Wheelock had moved his Connecticut missionary school to Hanover, New Hampshire, in 1769, and so founded Dartmouth College. The University of Vermont at Burlington opened in 1791; Williams, in its Berkshire valley in 1793; and with the founding of Middlebury, Vermont's new century began. In Maine, Bowdoin, at Brunswick, received its first class in 1802. To prepare boys for college, advanced private schools were established, such as Phillips Andover, Phillips Exeter, and Derby Academy at Hingham, even during the Revolution. The people of Deerfield, Massachusetts, "mostly farmers cultivating their own broad acres," set up their famous academy in 1782. Just a decade later at Litchfield, Connecticut, Sarah Pierce opened what is claimed to be the first school for girls in the United States.

Along with the organization of library associations, academies, and colleges, about this time publications relating directly to agriculture began to find a place in farmers' homes. Jared Eliot's *Essays upon Field Husbandry*, which took book form in 1760, was still influential. In 1790 another minister-farmer, Dr. Samuel Deane, put forth America's first cyclopedia of agriculture, his *New England Farmer; or Georgical Dictionary*, destined to go through three editions and to be the standard farm text for several generations. In this same fruitful period a third minister, Reverend Manasseh Cutler of Wenham, in Essex County, Massachusetts, offered the first systematic botanical classification of plants, appearing in Volume I of the *Memoirs* of the American Academy of Arts and Sciences; and at Hartford, New England's first dietitian, Amelia Simmons, in 1796 brought out her 46-page *American Cookery*.

Periodicals also took a hand in agricultural education. Almanacs had long been popular. The year 1793 saw the launching of the most famous and useful of them all, *The Farmer's Almanac* by Robert B. Thomas, offspring of a bookish farm household at Shrewsbury in central Massachusetts and a farm boy turned mathematician. For the next half century he was the New England countryside's farm adviser, philosopher, and sage.[4] In western Massachusetts the *Berkshire Chronicle* was publishing agricultural essays in 1787, and to the north the *Rural Magazine or Vermont Repository* in 1795 introduced articles on agriculture.

Agricultural organizations had their birth in the last years of the century. At Hallowell, Maine, Charles Vaughan and others on July 17, 1787, formed the Kennebec Agricultural Society, later revived in 1832, to continue a further useful life of over a century.[5] Five years later a group of wealthy Bay State men, chiefly farmers by avocation, were impressed with the need for more information as to good farming methods. In 1792 they incorporated the Massachusetts Society for Promoting Agriculture, still active today. Connecticut agriculturists set up a similar body in 1794. The Massachusetts group in 1797 awarded a prize to William D. Peck for his essay on the slugworm. It began in 1798 to circulate its informative periodical, *The Massachusetts Agricultural Repository and Journal*.

In this final decade of the eighteenth century ferment was also stirring in transportation. Boston and Cambridge bridged the lower Charles twice and Beverly and Salem were connected, moves important to farmers to the north in reaching market. New Hampshire bridged the wide Piscataqua. In 1796 the Tucker Toll Bridge between Windsor, Vermont, and Cornish, New Hampshire, began a life of 132 years, in the course of which innumerable Boston-bound animals and vehicles crossed from the farms of Vermont.[6] In the same decade another bridge spanned the stream at Springfield, Massachusetts; and in 1798 a bridge across the Deerfield at Cheapside became a boon to north-south Connecticut Valley traffic, already benefited by boat service which connected this trading point with Hartford. By 1796 the Merrimack was bridged in four places between Newburyport and Concord, New Hampshire.

Highways improved. Borrowing from English experience and urged on by local pride, capitalists began straight, well-drained turnpikes to speed travel. In 1792 the first in New England, some claim in the United States, connected Norwich, Connecticut, with New London. Before the century ended, Massachusetts had chartered three turnpikes and New Hampshire and Vermont each one, a start toward ending the isolation of interior towns. A stone-filled post road had connected Bennington, Vermont, with Albany, New York, since 1791, and progressive communities such as Holliston, Massachusetts, realizing the advantage of a stone foundation, provided an all-season road for swifter travel by the horse-drawn wagons and coaches now beginning to appear.[7]

Population, especially in the newer areas, grew rapidly toward the end of the century. Wilton, in southwest New Hampshire, had 623 inhabitants in 1775; in 1790 it had 1,105, most of the increase having come from Massachusetts. Chesterfield on the Connecticut River, first settled in 1761, counted 150 families a decade later and continued to increase. Peacham, Vermont, founded 1775, contained 1,187 inhabitants by 1800. Ashfield, in the western Massachusetts hills, settled in 1776, had 1,809 in 1800. Maine, with about 42,000 people in 1777, had 151,719 in 1800 and included 126 towns. Nearly all the newcomers to the infant towns did at least some farming. Meanwhile, the population in many of the old communities also continued to grow.

When the British fleet blockaded the New England coast at the start of the Revolution, one unintended effect was to give a tremendous impetus to local manufacture and inventiveness. Distilleries sprang up to turn local grain, potatoes, and cider into strong liquor. Ironworkers and toolmakers were no longer held back by acts of Parliament; war needs cried to be filled, and after the formation of the federal union a tariff on steel and nails gave the iron trade encouragement. Southeastern Massachusetts, for example, was already making ironplated shovels, and scythes and saws. In 1794 Jacob Perkins patented a nail-making machine and began manufacture in a small way at Byfield, Massachusetts, while countless farm people turned nails out by hand. In 1797 Charles Newbold of New Jersey patented a cast iron plow.

A woolen mill began operations at Hartford in 1788, a carding mill at Pittsfield in 1790, and Samuel Slater began American cotton yarn spinning at Pawtucket, Rhode Island, in 1790. In 1795 Arthur Scholfield and John Shaw started carding wool by machine at Byfield, Massachusetts, removing in 1802 to Andover. In 1798 at Providence, Betsey Metcalf plaited her first straw hat. Small beginnings all, but all destined to have marked effect on New England farm life.

Developments of great future importance began to appear in the field of agriculture itself. One was the conversion of considerable areas of interior New England to dairying. With Goshen, Connecticut, as its center, an export business was born that would turn western Connecticut and southwestern Massachusetts to wholesale cheese making, with the South as a market; further north, Cheshire and the northern Berkshire towns in Massachusetts began sending cheeses to Troy, New York, on the Hudson. Butter and cheese became staple products in central Massachusetts also, and were said to have made some farmers there wealthy by the century's end.

At Hadley, Massachusetts, in 1797 Levi Dickinson tried sowing broomcorn seed and opened the way for a new and valuable Connecticut Valley crop and industry. In Newton, John Kenrick began in 1790 to raise peach-tree whips for sale, the start of New England's earliest modern nursery. About that time came the introduction of the Hubbardston apple. To mark the final year of the century Vermonter Eliakim Spooner patented a corn-seeding machine.

What were New England's farm people like as persons, and what position did they hold in the world, as the eighteenth century came to an end? For evidence, to rely either on the addresses of orators at bicentennial celebrations or on the deductions of modern historical writers may be equally dangerous. The former incline toward ancestor worship; the latter, influenced by sociological theory, tend to divide post-Revolution people into sharply defined classes in a manner that would probably have greatly surprised the persons concerned. Records of the time, however, if used with discretion, can tell us a great deal.

In the years following the Revolution there lived on a Connecticut farm, stony like many others, a small family called Nott. The father was helpless from a long illness, and the two boys did the farming. Their mother, when her household tasks allowed, helped in the fields. A dozen sheep and a cow were the entire stock. Besides providing milk, the cow was used for plowing. The staples of the family diet were cornbread and bean porridge. Once, in midwinter, one boy suffered for lack of outer clothing. In the house there was neither money nor cloth, so the mother sheared a sheep, spun and wove its wool, and before long the boy had the needed clothes. Meanwhile, a covering was braided from straw for the shivering sheep. The family lived four miles from the meetinghouse, and walked each Sabbath to service. Yet they survived. Of the Nott boys, Samuel grew up to become a leading preacher. His brother Eliphalet, also a divine, eventually became head of Union College (now University).

Governor Treadwell of Connecticut, writing with regard to Farmington, which as the new century began was still almost wholly agricultural, gives this description of himself and his neighbors: "Industry and economy have characterized the inhabitants; labour has been held in reputation; none, however elevated to office have considered themselves above it. . . . Our magistrates have always been farmers . . . and have derived their support from labor as much as the meanest citizen . . . content . . . to be esteemed the first among equals."

In New Hampshire, according to W. Winterbotham: "Those persons who attend to husbandry are the most thriving and substantial," especially compared to "those who make . . . getting lumber their principal business."[8]

The verdict of one visiting Englishman: "The inhabitants of the country appear to be well-fed, cloathed, and lodged . . . nor is that distinction of the ranks and classes to be found which we see in Britain [and] infinitely more in France."[9] Another says in 1789: "They [the farmers] don't appear to work hard but I am told they live well [and] appear very civil, decent, well instructed people, possest with a spirit of religion."[10] Other similar comments could be cited.

Dr. Samuel Deane at Portland, like many ministers a farmer himself, took a gloomier view. He was troubled by "the low esteem in which husbandry has been held"—this in 1797. He thinks it is because farmers have not made much money and "too many have had the mortification of making but an indifferent figure in life even when they have used the strictest economy . . . The misfortune has been that a great proportion of their toil has been lost by its misapplication."[11] Yet three years later and only fifty miles away, Reverend Paul Coffin is equally impressed at the success of farmers in Androscoggin County. Among others he visits a farmer who had once fled Chelmsford, Massachusetts, to escape the debtors' prison. He now has 800 acres, 4 barns, 40 black cattle, sheep and horses, and two mills, and lives in plenty.[12] Brissot de Warville in 1788 praises the parish pastor at Andover, Dr. Symmes, as "a true model of a minister of religion . . . ; and the cultivation of his farm occupies those moments not necessarily devoted to . . . the care of souls committed to his charge," a double occupation which had marked earlier Symmes generations since the beginning of the colony.[13]

Such part-time farming was common. Brissot noticed that across Massachusetts "almost all the houses are inhabited by men who are both cultivators and artizans; one is a tanner, another a shoemaker, another sells goods, but all are farmers." On Nantucket in 1791 "it was no strange thing to see the same man . . . a merchant, at other times . . . a husbandman . . . or a number of similar occupations," and on Cape Cod both farmers and mechanics were on occasion seamen.

As the century ends it is clear that any swift generalization about the wealth or social status of New England's farm people is bootless. In many of the old settled communities families of well-to-do farm people held their property and stock unencumbered. They owed no man except such current obligations as lack of a reliable circulating medium made customary. In some new towns, on the other hand, there were families working under almost unimaginable handicaps, with barely enough to live on, who like Indians in a similar situation supplemented their few acres of corn and wheat and their hog or two with wild game, nuts, and berries, or went without. Call this poverty, as Kendall did in northern New Hampshire, or call it subsistence farming; it is doubtful if most of those who experienced it thought of themselves as either poor or especially deprived. Rather, as Robert Honyman had put it in 1775, though the land was rough, the people looked well fed and prosperous.[14] To quote a local estimate from an interior town toward the close of the century: "The people . . . have the reputation of being good husbandmen, frugal and industrious, and they live much independent."[15]

The period that succeeded the Revolution had been in general one of fluidity and change. Certain of the less well-established farmers had been dispossessed, partly as a result of the monetary chaos of the period. With the large size of farm families ("They double their numbers every twenty-five years," said the historian of the County of Worcester, describing the hill town of Lunenburg), a periodic swarming from the hive had to take place even from the best-heeled farms and the most fertile towns. Hence this era witnessed a heavy migration of farmers bent on making a new start, often with no great capital and sometimes with small idea of the hardships ahead for themselves, their wives, and children.[16] However, the farms they left went to some other member of the family; or if for sale, a customer, usually some other farmer, took over. Farming, family, and village life continued with little change in the old towns. At the same time new communities on a similar pattern took shape in Vermont, upper New Hampshire, and Maine. Though some farmers would prosper, others had hard work even to fill the mouths of their families.

The Revolution years had been a hard time: divisions between neighbors, continual calls for men and supplies, repeated raids from Canada, and on the coasts and islands, neglect of cultivation and upkeep of farms, huge public debts. Then followed economic misery, and in the interior widespread bankruptcy of farmers, which led to Shays's Rebellion.

Offsetting these in part, the four New England colonies, now states, had been joined by a vigorous fifth, Vermont. The confederation of thirteen colonies had become the United States of America.

By the end of the century New England's shipbuilding and foreign trade were expanding at a great rate, opening wider markets than ever for its farm and forest productions. Slavery had been ended. New towns were starting in the wilderness. Colleges were being founded; through highways and great bridges were planned; here and there a society for agricultural improvement was born.

Thus after all its wars and turmoil, for the majority of its farm people as well as for the New England community in general, the note on which the eighteenth century ended was one of hope: an expectation of better things to come.

18. Lines of Force

IN THE AUTOBIOGRAPHICAL *Education of Henry Adams*, this descendant of two presidents and a line of colonial farmers is struck by the "lines of force" of his era. For New England agriculture in the opening years of the nineteenth century at least four such lines became increasingly powerful; yet in the century's second decade their favorable effect was for a time thwarted by certain opposing events.

The helpful influences included encouraging growth in the market for farm produce; continuous improvement in highways and transport; a wave of intellectual activity; and the beginning of an outburst of mechanical ingenuity, of which the cotton gin of Eli Whitney, born on a Westborough, Massachusetts, farm had already appeared as the forerunner. All stemmed to a considerable extent from country people themselves.

Of adverse factors one was political. To avoid involvement in the Napoleonic Wars, especially with the chief contenders, England and France, Congress, beginning in 1807, passed two measures: the Jefferson Embargo Act and the Enforcement Act. These stifled foreign trade. The War of 1812, which followed, resulted in blockade by the British fleet, the prostrating of New England's shipping and commerce, and the drying up of the market for farm produce. Another blow to New England resulted from natural phenomena: the hurricane of 1815 and the unprecedented low temperatures of the succeeding summer of 1816.

To a farm population, whether working land often of mediocre natural fertility or, at worst, of near sterility, the prime consideration is its market. With good markets keen wits will work out a profitable agriculture on the poorest soils. When farmers lack a market, they soon decide that beyond providing for family needs the game is not worth the candle.

In respect to a market for his surplus, the New England farmer found himself increasingly well off as the new century opened. Despite continued heavy emigration to New York and the Western Reserve, the population of every New England state increased amazingly, with more and more mouths to be fed. Connecticut, with 237,940 people in 1790, by 1830 had added 60,000, bringing the total to 297,675. Rhode Island increased from 68,825 to 97,199. From 378,787, Massachusetts reached 610,408. By 1830 the new State of Maine contained over 300,000. New Hampshire almost doubled, from 141,885 to 269,328. Burgeoning Vermont counted 85,525 by 1790; forty years later this had grown to 280,652. From just over a million inhabitants following the end of the Revolution New England's total was to reach almost 2¼ millions by 1840, the completion of a half-century from the first census.[1] Many of these inhabitants, especially in the three northern states, were farm people, and the new fields and pastures they cleared added to both New England's agricultural capacity and its marketable surplus. Rising export trade, however, and the continual enlargement of the nonfarm population, both in numbers and as a proportion of the community as a whole, soon more than offset increased production.

Samuel Eliot Morison's *Maritime History of Massachusetts* and William Hutchinson Rowe's similar history of Maine vividly portray the expansion of the sea-borne trade of these two areas. Their shipping surged upward after the Revolution to reach by 1810 a registered capacity of 500,000 tons. New Hampshire, Connecticut, and Rhode Island increased their merchant ships proportionately.

A small port like Marblehead besides having its fishing fleet was the home of fifty to sixty merchant vessels; Salem was growing rich on its Oriental trade, and Newburyport was not far behind. Providence and the Connecticut ports were booming. In 1810 Merrimack River yards alone turned out 12,000 tons of vessels. Portsmouth across in New Hampshire, the North River in Plymouth County, and the Sound's shore echoed with shipbuilders' hammers and caulking tools.

Cargo for the West Indies and European ports included such agricultural items as potash and pearlash, lumber, beef, pork, barley, hops, butter, cheese, and beeswax. Outbound vessels from Rhode Island carried grain, flaxseed, lumber, horses, cattle, beef, pork, poultry, onions, butter, cheese, spirits, and linens. In Connecticut—from New London, Wethersfield, and New Haven with its newly opened Long Wharf—merchants shipped similar diversified cargoes; Windsor, Norwalk, Milford, Derby, Fairfield, and other ports forwarded farm produce to New York and southern ports by coasters. How all this might affect the agriculture even of a small town inland from the coast is evidenced by the historian of Ridgefield, Connecticut, fifteen miles north of Norwalk in the southwest corner of the state. Quoting a local minister, Reverend Samuel Goodrich at the opening of the century, he records that from the town's fourteen to fifteen hundred swine the annual export of pork amounted to 150 to 200 barrels (200 pounds each); of beef about the same. Butter sent out yearly reached 250 to 300 firkins, carried fresh to New York (a trade that was increasing); and 9,000 pounds of cheese went with it. That city also got about a hundred of Ridgefield's fat cattle each year. Such a list from a town of small population a half day's journey from salt water casts a clear light on the unsubstantiated statement echoed from one historian to another that New England's early nineteenth-century agriculture was almost entirely subsistence farming.[2]

Though provision for seamen was far from sumptuous, the crews even of coasting vessels and of the whalers from Nantucket, Martha's Vineyard, New Bedford, and New London offered a further substantial market for farm produce. A three-boat whaler carried twenty-one men; Marblehead fishermen off for the Banks carried eight to ten each; a vessel destined for Europe or Asia often had a much larger complement. The ship *Juno*, for Asia from Bristol, Rhode Island, in 1804, for example, took on board 3,800 pounds of salt pork, 8,420 of salt beef, 5,400 of wheat flour, and 10,000 of tobacco, besides Bristol onions and poultry.[3] (The flour may have been either of local Connecticut Valley production or from the Middle Atlantic states.) Crews of fishing schooners found the combination of salt pork and onions with their fish exactly to their taste.

Aside from the food for ships' crews, building and stocking vessels for foreign commerce and the fisheries required great numbers of shipwrights, riggers, blacksmiths, draymen, warehousemen, and others. Though numerous seamen and mechanics were themselves farmers in a small way and during off seasons, their agriculture, especially when times were good, would be chiefly a garden that the wife might attend to, a hog, possibly a cow or two, and a few apples. To supply daily food for the increasing numbers of nonagricultural merchants, tradesmen, and mechanics, market gardens began to appear near Boston, Providence, Hartford, New Haven, and other centers.

Away from the ports still another consuming group began to develop: the small industries springing up under the new republic in all directions. Rumbling charcoal wagons converged to feed the hungry furnaces of the ironworks at Taunton, Massachusetts, and Salisbury, Connecticut; woolen and cotton enterprises sprang up where waterfalls were dammed; paper mills, nailmakers, and shoe and leather enterprises increased. These and other industries, modestly begun, were destined for immense growth in the decades ahead. Added to the needs of the seaport population, they and their workers began to create for farmers a home market of considerable proportions.

Certain of these industries, in addition to the food needs of their employees, offered direct markets for farm products. For in a growing number of cases they added to rural income by "farming out" work to the countryside. For generations, in small shops alongside their homes, the people of Lynn and vicinity had produced shoes for market and export.

(By contrast, ordinarily a local or itinerant cobbler made each farm family's boots and shoes to order, perhaps from hides of home production.) In 1800 Lynn turned out 100,000 pairs of women's shoes, a decade later made it a million, and by 1833 reached 1½ million pairs, including 213,000 pairs for men. Leather for such as were not altogether of textiles was tanned largely in neighboring Danvers. The hides were from cattle that drovers brought in from both Essex County and the north. Soon Abington, south of Boston in what was to become the Brockton area, began to make men's boots. Brookfield in western Worcester County also got into shoemaking, the work farmed out in the neighborhood. So did many other towns even up into New Hampshire. All was on a small scale at first, but destined to grow to large dimensions in the second quarter of the century and to furnish a much appreciated income supplement for local farmers in addition to their nearby market for hides.[4] The fat from slaughtered animals went into soap or candles. At the end of the century's first decade a single year's production for Massachusetts was reported to be over two million pounds. Another product was combs made from horns: Worcester County, where the industry centered at Leominster, turned out 440,250 dozen in a year.

Distilling, given momentum by the Revolution, now reached considerable proportions. Entirely apart from the manufacture of rum from molasses at the ports, the distillation of whiskey, gin, and brandy, all merchantable and easily transported, consumed quantities of grain, potatoes, and local cider (especially in the Connecticut Valley), for which a market might otherwise have been wanting. By 1810 Connecticut was said to be furnished with 500 distilleries. Hartford merchants, even in the bad crop year of 1816, paid export duties of $40,000 on liquors from the area's 21 distilleries; East Windsor, itself growing up to 70,000 bushels of rye a year, paid $24,000. Gin and cider were Connecticut's most valuable exports. Four towns in the Springfield, Massachusetts, area in 1826 distilled 100,000 bushels of rye. Vermont counted at least 125 distilleries in 1810 (one writer says 200), of which 10, using grain, were in Putney; several were in Fair Haven. To supplement its income from spirits one distillery kept 40 cattle and fed them on the waste residue of the grain. Two distillers in Townshend, and doubtless others, made potato whiskey. Distilling went on across New England in places as scattered as Kent and Newtown in western Connecticut, Woodstock in the east, and Granby and South Oxford in Massachusetts. In addition to its local consumption, the product went to New York, Boston, Providence, the South and to foreign ports.[5]

Considerable of the brandy came from apples. Berkshire and Hampshire Counties in western Massachusetts in 1810 distilled 265,000 gallons of spirits from cider. About Windsor, says a Connecticut gazetteer, "Every respectable farmer had a small distillery upon his own premises." Orchards, "a source of profit . . . add greatly to the value of the lands." Newtown reported ten distillers of "apple jack," Canton eight.

Hartford distilleries developed a considerable agricultural by-industry. They fattened a thousand beef cattle yearly on their grain residue, besides a great number of swine.[6] In Vermont the grain residue went chiefly into pork, marketed for the most part to the north in Montreal.

Thus a considerable variety of factors: an expanding population; the increasing proportion of persons engaged in such nonagricultural occupations as fishing, shipping, and mechanical pursuits; the growth in export trade in farm products, and in domestic industries based at least in part on the use of agricultural raw materials—all these had a part in broadening demand for any surplus that the farmer could profitably produce.

Nevertheless, additional possible sources of income were about to appear: the rise of broomcorn growing and broom manufacture, straw-hat making, woolen spinning and weaving, hop growing, silk production, and other new enterprises involving merchantable crops, which had their beginnings in the early years of the century but became of increasing importance in later decades.

19. Turnpikes, Canals, and Bridges

D URING NEW ENGLAND'S first century and a half, most of its towns, established either beside the sea or on navigable rivers, were able to reach markets by water. After the Revolution, with water transportation so convenient, the incentive to improve highways was lessened. Connecticut roads remained so difficult that travelers by the southern route between Boston and New York preferred to board packets on the Sound for the stretch between Newport or New London and New York so as to hold the highway journey to a minimum. However, a public conveyance for passengers by the inland route is said to have begun operation as early as 1772.

Clearly, better roads were needed. Carriages and horsedrawn wagons were coming into use. A stage between New Haven and Boston had opened in 1783. Yet voters of interior towns remained reluctant to tax themselves to help traveling strangers and freight from elsewhere.

With prosperity returning, however, in the closing decade of the eighteenth century a vigorous movement for better through roads arose. Rather than wait for public appropriations, difficult to obtain and likely to be meager, groups of enterprising citizens began to form turnpike companies modeled after similar bodies in England. These secured charters of incorporation from state legislatures, with power to obtain rights-of-way by eminent domain. The roadways, built from the sale of capital stock, were to be paid for and maintained by tolls.[1]

In turnpike building the general rule of thumb was that a straight road is shortest. Hence marshes had to be filled and hills shaved, but not enough was done always to make the grade comfortable. Inexpert construction and high costs of building often precluded financial success. Yet the pikes, even where financially unsuccessful, opened back country, decreased isolation, reached markets, increased travel, and speeded mail. Many of them are thoroughfares today. Some became chiefly freight roads: six-horse wagon loads replaced plodding ox teams, unreliable in hot weather. Transportation benefited further when Lewis Downing of Concord, New Hampshire, in 1813 built the first of his famed Concord buggies. He followed this two years later with his even more noted Concord coach, the first public vehicle to give passengers a comfortable ride.

This period also saw bridges superseding ferries.[2] The lengthiest, already mentioned, "a most prodigious work 3800 feet long, 34 feet wide," "lighted all night by 40 to 50 lamps and with a draw for vessels," bore traffic from the north across the Charles River from Cambridge into Boston. A second, from Charlestown, soon followed. Not long after, four bridges, all of arched construction, spanned the Merrimack in its course from Concord to the sea. The Connecticut, already bridged at Bellows Falls, was now crossed downstream at Springfield.

While turnpike and bridge builders improved land transportation (fifty turnpikes were incorporated in Connecticut between 1803 and 1808), other entrepreneurs were extending water transportation to interior New England by excavating canals. First in importance was the Middlesex Canal, opened in 1803 from Chelmsford on the Merrimack to Boston. It was extended in 1811 to Manchester. In 1815 the canal transported its first regular freight south from Concord, New Hampshire's capital and its northern terminal. This canal was a marvel, termed the largest engineering work so far undertaken in North America.

Added together, the new roads, bridges, and canals had a remarkably stimulating effect on the farming of interior New England. Wagons and carriages began to replace saddles, pillions, and panniers. Teams for which a ton was formerly a load could now haul two. How far such inland transport business might extent under necessity is hinted by this item in an Albany newspaper during the blockade of the War of 1812: "Arrived 4 wagons, 4 oxen each, from Dartmouth [New Bedford, Mass.] laden with potatoes for a southern market."[3] By this date the highway from Pittsfield to Albany was of macadam all-weather construction, one of America's earliest stone roads.

Besides growing markets and improved transportation, a third strand of the line drawing agriculture toward a better day was the advance in education. In the new American nation, as Van Wyck Brooks has so well said, farming and learning went together. Nowhere was this so commonly true, every foreign visitor noticed, as in New England. "The education of youth in this state" (Connecticut), commented the critical observer John Harriott in 1815, "seems carried to excess: farmers, tradesmen, and mechanics give their children a college education which is as frequent as that of a common boarding school in England." A Connecticut widow's son bound out in 1786 to a farmer till he should be sixteen got only twelve days of school a year. "But," he wrote later, "I had the good fortune to live in a family where reading and writing were not deemed unimportant . . . I had a disposition for reading and I had the privilege of indulging it."[4]

In Massachusetts a hill farming town such as Harvard, in Worcester

County, in 1783 maintained eight district schools and beyond that offered Latin instruction. The Western Massachusetts town of Southampton, between 1765 and 1845, sent 48 boys to college, and its neighbor Easthampton sent 20. Yet as late as 1840 the population of the two did not exceed 2,000.[5]

In 1809 another visitor, Edward A. Kendall, describes some of the means by which country people learned. "There is . . . even in the remote societies and towns . . . a public library . . . common property and purchased by contribution." Education, he notes, is under "school societies," with power to levy taxes, place school buildings, and appoint visitors, and (this in Connecticut) the state turns over a certain proportion of the rates. "Hence every industrious man, who possesses a fair moral character is qualified to fill many important offices in the town, county, and state."[6]

Yet it would be a mistake to conclude that zest for education was universal. Many towns were far less wealthy than Deerfield and Woodstock. Litchfield and Killingly in Connecticut might each count four library societies, but in new farming areas plucked from the forest and in older towns whose soil was impoverished, sources of strictly agricultural information were scant, education was often neglected, and orders from state governments to provide it ignored. Even so, of New England's country people it could scarcely be said, as Elkanah Watson complained of New York State, "Thus far the German and Dutch farmers have been totally remiss in cultivating the first rudiments of literature."[7]

Education, specifically agricultural, got a slow start. Yale in 1802 did appoint Benjamin Silliman Professor of Chemistry and Natural History. Harvard also made a gesture toward formal agricultural studies in 1804 with the appointment of William D. Peck to a professorship in Natural History, and founded its Botanic Garden three years later.

In 1822 Thomas G. Fessenden began in Boston to publish the area's first farm periodical of importance, the *New England Farmer*, destined for a long and useful life; and James Thatcher of the same town started *The American Orchardist*. Two years later Solomon Drowne & Son published *The Compendium of Agriculture and Farmer's Guide*, and Daniel Adams, M.D., an *Agricultural Reader*.

Touring New England in 1793, John Drayton of South Carolina had observed: "On Sundays, which are days of rest and refreshment, when passing by the farmers' houses, I found many of them reading; and was told that they generally devote those days to reading religious books, the public laws, and the newspapers. Do you think it an easy matter to enslave such a people?"[8]

20. Combing the Back Country

I F GOOD MARKETS readily accessible are essential to good farming, New England's widening mercantile pattern was becoming a buttress to its agriculture. Well before the Revolution its merchants, keen on profitable cargoes for foreign trade and for sales through domestic outlets, had pushed their activities inland.

One of the Allen family, New London and Boston merchants, for example, had in 1757 set up a store in the central Massachusetts town of Shrewsbury. Their conveyances supplied the country people of that town and along the way thither with imported necessities; and on the return to New London bore back the farmers' surplus productions. The latter, along with what their coasters brought in, became freight for the firm's West Indies vessels.

What a variety of produce their vessels had carried even before the Revolution! Besides deckloads of horses, cattle, sheep, and hogs, the Allens' invoices included at one time or another (in addition to fish) corn, oats, flour, bread, potatoes, tobacco; fresh, salt, and smoked beef; pork, tallow, soap, lard, cheese, onions, beans, apples, hogs, geese, fowl, ducks, turkeys, tar, pitch, turpentine; together with shingles, hoops, staves, and boards.[1]

In Northampton, in 1780, Nicholas Garrett had acquired 300 bushels of wheat to be delivered for cash to merchant Andrew Lopez at his wharf at Newport. He got another hundred bushels for a barrel of rum, and bargained salt for wheat at the rate of one bushel of salt to four of wheat. At Pittsfield in 1788 Colonel Danforth advertised for lamb's wool and good shipping horses. In return for goods bought, he would take wheat, flaxseed, pork, beeswax, iron, and ashes. A special offer was that farm necessity, salt, for flaxseed. Merchants at Windham in northeast Connecticut just before the Revolution had been buying wool, hemp, flax, tobacco, cheese, and butter.[2]

At Lebanon, New Hampshire, merchant James Duncan built potash facilities and ground flaxseed. He also bought grain and other country produce for export from Haverhill on the Merrimack, to which a continual stream of ox teams delivered his purchases. The conveyances returned loaded with foreign goods and other supplies needed by country people.

The historian of Haverhill states that in just over two years shipments of this trader up country amounted to $96,000.

The many merchants who congregated at Deerfield about 1800 exchanged salt for flaxseed or white beans and offered cash for rye and Indian corn, or rum for barreled beef and pork. One ad in the *Greenfield Gazette* that year offered cash for beef bladders in which to pack snuff. Walpole, New Hampshire, stores sought to buy not only butter, cheese, beef, and lard, but mittens, socks, frocking, and tow cloth. A large proportion of such transactions involved little or no cash; entries on opposite sides of the merchant's books sufficed.[3]

All this was in addition to the farm produce that farmers took to market themselves. "Annually in October," said 91-year-old John Morse of Woodstock, Connecticut, regarding the century's early years, "my father went to Providence taking about 50 bushels of walnuts, a good many chestnuts and beans, and driving four or six large fat oxen to be sold for beef."[4] Nearly all histories of the river valleys of up-country New Hampshire, Vermont, and Maine tell of lines of loaded farm sleds on their winter way to Portland and similar markets.

Some merchants specialized in a single commodity, and by their operations influenced agricultural development across a considerable area. During the last decade of the 1700's Alex Norton of Litchfield, Connecticut, sought relief for failing health in a southern trip. Yankee fashion, he took along several thousand pounds of Connecticut cheese to pay his way. Finding the product welcome there, upon his return with health improved he began to buy and pack cheese for the southern market. At first he shipped it in hogsheads, then in specially designed round boxes with covers. His enterprise grew, others copied his methods, and before a decade had passed, the Litchfield County town of Goshen was marketing 270,000 pounds of cheese a year. Northwestern Connecticut and southern Berkshire County in Massachusetts were thus led permanently into extensive dairying. In 1810 Goshen managed to sell 588,124 pounds of cheese and 35,537 of butter. Cheese wagons combed the countryside, and for half a century Goshen remained the cheese capital of the nation.[5]

Across the line in the hills west of Springfield, another cheese operator, Amos W. Collins, in 1807 began to encourage the farmers of the poor Scotch-Irish town of Blandford to go into dairying. He helped them buy cows and taught them cheese making, transforming the economy of the place and causing it to prosper. The broad effect that such an enterprising dealer might exert on a community is evidenced by Jasper H. Stahl in his history of Maine's Waldoboro. Captain Smouse of that town made up a vessel's cargo from lumber purchased from thirty-two separate persons, plus oak staves from eight others. A single family of brokers at North Reading in Middlesex County, Massachusetts, between 1808 and 1837 assembled and sold 16.5 million pounds of hops gathered from a dozen or more towns in northeastern Massachusetts.[6]

Undoubtedly many, though by no means all, of these merchants made money. Some entered the ranks of the wealthy, whom modern economic historians are likely to place at the top of a social pyramid. However, country folks gained from these operations also. Evidences of well-being among the farmers who provided the traders with merchandise are frequently recorded by gazetteers and local observers, who mention some of those who attained wealth measured by the standards of their day.

Political factors, however, soon began to affect agricultural life in this era. The Jefferson embargo on foreign trade and the Non-Intercourse Act that succeeded it cut off New England's foreign trade, tied up its vessels, and idled crews, shipbuilders, supply and mercantile workers, and draymen. They destroyed or greatly impaired the outlets for farm products as exports and ships' stores. Distress resulted for many farmers as well as for the ports.

When 1812 came, the war laid up additional shipping, including fishermen and whalers, both of which had multiplied since 1800. A multitude of persons were left without means even to buy food. On Nantucket real poverty resulted, but a thousand-acre planting of corn gave its inhabitants at least subsistence. Part of the market returned with the commissioning of privateers, but the strict British blockade of 1813 cut even coastal traffic so severely that Maine and Cape Cod packets could scarcely reach Boston. Meanwhile prices of imported commodities and manufactured goods rose. The British occupied eastern Maine and Provincetown and bled Penobscot Bay, Cape Cod, and the offshore islands. In the middle of harvest in 1814, inland New Hampshire militia were called out to defend Portsmouth.

Yet few misfortunes are without gain to someone. With the war unpopular, in some sections of northern Vermont conscience scarcely bothered livestock men when drovers found markets for cattle by the hundreds across the line in Canada. It was reported that two thirds of Britain's Canadian army was living on New York and Vermont beef.[7] Cape Cod people, obliged to supply the British fleet with beef and vegetables, were said not always to do it unwillingly, for the British paid well. Block Island prospered on produce sold to British men-of-war.

To offset the losses, the war gave tremendous impetus to the development of American manufactures, a result from which New England as a whole, including its farmers, eventually was to derive immense benefits. When war ended it appeared for a time that the factories springing up at every waterfall on New England's innumerable rivers would bring unexampled prosperity to the whole region, farms included, but as cheap foreign goods once more poured in, the incipient prosperity collapsed. A money panic in 1819 caused wholesale mill closings. Trade stagnated and prices and wages fell on farms and elsewhere.[8] Before this occurred, however, Congress took one step that was to help invigorate both the industry and the agriculture of New England. In 1816 it enacted the first tariff designed to protect American manufactures and farm products. This, with other acts that succeeded, provided a base on which farmers speedily covered New England's pastures with sheep by the hundred thousand.

In its effect on rural life few events in the century's first quarter had more impact than the remarkable weather of the years 1815 and 1816. The great hurricane gale of September 23, 1815, proved "extraordinarily calamitous," especially in southern New England. It caused immense losses in the cities where trade centered. In the country, even far up into New Hampshire, timber trees were leveled by the millions, the year's crop of fruit was knocked off, and apple orchards destroyed. Stacks of hay and straw floated off the marshes all along the coast and were lost. Corn and grain fields were flattened, farm buildings unroofed and cattle killed. Farmers were especial sufferers from the tremendous gale.[9]

As though this were not enough, the whole year of 1816 which followed was one continuous disaster from cold. In many places frosts blackened vegetation every month of the year. Vermont had a foot of snow on June 8, a little in July and August, and a freeze September 20. Plowed land in Orange, Massachusetts, among Franklin County's eastern hills, was crusted with frost three fourths of an inch deep on June 7. On July 5 and again on August 5, ice formed in Maine. "The year of two winters," 1816 was called, or "Eighteen hundred and froze to death."

In some places drought further aggravated farm calamity. A historian of Keene, New Hampshire, records that in that same year the usual late spring rains failed, and for twelve weeks, while by the calendar spring became summer, no rain fell. Pastures browned, and corn replanted after spring frosts scarcely grew before August frosts cut it down. Distress ensued, for in addition to the bad weather depression came to industry. By 1819 almost every one of the textile mills that had sprouted at every waterfall had closed, and many capitalists lost all.

For a generation, tales of rich, cheap land to the westward had tempted the less prosperous farm people. Now, with New England experiencing

Arctic weather, could they be worse off in the Western Reserve? "The current of emigration from this state has swelled to a torrent," wrote Pease and Niles in their *Connecticut Gazetteer* of 1819. From Maine alone ten to fifteen thousand are thought to have removed between 1810 and 1820. From Vermont, where in some townships actual want and suffering were a consequence of 1816's frigid weather, many families headed for Western New York and Ohio. It was long before the influences of the disastrous years 1815 and 1816 were erased.[10]

21. Hay, Grain, and Livestock

As THE continuing emigration demonstrated, it has seldom been the nature of New England people generally, whether farmers or others, to rest content with a bare living. To understand how farm families managed in the first half of the nineteenth century it is necessary to consider the basic crops and animals found at least to some degree on nearly every farm, then to explore the specialized avenues along which New England farm people sought means to make a living and achieve economic advancement.

From the first settlement of Massachusetts Bay, the determining factor in New England's agricultural history had been that no crop is better suited to its climate, soil, and terrain than grass. The earliest Puritans rejoiced to come upon the intervales of their new countryside clothed with fresh water grasses, and on salt marshes that ringed shore and estuary to remind many of them of home. Wherever land had been cleared or was naturally open, it appeared designed for sheep and cattle, even as the woods, filled with nuts and acorns, seemed made for swine. To the tall bluejoint of the fresh meadows, nutritious for hay if cut early, fowl meadow grass had been added. This was a superior type of herbage which tradition claims was brought to the Neponset River marshes by a large flock of wild fowl before 1710 (from what source does not appear), and it had spread to other river bottoms.

Countless staddles (wood underpinning) for salt hay still dotted seacoast marshes from southern Maine to Cape Cod, along the shores of the Sound, and up the Connecticut and similar estuaries. In the fall, gundalows ferried the hay up every salt creek to the home farm. On such provender thousands of cattle and horses were wintered every year. The resulting manure, supplemented where possible from other sources, nourished merchantable crops of corn, potatoes, tobacco, flax, onions and other produce. As Lord Adam Gordon in 1765 wrote of similar salt meadows in New Jersey: "It will not fatten either Cattle or Horses, but it will keep them up . . . tis here of [un]Questionable Value for dung [plowed in] and other uses, and conveyed both by Land and Water many miles." One species called blackgrass, found in the upper reaches, was particularly nutritious.[1]

In the valleys of New Hampshire, Vermont, and Maine the beaver meadows, flats, and occasional open uplands that awaited new settlers were often reported to be luxuriant with native grass. Farmers in new country depended on such boggy meadows for scarce winter hay or for pasture. Governor Thomas Hutchinson's answer to King George III that nothing was more profitable in America than pasture, because labor was very dear, remained true in the nineteenth century.

Farmers had long since added nutritious English cultivated hay to the native grass. Well before the end of the eighteenth century timothy, red-top, and red and white clover had spread to every settled part of New England. On new land, crops of two to three tons of hay per acre were not unusual, dropping to less than a ton on old mowings. The latter, growing steadily poorer, were often turned into pasture.

Beginning with Plymouth Colony, Indian corn had been New England's staple grain from the first. In the nineteenth century nearly every farm continued to grow it, though coast-town mills ground large amounts of corn imported from further south. Many farmers continued to follow Indian growing methods, and pioneers in new plantations continued to spot hills between girdled trees or stumps. On Cape Cod and increasingly elsewhere, however, hilling had begun to give place to level culture. Careful cultivators planted corn in rows three feet apart, the hills at five-foot intervals, or vice-versa. The field was hoed three times. After the silk had become well fertilized and the ear had begun to fill, or at least by the time the kernels hardened, the stalk and leaves above the ears were likely to be cut and cured, to furnish a half ton to the acre of excellent winter fodder. Yields ranged from eight bushels an acre on poor, wornout land to the twenty-five to thirty bushel average of Rhode Island, and much higher where the crop had careful attention. Connecticut, with fish for fertilizer, and Massachusetts, under first-class tillage, called forty bushels a good yield.

Indian grain was a favorite food for both man and beast, and nearly always salable. Individual farmers usually saved their own seed; but in 1818 Salmon Dutton of Cavendish, Vermont, perfected and distributed a richly colored glossy flint that received his name.[2] This variety gave very high yields, heralding a long series of improvements by selection. Corn was of particular importance to Connecticut Valley fatteners of beef and hogs, and to Vermont, which besides marketing many in Canada as early as 1806 drove 15,000 cattle a year on the hoof to Boston.

Though not universally grown, wheat remained an important market crop for alluvial valleys and newly cleared towns for as long as their native fertility lasted. On newly cleared land this and other small grains might merely be harrowed in without plowing. On older fields, corn was apt to get the barnyard manure; wheat followed to pick up any residue of fertility. From seacoast areas, however, rust had long since nearly eliminated wheat. These areas now depended for flour chiefly on imports by sea.

Where wheat failed, there was always rye to fall back on. On poor soil rye would grow even without manuring if the land were first left fallow for three or four years. Grown properly on good soil, it yielded thirty bushels to the acre. In Maine a common rotation was potatoes, rye or wheat, then seeding to herdsgrass and red clover. Everybody mixed rye meal and flour with corn, barley, and wheat to bake into bread; and distillers bought rye by the thousands of bushels. A Connecticut Valley lady of this time describes the local rye harvest as a notable event and spectacle. She thrills at "the great turnout of reapers with their flashing sickles sweeping up the hills."[3]

Some farms in Rhode Island, others near the Sound in Connecticut, and to a small extent elsewhere still grew barley. Exported, New England barley had a good reputation to the southward. As horses became more numerous and wagons began to take the place of carts, oats came to be a desirable grain; but only where the Scotch influence was active did it become important as food for the table.

During the Revolution New England's livestock had been neglected and depleted. Numbers of the best beeves had gone to supply the Continental armies. The British had cleared sheep and cattle by thousands from Rhode Island, Connecticut, the offshore islands, and coastal Maine. With ports closed and foreign commerce almost at a standstill, little incentive had existed for improvement in any branch of livestock. Revival of trade following the peace treaty nevertheless brought renewed interest in stock. Here and there selection or importation of superior animals began. More care came to be shown also in farm products, and pride in their quality was renewed. An example of each will suggest the new trend. Both originated with ordinary country people rather than with wealthy innovators. The first concerns a famous horse.

During the 1790's a horse fancier of West Springfield, Massachusetts, named Justin Morgan, moved north into the new state of Vermont. He took with him to Randolph Center (or returned and took back) a modest-sized clever bay horse with broad forehead, short muscular legs, heavy mane and tail, and pleasant, spirited eyes. This horse's name was "Figure." He was a fast walker, smooth trotter, very strong, intelligent, and

14. "Old Green Mountain Morgan," foaled 1834. *Thompson,* Horses of Woodstock *(1881).*

willing. In Spooner's *Vermont Journal* in 1793 and 1794 and in the *Rutland Herald* in 1795 Morgan advertised service at stud "by the famous Figure Horse."[4]

Just what Figure's ancestry and bloodlines were has been a matter of endless debate and speculation, still unresolved and profitless here. Suffice it to say that the Connecticut Valley had long been breeding horses for export, and that at Cambridge in 1775, the horses of the Western Massachusetts cavalry had aroused General Washington's particular admiration. Figure may have been sired by an English horse owned by a New York loyalist.

What is certain, however, is that this stallion, who after his master's death came to be known by the latter's name, Justin Morgan, possessed precisely the qualities needed for Vermont conditions. Tradition says that he could snake logs out of the woods all day; or just as willingly set off at a smart trot with a rider or two for church or a frolic. Most important of all, in his long life of 29 years he sired a numerous progeny who inherited his characteristics. Many of his descendants, such as "Black Hawk" and "Sherman," became famous sires in their turn. One of the third generation was claimed to be the fastest trotter of his time. Morgan's offspring soon spread through Vermont, across New Hampshire, and into Maine, where conditions were similar, and horsemen bred them there as well.

The Morgans appeared at a time when the Narragansett Pacers were in decline, when wagons were replacing oxcarts on the smooth and speedy new turnpikes, and when the Concord buggy was superseding saddle and pillion. Stage drivers all over New England came to swear by Morgans. Soon the new West also, to which many New England people emigrated, turned to Vermont breeders, and was willing to pay high prices.

During the Civil War, U.S. Cavalry buyers very nearly denuded Vermont of Morgans. The 1st Vermont Cavalry charged at Gettysburg on Morgan mounts. It is said to have been a Morgan that bore General Sheridan on his famous ride in 1864 to turn the tide of battle at Winchester.

New England was not destined to be a wholesale breeder of horse-kind, but with Narragansetts, Morgans, and certain others to be later cited, it has no call to hang its head in the matter of horseflesh. In fact, in Vermont itself the original Morgan horse "Figure" was only one of a number of excellent stallions, some imported, advertised for breeding in this period.

A second example of the spirit of ambition among ordinary farm people of the time is the story of "The Great Cheshire Cheese."

In February 1801 Thomas Jefferson of Virginia was chosen president over John Adams of Massachusetts. Surprisingly, this was a cause of rejoicing in the Western Massachusetts dairy town of Cheshire among the Berkshire Hills, for a majority of its farmers were Democrats. Most ardent Democrat of all was Elder John Leland, who for a decade had been pastor of the town's Baptist church. He admired Jefferson among other things for his Virginian policy of separation of church and state, a hot subject then in Massachusetts. Why not celebrate Jefferson's election, asked Leland, and also call the attention of the nation to Cheshire and its chief product, by presenting to the president a cheese of a size never before seen on this side of the Atlantic?

The pastor talked up the plan; the farmers and their wives responded.

On a certain July day, it was decided, each farmer would bring in his whole milking. The curds from every cow in Cheshire would be merged into one giant cheese and that cheese transported to the nation's capital. How large a container would be needed to hold this mammoth? The town counted its milkers and calculated the result. Darius Brown prepared the materials and built a round wooden case four feet across and eighteen inches deep, to hold the product of 1,200 cows.

On July 20 the whole town brought in its milkings. The most skillful dairy women mixed the curds, sifted in their choicest herbs, primed and salted the mass to perfection. For eighteen days a cider press squeezed the cheese within iron bands. Then it was left to ripen. When ready for the journey it weighed 1,235 pounds.

The route took the giant cheese west across the hills to Hudson, New York, then by water to the nation's year-old capital, Washington. On New Year's Day in 1802 a six-horse team drew the gift through the streets of the new capital. Elder Leland proudly presented it to the nation's chief

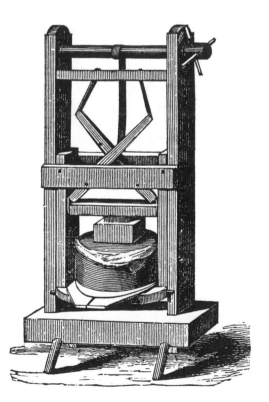

15. Self-governing cheese press: curds are pressed into wooden hoop. *Newell, Catalogue (1836).*

executive; and the assembled cabinet, diplomats, and distinguished guests partook of bread garnished with slices of Cheshire's pride.[5]

The productive limestone lands of the Taconics and the Berkshires were now permanently committed to dairying. Western Connecticut exported its cheeses through the Sound ports, Western Massachusetts via Troy and the Hudson. Williamstown, for example, by 1829 had deserted winter wheat, its former staple, and marketed 200,000 pounds of cheese that year.

Though farms with perhaps four or five milkers were the rule, by 1830 herds of 15 to 30 cows were becoming common in Berkshire valleys, and some ran beyond 50.[6] Farmers were building dairy houses and diverting springfed streams through wooden pipes to large tubs where night and morning milkings could promptly cool.

Goshen, Connecticut, the great cheese center, marketed 380,236 pounds—$38,000 worth—in 1811. Lewis M. Norton had in 1808 introduced there the pineapple cheese, and patented it two years later.[7] A second Norton manufactured circular boxes for ordinary cheese, their sides bent like a half bushel measure. For a limited time Rhode Island, where John Harriott reported the best milch cows he had seen in America, and neighboring Connecticut towns, such as Pomfret, could retain their reputation for export butter and cheese of superior quality. The rest of New England, however, was catching up. In any case a Northern visitor to the South at this period thought New England cows far superior as butter producers to any he saw there. Country merchants began to buy butter, heavily salted, as well as cheese; they cased it in firkins and sent it to market packed in straw. In winter, butter reached Boston safely even from northern Vermont.

Where dairy products had an outlet, better care was given the stock. Farmers began to provide more adequate shelter. One town after another voted not to leave its cattle and the town bull free to roam. Some farmers with a milk market had even decided that it was more profitable to turn their calves into veal than to raise them, and bought young animals, "springers," in the fall to serve as next year's milch cows. Stockmen began to take more pride in their animals. The Berkshire County Society's first exhibition in 1811 brought out sixty yoke of prime oxen. The French officer Marquis de Chastellux had been struck with admiration at the fine cattle he saw on the meadows at Greenland, New Hampshire; and the Connecticut Valley became noted for fat stock which another French observer, Brissot de Warville, called enormous. When slaughtered, such beeves helped the Boston market acquire a reputation for the high quality of beef offered there.

From the viewpoint of the family larder, the most necessary farm animal was the hog: few meals of this period anywhere were complete without some pork product. Nearly every farmer and some villagers had at least one or two. Concord, Massachusetts, in 1801, with 227 dwellings, counted 290 hogs. Dairymen making cheese or butter might have skim milk or whey enough to grow several, and a distiller could feed hundreds on mash. Thomas Badger, one of Boston's garbage contractors, in the early years of the century maintained a considerable herd right on Prince Street and fed them on garbage collected from among the town's 20,000 people.[8] Colonel Ethan Allen, one year, brought a Vermont herd down into the Franklin County hills of Western Massachusetts to fatten there on beechnuts.

In country towns swine, yoked or ringed, still ran at large and were expected to pick up a living in woods and from highways. More than one town maintained a swineherd still to look after the local herd during the warm months. In Vermont swine might be expected to forage for their living even into winter.[9] With such treatment hogs were apt to become bony and tough, and though perhaps fed some corn in the fall would dress only 150 to 175 pounds at slaughter, a total not much above a year's ration of pork for one person. Good farmers, however, fed their swine not only dairy and kitchen waste, but beans, pumpkins, sweet apples, small potatoes and other roots and vegetables; then finished them off with plenty of corn meal, beechnuts (for taste) collected by the family, or both. The bristles were sometimes the perquisite of the boy of the household, to be sold for pocket money.

Poultry for the table and for sale was a resource for numerous farm families. The rooster and his harem continued to be called "dunghill fowls." The clutch of eggs yielded in the warm months was scant indeed by modern standards, yet some farms must have found poultry profitable. W. Winterbotham, the Englishman, visiting New Hampshire in 1796, had found "poultry of all kinds . . . raised in great plenty and perfection."[10] He recognized in the lower towns the characteristics of a large-sized breed imported from England twenty years earlier, indicating that some attention was being paid to breeding.

In some sections of New England—the Connecticut Valley, southeast Massachusetts, and Rhode Island, for example—nearly every family raised geese. They scrounged their own food, ridding cultivated fields of bugs and weeds in the process. Geese were a source of valuable feathers, plucked two to five times a season (a merry time amid flying feathers for the children), to fill up the omnipresent feather beds. They also furnished quills for pens. Feathers and quills were each salable. The sloop *Tolera-*

tion, from Stratford, Connecticut, for Boston in 1825, carried an item of 10 bags of feathers. Geese were a favorite export from Bristol, Rhode Island, proverbial according to Birket, for "its plenty of [beautiful] women and geese." The Wolfeboro, New Hampshire, farm wife "from the profitable goose obtained for herself and her daughters many of the extras for their wardrobes."[11]

Turkeys were likewise a source of farm income. Reverend William Bentley's diary tells of his seeing a drive of several hundred turkeys reach Salem market on January 11, 1802. Guinea hens were in places still bred. Peacocks had been among Rhode Island's earlier exports, and Germans at Waldoboro, Maine, continued to raise them all through the nineteenth century.

Poultry, whatever the sort, were likely to be the province of the farm woman, even if she were the minister's wife; and income from them helped supply household needs. Plenty of poultry, live and slaughtered, went to market on the carts and sleds of Northern New England merchants and farmers. Substantial numbers went out by ship, also. Historian Percy Bidwell states that in 1810 New England sent to three southern states alone 4,000 dozen poultry. For ordinary marketing, up-country people might pack the dressed meat in snow until it could be forwarded.

Small woolen mills were appearing on New England's streams, and by 1810 there were 200 fulling mills, which cleansed wool of oil and impurities by use of hot water and fuller's earth. At a Northampton cloth mill opened in 1809, fifty workmen turned out fine broadcloth 1¾ yards wide which sold for ten dollars a yard. Even in the new and rough northern sections more attention began to focus on sheep. After the losses of the Revolution, the offshore islands, namely Nantucket, Martha's Vineyard, and Block Island, built up their flocks again to scores of thousands, only to have them swept off once more in the War of 1812. Some said these transactions were not altogether involuntary.

Kendall, traveling through Connecticut in 1809, reported small flocks on every farm in Middletown, up to 16 or 20 sheep per farm. Newtown's sheep at that date added up to 4,145; Litchfield's, a decade later, to 6,784. Towns like these generally employed one or more town shepherds, to whose care the farmer could turn over his entire flock, if small, or whatever limited number his proprietor's rights permitted, to feed on the town's common lands. This custom continued for several decades into the 1800's.[12]

Aquidneck Island and the rest of eastern Rhode Island were especially noted for the size and fatness of their sheep. Their pastures were considered particularly nutritious. In South County, on the other side of Narragansett Bay, "Nailer Tom" Hazard puts down in his July 1805 diary: "Put three Sheep in Clover field to Fatt." Meat rather than wool would appear to have been his main object, for in 1816, 25 of his fleeces weighed but 81 pounds in all.[13] "Sandwich mutton," from the town of Sandwich on Cape Cod, had a reputation in Boston's market for eating quality. Contrary to the preserving of beef and pork, salt mutton did not work out well. Hence, success in raising sheep for meat depended on easy access to the markets of Boston and other large towns where people had special fondness for roast lamb.

Besides the desire to produce wool for cloth and flesh for the table or for sale, a sheep man might have a subsidiary objective in his breeding. Where the three southern New England states meet in the Quinebaug Valley and in central Massachusetts, a breed "of good flesh" called "otter sheep" is said to have become popular. Some say a Brimfield farmer developed it; others, a Charles River shepherd. The breed's short fore legs, bowed outward like those of an otter, appeared designed to prevent the jumping of fences, and were considered a desirable characteristic.[14]

In the new century, however, the attribute most sought after came to be a long-staple fleece. The Spanish Merino, now introduced, had this as its prime characteristic. In the next half century and more, the Merino was to make New England a national nucleus for breeding stock and for still another century the continent's center of wool marketing and woolen manufacture. The first purchase of a pair of the Spanish Merino breed to be successfully imported is credited to a Massachusetts man, Seth Adams, in 1801. The following year General David Humphreys, minister to Spain, brought over in the well-named sloop *Perseverence* to Derby, Connecticut, 75 ewes and 25 rams, to become the foundation stock for the breed in southern New England. In 1806 he followed up by starting a mill with a capital of half a million dollars in the Naugatuck Valley to make woolens.[15] Another early Merino importer was Robert Livingston of New York. Both sold stock at very high prices.

A great advance in the fortunes of the new breed came in 1811. William Jarvis of Boston, United States consul at Lisbon, received official permission to purchase animals from the royal Spanish flocks, hitherto with few exceptions jealously held intact. He selected 200 rams and shipped them to Boston along with 200–300 other sheep, and had them driven to his farm on the Connecticut River's oxbow at Weathersfield, Vermont. On the rich intervale land there, these and their offspring "throve incredibly," the cold winters adding length to their fleeces. Jarvis helped multiply superior animals in the area by selling purebreds to neighbors at moderate prices. Merinos spread west across the Green

Mountains into the fertile Champlain Valley. All Vermont, for the next three quarters of a century became a cradle for superior sheep. They were taken east also into New Hampshire and Maine.[16]

Among the results of breeding superior sheep were increased prosperity and prestige for northern New England's farmers and added incentive to put capital into woolen manufactures all through the six states. In all this, at least as important to the well-being of farm people as the income derived was the eventual release of farm women and children from the burden of spinning and weaving to provide woolen clothing for their families.

22. Growth of the Land: New Crops

FRUIT GROWING was not yet a business in itself, but important advances were in the wind. Practically every farmer grew some apples, for cider was the universal beverage and easy to market. A Hampstead, New Hampshire, farmer who kept accounts recorded in 1817 that his 20 barrels of cider cost him 140 man hours and 28 team hours. With cider at a dollar a barrel, labor and team each at 50 cents per day, he appears to have had some profit. Up to 1820 or 1830 most families used that quantity at home as beverage or for vinegar. Apples fresh and dried were highly valued in the kitchen also. Farm families cut great quantities into quarters, dried these on boards or hung slices on strings for pies. Trees would grow among rocks and along stone walls and highways on land otherwise unproductive. Some observers noted orchards in the older sections which were neglected, the prey of cankerworms.

John Lincklaen, however, in 1791–92 speaks of "superb orchards" in the Connecticut Valley of Vermont, "but a worm eats the fruit." Colonel John Bellows of Walpole, on the New Hampshire side of the river, in 1805 had 30 acres of apples and made 4,800 barrels of cider. A town such as Woodbury in the western Connecticut hills had "many valuable orchards, so that the making of cider and cider spirits are important agricultural interests," so reads a typical report. Cider making did not reach its climax in Connecticut till 1830. Northern Worcester County in Massachusetts, too, abounded in large, fine orchards in this period. "Many farmers pay particular attention to raising all kinds of fruit which they have in plenty and of the best quality," an observer stated.[1]

A few orchards received cultivation, but most were in grass. In Rhode Island an April morning job for "Nailer Tom" Hazard's son was to manure his father's trees. Settlers on New Hampshire's hills and in inland Maine took seeds and scions to their new homes to begin fresh plantings.

New England was already well on its way in selecting fruit varieties. To the Roxbury Russet, Rhode Island Greening, Westfield Seek-No-Further, and Williams apples had been added the Baldwin, and in 1790 came the Hubbardston Nonesuch, the Mother (1800), and Porter (1800), all locally developed. The famous New York apple, Northern Spy, is said to have been a seedling from Salisbury, Connecticut, though it did not return to New England until later.

Roxbury and Dorchester gentlemen farmers were trying out and improving various pears; the Bartlett, Clapp's Favorite, Sheldon, and Seckel among them.[2] John Kenrick in 1790 opened a peach nursery in Newton, Massachusetts, and about 1832 introduced the superior Beurre Bosc. Isaac Hill, New Hampshire governor in this period, speaks of various kinds of peaches, from the yellow and crimson-cheeked rareripe to the ordinary fall clingstone, as growing in his native town, West Cambridge (now Arlington), Massachusetts.[3]

One never-to-be-forgotten fruit enthusiast was John Chapman, "Johnny Appleseed." Born in 1774 in the fruit town of Leominster, Massachusetts, his passion for apples led him to travel by water and on foot through the new country of the Western Reserve, his pockets full of apple seeds. He planted them by the highway, gave them to settlers, and in the course of forty years started a wealth of apple trees and of legends as well, in the New West. Less noted but not perhaps of less consequence were the efforts of David Church of Newington, Connecticut, who in 1810 wrote back from Newington, Chenango County, New York: "I have been carrying out appleseeds at the western little by little till I have carried out thirteen bushel and a half and put them in eighty nurseries and have got a hundred thousand trees I suppose." He had already sold 8,000 at 12½ cents each.[4]

Pedlars still hawked wild strawberries through the streets of the big towns in June; but near Boston and other large cities as the new century began, innovators were setting superior native plants in beds. Even in Western Vermont the historian of Salisbury mentions improved types brought there about 1810 from Salisbury, Connecticut. He states, however, that by 1860, when use of gypsum on the soil had become general, the quality and quantity of wild strawberries had improved, and as a result interest in strawberry cultivation flagged. Varieties propagated in early years by farmers included Early Hudson, Hudson's Bay, Hautboy, and Large Early Scarlet. Red and white field berry plants were set for cultivation also.[5]

Since colonial times cranberries had been harvested from eastern Massachusetts' natural bogs in marshy places in Norfolk, Middlesex, and other mainland counties. About the beginning of the century the purchaser of part of an island at Lincoln in the Sudbury Valley is reported to have sold enough berries the first year to pay for his real estate. In the year 1816 Captain Henry Hall of East Dennis, Cape Cod, began experiments in the cultivation of cranberries by transplanting to a neighboring bog vines from a marsh that produced extra fine berries. He also noticed the favorable effect of sand sifting in among the vines. His venture marked the start of an important present-day New England agricultural industry, the cultivation and processing of cranberries.[6]

By the end of the first quarter of the 1800's New England vegetable gardeners were growing great quantities of roots, especially potatoes, turnips, and parsnips, as well as onions, both for local use and for export. Greenwich, says Connecticut agricultural historian E. H. Jenkins, sent more potatoes to New York than did any other port, and became thereby a rich town. Johnston and other Rhode Island towns exported potatoes through Providence. The ship *Mary*, for example, in November 1810, put ashore at Richmond, Virginia, a shipment of 400 bushels (plus apples, cider, cheese, butter, onions, etc.). In 1812 the Providence packet ship *Rising States* landed 40 barrels as part of a cargo at Charleston, South Carolina.[7]

Coastal areas had the advantage of seaweed to manure their potato fields. In Madison, Connecticut, and other towns along the Sound, as has been noted, farmers spread whitefish on the land and plowed them in, a rich stimulant for this and other crops. Up country, on the fresh soil of new farms in New Hampshire and Vermont, potatoes might yield 400 bushels to the acre, their market frequently a whiskey distillery. In 1820 the Massachusetts Agricultural Society awarded a premium to Payson Williams of Fitchburg for a crop of 614 bushels from a single acre. The ordinary farmer's crop was on a much smaller scale, more like that of Deacon Amos Jewett of Rowley, who on March 30, 1816, planted "7 bushels of Red potatoes" in his sheep pasture. Each fall thereafter the deacon would sell a load of potatoes at Salem or Ipswich. The load in 1819, he noted, contained 41 bushels, sold for 30 cents a bushel. By 1829 his production had risen to 254 bushels. A farmer at Hampstead, New Hampshire, who in 1817 grew 442 bushels, at a valuation of twenty cents per bushel appeared to have a margin beyond expense of about one third. (Wheat at that time he valued at two dollars.) At Wilton, New Hampshire, Ezra Abbott is said to have worked out the process of making starch from the tubers, for sale to cotton manufacturers.

Maine had not yet turned to potatoes on any large scale, though Dr. Deane had earlier reported that even on poorly cultivated land a 100-bushel crop was not uncommon, and with better care 200. Maine already knew how to store them for later sale, for on April 7, 1825, the Maine sloop *Flora* delivered a cargo of 1,000 bushels at Boston from Orrington on the Penobscot.[8]

Wethersfield, Connecticut; Bristol, Rhode Island; and the farmer-fisher people of Barnstable on Cape Cod all continued to harvest quantities of onions. The Bristol ship *Juno*, outfitting in 1804 for the Pacific, had red onions among her supplies. Onions arrived at Boston and New York in single cargoes of as much as 18,000 bunches.

Close to Boston, where city manure or seaweed could be hauled and the market was lively, market gardeners, as they came to be called, even before the end of the last century had begun to develop skill in growing early vegetables of many sorts on southern slopes and under hotbed glass. Their crops included forced early potatoes, peas, asparagus, snap beans, cucumbers, lettuce, radishes, parsley, sweet corn, celery, horseradish, and others. Rhubarb was becoming popular, and tomatoes had made a start. Stored winter vegetables included squash, cabbage, and all the cultivated roots and bulbs. Cape Cod turnips were a byword among vessel crews for excellence.[9]

Cranston, Little Compton, and other towns in its vicinity supplied Providence with vegetables; Portsmouth's market was Newport. A ship captain in 1813 even picked up 1,300 cabbages on Naushon Island off Buzzards Bay. East Hartford was especially noted for watermelons, marketed in Hartford; and New Haven drew on its nearby towns for produce.[10]

Native-grown vegetable seeds were now on sale by, among others, those skillful horticulturists the Shaker colonies, one of whose farms, at Enfield, Connecticut, included a thousand acres in all. Joseph Belden in 1811 advertised in the *Hartford Courant* pea, bean, beet, carrot, and asparagus seeds "with a variety of others," all the growth of 1810. In 1820 James L. Belden of Wethersfield began his seed business, and in the *Courant* the next season listed 60 vegetable varieties. This firm, now Comstock, Ferré & Co., and the Joseph Breck Co., which began in a small way to sell vegetable seed in Boston in 1818, were still in business a century and a half later. In 1825 a Derby farmer and an Orange farmer each started seed growing in New Haven County.

William Downing, of Hancock in Massachusetts' Berkshire Hills, in 1821 offered a list of 54 items raised there, "put up in papers." Among these were red, white, and yellow onions and two varieties of summer and two of winter squashes. In Boston in 1825, John B. Russell's catalogue of seeds for sale at his warehouse of agricultural implements included the "Tomato or Love-apple," fourteen kidney or dwarf beans, four pumpkins, four summer squashes and the "Akorn." In addition to field corn, he listed "Sweet or Sugar (best for boiling ears)." Hovey & Co., Boston seedsmen, in their 1834–35 catalogue offered twelve varieties of dwarf kidney or string beans, eight of pole or running beans, eight of squash, two of tomatoes ("small and large"), four of pumpkins, and three of rhubarb.

Within five years their bush bean varieties had increased to twenty-one, pole beans to ten, and tomatoes to four.[11]

Not to be overlooked in any summary of the vegetables of this period are the general farmer's beans and field-sown pease. When thrashed out, they became mainstays in farm kitchens, as well as in the galleys of fishing vessels, cargo ships, and whalers. With the ordinary farmer, too, if Rodolphus Dickinson is to be believed, the kitchen garden, formerly often neglected, had "now become an object of great attention."

Several other specialty crops needing first-class land and manuring were grown for export. Flax, President Dwight of Yale thought to be "undoubtedly the most profitable crop which can be raised." Nearly every farmer had at least a small patch to provide raw material for his family's linens. Bronson Alcott, born in 1799 and brought up on Spindle Hill in northwest Connecticut, wrote: "Flax was cultivated by the farmers as generally as were oats and rye. Pulling flax was an employment in which women took part with the men. The linen manufacture was an important thing in every household. . . . My sisters were spinners both of wool and flax."[12]

The raw stalks, seed, and oil, all three, formed the basis of a substantial trade. Newport merchants made heavy shipments to Ireland. "Your flaxseed stands well in repute," a correspondent writes from Londonderry in 1785. Fairfield, Connecticut, on the Sound, alone in 1807 exported 20,000 bushels of seed, the product of about 3,000 acres. Nearby Milford sold yearly 100,000 pounds of flax and 4,000 bushels of seed, and Enfield was a heavy producer. In 1810 Connecticut could count 24 flaxseed oil mills within her borders. President Dwight mentions a New Bedford textile mill that annually twisted 50,000 pounds of Connecticut linen thread into twine. Household spinning was universal.[13]

The upper Connecticut Valley had been an important flax district since before the Revolution. Towns like Longmeadow, Sunderland, and Gill in Massachusetts; Walpole and Acworth, New Hampshire; and others in nearby Vermont now grew flax in quantity. Bennington was the market for western Vermont. Local mills crushed the seed. The oil and cake went east across the mountains to Hartford and Boston.

In Massachusetts, Worcester County towns such as Barre, Boylston, Lancaster, Lunenburg, and New Braintree were also big flax growers. The Merrimack Valley and eastern New Hampshire, where Scotch-Irish influence was strong, were heavily in flax. The little town of New Boston was nicknamed "Oil-Mill Village." Its mills crushed both flax and pumpkin seed. Portsmouth in 1796 had two oil mills. A bushel of seed made six quarts of linseed oil; the miller took one as toll. The oil cake residue found ready sale to fatten hogs and as feed for cattle.

Flaxseed was one of the few reliable sources of farm cash. Every store-keeper took it in trade. In the year October 1, 1790, to October 1, 1791, Massachusetts exported 6,036 hogsheads of the seed. Handmade linen goods produced beyond the needs of the family also furnished considerable farm income. Wansey, a visitor in 1794, mentions how the people of Northford, near New Haven, "raise a great deal of flax, and spin and weave it into sheeting, curtains, bed furniture Ec [etc.] of which I saw a great deal manufacturing." Newport got cloth from Western Massachusetts. Victor Clark, in his *History of Manufactures*, states that in 1788 Philadelphia was the market for 50,000 yards of New England linens, all hand-produced. In Vermont the Scotch at Ryegate built up a reputation for superior linens like that of the Scotch-Irish of Londonderry, New Hampshire.[14]

Another merchantable crop was hops. Judge Samuel Sewall records going "to View ye Hop-yards at Woburn" (Massachusetts), in 1702; and hop growing must have reached some magnitude before the Revolution, for shipping records show 3,000 pounds going to New York on the schooner *Bernard* in February 1763. To Massachusetts the crop became of such importance that in 1806 the state set strict standards of quality and required official inspection. A dozen towns, chiefly in northern Middlesex County, were the center of production not solely for New England but for the United States. "Tewksbury" (Massachusetts), says President Dwight, "yields more of this commodity than any other spot of equal extent in the United States." Old kilns where hops dried over pine and oak charcoal fires are said still to be found in that town. Much of the crop went to Europe, which preferred the Massachusetts-inspected product, though Boston itself had two breweries. The port of Charlestown (now part of Boston) in three decades, 1806–37, inspected 76,860 bags weighing 16,467,162 pounds.[15]

The price was volatile. On September 30, 1802, a journal-keeper in the town of Shirley, Massachusetts, wrote: "Hops in great demand at six cents per pound; thousands bought and sold this day." In 1817 it is said that the price reached 37 cents. A hop fever set in, however, which by 1819 pushed the price back to 6 cents once more, or even less. The average price over these decades was 13 cents. Southern New England continued to grow the crop up to the time of the Civil War. Despite competition from other New England states and the West, in 1840 Massachusetts still produced one fifth of the nation's crop. A valuable benefit, just as in

Kent, England, was the employment hop growing provided for local young people. To gauge the importance of the business, one family firm, the Blanchards of North Reading, between 1808 and 1837 brokered 16½ million pounds of hops.[16]

Western New England, in addition to cheese, dairy products, and fat stock, developed several marketable farm specialties. One reliable income producer was broomcorn. Cultivation of this grasslike form of maize began toward the end of the eighteenth century—first, it is claimed, in Connecticut. In the nineteenth century it became a staple for a tier of towns to the north in Hampshire and Franklin Counties, Massachusetts. Previously householders had relied on round brooms of birch twigs, hemlock tips, or split ash; some made by Indians, some by country people. Benjamin Franklin, that keen observer, is credited with planting America's first broomcorn seed. One story is that he brought it from England; another, that he picked a single stray seed from an imported whisk broom. The earliest recorded grower in New England seems to have been Samuel Hopkins of Hadley, who is said to have planted the seed in 1778. The broom trade's beginning has been credited to the year 1787.[17]

However, it was another Hadley farmer, Levi Dickinson, originally from Wethersfield, Connecticut, who developed the broomcorn industry. Beginning in 1797 and 1798, he gathered the straw from an experimental planting, bound it to handles with homegrown flax cord, and sold his few brooms to neighbors. His first brooms were circular, like those the Indians had made of birch brush, but of superior quality. Encouraged by their quick sale, he saved seed, the next year grew an acre, and peddled his brooms from a cart. From small beginnings he expanded operations till his sales route reached from Boston to Albany.

Noting Dickinson's success, other farmers in Hadley, Hatfield, Whately, and Northampton took up broomcorn growing and manufacture. Flat brooms replaced the round. Shops were opened where tiers became expert and the product uniform. Northfield took up the crops in 1813, then Deerfield; and Wethersfield in Connecticut was another center.

Broomcorn was grown much like field corn but required heavy manuring and more labor. It was planted in rows about 2½ feet apart, with hills at 1½ foot intervals. When nearing maturity, but before frost, the valuable upper two or three feet of the stalk was cut, allowed to dry, and the cuttings tied in bundles. The seed, if it had matured, was "hatcheled" out and the "brush" stored for manufacture. The stalks left standing in the field might be plowed in, burned, or cut as feed for young stock, any remainder trampled into manure. Each September, from Northampton to

Northfield, the Connecticut Valley was said to look like one continuous broomcorn field.[18]

Between growing the raw material, and manufacturing and selling the finished products, country people had employment winter and summer. Nearby hill towns cut stock for the broom handles. "Broomcorn is valuable," commented John Harriott, an 1815 visitor, "and the seed is excellent for poultry"—a correct observation, though seed did not always mature.[19] Some farmers had the seed ground and fed it to cattle and hogs. The greatest virtue of all, from the farm point of view, was that for over three decades broomcorn became the money crop for the farm people of Hampshire and Franklin Counties of Massachusetts.

In this period the cigar industry developed also. Rhode Island merchants had long been exporters of tobacco. When the Revolution ended, the business took on life once more. The brig *George* from Newport for Surinam in 1782 carried 29 hogsheads and two tierces—almost twelve tons in its lading. In 1783–84 the observant Spanish visitor Francisco de Miranda reported fields of very good tobacco on the light soils about Providence. Connecticut had also earlier grown tobacco in quantity, both for home consumption and for West Indies sales. Colonel Alexander Harvey of Scotland back in 1774 had noted excellent tobacco even at Ryegate, Vermont.[20]

About 1801 a Mrs. Prout of East Windsor, Connecticut, originally from Virginia, began to twist up tobacco leaves into cigars, whether from local or imported leaf is unclear—perhaps both. Previous local New England uses had been for pipe smoking, and for chewing. Other women soon took up cigar making, exchanging cigars made in spare time for goods at local stores, or selling through traveling pedlars. These Connecticut Valley cigars got the name of "long nines"; in Massachusetts they were called "barnyard cigars."

In 1810 Simeon Viets of Suffield built a shop and started to roll cigar leaf in quantity. He also began pressing plug tobacco, called fudgeon. From Edward A. Kendall's description of a local church service, the chewing habit appears to have been already well established. Viets's brother Roswell built another shop at East Windsor, a town that had not only soil suitable for the crop but hog manure to fertilize it. The manure was a by-product from the large herds maintained on refuse grain at its distilleries.[21] Some leaf was imported from Cuba. The narrow, locally grown leaf known as "shoestring tobacco" was often bartered with village storekeepers.

Hadley, Sunderland, and Deerfield, Massachusetts, further north in the

Connecticut Valley, were by 1835 growing leaf as a field crop, and town governments there (and even in the Merrimack Valley) accepted it in payment of taxes. Considerable leaf must have been exported, for among Hadley's regular town officials were Packers of Tobacco, an office known also in Connecticut at least as far back as the regulatory act of 1753.

Production increasing, a packing house to handle harvested cigar leaf was built about 1825 at Warehouse Point, Connecticut. The leaf was then shipped in hundred-pound bales to New York. The enlarging tobacco trade opened what was to be a century and more of substantial prosperity for growers in the Great Valley and its neighborhood.

A quite different but likewise successful agricultural specialty became a reliance of farmers in the Franklin County hills northwest from Northampton. Peppermint had already, after the Revolution, been distilled in Agawam, across the river from Springfield. About 1812 Samuel Ranney, an Ashfield man from New York State, began to raise peppermint for which the stolons or shoots are thought originally to have been imported from England. He set up a small plant to distill the oil from his crop, for the success of which a moist soil rich in potash and long days for distillation were among the requirements.[22]

Sales of peppermint were good; growing expanded. By 1821 Ashfield's stills had increased to five; by 1830 to ten. Young salesmen from Ashfield and other hill towns set out each season in all directions bearing baskets, to quote Ashfield's historian, heavy not only with peppermint but with spearmint, hemlock, spruce, wintergreen, tansy, and other essences. Essence growing spread to Lanesboro, Pittsfield, and Lenox in the Berkshires; later to Warren, New Hampshire. Such products of their soil and labor, of high value in proportion to quantity, continued for years to afford welcome income to these hill towns. At length migration of experienced natives bore the skills and secrets of growing and distillation first to western New York, later to Michigan. In both states superior conditions resulted in competition that the Massachusetts growers could no longer meet.

Another specialty crop to which gentleman farmers and home gardeners especially began to show marked attention was silk production, though it was not destined for commercial success. The enthusiasm for silk during this period and succeeding decades is one example of the determination of Americans of that era to search out every possible salable crop.

Propagating mulberry trees to feed silk worms had been an objective of the governments of Virginia and Georgia almost from the beginning; and, during the previous century, of other colonies also.[23] The Revolution over, the state of Connecticut in 1784 offered bounties for growing mulberry trees and producing raw silk from cocoons spun by silk worms feeding on their leaves. A Connecticut Silk Society, formed the next year, generated enthusiasm, and in 1789 the town of Mansfield produced 200 pounds of raw silk. At Northford, near New Haven, Henry Wansey in 1794 observed a great many plantations of mulberry trees and met a young lady who with her sister's help had the previous year raised and spun enough cocoons for 18 yards of Florentine silk. Mansfield, where by 1819 production of at least 2,500 pounds of raw silk was reported, and 3,000 in 1825, set up what is called the first silk mill in the United States. Sewing silk became part of the circulating medium. The following year Connecticut growers held a silk convention.[24]

Massachusetts and Rhode Island, even Vermont, also had their mulberry and silk enthusiasts. The sincere endeavors to establish a new type of crop for which the market was hungry, the speculative craze that grew from it, and the collapse that followed will be the subject for fuller discussion later. From the century's opening decades at least, the prospects appeared quite promising.

Meanwhile, wood and its products continued among the area's most reliable farm resources, although conditions as to forest products varied remarkably from one part of New England to another. While trees were being burned to clear land in the hills of Vermont and in interior Maine, providing potash as their only contribution to the economy, Cape Cod was already importing firewood, and in Truro pine seed was being planted in plough furrows to try to bring back a forest there. Eastham on the Cape had used up its oak and white pine to build vessels, and pitch pine was taking over. Orleans, lacking wood, was reduced to burning peat for cooking and heating, a custom long prevalent on Block Island. In interior Essex County, Middleton and Topsfield cut peat for fuel from 1800 on; and during the War of 1812 when the British shut off the Maine woodboats that ordinarily kept Boston and Salem warm, Essex County farmers sold peat outside at a great rate. At Bedford also, in Middlesex County, the extensive peat beds were highly valued for their coal-like quality.[25]

In southern New England, Rhode Island had little old-growth timber left. New Haven in 1806 imported 2,500 cords of firewood from Long Island, and drew on Maine for ship timber. Yet on that same Connecticut shore and further west, Guilford and Derby marketed in New York City both firewood and lumber. Up the Housatonic, the Salisbury iron works, their fifty blast furnaces fed by charcoal, devoured the woods for miles around. All in all, much of New England was rapidly clearing its original forest and changing its landscape to one of open country. Some sense of the importance of what in the twentieth century came to be called conservation is indicated by a letter home from Ambassador James Bowdoin of Boston, advising the sale of some timber on Naushon Island off Buzzards Bay. Though he is anxious that harvesting yield the greatest quantity of timber, he advises cutting the old and decaying trees only, leaving the rest for future growth. In New Hampshire, as early as 1822, the Board of Agriculture recommended what is now called selective cutting, and the propagation of forest trees. "If land be not useful for pasturage or tillage let it be forest."[26]

Maine's immense forests were the basis not only for the remarkable surge of shipbuilding that during the first years of the nineteenth century lined its shores with shipyards (an industry resumed after the War of 1812), but also for many of the keels laid down in Massachusetts. On Plymouth County's North River, shipbuilders reached continually further back for stock and masts. After they had taken out the oaks and hardwoods, white pine seed filtered in to replace them. This new crop was to become salable generations later. Up the Merrimack Valley in New Hampshire, lumbermen cut steadily into timber made marketable in Boston by the Middlesex Canal, completed to Concord, New Hampshire, in 1811. The great new mills and other structures of the new city of Lowell in 1822 also furnished a useful market. The upper Connecticut Valley floated its lumber down the great river, while the Champlain country shipped oak and pine as lumber by river north into Canada. Potash and pearlash (more refined and a source of baking soda) continued a chief source of outside income for mountainous areas away from water transport.

As the new century advanced, another forest crop began to contribute to the economy of hill farms: maple sugar. Goshen, Connecticut, settlers had made sugar there before the middle of the previous century. As early as 1754 a Hatfield, Massachusetts, farmer is recorded as having had a "sugar place" in the hills west of Northampton. By 1763 hill farmers were selling sugar in that shire town at five and six pence per pound, and maple "molasses" at two shillings five pence per gallon. Sugaring was also reported to the north, on the state line in Bernardston. This was just about the time that Reverend Samuel Hopkins was describing in print the process of sugar making as he observed it carried on by the Indians at Great Barrington in southern Berkshire.[27] A London publication of 1765 spoke of the method of getting sugar from trees as having been "lately" introduced into New England. About 1774 Norfolk, in the northwest Connecticut hills, was making 16,000 pounds a year; after another ten years 21,000, with three out of four families tapping trees. A decade later

Dr. Stiles remarked that the process had been in use for forty years. Henry Wansey, passing the low mountains of Durham, Connecticut, in May of 1794, took note of taps still left in tree trunks and troughs beneath.[28]

In New Hampshire, Matthew Patten, a Bedford farmer, had his boys out "shugaring" in early April 1776. Later in the month they boiled sap to "molasses," but not to sugar. New Hampshire families often made as much as two to three hundred pounds. In newly opened Vermont, Pittsford's first settlers had made sugar in 1770. After the Revolution, John Lincklaen, traveling in the state's western section in 1791, had found to his surprise that the people did not seem to think the sugar maple of great advantage to them; chiefly, he suspected, from lack of a market for the sugar and the difficulty of getting utensils. Yet in Cavendish in eastern Vermont, 83 families are said to have made 80,000 pounds of sugar in 1793, and nearly as large a total the following year, selling much of it to storekeepers.[29]

In any case, early nineteenth-century western and northern New England towns, far from the sources of imported cane sugar, began to produce tons of sugar for sale. Decade by decade the maple was to be of increasing importance to the whole hill country. In seaboard New England, on the other hand, the sugar maple tree was almost unknown. Even if available, at that period, its product could scarcely have competed for sweetening with molasses imports from the West Indies.

Another prime farm resource, often overlooked by historians, was the wealth of nut-bearing trees. The chestnut, hickory, black walnut, butternut, and beech grew thick on many a hillside. Their nuts made good eating in their natural state: dried and stowed away for winter use, they gave distinctive flavor to cakes and sweets. Swine throve on them, as the name "pignut" for one hickory variety attests. Of all forest species, hickory made one of the hottest fires. Properly shaped and smoothed it also became an excellent scythe or axe handle. Chestnut was easy to work, and popular with farmers for building timber and for fence rails; it would last for generations in all but moist situations. Walnut and butternut provided not only tool handles, gunstocks, and fine furniture, but also essential dyes to color textiles and clothing. These values were in addition to the food the nut trees furnished.

Every species of tree had its individual virtues. The several varieties of oaks and pines included numerous types of building and shipbuilding stock. Other trees had value right on the farm. The ash appeared to be especially designed by its straight smooth grain for long tool handles. Split into thin strips, ash was perfect for plaiting into baskets. The red cedar, which throve on the poorest gravel hillside pasture, served as a fence post that would last for generations; while the white cedar of the swamps, like white pine, became valuable for shingles. The cherry not only offered wild fruit, but was coveted by furniture makers. And no teeth for a hayrake or harrow were as tough as those made from hop hornbeam: a wood, when dry, almost as hard as iron. From even the soft gray birch, commonly considered a weed tree, the flexible small branches would make a good broom. When several of the long spidery branches were hitched so as to trail behind the width of a log, the result when this was drawn by a horse or ox was an excellent smoothing harrow.

These are but a few examples of the multitudinous uses that made the woods an invaluable asset to the New England husbandman, not only in the days of early settlement, but for generation on generation thereafter.

Tillage methods had not changed much since the Revolution, nor the tools which did the work. Charles Newbold of New Jersey patented an iron plow in 1797. In 1814 Jethro Wood, born and brought up in Dartmouth, Massachusetts, but then of New York State, patented a cast iron plow with replaceable parts designed for more efficient soil breaking and scouring, and followed this five years later with an improved model. His plow was so superior that it was soon copied by numerous manufacturers without credit to the inventor. Despite his great contribution to agriculture he never reaped financial reward, though Congress in 1833 extended his patent. In 1822 Vermonter John Conant invented a lock coulter, and in 1825 Russell's Boston agricultural warehouse stocked a "greatly improved sidehill plow." Here and there a progressive farmer might hear of the novel all-iron plow, but of three plows entered at Berkshire County's first plowing match in 1818, two had wood mouldboards, though their shares were of wrought iron and the points steel. The exception was an imported iron plow. At a Brighton contest in 1825, four out of fifteen were of cast iron. For hay, a type of wooden horserake had been worked out, but its acceptance was yet to come.[30]

In hand tools the advance was greater. The wood shovel that a farmer could make himself remained useful for some purposes (handling grain, for example), especially when given a metal edge, but the Ames firm at North Easton, Massachusetts, in 1814 began to turn out nine to ten dozen a day of excellent iron shovels. Numerous small manufactories made greatly improved scythes, hay and manure forks, churns, and cheese presses.[31] An export trade in such tools was developing also. The cradle, of European origin, had begun since the Revolution to quicken grain harvesting, which for thousands of years had been dependent on the sickle. Any general use of it in New England was nevertheless still ahead. One farm necessity, attention to which was continually required, was the stone wall. Not that walls were anything new. All through the previous century industrious farmers had been building walls and more or less permanent barriers of other sorts to replace original short-lived wood fences. As has been noted, on sandy Cape Cod and in alluvial plains where stone was scarce, ditches confined sheep and other animals—the banked earth that was thrown out forming an extra barrier on one side. Wherever stone was available, however, walls were preferred. A well-laid stone wall such as still surrounds many a barnyard and nearby lot is a work of skill, often of art. Most walls, however, were purely for utility, laid up to keep cattle out of a field or within it, or to mark a boundary. At the same time they rid cultivated land of a nuisance.

The end of common herding, marked by the division of proprietors' remaining common lands, and an increase in the number of sheep both helped to make the decades succeeding the Revolution an active period of wall building. A good man with a good team might build four rods a day. Such a statement illumines the investment of human labor involved in building and maintaining the thousands of miles of stone walls that, despite all efforts of modern bulldozers, still crisscross New England. Often they enclose one-time pastures, today become deep woods, or, as in Robert Frost's "Mending Wall," serve as boundaries: "Good fences make good neighbors," his next door farmer quoted.[32]

In long-settled sections of New England, once the riches of the natural leaf mould were exhausted, farmers recognized the need to supplement the land's slim fertility. If they were within reach of salt water, they hauled rock-weed, kelp, and eelgrass in fall and winter for stable bedding, and again in spring as fertilizer for corn, potatoes, and roots. Industrious farmers were said to lay down from 30 to 60 loads to the acre. It was generally considered to be of great utility in enriching the land. Diaries of seaboard farmers like "Nailer Tom" Hazard of Rhode Island are full of seaweed hauling. Massachusetts' North Shore towns jealously guarded their beach rights against encroachments by inlanders seeking means for building up their soil. Rhode Island and Connecticut farmers at least were becoming great users of peat also. They dumped it on the land in piles to decompose, or put it in the pen for hogs to work into manure.[33]

Waterside cultivators had a second valuable manure, fish. Along the Sound, Connecticut farmers made immense hauls of whitefish, which they either spread directly on the land 10–12,000 to the acre before plow-

16. A noble stone wall serves to fence and clear a hundred-acre cornfield: (above) side view; (below) top view. *Howard S. Russell collection.*

ing, or composted with layers of earth for later use. This compost was deemed efficacious on all soils and for almost every type of vegetation. The lightest soils, enriched by fish, a writer maintained, have produced forty bushels of rye to the acre. Near Gloucester, Massachusetts, farmers obtained fish heads, the refuse of fish drying and the export business. At Plymouth and on the Merrimack, Mystic, and other estuaries leading to fresh water ponds, numerous reports of the early eighteenth century testify that the ancient Indian practice of putting herring in the cornhill still helped ensure an adequate crop.[34] Cape Cod had good returns from the king crab. The grain was reported to fill out well. Though the stalk was of low stature, it yielded twenty bushels to the acre on light land, one writer reports; another speaks of 35–45 bushels of corn and 20–30 of rye. On the shores of Buzzards Bay farmers plowed in what was locally called "menhaden," probably herring but perhaps whitefish.[35]

On most farms, if we are to believe available diaries, barnyard manure was ceaselessly hauled, spread, and valued. The ancient jibe about manure being allowed to accumulate till it was easier to move the barn than the manure pile, if it applied in New England at all, was possibly true only in the midst of new-land fertility or during hard winters. Eighteenth- and early nineteenth-century diaries abound in entries about carting, "beating," and spreading dung, though little thought was yet given to protecting it from the weather.

Travelers unanimously remark on the well-tilled, fertile appearance of country about Boston, New Haven, and other large ports. The many draymen's and private stables of such commercial centers were now the source of great quantities of manure. Nightsoil, brought from the city in tight covered wagons, was deposited in open basins and mixed with what Coleman calls "mould," presumably what would now be termed humus, to absorb the liquid parts and to put the whole into condition to apply to the soil. Slaughterhouse and tannery wastes also were hauled out for use in neighboring towns as these areas developed market gardening and commercial fruit growing. Near Boston a large farmer might contract for a stable's output by the year. Others bought manure by the load in winter, often hauling it on the return trip after sale of a load of wood or hay. In summer when Boston's Board of Health was hot after stable owners, forbidding accumulation of over two loads, farmers had to be "invited" to come in and clean the town.[36]

Presaging the coming of commercial fertilizer, trade sprang up in crop stimulants. Boston merchants sold French and Nova Scotia plaster of paris before the eighteenth century ended. In 1801 a Greenfield, Massachusetts, dealer offered plaster of paris by the ton or bushel. Soon President Dwight reported rich crops of clover and grain from treated fields in Massachusetts' Connecticut Valley. "The use of gypsum alone has wonderfully meliorated this soil," he concluded. Even in the limestone valleys of the Berkshires and Taconics plaster was used. Rodolphus Dickinson in his 1813 survey of Massachusetts remarked on the extensive spreading of plaster, which he considered especially useful on light soils. The idea was also abroad that after cropping land a few years a good farmer did well, as Eliot had advised, to sow clover and leave the field as a meadow to recover before planting again.[37]

Yet with all such additions to productiveness, and notwithstanding the praise of abundant crops that traveler after traveler gave the Connecticut Valley and the environs of Boston, Providence, Hartford, and other marketing centers, much of the older acreage was undoubtedly going downhill. Remaining native fertility was slight. Available manure and other soil complements went chiefly to fertilize corn land and money crops. Carelessness in conserving and returning fertility, however, might result more from lack of capital and the high cost of labor than from ignorance of the need to keep land in good heart.

23. Comfort and Struggle

ONCE MORE we come to a discussion and assessment of the farm people and their situation in the early nineteenth century, as the era of industrialization was about to begin.

Farm living continued to be laborious, but that did not necessarily imply discomfort or deprivation beyond that of other people. In new towns in northern New England the farmhouse might still be of squared logs, as Benjamin Silliman reported in 1819; but old people, questioned in a later era, looked back on life in them as very happy.[1] Or if framed and clapboarded, the house might still lack paint, especially in hill towns. But in 1809, of the dwellings he saw on the comparatively poor soils between Providence and Boston, English traveler Edward A. Kendall remarked: "the farmhouses (which are almost universally of wood, and painted either white or yellow) are frequently large, well built, and generally well furnished." Widespread production of linseed oil was one reason for the increasing use of house paint. John Lambert, traversing southern New England, gives further testimony: "A small town composed of these neat and ornamental edifices, and situated in the neighborhood of well-cultivated farms, large fields, orchards, and gardens . . . gives the traveller a high opinion of the prosperity of the country . . . The farms appear in excellent order, and the inhabitants sober, industrious, religious, and happy."[2] John Melish, a first decade English visitor, thought the white paint gave the country an appearance of great cleanliness and neatness.

Other improvements were beginning to appear. Most farms would for a long time depend for water on wells with their buckets and sweeps, but farmers near hillside springs were bringing in water through logs bored and fitted, to lighten the burden of the housewife as well as to water the stock. Here is the description of two farms advertised for sale in 1803 in the dairy town of Cheshire, Berkshire County, Massachusetts, source of the Great Cheshire Cheese: "They are situated one-half mile south of the meeting house, have all conveniences, have dairy, cheese, milk and press house, two dwelling houses, good barns, cornhouses, and two good fruit orchards. . . . Two aqueducts carry a plentiful supply of water to houses and barns." For village farms, as in 1798 at Keene, New Hampshire, a citizen might bring water in a wood pipe for several families; and soon aqueduct companies were being formed here and there to provide piped water for a whole neighborhood.[3] A Massachusetts gazetteer of 1813 said that wells were almost universal and subterranean aqueducts numerous.

By contrast, Horace Greeley later wrote of the struggles of farmers in the Scotch-Irish section where he grew up in southern New Hampshire. It was an area with strong but rocky soil and small struggling farms: "Its people all live by farming," Greeley wrote, "and own the land they cultivate; three-fourths of them were born where they live and there they expect to die . . . Poor as we were, no richer farmer lived within sight of our humble homestead, though our western prospect was only bounded by the Chestnut Hills, two or three miles away." For water supply Reverend Warren Cochrane, writing of another nearby town, tells us that even after wells were dug, water was drawn up with a pole, and well-curbs and well-sweeps were "precious inventions." "Many will remember when there was not a well-sweep in town," he says in 1845.[4]

As to food, except occasionally in the latest settled, most remote sections, it was seldom that a farm family suffered; and for most families the amount was ample, though variety was not always great. However, differences between areas and even within the same neighborhood might be considerable.

An observer in the town of Sandwich on Cape Cod, favored with marsh hay for stock, reports in 1802 that "the inhabitants in general are substantial livers." If a Sandwich farmer ran out of beef, lamb, pork, and cheese, he and every inhabitant had access to a supply of clams, flounders, and dried herring.[5] A surprising proportion of country people, even far inland, could also rely on fish for at least part of the year, as salmon, sturgeon, and herring sought ponds at the river sources to spawn.

During that same decade at the opposite corner of New England, John Lambert, from overseas, came ashore from a Lake Champlain craft in the early dawn of a snowy morning. He and his party knocked at the first farmhouse door they met and waked the family. Though the town of Shelburne was new and Vermont country rough, the household welcomed the visitors. The women stirred the fire, and with only a short delay, the travelers had the pleasure of sitting down to a substantial breakfast of eggs, fried pork, beefsteaks, apple tarts, pickles, cheese, cider, tea, and toast dipped in butter and milk![6]

Yet in that very same Vermont a native of Peacham, born in 1807, recalled that frequently during his childhood all that his father's household had for a meal was stewed pumpkins and milk. The historian of Francestown, New Hampshire, where the Scotch farmers mentioned earlier were for a time so poor that, lacking draft animals, they carried stable manure to the fields on their shoulders, comments: "A constant dish . . .

was broth: corn broth, bean broth, barley broth and sometimes . . . a mixture." In New England as a whole the most common dishes seem to have been hasty pudding and pie. The diary of youthful Miss Elizabeth Fuller of a well-to-do family in Princeton, Massachusetts, records: "November 24. We baked two ovens full of pyes. . . . Nov. 25. Thanksgiving today. We baked three ovens full of pyes . . . They were better than last Thanksgiving for I made them all myself."[7]

Coming back once more to Cape Cod, but to the lower end, we are told that even among the poorest at this period a breakfast would include salt or fresh fish, brown bread generally with butter, and tea or coffee. At dinner, though the family would be likely to enjoy fresh butcher's meat not more than a dozen times a year, there would be fish of different kinds, salt pork baked with beans, "roots and herbs" (meaning, besides potatoes and very likely turnips, there might be carrots, parsnips, pumpkins, beans, and perhaps cabbage), followed by Indian pudding, and again tea and coffee. In rural Vermont at that period, however, the sole root mentioned in a store account book was turnips.[8]

An example applicable to many if not to most of the farm families of New England would be the recollection of Lucy Stone as she looked back at the West Brookfield hill farm where her mother had regretted the birth of a daughter because farm life was so hard. Lucy's recollection was of a copious larder: barrels of meat; milk, cream, butter, and eggs; several kinds of cultivated fruit and many wild berries; delicious honey; and fresh rye and Indian bread.*[9]

Independent, industrious, ingenious, shrewd, thrifty, often sagacious and active in the pursuit of knowledge; "raising [even in rural New Hampshire] ordinarily a little surplus with which to furnish their families the little necessaries which common custom or inclination invite them to procure"—the farm people of New England were the wonder of foreign travelers. "There is no class like that which the French call peasantry," William Cobbett wrote in 1818.[10]

President Dwight, leaving Yale to roam New England, is equally impressed. "Even a poor man," he says, "has usually a comfortable house, a little land, a cow, swine, poultry, a few sheep, and not infrequently a horse." The family eats well, has decent clothes, educates its children, and goes to church, he adds.[11] In the Housatonic town of New Milford ministers, doctors, lawyers, storekeepers all did some farming. One of

---

*As with numerous similar matters related to farm history it appears to this writer that despite the many popular and not too critical writings on undated "old times," the field deserves much more detailed and systematic attention than it has ordinarily received.

Dwight's Connecticut contemporaries acutely summed up the quality of New England's rural people: "Competence among the rocks," he called it.[12]

Nor should it be overlooked how many boys and girls destined to superior attainments, to become what the present generation priggishly designates as "intellectuals," were growing up during these years following the Revolution on farms among those rocks. As examples from those decades, set down Daniel Webster (born 1782), Horace Mann (1795), Mary Lyon (1797), William Cullen Bryant (1798), Bronson Alcott (1799), Dorothea Dix (1802), Hiram Powers (1805), John G. Whittier and Emma Hart Willard (1807), Theodore Parker and Asa Gray (1810), Horace Greeley and Henry Barnard (1811), Henry D. Thoreau and Sylvanus Thayer (1817), Lucy Stone (1818), Susan B. Anthony (1820), Clara Barton (1821), William Morris Hunt (1824).

In addition there was the host of inventors and innovators of these years, for whose practical, ingenious minds New England farm shops served as training ground—such men as Eli Whitney, inventor of the cotton gin and deviser of interchangeable parts for machines; John Fitch, who put steam to work for navigation; John Deere, father of the modern steel plow; Elias Howe, Jr., who devised the lockstitch sewing machine; William Howe, the truss bridge; Tyler Howe, the spring bed (all of one farm family); Simeon North, the revolver; and Eli Whitney Blake, who worked out the power stone-crusher with which it became possible to build all-weather roads. The list could continue.

For farm boys the options, besides farming, had for generations been the ministry, the law, teaching, a merchant's warehouse, or the sea, and these still attracted some of the best. But now almost limitless choices were opening. John Warren became a surgeon, and the father of Harvard Medical School; Oliver Hazard Perry, naval commander, and hero of the Battle of Lake Erie; and Henry Ellsworth, United States Commissioner of Patents and architect of the Department of Agriculture. Joseph Smith founded the Mormon Church. Collis P. Huntington was to build the Southern Pacific. More options were to open for girls also. The soil of New England farms might appear thin, but like the splendid forests that sprang from it, that granite soil nurtured a human harvest such as far richer ground might have been proud to sponsor.

In place of the term "subsistence farm," sometimes applied to the New England homestead of this half-century, a more accurate description would be "the multipurpose farm," and one of its primary purposes seems to have been the development of persons of superior capabilities and attainments.

Thus the first quarter of the nineteenth century, though interrupted by an unpopular war that for a time shattered New England's economic life and then by two years of climatic misfortunes, had been a time of seed-sowing: in trade, in transportation, in intellectual life and ingenuity.

Trade opportunities occasioned by the Napoleonic wars brought on a surge of shipbuilding, creating a market for forest products. Shipbuilders and the crews of vessels trading in the Atlantic and across the Pacific, and hunting cod and whales in many seas, had to be fed. Meanwhile, in their holds these ships carried not only barreled beef and pork, distilled spirits, lumber, staves and fish, but apples, cheese, lard, flaxseed, soap, onions, potatoes, and poultry; a diversity of minor products of the soil.

In assembling such cargoes merchants had the help of coasters from every little harbor, and of the first strands of a web of new turnpikes aiming straight at the ports from many directions.

Among the goods backflowing from port to farm was a trickle of blooded cattle, sheep, and poultry brought from foreign lands by observant travelers and sailors, and destined in time to come to make New England a seedbed of superior livestock.

Meanwhile, wars over and the new nation buoyant, the countryside showed increased well-being: paint shielded and decorated the wood of buildings, horse-drawn vehicles were more numerous, clothing more adequate, food less monotonous. Education was gaining, and ingenuity and thrift were creating on the farm and in the village a better life. For country people it had been a time of innovation, of seed sowing. Growing weather in both farming and intellectual life lay just ahead.

IV. GOOD GROWING
WEATHER, 1825-1860

24. Things to Come

IN THE EVENTFUL YEAR 1825 the waters of the newly dug Erie Canal joined Albany, head of navigation of the tidal Hudson, to Buffalo and the Great Lakes. That same year the new president of the United States, John Quincy Adams of Massachusetts, recommended to Congress exploration of the 2,000 miles of unknown country that lay between the Mississippi and the Oregon coast. The year following, 1826, was the fifty-first anniversary of Bunker Hill. It saw one of the country's first railways carry Quincy granite the few miles to the Neponset shore, thence to be floated across the harbor for the 220-foot memorial at Charlestown planned to commemorate the battle; and 1829 saw incorporation of the Boston and Lowell, earliest New England steam railroad company. These events were harbingers of forces, historical and economic, destined in the four decades ahead to transform New England farming—and the life of the entire nation as well.

Of less national import yet examples of the striking changes impending in agriculture were these: the first importation of guano (the accumulated dried droppings of Pacific island seabirds) and Chilean nitrate of soda, and a beginning in the manufacture of ground bone, both of which would open the era of extensive use of crop stimulants; the patenting by Silas Lamson of Sterling, Massachusetts, of the graceful and effective curved scythe snaith; the setting up at Canton, Connecticut, by the Collins brothers and William Wells of the world's first axe factory; the publishing by Dr. Daniel Adams of the earliest American agricultural textbook; at Millbury, Massachusetts, the opening of the first Lyceum; and the establishment in Massachusetts and Vermont of the country's pioneer teacher-training institutes. At the new town of Lowell in these same few years the Merrimack Manufacturing Company started the machines in its great new brick mills, to turn out two million yards of cloth in its second twelvemonth; and at Sandwich on Cape Cod a new factory began to make attractive, inexpensive glassware available to American households everywhere.

This period also saw Boston open its monumental Quincy Market, unmatched in the New World. Worcester citizens, wishing to insure their dwellings and farm buildings, incorporated what has become Massachusetts' oldest fire insurance company. The Lake Champlain, the Blackstone, and the Farmington canals all began to transport freight. Lest the picture appear too rosy, a thousand miles away in Wisconsin the Colorado beetle began an eastward journey that presaged catastrophe for one of New England's most prized crops, potatoes.

Such crowding events were symptoms of the changes about to engulf New England farm people. Some of these farm folks would be made wealthy; some would be brought to national prominence. On the other hand, thousands of families would be uprooted from ancestral homes and occupations, and the ways of life of all would be altered at a hundred points.

The four keys (page 136, above) to the character of New England's agricultural history and the life of its farm people all increased their influence during these years preceding the Civil War. They are the rapid expansion of the means of transportation; marked improvement in education and information; a turning to better tools and machines; and a tremendous growth in industry and population in the area. Each brought benefits to New England farms; each created problems. Powerful additional factors exerted influence also, especially emigration from the hills; immigration of new peoples from Europe; the continual necessity to adapt to economic changes; and the beginnings of the era of farm as well as industrial organization.

By 1825 a widespread web of turnpikes and canals had substantially reduced transportation costs for the back country, made travel more swift and comfortable, and the exchange of goods much easier. For interior towns they opened new markets for farm produce. Every state in New England benefited. Even Maine, though its rivers and sea routes made canals less necessary, and only a few turnpikes were built there, felt the influence. Military roads chopped through the woods linked Lincoln with Houlton and Houlton with Fort Fairfield. Thence a road eventually reached Calais, portending the opening of the Aroostook country. From the west, turnpikes through the White Mountains increased Portland's commerce.

From the Champlain Valley and western Vermont, butter, cheese, beef, pork, wool, and lumber flowed south by water to Albany and tidewater via the Champlain Canal and Lake George, in greater volume than they had ever gone north by the Richelieu River to Canada. In the decade 1823 to 1833, traffic south through Whitehall from both shores of the lakes increased greatly: in butter and cheese, five times; in sawed lumber, over three times; in wool, about fifty times. Most of this wool and half the dairy products came from the Vermont side.[1] On the Connecticut River a

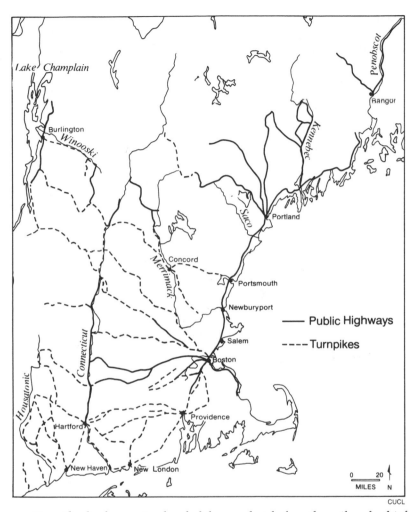

Lake Champlain

Penobscot

Bangor

Burlington

Winooski

Kennebec

Saco

Portland

Merrimack

Concord

Portsmouth

Newburyport

Public Highways
Turnpikes

Salem

Connecticut

Boston

Housatonic

Providence

Hartford

New Haven   New London

0   20
MILES   N

CUCL

17. How the back country headed for market before the railroad: chief
travel routes for stock, produce. In addition to these, all coastal areas
made the sea their common route to market. *Cartography Laboratory,
Clark University.*

system of locks completed in 1835 by-passed the falls to help the produce and lumber of the great central valley reach tidal Connecticut. In turn, during the ice-free months, flatboatmen worked supplies north to the traders at Deerfield's Cheapside and as far as White River in Vermont. A sailing sloop, even, is reported to have unloaded freight at Brattleboro in 1837. Farmington Canal was extended from its Springfield terminal to Northampton, its total length 76 miles.[2] Maine, not to be left out, tied Lake Sebago with Portland. Directly or indirectly, each of these developments brought aid to interior farms.

The increasing mileage of through turnpikes stretching in all directions did even more to speed inland transportation. Their centers were elevated for drainage. Ox-drawn scoops and tree-branch graders kept their surfaces smooth. In wet places willows planted alongside held fill and eliminated bogholes that had previously cursed travelers. The multi-horse team now superseded the plodding ox, though in an occasional tandem rig a horse might act as leader for a pair of oxen.[3]

Meanwhile, more than ever, coastal New England merchants and farmers used the sea for conveyance of goods to market. Like automobile truckmen in the twentieth century, regular coasters, small and large, connected every shore town with larger ports.

From Portland, Wiscasset, Hallowell, and other Maine harbors schooners christened *Sea Flower*, *Syren*, *Olive*, put off for Boston with potash, clapboards, shovel handles, bedposts, apples, cider, hay, butter, potatoes, sheepskins, cordwood. On New Hampshire's sixteen-mile coast the *Sarah* or the *Polly and Clarissa* would leave Portsmouth or Rye for the big market loaded with potatoes, beans, butter, eggs, and cider. Cape Cod packets slipped across Massachusetts Bay bearing the Cape's fish, and along with it, thousands of ropes of onions. In 1835, from Portsmouth to Provincetown, Massachusetts Bay arrivals of coastwise vessels numbered 3,879.[4] In Narragansett Bay packets plied regularly from Newport, Bristol, and Warren to Providence, and others from the Bay's western shore. They bore to market the countryside's fresh eggs, poultry, onions, turnips, cheese, and butter. Even though by 1840 Rhode Island's direct foreign commerce was a thing of the past, the population and trade of Providence kept growing.[5]

If to farmers in interior New England canal and turnpike traffic was a boon, their effect was minor compared to the revolution that resulted from the coming of the railway. In 1835 the Boston and Worcester railroad opened; four years later it reached Springfield; and in 1842 by what was for that time superior engineering, the track was pushed up through high Berkshire valleys to the Hudson. By 1847 this "Western Railroad," linking Albany with Boston, carried 88,438 tons of freight. Meanwhile, the Boston and Lowell, completed in 1836, by lower rates and higher speed almost at once cut Middlesex Canal traffic by two thirds. Further south the Boston and Providence, and the Stonington and Providence railroads began business about the time Boston got its link to Worcester. In 1840 rails connected New Haven with Hartford, four years later with Springfield, in 1845 with Northampton, then in 1849 with New York.[6]

This was only the beginning. The railroad builders opened northern New England. The track crept up the Merrimack Valley into New Hampshire, then into Vermont. By 1845 the *Boston Cultivator* could report "an enormous train of 44 cars from the center of Vermont" arriving at Boston's Lowell depot. By 1850 Burlington on Lake Champlain was tied to Bellows Falls on the Connecticut. On November 13, 1851, Henry D. Thoreau, watching from Walden Pond, recorded in his journal: "The cattle train came down last night from Vermont with snow nearly a foot thick on it."[7] In 1853 Portland was connected to Montreal. Rails were reaching into Central Maine.

Canals and turnpikes found themselves superseded. The Middlesex Canal suspended operation in 1853. Dependent on tolls, most turnpikes lost money and eventually became public roads. The stages between the leading cities were given up, although certain short lines from interior towns to railway stations lasted through the rest of the century.

By the middle of the nineteenth century New England's network of railways surpassed in density anything to be found elsewhere in the United States. It was claimed that few farms in Massachusetts lay more than twelve miles from a railroad: the effects of "the steam train" reached every corner of New England. Towns previously important as stagecoach stops found themselves high and dry, while land values near the railways doubled and tripled. Before long the cost for freighting produce from Vermont to market dropped by three fourths from that of old teaming days.[8] Back-country farming towns, formerly a week distant from market, could now reach potential customers the next day. In the meantime, close-by farmers in Roxbury, the fruit and vegetable town nearest Boston, could get in and out by the new horse car if they wished.

As rails stretched west and south, the entire United States tended to become one vast market. This was a boon for New England manufactures; and since nearly every town, however rural, provided at least some small portion of these, their industries promptly took eager advantage.

Conversely, New England's commercial centers now became wide open to farm products and livestock from every direction, most importantly from the West with its rich virgin soils.

Despite the opening of the Erie Canal in 1825 New England farms had up to this time continued to grow considerable small grain. The Champlain Valley remained a wheat district until the midge appeared. The newly cleared intervales of northern New Hampshire grew wheat and rye for several decades more. Maine, spurred by a wheat bounty offered in 1837 by the state legislature, harvested over a million bushels the next year. Houlton in Aroostook claimed to produce 25 to 40 bushels to the acre.[9]

Western competition did not hit all farms at once. Fenced off as it was by the Berkshires from the Erie Canal, Charles W. Eldridge in 1833 found the alluvial plain of Westfield, Massachusetts, "every inch cultivated" and "groaning under the weight of its rich but honest burden," principally of wheat and rye. East Windsor, Connecticut, produced 70,000 bushels of rye yearly for its distilleries. In Western Massachusetts straw from which the grain had been thrashed had a special market at $5 a ton at the paper mills.[10] At Winchendon in Worcester County a grower who got 31 bushels of wheat to the acre was able to sell his straw to local woodworkers for $20 a ton to pack woodenware in. Straw went also into mattresses, and near ports found use for bedding horses. The manufacture of straw bonnets grew important. Thus industry, if the loss of fertility to the soil is left out of consideration, for a time and in several minor respects was a help to local grain growers.

When, however, the Western Railroad in 1842 extended its track to the Hudson, Erie Canal terminus, western competition doomed any extensive New England wheat growing even more certainly than had the Hessian fly. Flour receipts at Boston increased from 530,000 barrels in 1840 to 761,000 barrels in 1850. By 1860 the amount of wheat produced in New England had sunk to a third of a bushel per capita. Maine's wheat crop dropped by over two thirds during these two decades.

Corn, though importations increased, proved less vulnerable. True, a historian of Plymouth by 1835 could already write that the principal part of the corn and rye and all the flour used there was imported by sea from the southern states or from Boston. At Sturbridge in central Massachusetts the record shows western corn coming in 1844 by railroad. Thoreau found one of his neighbors selling his own corn, and buying the corn from the South, and "shorts" or middlings from the flour mills. Yet between 1840 and 1860 production of corn in every New England state increased. In 1860, though less by a million bushels than that of a decade earlier (the largest crop ever), New England's total yield still went more than two million bushels beyond production of 1840.

It was otherwise with livestock, especially the hog market. Competition from rail shipments rose promptly. The decade previous to 1840 saw annual hog sales at the Brighton market average 22,700 head. By 1849 receipts of western hogs had pushed total sales to 80,120. Moreover, during the cold months bulk pork from interior New York began to arrive by rail. In the following decade, Western pork shipments tripled.[11] Though other factors entered, such rail competition forecast the eventual decay in New England not only of hog growing in quantity but of the cattle fattening that had been so lucrative for many productive corn and pasture areas. It helped to hasten the decline of the sheep industry also.

Yet, notwithstanding all the problems they brought to New England's agriculture, the railroads, as has been suggested, provided at least an equal freight of blessings. New, well-financed corporations were organized to take advantage of great river falls that had been too big to harness. A joint-stock company formed in 1822 dammed the Merrimack at East Chelmsford. In 1831 the Amoskeag Company, with a million dollars capital, threw a granite dam across the river to the north at Manchester in New Hampshire. At both locations the companies laid out new planned towns. For these industries, manufacturing cotton goods, the railroads provided the transportation essential both before and after fabrication. The mills offered employment and regular wages, and thousands of eager country people responded. In 1845 large-scale manufacture of woolens began further down the Merimack where the river plunged again, and the vigorous textile city of Lawrence was born. These tremendous enterprises, at Lowell, Lawrence, Manchester, and elsewhere, unmatched in America up to this time, supplemented earlier but smaller factories at Waltham on the Charles and Pawtucket on the Blackstone, at Fall River, and at other sites which for a considerable time had been making fabrics by machinery.

Textile enterprises were not alone. Metal-working industries grew fast in Connecticut. On mountain streams in the Berkshires water power rolled out paper. In 1848 the white waters of the wide Connecticut were impounded at South Hadley for paper and more textiles, and the town of Holyoke grew beside the great dam. By means of the ever-expanding railways of the nation, the new mills found country-wide markets for their production.

To New England's farms, especially those inland from the sea, such enterprises offered new outlets; customers for food and fiber, with cash incomes, right at home. With regard to the textile factories at Palmer,

18. Family cow and farmer's daughter, York, Maine, 1883. *Society for the Preservation of New England Antiquities.*

Massachusetts, a gazetteer writer in 1846 put it thus: "The farmers are striving to meet the demands of factory villages for their productions. How much better this state of things is, than when they had to lug their beef, pork, butter and cheese to Boston to purchase foreign goods, at a dearer rate than such can now be made at their own doors, and of a better quality."[12]

Effects of the change appeared in countless directions. Water-powered machines, turning out inexpensive cottons and woolens, in a few decades freed farm women from the necessity to spin and weave which for generations had overburdened them. Farm girls, especially from New Hampshire and northeastern Massachusetts, released from home drudgery, thronged to the mills. At Manchester, Lowell, and Lawrence, for the first time in their lives, they could enjoy a reliable cash income. Despite the long factory hours, at a cost of but little more labor and time girls could now afford much better clothes, as well as comforts and luxuries previously out of reach.[13] At the same time, their fathers and brothers at home had found a brand new market not only for food products but for fiber and fuel and timber—one far easier to reach than the West Indies, the British Isles, or the Baltic: organized industry and its employees.

The new factory system might even help in the production of strictly agricultural products. At the nation's cheese capital, Goshen, Connecticut, for instance, Lewis M. Norton put machines to work to turn out factory-pressed cheese. Cream could now be set in Connecticut's machine-made tinware, and milk go to market in machine-rolled cans, while factories made scythes, forks, hoes, and axes better and lighter than any the local blacksmith had been able to turn out.

Still another of the almost countless side effects of the opening of the railroads and the accompanying industrial upsurge was a tremendous increase in the demand for wood for fuel to feed metal forges, railway engines, and furnaces of many sorts. Besides the enormous quantities used by locomotives to make steam, their balloon smokestacks caused fires along the right of way, to destroy more timber. To a farmer with salable wood, however, the advantages of a railroad siding as a market place and the additions to pasture that resulted from his cutting timber outweighed anxiety over future forest cover. Beyond all these factors, he and his family could enjoy the lifting of former rural isolation that attended each rail extension and each developing manufacturing community.

25. The Eager Young

NEW ENGLAND FARMERS in this first half-century might be reputed to be deeply conservative and subject to criticism for backwardness in agricultural practice, yet many, ambitious for their children in particular, placed high value on education. In 1827 the Massachusetts legislature, a majority of its members farmers, decreed that henceforth the public school system was to be supported by public taxation and open to all. Each town of 500 families or more was required to have a high school.

The quality of general education was not high and in some places was called by local observers deplorable. Most conscious of the need for better schools was Horace Mann, a farm-raised boy, in 1837 a lawyer and president of the Massachusetts Senate. He persuaded the legislature to establish the country's first State Education Commission, and the next year abandoned his own prospects for higher office to become the Commission's secretary. Connecticut followed in 1839 with the similar appointment of Henry Barnard. Massachusetts next passed a law requiring at least six months schooling for all, appropriated two million dollars for better school buildings, and at Lexington set up its first normal school to train teachers.

The country schools sorely needed the improvements that Horace Mann and other innovators began. Yet despite the shortcomings of the schools, farm-bred boys and girls, spurred by ambition, were making their mark on the intellectual life of the time. William Cullen Bryant got his love of poetry from his Berkshire-farmer grandfather. In a neighboring hill town Bryant's schoolmate, Charles Dudley Warner, filled his memory with verses and Latin while he milked. At an Amesbury farm fireside John G. Whittier absorbed the history and legends of Indians, Quakers, and Essex County witches. Horace Greeley tells how on the New Hampshire farm and in country schools there and in Vermont, he learned, borrowed books, and laid the foundations for his editorial career. When he came to conduct the Concord School of Philosophy to which flocked that era's eager intellects, Bronson Alcott could look back to inspiration from his boyhood reading on the farm on Spindle Hill in Connecticut. Among Alcott's prized associates at Concord were country-born Henry Thoreau

19. Ancient hay wain, Martha's Vineyard. *Howard S. Russell collection.*

and Edward Everett, the latter's brothers still farming after he himself
had become a leading orator and public figure.

Hawthorne, Salem reared, twice in his "Note-Books" poked fun at the
country graduates of Williams College, "great unpolished bumpkins,
who had grown up farmer-boys"; but that very same year British-born
Captain Frederic Marryat in his diary thought it remarkable how in New
England a farmer with three or four sons would educate one to be a lawyer, another a doctor, a third a minister, while one stayed at home to take
over the farm. "Thus, out of the proceeds of a farm, perhaps not containing fifty acres, all these young men shall be properly educated," and some
started on the road to high position. Emerson in his essay "Self Reliance"
holds up for praise the "sturdy lad from New Hampshire or Vermont,
who teams it, farms it, peddles, keeps a school, preaches, edits a newspaper, goes to Congress, buys a township . . . and always like a cat falls
on his feet." In 1847 Connecticut-born Henry Ward Beecher wrote: "Farmers' sons constitute three-fifths of the educated class."[1]

Nor were country-bred girls less eager. A Connecticut girl, Emma Hart

Willard, pioneered women's education first at Middlebury, Vermont, then in the first woman's institution of college grade, at Troy, New York. Mary Lyon, "born upon a little rockbound farm" in Buckland in the western Massachusetts hills, founded Wheaton Seminary (now College), and in 1838 graduated the first class from what is now Mount Holyoke. Clara Barton's *Story Of My Childhood* warmly pictures the refined farm home at Oxford, Massachusetts, that nourished this teacher and nurse who was to found the Red Cross. Lucy Stone was later to recall in print her family's struggles on the West Brookfield farm that prepared her to fight for woman's rights. "There was a good farmer spoiled," she said, "when I went into reform." At Hatfield in the Connecticut Valley, reading, plus a season at an academy (in many country towns open to girls as well as boys), opened for Sophia Smith a window on life that helped lead later to the bequest of her family fortune to found Smith College.[2]

The village "social libraries" already flourishing continued to grow in numbers and volumes; but an additional concept developed. In 1833 the New Hampshire farming town of Peterborough established the nation's first tax-supported public library, and in the middle of the century Massachusetts authorized tax support for a library by any town. A desire for strictly agricultural information led to organization of agricultural library associations. Deerfield farmers founded one in 1814, a second toward the middle of the century. Oxford, Massachusetts, farmers in 1854 raised $225 for 148 books on farming to be kept at their post office. Winchester, ten miles north of Boston, formed an Agricultural Library Association in 1856. In Vermont, Pomfret's Agricultural Library Association bought a hundred agricultural volumes in 1862. Undoubtedly careful local research would discover plenty of others across New England.

Another popular rural educator was the Lyceum. This type of forum originated in 1826 at Millbury, a farming and manufacturing town in southern Worcester County, and spread rapidly. By 1837 there were said to be 137 in Massachusetts alone. Local orators and pundits "debated everything: huge philosophical questions, trivialities, morals, religion, politics, farming, cattle raising. Excitement often ran high . . ." At Hubbardston debates led to a biweekly paper, *The Winter Wreath*, filled with original compositions by the ladies.[3] Benjamin Silliman, Yale Professor of Agriculture and Natural History, was one popular forum speaker on agricultural topics in the decades before the Civil War. The new scientific interest of the time found in the Lyceum a powerful means of extension.

Agricultural magazines began to appear—and to be read. Besides the *New England Farmer* published in Boston, already mentioned, in 1833 Ezekiel Holmes established the *Maine Farmer*, at first called the *Ken-*

nebec Farmer, an excellent practical journal which enlisted farm support in that growing state and lasted nearly a century. Over in New York State, Jesse Buel from Connecticut founded the widely influential *Cultivator* at Albany in 1834, and published the *Farmer's Companion*, a book that also sold well in New England. A firm of Cambridge nursery and seed men, the Hoveys, in 1835 entered the horticultural field with the *American Gardener's Magazine*. By 1856 the Natick, Massachusetts, postmaster counted 59 copies of the *New England Farmer* and 22 of the *Massachusetts Ploughman* (founded 1841) to be distributed each week. Clarence Danhof estimates that in all New England agricultural publications may have had 50,000 subscribers.[4]

Such publications, however, failed to reach some who needed them most. The *New England Farmer* complained about the prejudice among ordinary farmers against agricultural periodicals. Many felt the methods and "fancy manures" they advocated to be impractical, and disbelieved in "the curculio and other new notions." Horace Greeley looked back late in life from his editorial desk in New York at the small, poor farms of the Scotch in southern New Hampshire and similar farms in Vermont among which he grew up. "I know," he declared, "that I had the stuff in me for an efficient and successful farmer," but "during the whole period, though an eager and omnivorous reader, I never saw a book that treated of Agriculture and the natural sciences . . . never saw even one copy of a periodical devoted mainly to farming; and I doubt that we ever harvested one bounteous crop." Plenty of farm people were readers, however. Lucy Stone's family took the *Massachusetts Spy*, the *Advocate of Moral Reform*, the *Liberator*, and others. Cyrus Hamlin, founder of Robert College at Constantinople, tells of much reading in his farm home. "My father and mother," he comments, "took great pains to keep up Massachusetts culture down in that new settlement in Maine," and despite the hardships in their new surroundings, the results showed in their children.[5]

A movement gathered force, though opposed by some farmers, for educational institutions to teach agricultural subjects specifically. To the two-year-old state of Maine, under the leadership of a prominent citizen, Robert Hallowell Gardiner, goes the honor of having in 1822 incorporated the nation's earliest school for teaching agriculture, chemistry, and the mechanic arts, the Gardiner Lyceum, and for making the earliest public appropriation in aid of agricultural education. The first class entered in 1823.[6]

In Connecticut, always educationally minded, Josiah Holbrook opened an agricultural school at Derby by the Housatonic a year later, but its life was short. In 1833 the Farm School on Thompson's Island in Boston Har-

bor began in a small way a long and useful life, its purpose "to teach indi-
gent city boys mechanic arts and agriculture." The Manual Labor School
at Shelburne Falls, Massachusetts, had "a considerable and valuable
farm."

Connecticut's interest in agricultural study caused Yale College in
1846 to appoint John P. Norton as the country's first professor of agricultural chemistry, and the next year to establish a School of Applied
Chemistry with Professor Benjamin Silliman, Jr., at the head, where agricultural experiments became an important feature. From these came
other advances, and eventually Yale's Sheffield Scientific School.[7]

Many agricultural enthusiasts wanted to go further. In state after state
all through these decades proposals were offered for colleges to be devoted specifically to agricultural subjects. Governor John Ball of New
Hampshire in 1828 even proposed a state experimental farm. There in
1856 Benjamin Thompson of Durham made his will bequeathing his
property to the state for a school of agriculture and mechanic arts, now
the seat of the University of New Hampshire. But despite agitation and
debate real progress had to await the impetus of the Civil War, while the
honor of opening the nation's earliest agricultural colleges went to Michigan and Pennsylvania.

Important influences of this era were the county, state, and local agricultural societies. County societies had sprung up in the early part of the
century under the influence of Elkanah Watson, who in 1811 founded the
Berkshire Agricultural Society. An autumn exhibition followed that drew
thousands. In 1819, Watson persuaded the Massachusetts General Court
to pass a general act for the incorporation of such bodies. The movement
began to gain new impetus later when state legislatures were induced to
appropriate funds to assist in financing such exhibitions, and county
groups bought land for fair grounds. By 1857 there were said to be ninety-
five such societies in New England.[8]

The exhibitions offered country people a chance to show their best
stock, products, and handiwork, and provided a basis for comparison and
competition. There were horse-racing and fun as well. Organization and
management were usually in the hands of the well-to-do and gentlemen
farmers; and they were often among the successful exhibitors and collected a considerable proportion of the prizes. This sometimes led to
disparagement of the shows by ordinary farmers. Yet the opportunity to
observe the best quality available in each phase of agriculture, livestock,
and household manufactures, as well as to hear speakers of national repute, could hardly fail to stimulate new ideas and methods. Full reports in

the local and agricultural press widened the influence of the speakers. State agricultural societies were revived or newly developed. The original Massachusetts Agricultural Society had in 1816 established the Brighton Cattle Fair. During the next decade this brought together yearly several hundred of the best livestock in New England for the edification of thousands of visitors, including Nathaniel Hawthorne. Maine organized a state society in 1818, New Hampshire one in 1849.

Agricultural enthusiasm spilled over into town organizations. Deerfield formed a Farmers Association in 1821; Middletown and West Cornwall, Connecticut, started Farmers Clubs in 1842; Lenox and Stockbridge, Massachusetts, in 1846; Newport and Bethel, Maine, by 1853. Such local groups put on their own educational meetings and shows. The Belmont, Massachusetts, club sponsored a highly successful local strawberry festival.

The new energy influenced state governments, which took steps to examine the resources and needs of their countrysides more carefully. First came geological surveys. Massachusetts opened the field with the nation's first, carried out by Edward Hitchcock. Connecticut followed in 1835 and the other New England states by 1844.[9] Next, Reverend Henry Colman of Deerfield was commissioned by Governor Edward Everett to survey the agriculture of Massachusetts. In 1838 he published the first of four official reports packed with information concerning practices on Massachusetts farms and markets and with suggestions on how they might be improved; two volumes more resulted from his observations of agricultural advances in England and on the Continent. People read and discussed these interesting and informative reports and the questions he raised.

The state agricultural societies (Massachusetts in 1852, and Maine in 1853) were influential in getting official state boards of agriculture appointed, which in turn appointed paid secretaries. The reports of these officials and the proceedings of the Boards, when published, contained authoritative essays and data. Among influential articles were those by Secretary Stephen L. Goodale of Maine on animal breeding, cultivated grasses, sheep, and fertilizers. The Massachusetts reports by Secretary Charles L. Flint on milch cows, dairy farms, and the state's first hundred years of agriculture were also eagerly read.

Destined in their special fields to have great influence on the course of New England agriculture were certain corollary organizations formed in this period. Most influential in their effects were the Massachusetts Horticultural Society, founded in 1829, its smaller sister the Worcester County Horticultural Society, and the Pomological Society of New Haven.

The first two established permanent headquarters, with useful libraries, held public lectures, and frequent exhibitions with awards and prizes. Their efforts stimulated the development of improved fruits and plants. They assisted with imports of nursery stock and seeds from all quarters of the globe, and provided valuable public recognition to local innovators in the fields of fruits, plants, and flowers.

The decades preceding the Civil War saw also the formation of numerous mutual savings banks and fire insurance companies all through the six states. Among their corporators were the more well-to-do farmers. Both banks and insurance companies, organized without capital stock to meet the needs of their communities, were to prove towers of strength during the century that followed. The banks especially helped save rural New England, including its farm people, from the sharpest effects of recurring financial crises.

26. Sheep and Other Livestock

WHEN IN 1811 Consul William Jarvis had sent his purchase of Spanish Merino sheep from dockside to his Weathersfield acres in Vermont he started New England's hill country on a marked change in course. To many farmers it brought profit, even wealth; others it dispossessed. To many an upland community one longtime result was loss of population and a return of the woods.

As the blood of the Merinos and the related Saxony imports spread, the lengthy fleeces of these breeds offered a quality of wool that precisely met the needs of the increasing number of woolen mills, especially those producing high grade yarn and cloth. Thus sheep herding and woolen manufacturing complemented each other. Once the slump that followed the War of 1812 was over, both flourished under increased tariff protection.

When, however, the tariff on the poorer grades was removed and prices dropped, many growers became discouraged. Those near population centers, especially in Maine, eventually turned to the heavier-fleshed English meat breeds to take advantage of the growing city demand for roasts, chops, and spring lamb. The hill country reduced flock numbers for a time, and discouraged farmers left for the West; but the better-founded sheep men soon built up their flocks again and, as prospects improved, added land. A Vermonter sized it up: "As fast as one farmer caught the Western fever, his neighbor would buy him out, and . . . add to his flock of sheep. Thus we were depopulated and the West settled."[1]

With the 1830's, tariff protection had been increased for a time on both wool and woolens. During much of the next two decades long-staple Merinos and Saxonies became highly profitable. They multiplied in the Champlain Valley; in the hill country, too, sheep cropped nutritious mountain grasses from lands cleared to the summits.

Meanwhile skilled breeders were at work. In 1812 Vermont's average fleece had accounted for only 6 percent of the sheep's live weight. By 1844 the proportion of weight in fleece had been boosted to 15 percent, and by the end of the Civil War, in 1865, it reached 21. Though sheep numbers had dropped somewhat by 1850 when the United States published its first agricultural census, Vermont's wool production for the preceding year had been 3,400,717 pounds, almost half that of all New England and one third that of the great Empire State of New York. It was not uncommon in the 1850's for a prize ram to shear 12 pounds of wool, and Brigham rams from Cornwall turned in as much as 20 pounds or more. Vermont's reputation for superior stock brought buyers from all over the country seeking the rams and ewes of its noted breeders. Prices ran into the thousands for the best animals. Vermont sheep went west in great numbers.[2]

In the 1830's New England's three northern states between them could reckon almost three million sheep, and the number increased rapidly. In 1840 in Addison, Vermont's and the country's leading sheep county, there were eleven sheep for every human, or 1,681,000 in all. There beside Lake Champlain the density at one time reached 373 sheep per square mile. The town of Shoreham alone counted 26,584 in 1837 and Salisbury 81,166 in 1850. Springfield, on the opposite side of the state, had 17,872 in 1837.

Southern New England also showed some well populated sheep areas. In 1837 Newport, Rhode Island, had 37,340, and next door Portsmouth just short of 14,000. In 1840 the state of Connecticut counted over 250,000 and Massachusetts toward 400,000, mostly in their western counties, where several towns had 10,000 or more. In New Hampshire, wool shearings passed a million and a quarter pounds in 1840 and remained well over a million through 1860.[3] By contrast, Nantucket, once a big sheep county, was by that date down to 1,200 inferior animals.

At length loss of tariff protection, business depression, and increasing western competition knocked down wool prices. After the tariff changes of 1846, discouraged speculators sold whole flocks to the butcher the next season. Yet skillful selection for heavier fleeces by real sheep men continued. This held the loss of total clip to only 15 percent; and the healthy market for New England's high quality breeding stock lasted for decades after what was dubbed "the sheep mania" had subsided.[4]

Sheep raising might flourish in favorable areas but for the majority of New England farms cattle remained the backbone. The small general farmer pridefully trained and used his yoke or two of oxen, which he might turn into beef after a few seasons' work, or more likely sell to a dealer to fatten. He also kept from three to ten milch cows (the common count in 1840 for Walpole, New Hampshire farmers, for example). Maine's farms in 1860 averaged seven cows each. The usual country cow gave perhaps five to six quarts of milk a day, mostly in warm weather. The surplus beyond family needs was turned into cheese or butter. Many villagers kept their own family cows. In Walpole in 1840 a hundred households had only a cow apiece, and 69 families kept two.[5] Usually such native cattle were descended chiefly from the original red Devon stock, which made excellent draft animals and gave a modest supply of milk.

Within reach of the great cheese market of Goshen, Connecticut, cheese making grew to the point where in 1844 Lewis Norton, of the enterprising cheese family, could open a factory—a new departure. Litchfield County as a whole was making 2¾ million pounds of cheese yearly, and Goshen had become wealthy on it. Here and among the Berkshire valleys of Massachusetts, herds of fifteen to twenty cows were not uncommon, with some larger. Eastern Connecticut was also a prolific cheese area, and in the middle of the century Vermont turned out almost 9 million pounds yearly.[6]

By midcentury competition from Vermont and from western cheese shipped in by rail gradually curtailed Connecticut's market. Next, New England's production, as a whole, instead of increasing from the 27 millions pounds a year in the 1850 census report, dropped below 22 million in 1860, a decrease of toward 20 percent in a single decade. The largest percentage drop occurred for that formerly famous cheese producer, Rhode Island. Still, a lot of cheese continued to be made. In midcentury, for instance, the Berkshire town of Monterey sent 400,000 pounds to market yearly, and 25–30,000 pounds of butter in addition. The nearby mountain town of Sandisfield, where Durham, Ayrshire, and Devon blood had been infused into the native cattle, exported 300,000 pounds of cheese. By 1860 a thousand tons traveled to market over the Vermont and Canada Railway, quadrupling the freight load of 1851. In northern New Hampshire the new and fertile Lancaster area grew prosperous on cheese and butter, and some farmers there were termed rich. Nearer Boston, "Every farm had its cheesepress and every housewife her reputation in Faneuil Hall Market as a dairy woman."[7]

If, in the 1850's, New England dairy women decided to press less cheese, the amount of butter they churned grew by 7½ million pounds—the largest increase, 30 percent, being in Vermont—while Maine's total grew by over one quarter. At the end of the decade Vermont's butter production stood at 15,900,000 pounds, Maine's at 11,687,000, and the New England total almost 51,500,000.[8]

Most country stores took butter in exchange for groceries. It was likely to be heavily salted to make it keep, and of poor quality. Within reach of populated centers a market wagon might make the rounds of the neighborhood collecting butter and cheese, and along with these, poultry and eggs, for which cash returns were made the next week. As early as 1833 a traveler in Connecticut reported a hotel as icing the butter served on the table. By 1854 iced butter cars began to run to Boston by rail from as far as Franklin County in the northwest corner of Vermont. Butter dealers met farmers at the station, where the street would be packed with vehicles.[9] With icing, less salt was needed, and as a result light-salted butter of better quality reached Boston's tables from the three northern states. Another factor contributing to improvement in dairy returns was the practice—reported from Addison County, Vermont, and elsewhere—of growing beets, carrots, and similar roots for stock feed to supplement hay and corn fodder.

Butter and cheese production up to Civil War times was still largely on an individual basis, and usually the province of the women of the household. An Essex County, Massachusetts, farm boy, looking back to this period, wrote: "My mother's department on the farm was the dairy and no person took more pleasure than she in this line of work and the profits were all her own." (Clearly this was a farm more successful than the average.) "We always," he added, "had twelve to fifteen cows and we boys did the milking."[10]

As cities and manufacturing towns swelled in population, they called for more and more fresh milk. Farmers in town or within hauling distance turned from general farming to milk production and built up herd size to as many as 40 or 50 cows. They found it more practical to buy milkers from drovers bringing cattle from up country than to bother with raising calves. When purchased animals passed the stage of profitable milk production, they were sent to Brighton for beef and replaced with fresh milkers. It paid also to feed roots, cottonseed meal, and shorts (a type of milled grain) to supplement hay and pasture, so that the cows might average six quarts of milk daily for the year rather than four or perhaps five like neglected country stock.[11]

Often nearby dairies delivered the milk directly to consumers, but many farmers sold to milk dealers, whose cans the farmer filled and cooled in a well or with ice for delivery the following day. As railroads stretched out, dealers engaged farms at greater distances to supply their needs, at lower prices. The first New Hampshire milk flowed into Boston in 1845. The Fitchburg railway, a little later in the same decade, was daily delivering 14,400 quarts of up-country Massachusetts mik to Boston.[12]

Henry Colman in his *Fourth Report* in 1841 thought a good, nearby retail milk farm "profitable husbandry, where the milk brings 5 cents in summer and 6¼ cents in winter."[13] He had strong doubts, however, about any profit from milk that had to be sold at 3 cents to a milk dealer by a small farmer with only 4 to 6 cows.

Abuses in the cities, such as adulteration, dirt in milk, and the sale of unfit milk from cows fed on distillery slops led Massachusetts in 1856 to pass the nation's earliest pure milk law. Three years later Boston established the country's first systematic milk inspection.[14]

If the sale of fresh milk was to be a farm's objective, it became apparent that more attention needed to be given to selecting cows of superior milking characteristics. Patrick Shirreff, a Scottish farmer, entering New England via the Berkshires in 1833, thought the cattle he saw in the fields there invariably too thin, though at Northampton he met with "some beautiful cows apparently descended from the North Devon breed."[15] The "native" cattle, most of them originally of Devon blood, had remained for generations New England's favorites. But in this first half of the nineteenth century forward-looking stockmen, often wealthy, here and there turned to animals of superior type from abroad. Selected imports: Devons, Herefords, Ayrshires, Alderneys; Shorthorns especially (even Longhorns were brought in), had succeeded and, according to the *Boston Cultivator* in 1848, had been of great advantage. Connecticut's Hurlburt family distributed as many as 1,500 of the progeny of their fine imported Devons.[16] Maine was keen on Devons as well as on the Shorthorns that had begun to arrive in the first quarter century. Two of the first Ayrshire importers were Massachusetts men, and the Massachusetts Society for Promoting Agriculture brought in two valuable Ayrshire bulls.

Connecticut got its first Jersey, or Alderney, from the Channel Islands in 1846; then in Massachusetts Thomas Motley's herd of 25 created a great impression at the 1858 Norfolk County Agricultural Show. Nevertheless, it was said in this decade that the whole number of Jersey cattle in the state was not over 75. Thirty of Maine's first Jerseys were shown at the State Fair in 1860, though only three were known to be in the state five years before.

In 1852 and at intervals in the next decade a Belmont, Massachusetts, farmer and fruit grower, Winthrop W. Chenery, imported Holstein or "Dutch" cattle that proved to be remarkable producers, and began to record them in a herd book.

Despite efforts to improve hog quality and the introduction from England of the Berkshire breed in 1832 and of the Suffolk in 1844, few New England farms bred superior swine or raised hogs in a wholesale way. They were grown chiefly for family and local consumption. On farms that made butter and cheese in quantity, whey, boiled small potatoes, pumpkins, and other farm wastes could be turned into pork advantageously. Swine were useful also in composting peat, sand, seaweed, kelp, and straw into enriching manure. The ratio on dairy farms specifically was one hog to every four cows. One other type of pork production could

20. Thursday was top day at the great Brighton Cattle Market. Ballou's Picto

56).

be made profitable. Near Boston and Providence and in similar situations, garbage collected from city homes, hotels, and markets or refuse from distilleries provided food for hogs by the hundreds, though hog cholera sometimes played havoc. Five hundred to a thousand would be concentrated in some spot to which garbage could be delivered conveniently by road or rail, though this often caused local protests. The manure that resulted went to market gardens to grow vegetables.[17]

One good type of local hog, the Byfield, was developed in Essex County and spread into Rhode Island, but from lack of care in breeding soon ran out. A sea captain sponsored the Mackay breed. A few wealthy men imported Chester Whites, Poland Chinas, and Yorkshires, larger types that would dress five hundred pounds at sixteen months. Competition from the West, however, soon made large-scale production under ordinary farm circumstances uneconomical.[18] Before the railroads came, drovers brought hogs, two hundred or more in a herd, to market over the highways from New York State or even further. A day's journey would be about thirteen miles. The drover would have a dog to help, as Nathaniel Hawthorne recorded in his *Note-Books*, and would peddle some porkers by the way.[19] In 1849 one drover started his herd over the road in Kentucky. Buying and selling as he went, he eventually reached Albany. There he loaded his accumulated swine onto railroad cars and let the engine haul him and his charges the 170 miles to Brighton, where they all landed two months from the beginning.

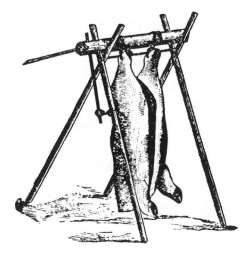

21. A farm family's roast, ham, bacon, salt pork, and lard. *Martin*, Farm Appliances *(1887).*

With the coming of transportation, driving by road gradually ceased. Chilled hog carcasses began to arrive, in winter, from western New York; in 1850 their number reached 37,778. In 1855 a processing plant opened at East Cambridge; it was enormous for that era and for a century was to be an important factor in packing both New England and western pork and dressed meat.

Between 1840 and 1860, however, western competition, plus greater opportunities in other lines, brought about a drop in hog numbers in southern New England of over 40 percent.[20] Maine and Connecticut farms showed the greatest stability. Hogs, except as they long persisted in domestic farm economy and garbage feeding, were never to become a major farm enterprise in New England.

In the three northern states Justin Morgan's progeny more and more made a name for themselves. From the strictly agricultural point of view, to quote a local historian: "Morgan horses were perfectly adapted for working on the small Vermont hill farms and for driving over the hilly roads."[21] They were special favorites of stage drivers. A regiment of British cavalry, sent to Canada in 1837 and there fitted out with Morgans, was so taken with them that it shipped many of its mounts back to England. "Black Hawk," a Morgan, was called by a writer for the *Louisville Journal* "the finest stallion I ever saw."[22] His son, "Ethan Allen," and other Morgan sires became famous. A six-year-old "Black Hawk" colt, accounted not too fast either (though doing a mile easily in three minutes), was reported sold in 1857 to an Illinois buyer for $5,000, to be driven west. Eager purchasers from as far away as California bought Morgan stock and drove or shipped them out. Western Vermont, touched by New York influence, bred Hambletonians also. When the Civil War came, army cavalry buyers almost stripped Vermont of mature horseflesh.

This was a period when county fairs were finding race tracks a popular drawing feature.[23] Increasing public interest in horses resulted in a three-day "First National Exhibition of Horses" at Springfield, Massachusetts, October 19–21 in 1853. The over 400 horses exhibited from eleven states and Canada brought visitors from nearly every state, and the event created a sensation. The exhibit, however, was considered more of a gentleman's than a farmer's affair. Not to be surpassed, the Maine Horse Association in 1860 exhibited a hundred at that state's capital, and Maine continued for some years to be a source of excellent driving horses, Drews, Eatons, and trotters, with Morgan and Messenger blood.[24] But for the long run, horse breeding was not to be New England's forte.

During these decades preceding the Civil War New England began to develop an interest in poultry that went beyond anything found elsewhere on this side of the water. This was in part because its population liked chicken and eggs and offered a good market for them, in part because of its world-wide trading.

Most farms had been in the habit of keeping some geese or turkeys, and a flock of nondescript hens; but as Yankee ships came back from harbors all over the world, their captains and crews, many of them farm-raised, brought home European and Asiatic fowl that caught their fancy. These were bred and cross-bred by the local folks. Poultry fanciers began to mate for special characteristics and to keep distinct the different breeds; though with the wealthier breeders, looks and plumage often counted more than laying records.

Instead of being left to roost haphazardly in barns or trees, as had often been the custom, fowl were now given better quarters, and improved care. "Nailer Tom" Hazard's South County, Rhode Island, diary, on June 3, 1830, records one development that was to be repeated again and again through the succeeding century: "helpt Son Benja. build a Hen House." On the 15th of November: "Glased the Hen House Window." All through the next few years his son Benjamin was carrying eggs to the packet landing to be picked up by the boat for Providence. Daughters, too, had a part. On December 7, 1835, the father records: "The Girls kild 29 Chickens Thay weight 48 lbs. carried them to Rodman's Pier and Sold them for 9 cents a lb."[25]

That the poultry business deserved attention became continually more apparent. In 1848 sales of poultry in Boston's Quincy Market reached a total of $694,483, and for the entire city went beyond a million dollars. The Market also handled well over a million dozen eggs that year at prices of from 11½ to 30 cents a dozen. From Maine, the Penobscot and Kennebec steamers were bringing to Boston $340,000 worth of eggs yearly. Three of the city's hotels alone used 200 dozen eggs a day. Even London steamers, after the Cunards in 1840 had established regular service, might take eggs on board for Great Britain.[26]

An incubator exhibited on School Street, Boston, in 1846 "delighted" the *New England Farmer*, but it would be another twenty or more years before use of these became practical. Meanwhile, farmers were experimenting on how best to feed birds. Besides providing corn from the fields, wastes from the kitchen, and pickings from the barnyard, we learn from Henry Thoreau's journal in 1851 that: "in Concord . . . they chop up young calves and give them to hens to make them lay, it being considered the cheapest and most profitable food for them."[27]

Many a farm still kept geese and turkeys. Deacon Jewett of Rowley, Massachusetts, on January 11, 1833, entered in his diary: "Kill & dress 8 turkies. I go to Ipswich P.M. Carry turkies 54 lbs. sold them for 10 per lb 5.40." At times thousands of turkeys were driven to market from the north over the turnpikes, their feet sometimes coated with tar to stand the long journey.[28] The German farmers at Waldoboro, Maine, raised peacocks.

Interest in poultry reached a peak in 1849 with a proposal from the editor of the *Boston Cultivator* and *Massachusetts Ploughman* for a convention of domestic fowl breeders and fowl fanciers. The response to this proposal surprised everyone. On November 15 and 16, 1849, the convention became a reality. In a marquee on Boston's new Public Garden, fowl fanciers exhibited 1,423 birds in 219 cages. The event attracted the unheard-of total of over 10,000 people (some said 20,000).

Meantime down at Little Compton, Rhode Island, on the east shore of Narragansett Bay, two farmer marketmen, William Tripp, and a neighbor, John Macomber from across the Massachusetts line in Westport, teamed up. About 1854 they cross-bred certain of their best birds, good layers but meaty also, of Shanghai and Cochin-China blood. Within a dozen years the strain produced more and larger eggs, yet at the same time fowl whose carcasses dressed well. Though for the present, only the customers of Tripp and Macomber and neighboring poultry keepers were impressed, their selections for cross-breeding became the foundation for New England's second noted strain of poultry, the Rhode Island Red.[29]

27. Backbone Crops and New Departures

For generations, to carry stock through the long winters, New England farmers had depended on hay, though corn fodder, now frequently cured in shocks, was a useful supplement. It had been considered good cultivation practice to plant crops for three years running and follow them with three years in herdsgrass and clover sod. With the common tendency to delay replowing, however, the period in hay might stretch on and on. Clover would disappear, weeds creep in, and land that cut two tons or more at the beginning would at length cease to yield enough to pay for cutting.

Pastures had often been neglected. Brush might be cut occasionally but that was all. The herbage would eventually become so slim that a report to the North Middlesex Agricultural Society in 1855 lamented: "Very few animals are now pastured in this section that do not find it necessary to labor as hard and as many hours per day . . . as do the farmers who own them."[1] To secure nutritious summer grazing, Massachusetts cattlemen often drove their dry stock to verdant mountain pastures in New Hampshire and Vermont. For hay, salt marshes remained a valuable asset to shore towns, while fresh marshes along the rivers were still a resource inland. Some diking was done to turn salt into fresh meadow. The better farmers manured, plowed, and reseeded their hayfields in regular rotation. Here and there hillside hayland got irrigation by cross channels gently sloping from a spring or brook above. Leading grasses cultivated for English hay continued to be herdsgrass, red clover, and redtop.

City dray and driving horses and work oxen offered farmers within hauling distance by wagon or by sea a cash market for their hay. Ipswich "green" hay topped the Boston market. Hay prices rose during the 1830's; and between 1840 and 1860 hay production in the six states increased one fourth. In the decade of 1850–60 its value rose in every New England state. The biggest jump was in Maine, from whose fresh fields farmers shipped hay to Boston in large quantities for sale. A report in 1857 warned them that many were exhausting their land by the practice. Yet it continued.[2]

Indian corn was always by far the leading grain, and frequently got the bulk of the farm's manure. As horse cultivators came more into use, level culture for corn began to replace hilling. With good care the average crop was around thirty bushels per acre. Fertile Connecticut Valley soils sometimes yielded seventy bushels year after year; and crops well over a hundred bushels on specially treated fields were by no means unknown. New Hampshire in particular reported high yields. Since early in the century separate corn-cribs had become customary farm buildings to store the ears. Jesse Buel's *Farmer's Companion* in 1839 urged leaving the entire cornstalk on the hill until fall, rather than topping above the ear to make the grain mature. At harvest the corn, stalk and all, was to be cut and allowed to cure in stooks (standing bundles). After husking, the stalk and leaves remained for winter fodder.

Importation of grain went on by the millions of bushels, not only through the ports but over the rails, to be unloaded at mills in towns well in the interior. Nevertheless, the harvest of New England's superior hard flint corn continued to grow through 1850, when the six states reported a crop of over ten million bushels. The 1860 census, however, showed a decrease in all except Connecticut. Yet Eastham, though on sandy Cape Cod, in 1860 raised enough for its own needs and exported 3,000 bushels besides.[3] Corn dishes were a cook's standby for farmers everywhere. Beyond that, the rest went to feed the livestock or was sold. Some farmers sold their own corn, then bought imported grain at a lower price and had it ground to feed to their animals.

In contrast, wheat growing was in decline. The wheat midge, which arrived in the 1830's, made serious inroads. Yet despite a heavy drop in production in most places, northern New Hampshire and Vermont and interior Maine did well with wheat long after it had ceased to be of importance in southern New England. Upland valleys were green with wheat up to Civil War days and beyond. The finest wheat farms in New England, it was said, were to be found in the White Mountains.[4]

Rye held its own at about a million and a half bushels yearly, with Connecticut the largest producer. The growing of oats increased as farmers and draymen turned more and more to horses. New England's production expanded from 8,101,268 bushels in the 1850 census to 10,885,267 a decade later. Peas were a favorite companion crop. Perhaps a liking for oatmeal, developed from the admixture of Scots in parts of New England, also had an influence. In Barnet, Vermont, where Scots were strong, an 1838 diarist, sifting the meal from 57 bushels that the mill had ground for him, wrote: "Oatmeal constitutes one-fourth of the breadstuffs of this

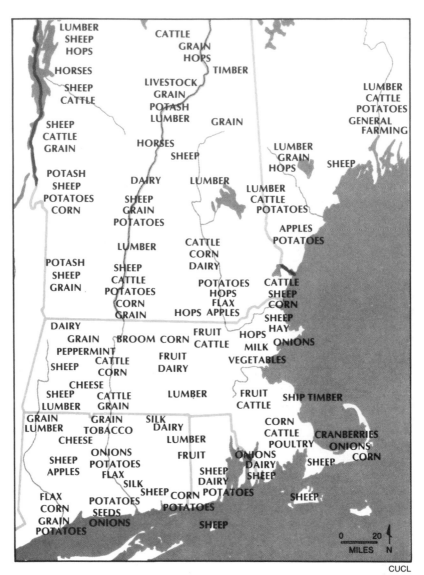

LUMBER
SHEEP
HOPS
HORSES
SHEEP
CATTLE
SHEEP
CATTLE
GRAIN
POTASH
SHEEP
POTATOES
CORN
POTASH
SHEEP
GRAIN
DAIRY
GRAIN
PEPPERMINT
SHEEP
CHEESE
SHEEP
LUMBER
GRAIN
LUMBER
SHEEP
APPLES
FLAX
CORN
GRAIN
POTATOES

CATTLE
GRAIN
HOPS
TIMBER
LIVESTOCK
GRAIN
POTASH
LUMBER   GRAIN
HORSES
SHEEP
DAIRY   LUMBER
SHEEP
GRAIN
POTATOES
LUMBER   CATTLE
CORN
SHEEP   DAIRY
CATTLE
POTATOES
CORN
GRAIN   HOPS APPLES
BROOM CORN   FRUIT
CATTLE   FRUIT
CORN   DAIRY
CATTLE   LUMBER
GRAIN
GRAIN   SILK
TOBACCO   DAIRY
CHEESE   LUMBER
ONIONS   FRUIT
POTATOES
FLAX   SHEEP
SILK   DAIRY
SHEEP CORN POTATOES
POTATOES   POTATOES
SEEDS
ONIONS   SHEEP

LUMBER
GRAIN
HOPS   SHEEP
LUMBER
GRAIN
HOPS
LUMBER
CATTLE
POTATOES
APPLES
POTATOES
POTATOES   CATTLE
HOPS   SHEEP
FLAX   CORN
SHEEP
HOPS   HAY
MILK   ONIONS
VEGETABLES
FRUIT   SHIP TIMBER
CATTLE
CORN
CATTLE   CRANBERRIES
POULTRY   ONIONS
ONIONS   CORN
DAIRY   SHEEP
SHEEP
SHEEP

LUMBER
CATTLE
POTATOES
GENERAL
FARMING

0   20
MILES   N

CUCL

22. The principal farm productions, by area, 1800–60. *Cartography Laboratory, Clark University.*

town."[5] Buckwheat was a useful cash crop, blossoming promptly to furnish food for bees, then grain for poultry. It was popular only in a few places. Norwich, Vermont, in the Connecticut Valley, for example, in the 1840 census reported a harvest of 11,119 bushels of corn, 20,727 of oats, and 11,182 of buckwheat. Down river, Amherst, Massachusetts, busy with brooms, tobacco, and dairying, five years later reported 18,930 bushels of corn but only 500 of buckwheat; and of wheat, rye, and oats a little less than 16,000 bushels. Added to its small grains, however, was an item of 4,526 bushels of broomcorn seed. By contrast, in the 1850 census Rochester, a large town in southeast New Hampshire, grew of small grain altogether only 4,000 bushels, while Indian corn totaled nearly 14,000. Back on the Connecticut River but on the opposite side from Norwich, as late as 1872 Walpole, New Hampshire, was topping its huge total of 38,000 bushels of corn with 33,000 bushels of barley. This variation in small grain was to be found within a circuit of seventy-five miles![6]

Potatoes were a crop on nearly every farm, large or small. Like corn, the potato was a standby in the kitchen and good food for stock as well. From one to four acres was a common planting, but many farms grew up to a dozen acres for sale or export.

Potatoes for the South, according to James G. Bonner, writing on southern agriculture up to 1850, came almost wholly from New England. Connecticut's Greenwich area, growing 200 bushels to the acre, sent heavy shipments by water to New York. Smithfield and Johnston, towns in Rhode Island, were also among substantial exporters. Massachusetts, with a population by 1850 of almost a million, was growing three and a half million bushels for its own use and export. In all these states, towns near the shore, by fertilizing with fish, kelp, and rockweed, had excellent yields.[7]

In Maine, when wheat became unreliable, farmers turned to potatoes, often getting 250 bushels to the acre. A single year's production from the Kennebec Valley alone might reach a half million bushels. Where markets were too distant, newly built starch factories, opened in the 1840's, took up the slack, though at low prices. Starch was easily transported. It had only one tenth the bulk of whole potatoes and was salable both in textile cities and for export. In northern Maine Houlton already knew that it could grow potatoes; but to produce in quantity, Aroostook had to wait for rail transportation.[8]

Northern New Hampshire was making starch on a considerable scale. Some Vermont towns made starch, others turned potatoes into whiskey, which was salable and easily transported. Across the line in Massachusetts the town of Rowe in the Berkshires also had a potato still.[9] Near good markets, however, most potatoes were sold for food.

In all the northern states new land produced bountiful potato crops. On the wide Keene, New Hampshire, plain, yields in the century's first third were said often to reach 400 bushels per acre—in White Mountain valleys in the 1850's, 500 to 600. On older land, manure, muck, and turned-over sod helped production. In any case well-populated New England harvested double the amount per inhabitant that was grown by the country as a whole. There were, however, wide variations. Norwich, Vermont, in 1850 harvested 53,480 bushels; yet only 90 miles south in the same rich Connecticut Valley and but five years later, Amherst, Massachusetts, grew a mere 1,691.[10] All through the middle decades a substantial factor in demand was the tremendous immigration of Irish to the mill towns of southern New England.

During the 1840 decade an unwelcome disease brought calamity, destroying whole crops either in the ground or after they were dug. Blight of some sort was not an altogether new phenomenon; it was said to have been reported several times, beginning in 1770, and control had been sought by reverting to the planting of potato seed balls. Now, in many sections, especially from 1843 to 1845, the effects of an imported disease, late blight, were disastrous. From over 35 million bushels in 1839 New England's production dropped by 40 percent in that decade. In Massachusetts the legislature offered $10,000 for a remedy. The only New England areas wholly to escape the blight appear to have been Martha's Vineyard and Nantucket.[11]

Recovery brought total production back to 21 million bushels in time for the 1860 census report. Maine's crop alone the previous year was 6,384,317 bushels, two thirds of the 1839 crop, yet its production nearly equaled that of the whole eleven states of the South and was almost double the amount reported in 1850.[12]

Among varieties grown about 1840, Henry Colman lists for Essex County, Massachusetts: English Whites, a round sort; Biscuits, round, with a rough skin but mealy and productive; La Plata, a long red; Chenango and Mercer, or Pennsylvania Blue, early and heavy producers which Clarence Day calls special favorites in Maine. There were half a dozen other sorts. The blight, however, was to cause radical changes in varieties planted.[13]

To a Vermonter, Albert Bresee of Hubbardton, is accorded the credit for developing a promising new variety, Early Rose. Its fame began about 1860, and shortly it became the leading American potato. Its ancestor was said to be Garnet Chili, one of thousands of seedlings grown from

South American stocks by Reverend Chauncey Goodrich of Utica, New York. By selection and propagation Bresee fixed the type of his stock until, after the end of the Civil War, it was ready for introduction.[14]

Through the country's early years cider had continued to be a major product of New England apple orchards. As one instance, Hartford, Vermont, farmers worked together in a cider club, making twenty-four barrels average per member. However, the temperance crusade of the century's second quarter dealt a blow to old-fashioned, nondescript apple orchards. Yet long after rum and brandy fell into disfavor, cider drinking hung on in country towns. By 1840, nevertheless, many plantings started for cider had been cut down or abandoned. Good Baldwins, Greenings, Russets, and Pearmains continued to sell, and alert apple men top-grafted scions of these varieties on their ordinary trees, or, as Henry Thoreau noted, set new orchards in fenced plots. Baldwins especially were market favorites, but trees of this variety suffered severely in the hard winter of 1833–34 and were hurt again by cold in the 1850's.

In addition to the domestic market, apples went in coastwise vessels to Atlantic ports as far south as Mobile, as well as to the West Indies. Thousands of bushels also crossed to England, 120,000 from Boston alone in 1858–59. Iced, they were delivered to Calcutta.[15] In this period Massachusetts added the Sutton Beauty to the list of excellent varieties originated in New England, and at about the same time the Northern Spy was introduced from New York. Another fruit popular with apple growers and home gardeners alike was the quince, valuable for jelly.

Pear orchards were favorite projects both for gentlemen with estates in Roxbury and Dorchester (1,200 varieties on one such, it was said), and with ordinary farmers and householders. This fruit sold well in the markets. Farmers in the town of Lincoln, north of Boston, clothed their hillsides with peach trees, and did very well financially. The value of Massachusetts' fruit crop tripled in the quarter-century ending in 1860.[16]

Experiments with small fruits resulted at Lynn in the first domesticated native gooseberry variety; and in cultivated blackberry varieties at Beverly and Dorchester. At Concord, Ephraim Bull, after years of patient experiment, in 1843 selected a seedling grape destined to become the most famous, popular, and useful of American grapes. He received the Massachusetts Horticultural Society's gold medal, and named the grape for his town.[17]

Demand for strawberries increased. To meet it, in 1838 the Hovey firm of nursery seedsmen in Cambridge introduced the first really successful American variety, the Hovey. The popular Wilson followed in 1853. Market gardeners began to grow berries in quantity; they even forced them under glass hotbed sash. Such early berries sold at sensational prices. From their field beds gardeners picked up to 4,000 quarts to the acre. The Farmers' Club of Belmont, Massachusetts, a market garden and fruit town, in 1859 invited the public to the first of what were to become innumerable strawberry festivals.[18] With rail transportation, specialization in early berries developed at Dighton, Massachusetts, near Providence, and at Concord. The railroad's coming forecast eventual trouble for local growers, however. Already a Connecticut farmer was at work in Alabama adapting strawberry growing to southern conditions.

On Cape Cod and in Plymouth County increasing interest in cranberries led in 1843 to the selection and propagation of the valuable Howes variety. Next came the Early Black by Cyrus Cahoon in 1847. As sales increased, towns had to adopt local bylaws for the preservation of the wild vines.[19]

The great bulk of the crop still came from the large natural meadows of the inland counties. A single bog of 25 acres in Franklin, Norfolk County, Massachusetts, was reported to yield 1,050 barrels in 1863. This was at a time when Harwich, with 2,697 barrels, was the only Cape Cod town picking more than a thousand barrels. A traveler to Portland, Maine, in October 1857 tells of a drained pond bed at Cape Elizabeth, bigger, he said, than Boston Common, with 50 to 60 pickers at work, and an expected crop of four to five hundred bushels. The owners of such natural bogs did very well financially.[20]

As population doubled, both in New England's cities and centers of manufacture and in the Atlantic states generally, much of the growth was in the families of workers receiving cash wages and those of businessmen active in trade and industry. They bought increasing quantities of vegetables of all kinds, and New England farms began to raise more, both of old staples and of novel sorts that grew popular.

By 1840 farmers in the Bristol area of Rhode Island, Wethersfield and Fairfield in Connecticut, and Barnstable and Danvers in Massachusetts were deep in onion growing. Their crops went to New York, Boston, and more distant markets. At Barrington and Warren, Rhode Island, about 1839, good growers working heavily manured land were producing 600 to 800 bushels per acre of onions, and of carrots up to a thousand bushels. Nearby Bristol grew not only these crops but rutabaga turnips as well. From Wethersfield, Connecticut, the South was said to get three fourths of all its onions. The cargo of a single outbound coaster that struck a Connecticut reef contained 65,000 ropes (about 4,000 bushels). Southport, in the town of Fairfield, had for years grown some onions for export.

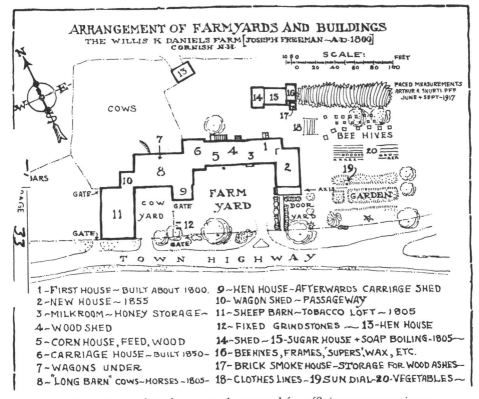

ARRANGEMENT OF FARMYARDS AND BUILDINGS
THE WILLIS K DANIELS FARM [JOSEPH FREEMAN~A.D.1800]
CORNISH N.H.

SCALE:

PACED MEASUREMENTS
ARTHUR A SKURTLEFF
JUNE + SEPT~1917

COWS

BEE HIVES

FARM
YARD

GARDEN

TOWN HIGHWAY

1~FIRST HOUSE~ BUILT ABOUT 1800.   9~HEN HOUSE~AFTERWARDS CARRIAGE SHED
2~NEW HOUSE~1855   10~WAGON SHED~PASSAGEWAY
3~MILKROOM~HONEY STORAGE~   11~SHEEP BARN~TOBACCO LOFT~1805
4~WOOD SHED   12~FIXED GRINDSTONES ~ 13~HEN HOUSE
5~CORN HOUSE, FEED, WOOD   14~SHED~ 15~SUGAR HOUSE + SOAP BOILING~1805~
6~CARRIAGE HOUSE~BUILT 1850~   16~BEEHIVES,FRAMES,'SUPERS'WAX, ETC.
7~WAGONS UNDER   17~BRICK SMOKE HOUSE~STORAGE FOR WOOD ASHES~
8~"LONG BARN" COWS~HORSES~1805~   18~CLOTHES LINES~19 SUN DIAL~20~VEGETABLES~

23. A New Hampshire homestead arranged for efficiency, convenience, and comfort, winter and summer. *Landscape Architecture (1917).*

Now it increased its plantings to become for the next four decades, with its red, yellow, and white Globes, an important factor in the New York market. During the 1840's, the crop at Danvers, near Salem, increased from 25,000 bushels in 1838 to 120,000 in 1848. Despite the destructive onion maggot, this one town grew 200 acres in 1857, though producing only 300 to 400 bushels per acre. The crop for all Essex County was estimated to be worth several hundred thousand dollars annually.[21]

A demand for fresh produce had encouraged wide-awake farmers near the larger cities, particularly Boston, to grow a variety of vegetables. In addition, they extended the natural season at both ends. In early spring they used glass sash laid across plank frames. These were heated from beneath, at night and when sunlight failed, by fermenting horse manure. From those hotbeds they marketed radishes, lettuce, cucumbers, and

24. Boston's Faneuil Hall (or Quincy) Market, heart of New England meat and produce trade. Ballou's Pictorial *(1856–60)*.

melons months ahead of the outdoor season. In the fall, with underground pits and tight storages, they stored cabbages, squashes, potatoes, and all sorts of root vegetables far into winter and even the following spring. The pioneer Boston "market-gardeners," as this type of grower had also been called in England, were located in adjoining Brookline, Roxbury, and Jamaica Plain. These towns, all in the area called by geologists the Boston Basin, enjoyed a frost-free season longer by a month than most of Massachusetts. Garden-farmers vied to be first in the market with green peas for June 17, Bunker Hill Day. They sprouted potato sections under glass and as soon as they dared set the started sections on warm south slopes so as to market new potatoes by July 1.[22]

For early spring transplanting outdoors, in late winter they sowed seeds of many vegetables under sash. A few gardeners experimented with greenhouses. By starting early and by companion-cropping of quick- with slow-growing vegetables, enterprising gardeners hustled two to four crops a season off each highly tilled and fertilized acre.[23] Most of this produce finally landed in South Market Street, beside Boston's imposing new Quincy Market. It was 535 feet long, all of granite, dedicated in

1826. "I know none that can equal it in any part of the world except one at Liverpool," wrote Henry Tudor, an English visitor. The open-air farmers' market, alongside, was entirely wholesale. It began its trade long before dawn. Later in the day the building's long corridor welcomed society matrons, hotel chefs, and ordinary householders to fill their needs from stalls full of choice meats, fowl, and fish as well as fruits and vegetables.[24]

Before the middle of the century, the city's growth had already turned some close-in market gardens into house lots. Growers then pushed farther out into Watertown, Newton, Arlington, and similar towns favored with the same long season. By ditching and heavy manuring, sometimes with seaweed to help, they turned poor, light sands and blueberry swamps into black loam on which to grow tennisball lettuce, white-stalked celery, and a dozen other vegetables, not only for Boston and New England's smaller cities but for New York.

Market gardens spread in a similar way in Rhode Island about Providence—where the great Budlong farm started business at Eden Park in 1854—and about Hartford and New Haven in Connecticut. By the

25. The Boston hotbed: lettuce, radishes, even strawberries in March. Skilled market gardeners grew them in these beds, often hundreds of feet long, sheltered by tall fences, and kept warm at night by hot horse manure underneath and straw mats above the sash. New England Farmer (1853).

1850's Cape Elizabeth, close by Portland, Maine, was becoming a vegetable center. The 1860 census valued New England's market garden produce at over two million dollars, two thirds of it from Massachusetts. A Boston wholesale market report in February 1852 listed midwinter prices for nineteen different vegetables, including glass-grown lettuce and radishes.[25]

By that time new crops such as rhubarb and dandelions were well established in popular taste. Tomatoes had grown in favor for twenty years and sold in large quantities. Lima and sieva beans had been among the century's early arrivals. They are mentioned in the diary of Benjamin Goddard, a Brookline gardener, in 1812.

About 1835 John M. Ives of Salem introduced the Boston Marrow squash, said to have originated among New York State Indians. A decade later J. J. H. Gregory, Marblehead seedsman, brought out the Hubbard, which, he said, had been grown in a Marblehead garden since the end of the previous century. For at least the next century these two were to remain among New England's favorite winter vegetables. Improvements were taking place in sweet corn, another vegetable destined to become highly popular on New England tables and elsewhere. In 1839 Noyes Darling of New Haven crossed "sweet sugar corn," of the type that Captain Bagnall had brought from western New York in Revolutionary times, with white flint corn. The result, after selection, was "Darling's Early." This, the first variety specifically named, soon became popular. A decade later another New England variety appeared, "Old Colony," a cross with a dent corn. It was larger and held its sweet taste longer. A still better corn, "Crosby's Early," was the selection of an Arlington, Massachusetts, market gardener. This was destined to become for a half century the favorite both of vegetable consumers and of corn canners.[26] All these varieties had white kernels.

Increases in the production of vegetables and of flowers as well created a demand for reliable seed. The nine Shaker colonies in New England continued to grow excellent seeds of both types, which they distributed in packets by wagon and through country stores.[27] James L. Belden, the Wethersfield, Connecticut, seedsman, in 1838 sold his business to Frank G. Comstock. The new proprietor began to decorate his packets with pictures of the hoped-for vegetables and flowers, a practice that seedsmen everywhere were prompt to take up. With his partner, Henry Ferré, Comstock sent seed wagons all through New England and into the Provinces. (This firm still publishes its annual catalogue.)[28] B. K. Bliss & Sons of Springfield, Massachusetts, are said to have published in 1853 the country's first catalogue illustrated with colored plates, and to have intro-

duced the seed trade's mail order practice. By 1850 Connecticut contained at least ten seed farms; with neighoring New York it produced
more seed for sale than all the rest of the United States.[29] About 1857
E. B. Clark of Milford, Connecticut, began to make sweet-corn seed his
specialty. Several other growers entered this field, and corn seed became
for years a valuable Connecticut product.

Though New England's soils have often been dismissed as inferior,
their special qualities together with certain aspects of the region's climate have been determining factors in the flavor and crispness of apples,
cranberries, and other fruits. Among field crops, and with cigar tobacco
in particular, such local characteristics have had potent influence.

Southern New England had grown and sold tobacco from the beginning, but in the early nineteenth century Connecticut increased its
plantings. About 1833 a grower at East Windsor brought in seed of the
delicate-leaved Maryland Broadleaf. The variety did well, and acreage
spread. In a shipment of leaf to Germany it was discovered that sweating
in transit greatly improved its flavor and quality, making it of exceptional
value as a binder for the outer layers of cigars. Taking this as a cue, growers dropped production of chewing and pipe-smoking varieties and began
to concentrate on this type of cigar tobacco, which by selection came to
be called Connecticut Broadleaf.[30]

The census of 1840 put Connecticut's tobacco crop at 471,000 pounds.
Another source, an actual survey, put that of Hartford County alone at
417,380 pounds.[31] At the 1850 census the Connecticut crop had risen to
1,267,624 pounds, and cultivation had spread into the Housatonic Valley.
By 1860 the total was just over 6,000,000 pounds. Further north, Massachusetts farmers in Hatfield and Whately, near Northampton, in place
of their former modest plots began to set substantial acreages. The
enthusiasm spread to Hadley, Amherst, and Granby. At Westfield two
growers experimented successfully with another type, Havana Seed, destined to become the favorite variety for the upper Connecticut Valley.
From 138,000 pounds in 1830, Massachusetts' harvest bounded up to
3,233,198 in 1860.

Prices paid by New York buyers varied widely from year to year, but on
light soils suited to producing high grade leaf the returns to skilled growers were sometimes remarkable. This crop was not one for slovens, however. Its requirements were strict: early sowing in a seed bed, transplanting to the field, good manuring, careful cultivation, keeping the soil clear
of weeds, continual expert attention to the curing process.

Details, especially fertilization, had a bearing on a crop's success. East

Windsor, where Broadleaf got its start, was the seat of a number of distilleries. As a sideline, it will be recalled, distilleries kept large herds of hogs to profit from the grain waste. Their manure became an important factor in successful tobacco growing in the vicinity. Further up the Valley it was fertilizing the fields, with the manure of sheep that on some tobacco farms added special quality to the local leaf. Farmers kept flocks of sheep or herds of cattle as much to benefit their tobacco crop as for the fleeces, milk, or meat that their stock provided. One consequence was that in order to feed the stock additional rough land had to be cleared of trees and sown to hay or used as pasture. Moreover, it was not tobacco alone that benefited from the liberal use of manure; subsequent crops grew bountifully.[32] Tobacco growing had effects on the general community also. By 1856 local cigar factories were employing 400 men and 200 women. The returns from this crop added to that air of comfort, even opulence, that visitors frequently noticed in Connecticut Valley farming towns. Eventually some modest fortunes built on tobacco growing went to the endowment of local schools, colleges, hospitals, and libraries.

For one group of Massachusetts towns in the Connecticut Valley, broomcorn continued during these decades to be largely the farmer's "money crop" to buy necessaries not readily bartered for with other farm produce. In 1845 Hadley reported a half-million pounds of broombrush and made almost 600,000 brooms. By 1850 with adjoining towns it had an output of 770,000 brooms and 70,000 brushes, with 41 shops doing the manufacturing. Ashfield, Goshen, and neighboring hill towns supplied wood handles for the brooms. Five years later Massachusetts' broomcorn crop was valued at $187,000, about equal to its onion crop and exceeding the worth of its wool clip by over $30,000.[33] There were other income producers, though less important. The center of production had already moved west, but in the Berkshire Hills a few farms still found peppermint, spearmint, and other oil-bearing and scented plants worth growing or collecting for essences. The expansion of woolen manufacture to large proportions created a ready market for teasels, the rough flower heads of a tall plant. When dried, they were employed to raise the nap on the cloth. New England's 1835 crop of teasel heads was 30 million, almost three fourths of the nation's production. At about that period Concord farmers in Massachusetts alone grew 880,000.

The effects of textile manufacture became evident in other directions. Flax growing for home use was on a steep downgrade. A linen mill with up-to-date machinery opened in Andover, Massachusetts, in 1836, an-

Brooks' Patent Silk Spinning Machine.

Brooks's silk spinning and reeling machine, which was invented by himself, is found to be a very simple and easy operating machine, and yet one of the most perfect that has been invented for the purpose of reeling and twisting silk from the cocoons, and manufacturing it into sewing silk. By the different arrangements of this machine, it will operate upon a single or double thread, as may be required, and prepare it for twisting or weaving. Experience has fully proved that by uniting the filaments of silk as they are drawn from the cocoons, wet in their natural glutinous substance before they are dry, the thread is more firm, smooth and stronger ; from the simplicity of the machine, and the very easy way in which it is used, brings it within the comprehension and capacity of any person to use it. Mr Brooks has received a premium for his invention, from several societies, and of late, a premium and medal from the Scott's legacy, in Philadelphia.

26. Connecticut led the nation in mulberry trees and in silk production from cocoons grown by worms that had been fed on their leaves. *Newell,* Catalogue *(1836).*

other in Dudley in 1840, and one of 10,500 spindles at Fall River in 1852, to make linens by machinery. By 1860 local cultivation and household spinning of flax had nearly disappeared before the influx of inexpensive cotton goods from Pawtucket, Lowell, and Manchester. Farm people had little regret, however, at dropping the hard, dirty work of retting and swingling flax, or the monotonous grind of spinning and weaving that occupied every spare moment of the household.

Hops remained for some decades an important crop, especially in Middlesex County, Massachusetts, said to grow more than any similar area in the United States. In adjacent New Hampshire in the 1830's, Bedford in the Merrimack Valley was said to be the largest hop-growing town in New England. In the Connecticut Valley, Northfield, which began to raise the crop in 1833, was credited with nearly $30,000 worth in 1855; and in 1858 hopyards in Vermont's three northern counties produced 121,512 pounds, worth nearly as many dollars. The price, though high at times, was extremely volatile, and the crop was thought to rob the soil and absorb the bulk of a farm's manure, to the detriment of all else.[34]

By the second quarter of the nineteenth century the interest in producing silk from cocoons spun by worms fed on mulberry leaves, begun in the eighteenth century, had increased remarkably. The Cheney brothers in South Manchester, Connecticut, William G. Comstock in Wethersfield, and Samuel Whitmarsh in Northampton, Massachusetts, were among the leaders in the movement. The Connecticut Valley, even as far up as New Hampshire and Vermont, was the area where enthusiasm became most intense, though the rest of New England shared the excitement. Connecticut, Massachusetts, Vermont, and Maine all offered bounties for silk production. (New Hampshire and Rhode Island refused.) Massachusetts published J. H. Cobb's *Manual . . . Respecting Growth of the Mulberry Tree, With Suitable Directions for the Culture of Silk.* Several states started silk societies. The federal government printed 6,000 copies of a *Manual of Silk Culture* to forward the movement. Special magazines whipped up what became a speculative mania.

One Wethersfield nurseryman grew mulberry trees in Cuba and shipped them home for sale. A Northampton stand was said to cover 500 acres: a Providence company grew 30,000 trees. Some nurserymen became rich. Householders filled their backyards. Plantings of a thousand were common; one of 6,500 trees is recorded as far north as Walpole, another of two acres in Sanbornton, New Hampshire. In Springfield, Vermont, enough were set to produce in one season a half ton of cocoons.[35]

Connecticut and Massachusetts were by far the greatest centers of interest. By 1825 the Mansfield area of Windham County had produced an estimated three to four tons, and its crop reached five tons in 1834. Its 1829 production was valued at $25,000. Silk was regularly accepted at stores in exchange for purchases or paid for in cash. Growing cocoons and spinning silk did not interfere with regular farm work, and it brought extra income.

The banking crisis of 1837 dampened the speculative fever. Terrible storms occurred in 1839, and the hard winter that followed killed thousands of mulberry trees. In the next year, 1840, to add discouragement, a mulberry blight set in and the boom faded. Still, on March 20, 1843, a grower in Vermont could record in his diary: "Bot 18¾ gallons of molasses of Mr. Willey [of Saxton's River] and paid him 300 skeins of silk."[36] Even a century later mulberry trees were occasionally to be found as reminders in city back yards and in country towns.

By far the most enduring result was that even though the mulberry boom soon faded, Manchester, Connecticut, and Northampton, Massachusetts, by importing raw materials, remained prosperous for a century as two of the three centers of silk manufacture for the United States. Manchester's large, successful mills were developed by able enterprising young local farmers and silk growers. Enough had been done also to prove that with due precautions raw silk production could be carried on as far north as Boston, should economic conditions ever warrant it.[37]

28. Marketing the Woods

THE HARVESTING of New England's woodland wealth went steadily on. Near railroads "the locomotives [were] sweeping away thousands upon thousands of acres yearly to say nothing of the millions upon millions of cords consumed for family and domestic purposes," a writer in the *Boston Cultivator* warned in 1848. (A cord is a horizontal pile of four-foot logs or split sections, four feet high and eight feet long.) Boston alone bought 120,000 cords in 1825, one sixth from nearby farms, the rest by sea from Maine, sledded to the waterside in winter. Salem in 1840 used 30,000 cords. Parts of Cape Cod might be sandy, but Falmouth marketed 5,050 cords of firewood in 1855. Lest all this seem exaggerated, Vermont's railways burned 63,000 cords yearly. (It was the late 1850's before Connecticut railways tried coal.) Rhode Island's lime producers burned 90 cords for each 500 barrels they made from the rock, and by 1839 they had been at it for eighty years. Glass factories, brickyards, and iron works burned wood or charcoal long after the 1830's, when cotton factories near the sea began rapidly to turn to mineral coal. The Boston & Sandwich Glass Works on Cape Cod, which owned 2,300 acres of woodland, used 3,000 cords a year. Like the foundries in western Connecticut, they employed farmers and their ox-teams off-season to haul the fuel.[1]

Up country the best stands were turned into lumber and shingles, defective trees into potash. Spring floods on the Housatonic floated down pine and hemlock logs to be sawed at Derby on tidewater. In Massachusetts, with railroads handy, towns like Hubbardston, Middleboro, Milford, and Montague turned out over 2½ million board feet each a year; and in 1855 there were a dozen towns like Holland where fifteen mills each sawed a million feet.[2]

From eastern Maine to Cape Cod shipbuilders bought oak and hard pine knees for cash; and once the rails reached northern New Hampshire that area's knees and ship timber found a market in Maine's busy yards. Within drawing distance of Massachusetts Bay yards, a single, well-branched pasture white oak, skillfully cut up under the eye of a shipbuilder, might bring a farmer fifty dollars (a large sum then) and still leave him the minor branches for his own use. Nevertheless, as Thoreau and others commented, some farmers were not to be persuaded to part with a fine pasture oak for mere money.[3]

The results of deforestation showed, however. When Charles Dickens took the railroad north from Boston in 1842 he commented on the mile after mile of stunted growth that greeted him. Fires started by engines took heavy toll along all railway lines. In Petersham, now the seat of the Harvard Forest, in a bit over three decades the area in woods decreased by two thirds: from 9,270 acres in 1831 to 3,385 in 1865, the latter a mere 15 percent of the town's total area. The northern states had immense resources yet untouched; but Connecticut, which in 1844 still retained its impressive hemlock "Greenwoods" in the Taconics, was three fourths open land by 1860. Bronson Alcott, revisiting the Connecticut farmland of his boyhood, called the second growth there the most productive crop the owners could grow for the market. That market was the Naugatuck Valley, busy with clockmaking and copper and metal manufactures.[4]

All this available lumber brought certain concrete advantages. Histories of town after town in every state relate the amazing number of wood products, manufacture of which afforded income to farm people whose time at certain seasons was otherwise of small cash value. Endless wooden articles made with hand tools or in small mills during winter months were constantly being exported in all directions. Timber was the most reliable cash resource for many a small farmer, though its cutting and sale might provide little beyond winter wages for himself and his team. If his own wood was gone, he could cut on shares for a larger owner, chopping perhaps as much as two cords of firewood a day. The clearing of woodland fortunately coincided with a steady increase in the market for dairy products, so that the added pasture, even though poor, became for a time a useful asset to the farms. On Cape Cod,however, it was not pasture that resulted, but sand dunes and wastes. Frederick Freeman, the Cape historian, in 1860 told of seeing large tree stumps on tidal flats a mile out from shore, apparently at Provincetown. At Eastham, just beyond the crook of the Cape, no forest remained except near its boundary with Wellfleet. Sand continually encroached.

Meanwhile recuperative forces were here and there beginning to appear. An occasional voice such as those of Theodore S. Gold of Connecticut and John Lowell of Massachusetts warned of waste or advocated reforestation.

Said one prophet in the *Massachusetts Agricultural Journal* in 1831: "We are fast consuming these rich treasures of our woods, and I fear that our prodigality will be followed . . . by the usual consequences of prodigality." Fifteen years later an official report commissioned by that state's legislature warned that unless pains were taken to replace the forests, manufacturers of products based on wood, with a payroll of over two mil-

27. Charcoal burning from 1650 to 1900 turned woods waste into wages and provided the fuel for metal manufacture (1884). *Society for the Preservation of New England Antiquities.*

lions, were likely to leave the state. "A prudent foresight may prevent this by planting [trees] in season."

Massachusetts and New Hampshire passed laws to protect shade trees. Far-sighted towns like Sheffield, Stockbridge, Lynn, Deerfield, Greenfield in Massachusetts, Walpole in New Hampshire, and numerous others were planting them along the highways. Already in places they were so plentiful that when architect Charles J. Latrobe in 1835 recorded his visit to the area, he called the great elms that frequently lined village streets on both sides and clustered about the dwellings "the glory of New England."[5]

What happened to fertility depended largely on location, on what could be found to augment manure made by the farm's livestock, and on whether available markets for the farm's products made worthwhile the labor and expense that extra manure entailed. Barnyard manure was likely to go largely to the crops that brought direct income.

Still, on many a farm, a large part of the manure's potential was lost through lack of care. Investment in a barn cellar to cover it from the weather commended itself to some, but Henry Colman in 1838 complained that one would go far to find one in Berkshire County, Massachusetts. Those who had cellars, though, in a few years began to sell hay, he said.[6] Many, nevertheless, pitched the manure out the window into the weather.

Near cities, market gardeners hauled from city stables every load of manure available. Colman said it cost about as much as good cordwood, and mentioned one gardener who paid out the (then) very large sum of a thousand dollars a year for city manure. Farms within smell of salt water had great advantages. Two or three barrels of menhaden (a fish available in abundance), so a Bristol, Rhode Island, farmer testified in 1844, when spread on the land 6–10 inches apart and plowed in, were equal to a whole load of manure. The fish decomposed rapidly. Even on a poor, wornout sod an amazing growth of timothy and clover resulted, he continued, and cattle loved the sweetness of that grass and hay. The effects showed for years. For onions, when fish manure was plowed in during the fall, a great crop would be harvested next season. One Bristol, Rhode Island, farmer reported 800 bushels to the acre, plus some beets; another, 600. Crops of carrots went as high as 1,000.[7]

Seaweed was an excellent feeder for potatoes, several Rhode Island farmers testified. At Newport on a one-and-a-quarter mile beach 3,000 wagon loads worth two dollars each were thrown up yearly. Sea wrack (flotsam and jetsam) did best "composted with rich, unctuous, and viscid" sand from along the shore or mixed with riverside sediment and broken shells ("coral"), a source of lime. Such a manure was often called mussel (or muscle) bed, sea mud, or flats, and might contain black clams. Like the Rhode Islanders, a Cape Cod farmer told of stacking all such materials in a pile and adding lime to the heap. When this mud plus seaweed, rockweed, and seamoss were put into the hog pen to be worked over, not only did excellent land dressing result, but the hogs, feeding on the gelatinous sea plants, were healthy and ended in good shape for fattening.[8]

Where slaughterhouses, tanners, and curriers were found, their waste and offal made a valuable manure for farmers nearby. Nightsoil (human excrement) from the large towns, mixed one part to four with loam or sand, had "extraordinary efficacy" on meadow land. At Hamden, Connecticut, in 1856 a factory began to press out fish oil and built up a fertil-

28. Gathering kelp for fertilizer, York, Maine, 1882. *Society for the Preservation of New England Antiquities.*

izer market among farmers for the waste. Other such factories opened in Rhode Island and near Boston. Peat dug from bogs in summer was hauled in winter by the hundreds of loads, spread directly on land to be cropped, or deposited in barnyards to be trampled into mud, which would be spread later. In his journal Thoreau describes this process.[9]

Everyone recognized the virtues of wood ashes, even after much of the potash had been leached from them, and plaster of paris had come into vogue well before 1830. A farmer in Poultney, Vermont, with a pailful in his hand, wrote his name in big letters with plaster on a piece of grassland, and let the results speak to his neighbors. By 1830 Boston received its first experimental Peruvian guano (sea bird droppings) which, placed under cornhills, was reported to do wonders. Thirty years later, three shiploads came into New London and a little began to be imported to Maine. Clarence Day states that in 1857 a Portland dealer advertised 150 tons.

Among the better-informed farmers, interest in chemical fertilizers grew. In 1848 the *Boston Cultivator* reported English experiments with phosphoric acid, lime, and potash, and in 1850 there were German trials of nitrate of soda and sulphate of ammonia. In the same year mixed fertilizer was produced at Baltimore, and Charles T. Jackson clearly outlined the properties of these and other sources of fertility before the Plymouth County Agricultural Association. A Berkshire farmer inquired of the *Cultivator* about poudrette (a dried product of human excrement). The important stimulus that commercial fertilizers were to offer New England crops was, however, still ahead.

Meanwhile, except near good markets, ordinary farmers often attempted to work too much land and, as one visitor after another pointed out, without sufficient labor or manure. On poor soils in long-settled areas plenty of fields—and farms—were by this time worn out. Visitors, however, continued to praise and to compare favorably with England the "delightful" farms and villages they met with near Hartford, in the Farmington Valley, about Springfield, and around Boston.[10]

The unprecedented advances in transportation, education, manufacturing and available markets, added to the populating of the West, continued to give New England life and farming in particular a tremendous shakeup, economically and socially.

In a farming town only one son, obviously, could take over the ancestral homestead. A second or third son would need considerable capital in order to buy and stock a local farm, assuming that he could find a good one for sale. On the other hand, a job in a factory, store, or school, or on a vessel, called for little or no investment. Wages or a share in trading or fishing profits offered a chance to accumulate money. This prospect appealed to many, for the farm, with its necessities and its variety of tasks, bred young people of industry and resourcefulness. Thousands of such eager youngsters, from the hill towns in particular, set out for the manufacturing and commercial centers of New England and New York. From a New Hampshire farm went Henry Wilson, to become a shoe manufacturer in Natick, Massachusetts, and to go on to be Vice President of the United States; Marshall P. Wilder left New Ipswich, New Hampshire, to build a leading Boston mercantile business and continue his agricultural bent as a farmer and president of the Massachusetts Horticultural Society; Jonas Chickering set forth from the same state to make famous pianos.

The West too was alluring.[11] It promised opportunity to take up a farm, on rich soil perhaps, with only a modest outlay; or to use education, skill, and ingenuity in trades and professions. So other thousands of farm boys—and girls—headed west to seek their fortunes. From a Vermont town John Deere set forth to Illinois to manufacture there steel plows to break the prairies. A Vermont farm boy, Stephen A. Douglas, went west to become Senator from Illinois and candidate for President; Marshall Field, to found Chicago's greatest mercantile house; and Gustavus Swift, from Cape Cod, to build a meat business in Chicago which, like Field's, still prospers. Farm-bred boys founded enduring colleges, churches, and institutions in Ohio, Michigan, and other new states. In 1830 Tocqueville was told that thirty-six of the nation's congressmen had been born in Connecticut. These sons were New England's most valuable farm export.

Girls, no longer tied to the spinning wheel, went by the hundreds into the new mills of Lowell and Manchester; in 1846, in Lowell, there were 1,200 Vermont girls at work. They and their "Lowell Offering" were the wonder of foreign visitors. Some taught school in the new states; some, like Mary Lyon, Lucy Stone, and Clara Barton, prepared for great public achievements and national and international fame.

By 1850 half of Vermont's natives were said to have removed. Hill towns lost not solely from outward emigration but by removal to valley towns with better soil, industries, and railroad service. There new villages grew up and old ones enlarged. Athens, Vermont, dropped from 507 in 1820 to 309 in 1850. Russell, in western Massachusetts, with 1,000 in 1840, counted only 532 a decade later; adjoining Montgomery decreased from 656 to 401. Foster, Rhode Island, dropped from 2,900 in 1820 to 1,935 in 1860. In those same years, however, railroad and mill towns doubled.

Yet it would be far from the truth to conclude, as some writers have done, that those who set forth were necessarily the ablest or most ambitious and that agriculture suffered. Nearly all really good farms remained occupied, and not infrequently in succeeding decades continued to breed superior men and women. Agricultural production in New England increased rather than decreased. Moreover, if a so-called farm had been treated actually as a mine, its timber and its natural fertility exhausted, or if it should never have been farmed at all, no private or public end was served by trying to exist there. Another farm was waiting to be exploited in the West, or the family members could better themselves by changing occupation while staying close by. Lewis D. Stilwell has acutely pointed out that "the bulk of the emigrants [from Vermont] were simply surplus . . ." In general this was true in every New England state. Swarms left the home hive regularly; yet a healthy nucleus remained, to swarm again and again.

29. Yankee Inventors

THE DECADES between the War of 1812 and the Civil War were years of amazing invention and improvement in farm tools. Of greatest import after the cotton gin was the development of the steel, self-scouring plow. The iron plow first in use was not wholly satisfactory, even with Jethro Wood's redesign and casting it in sections. A Hanover, Massachusetts, firm, Prouty & Mears, made a thousand iron plows a year that were reputed effective, and William Hussey of North Berwick, Maine, about 1825, began a line of Hussey plows that for years had a high local reputation. John Lane about 1833 put one together from sections of a steel saw. Then, four years later, John Deere, an emigrant to Illinois from Derby, Vermont (as noted), and a skilled blacksmith, succeeded in joining portions of discarded steel circular saw blades which he had painstakingly heated, bent, and bent again until the share automatically scoured away the sticky prairie earth; and the modern plow was born.[1]

Back in New England, Joel Nourse of Worcester offered five sizes of regular plows besides a swivel or side-hill plow and a cultivator. About 1842 he brought out his Eagle plow, its mouldboard skillfully shaped both to stand rough ground and gravelly fields and to turn tough sward. Nourse's Eagle not only remained for generations the local standard, but became an item of export. From Vermont, Cyrus Warren's and Frederick Holbrook's side-hill swivel plows proved a boon for hill farmers, though swivels had long been in use in England. Holbrook also invented a subsoil plow.[2]

By 1855 numerous New England foundries were manufacturing plows. Massachusetts was the core, in particular Worcester, which made Nourse's Eagle and was called the largest center for the manufacture of agricultural implements in the United States. The state had in 1830 turned out perhaps a few thousand plows (1,000 in Worcester that year); in 1845, 61,000. By 1855 its output, from 22 foundries, was 152,686. Of that year's production, worth over $700,000, one fifth stayed in the state and the rest were sold elsewhere, some in England.[3]

Other large tools made their way into use. For hauling manure and the omnipresent field stone, the dumpcart, which had become more common by the middle of the century, was a boon. A potato digger was tried out in 1833. Jesse Buel's *Farmer's Companion* in 1839 mentions the

29. (a) Discharging and revolving horse rake; (b) Nourse's famous Eagle plow. Sources: (a) *J. R. Newell,* Catalogue *(1836);* (b) *Russell, Nourse, and Mason,* Catalogue *(1846).*

(a)

(b)

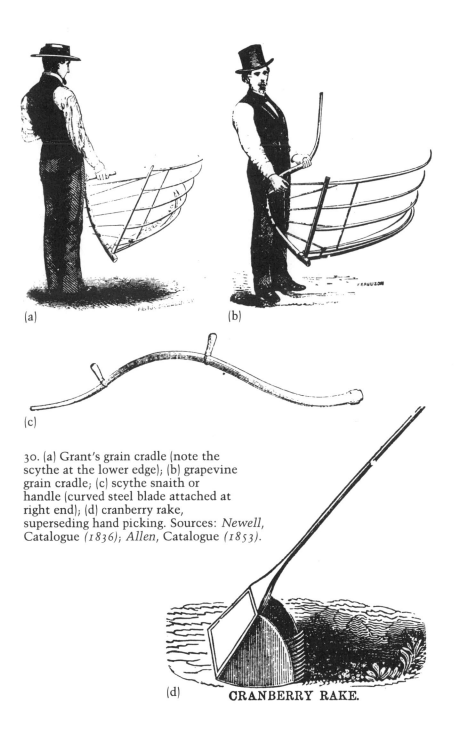

(a)

(b)

(c)

30. (a) Grant's grain cradle (note the scythe at the lower edge); (b) grapevine grain cradle; (c) scythe snaith or handle (curved steel blade attached at right end); (d) cranberry rake, superseding hand picking. Sources: *Newell*, Catalogue *(1836)*; *Allen*, Catalogue *(1853)*.

(d) CRANBERRY RAKE.

roller and drill-harrow as new implements. Buel thought that because of improved implements a farm could be run at half the expense of forty years earlier. George Page invented a revolving tillage tool in 1847, foretelling the disc harrow. The horse cultivator had begun to take over the job, formerly done by the plow, of eliminating the weeds between corn rows. It proved valuable also for other row crops. Charles W. Billings of South Deerfield invented a corn planter. Seed sowers were tried out for small seeds. In the barn, corn shellers, seed winnowing machines, and straw cutters began to come in. Nathaniel Hawthorne describes a hay chopper he saw about 1841; in 1855 Boston firms sold 11,900 hay cutters in that one year. Rhode Islanders patented a corn husker, grain drills, and haying machines.

Horse-drawn wooden rakes of various simple types locally invented, some in New England, had come into gradual use to handle the universal hay crop in the field. The first good riding rake was the idea of a Maine man, Calvin Delano, who patented it in 1849.[4] Mowers and reapers of various sorts began to appear. Nantucket-bred Obed Hussey had patented his reaper in 1833. The Walter A. Wood firm sold 500 such machines in 1853.

Hussey had worked out also the principle of the cutter bar which was to be used in the horse-drawn mower, and in Maine R. T. Osgood conceived an even better arrangement, which the driver could raise and lower. Numerous other inventors were at work on mowers. Yet in 1847 it was said that in Norfolk County, south of Boston, not one farmer in ten used a mechanical mower. They were often crudely designed, always costly. From 1859 on, however, the close-cutting Wood mowing machine proved a thoroughly practical implement to help New England farmers through the war years.[5] The hay-tedder was scarcely known until the Massachusetts Society for Promoting Agriculture imported two English machines in 1858.

For grain, the Pitts brothers, Hiram and John, of Winthrop, Maine, concocted a combined thresher and separator. Though expensive, it would thresh 300 bushels a day, a wonderful advance over the flail.[6] In the hands of western farmers this combine, with McCormick's reaper, was to prove a boon on wide prairie landscapes. At the same time it made the growing of small grain in New England uneconomical except for local use. Worcester's Richardson Manufacturing Company claimed to be the oldest maker of the manure spreader, another machine destined for wide acceptance.

Improvement of small tools made great strides. They became more effective and in most cases lighter than any previously known. The Col-

31. A midcentury invention: Hussey's reaping and mowing machine. *Allen*, Catalogue *(1853)*.

lins weighted axe, already mentioned; the Ames steel shovel and spade from North Easton, Massachusetts (2,400 made daily in 1857, one third of all shovels manufactured in the country); a cast steel garden hoe invented by C. Bulkeley of Colchester, Connecticut, and Buxton's onion hoe; Charles Goodyear's spring steel pitchfork, patented in 1831; the Wyman Brothers' cast steel forks for horse manure—all were great improvements. From a small beginning in 1835, making steel pitchforks became for a century the big industry of the little village of Wallingford, Vermont, which exported large shipments to the Middle Atlantic states and England. In no more than a half century the efficiency of hand tools was doubled.

A gracefully curved ash snaith (or handle) for the scythe, patented in 1828, was the invention of Silas Lamson of Springfield, Vermont. A factory near Shelburne Falls, Massachusetts, came to put out 75,000 snaiths a year. Scythe factories dotted New England: one large producer in Litchfield, Connecticut; another at Smithfield, Rhode Island; a third at West

32. Another midcentury invention: Wood's Reaper and Mower. *Walter A. Wood Co.*, Catalogue *(1868)*.

Fitchburg, Massachusetts. In 1849 R. B. Dunn's factory at North Wayne, Maine, claiming to be the largest in the world, turned out 12,000 dozen annually.[7]

Grain cradles were slow in arriving in New England. A traveler records the cradling of oats at Leicester in central Massachusetts in 1820, but use of the cradle did not become general before 1840, and in a few years the harvester superseded it. A writer in the *Boston Cultivator* of August 26, 1848, advocated the use of wire for fences. "They will yet supersede all others," he correctly prophesied, for a quarter century later Joseph F. Glidden, farm hand and schoolteacher transplanted to the West from Charlestown, New Hampshire, patented barbed wire.

An especially valuable invention was the stone crusher worked out in 1852 by farm-born Eli Whitney Blake of Westborough, Massachusetts, nephew of the inventor of the cotton gin. It supplied not only the material for the hard surfaced roads so badly needed, but a market for the loose fieldstone with which the area's farms were all too well provided.

Other useful additions to farm equipment were the air-tight Mason fruit jar and a jar with a spring-fastened glass top patented by W. W. Lyman of Meriden, Connecticut (1858); the movable frame beehive (1852) designed by Lorenzo L. Langstreth of Pennsylvania, "father of modern beekeeping," who lived for a time in Massachusetts; the Eddy ice chest (1840's) and the ice cream freezer (1854); the hand-pushed wheelbarrow (1828); the platform scale, patented 1831 by Thaddeus Fairbanks of St. Johnsbury, Vermont; the steel square, credited to Silas Harris of Shaftsbury in that state; the safety fuse for blasting, conceived by Ensign Bickford of Granby, Connecticut, in 1836. Not to be forgotten for his influence on the household, Elias Howe, a clever farm-born mechanic, in 1846 patented his sewing machine.

Massachusetts could report in 1855 that five Boston agricultural warehouses sold 36,950 plows, 5,815 cultivators, 93,000 shovels, 60,000 hoes, 60,000 forks, 138,600 rakes, 33,600 scythes, 12,000 axes, 6,750 wheelbarrows, 11,900 haycutters, 12,165 corn shellers, 5,100 grain cradles, and 1,850 horse rakes: evidence of a healthy desire for improved tools on the part of New England farmers.[8]

Though these advances sound and are impressive, many a small farmer lacked cash to buy the new implements; or, recalling the depressions of the 1840's and 1857, thought it less practical to spend money for them than to hang onto his savings and deposit them in his trustworthy local savings bank. But the Civil War just ahead was to cause swift changes in attitudes toward machinery and other aspects of farming.

V. WAR AND
READJUSTMENT
1861 AND AFTER

30. For Better and Worse

AGRICULTURALLY SPEAKING, the Civil War years 1861–65 were notable for trends rather than for changes in crops. Nor, except for a few products, were there such increases in prosperity or such profits as those in the world of manufacturing and commerce.

From the point of view of rural well-being the most striking aspect of the war was the departure of the finest young men of the villages, many of them called in the haying season. A disheartening number were never to return. Vermont saw 34,328 march off, one in nine of its whole population; New Hampshire, one in ten. Of Vermont's youth, 5,128 died in service; of Maine's 73,000, 7,322 were lost.[1] Jaffrey, in New Hampshire's green pasture area, sent 151: of these, 28 died, or 18.5 percent. Goshen, Connecticut, saw 146 go: 29, almost one in five, never came back. From Amherst, Massachusetts, 93 out of 345, about 27 percent, are said to have died of wounds or disease. These farm communities were typical of New England, though not all towns lost so heavily.

For those who returned, ties to the old town had been loosened by absence and travel. The urge to make a new start elsewhere was compounded by inducements to go West. Through the Homestead Act, passed in 1862 and liberalized in 1864, Congress offered 160 acres of public land for a small payment to any settler who would occupy it for five years: but in the case of a soldier who had served two years, four fifths of the residence requirement was waived. Railroads, pushing ever westward and anxious for settlers on the immense acreages granted them by Congress, held out lures of their own.

All this hastened the decline of the less favorably situated New England country villages. A town such as Sutton, in west central New Hampshire, which counted 1,431 people in the 1860 census before the war began, by 1870 was down to 1,153, and a decade later to 880. Ashfield, Massachusetts, in the Berkshire foothills, lost 122 inhabitants, almost a tenth in the 1860–70 decade, and another tenth by 1880. In a town such as Sanbornton, upriver from Concord, New Hampshire, its historian claimed in 1876 that a dozen contiguous farms there had each a record of three fourths of a century in the same family. In such cases, however, it was chiefly the older folks who remained.[2] Statistics alone may conceal what was happening. Half of Maine's counties and half of

New Hampshire's in the two decades 1860–80 made population gains, and in Massachusetts all mainland counties except two had increases. Vermont's total stayed about even, while every Rhode Island and Connecticut county added inhabitants. Usually, however, it was the mill villages, railroad towns, and suburban and commercial communities that increased, perhaps even added farms; while at the same time the isolated, frosty, hilly towns and infertile areas gradually contracted and lost population.

A favorable feature of the war for agriculture was final success in establishing agricultural education of college grade. One of Vermont's representatives, Justin S. Morrill, a merchant-farmer, had the distinction of getting Congress in 1862 to endow every loyal state with a generous land grant from the national domain for establishing a college to teach "such branches of learning as are related to agriculture and the mechanic arts." For decades New England had talked of such colleges. Now four states promptly acted. Before the year ended, New Hampshire had accepted the grant; Massachusetts followed in 1863, Vermont in 1864, and Maine in 1865. All the new institutions except Vermont's opened for enrollment before the decade was out. Attempting to graft agricultural education on existing institutions, Connecticut waited until 1881, Rhode Island until 1888, before establishing separate agricultural colleges.

Agricultural progress came during the war in a related area of governmental action. Back in 1839, on recommendation of Henry L. Ellsworth of Connecticut, Commissioner of Patents, Congress had appropriated $1,000 to secure promising seeds and cuttings from foreign sources for trial, and to conduct agricultural investigations and assemble statistics. The first national agricultural report, a document of 59 pages, was one result. The public approved, and appropriations and activities increased. The Patent Office's annual report proved so popular that by the end of a quarter-century its edition exceeded a quarter-million copies. In 1862 with the war on, Congress advanced the agricultural bureau to the status of a government department. Divisions of chemistry, statistics, and entomology were soon set up.

Another decisive intervention of government, this time by a state, took place in the animal husbandry field. Resolutely meeting what might have become a frightful disaster to the whole nation's cattle, Massachusetts provided a precedent that was to prove highly valuable later.

It came about in this way. Winthrop W. Chenery, a progressive Belmont, Massachusetts, farmer, had for some years been importing superior Holstein cattle. Suddenly, in May 1859, deadly pleuropneumonia was discovered in Worcester County and traced to one of Chenery's importa-

tions. The disease spread. Consternation ensued. The Massachusetts legislature, acting promptly, set up a cattle control board with broad powers
to quarantine and destroy, and made reporting of livestock diseases compulsory. Maine and the other states to the north promptly followed, so
that the disease did not spread at all in that direction. In fighting the disease Massachusetts alone spent $20,000 and slaughtered hundreds of ani-
mals. So thoroughly was the situation met that by 1867 the plague had
been wiped out in New England.[3] Moreover, a pattern of government action had been drawn that was to bear fruit nationally in control of foot
and mouth disease, which appeared in Massachusetts in 1870, and for the
later battle against bovine tuberculosis and other animal infections.

During the war years food processing, a field closely related to agriculture, opened a new era. Back in 1851 Gail Borden, a Texan transplanted
to Connecticut, had patented a method to condense milk to a fraction of
its normal bulk; but the process failed to gain popularity. Now, with war
on, the need to feed troops put a different face on the innovation, and a
hungry military outlet for the new product opened. In 1863 Borden's
Condensed Milk Company was organized at Winsted, Connecticut. For a
time it offered a market for local milk, but its stay in Connecticut lasted
only a few years, then Borden moved his operations to the Harlem Valley,
New York, later licensing another plant at Livermore Falls in Maine.[4]

In still another type of food processing the war brought advances. To
some extent meat and other foods had been preserved in tin cans ever
since Nicolas Appert discovered the process in France during the Napoleonic wars. The British had tinned meat and vegetables for their army and
navy in the century's early decades. William Underwood, a young Englishman who came to Boston in 1822, had used Appert's methods to
pack fruits in bottles, later in cans. In Maine about 1840, Isaac Winslow
had tried canning sweet corn and in 1853 secured a patent on his process.
Soon he was selling canned corn to S. S. Pierce, the Boston grocer. In the
war's first year, a Baltimore canner, using a method invented in England,
cut the boiling time for canning to a half hour.

The needs of the Northern forces and the difficulties of supplying great
armies under southern field conditions opened the opportunity for canned
rations of all kinds. Clarence Day recounts some of the effects in Maine.
Though the best of Maine's beef continued to go to Boston, local canneries furnished a welcome nearby market for ordinary beef and for other
farm products. One of these, the Portland Packing Company, put up mutton, veal, and sausage as well as beef. (The company is still active at this
writing.) Quantities of Maine sweet corn went to the troops. When the
war ended, wild blueberries by the hundreds of bushels also began to go

off in cans. By the time the troops had dispersed, canning was well established, and thus began an important local industry.[5] By 1873, 13 Maine firms were turning out 5,700,000 cans of corn alone, as well as other vegetables. By 1881 the pack had almost doubled. That year it took 12,500 acres of Maine farmland to supply the canneries with vegetables.

During the war, between the draft and bounties to recruits, farmers unable to find help were forced to get along with youngsters and old men, and to turn to the new machines. Already, from 1850 to 1860, the value of farm tools produced in the nation had grown over 65 percent, more than one fifth of them made in New England. With the war demand soared. By 1864 mowing-machine production in the North had increased two and a half times. On one Norfolk County farm in Massachusetts an 1863 report mentions in addition to the mower, a hayspreader, a horse pitchfork, and a wheel horserake. The fork would unload a ton of hay in only six minutes, and with no sweat! Other wartime innovations included the checkrow corn planter, and a combined wheeled onion seed-drill and cultivator introduced by S. E. Harrington of North Amherst, Massachusetts. Connecticut inventors developed other seeders and special onion tools. On the less fortunate farms old standbys such as the bull rake and the wooden hand rake might still be the chief recourse in hay time, but the day of the blacksmith-made and home-whittled implement was past.

The war years saw also substantial advances in the volume of agricultural information and ways of spreading it. A gathering of notables attended the nation's first college "Short Course," the Yale Agricultural Lectures, from February 1 to 25 in 1860. A series of useful books was published. In 1862 George B. Emerson and Charles L. Flint printed a well-received *Manual of Agriculture*. The respected Fearing Burr of Hingham in 1863 brought out his excellent *Field and Garden Vegetables of America*. New York's Peter Henderson supplemented this in 1866 with his popular *Market Gardening for Profit*. For sheepmen, Henry S. Randall wrote *The Practical Shepherd*, published in 1863.

Toward the decade's end Professor Samuel Johnson of Yale tapped a new source of scientific information. He analyzed various fertilizers and told about the need for fertility in *How Crops Grow* (1868), and *How Crops Feed* (1870). Agricultural periodicals continued to circulate widely.

In dairy practice the midcentury saw continued changes. The compulsory reporting of diseases in cattle prompted by the pleuropneumonia epidemic was but the first of a series of official acts related to animal and human health. In 1859 Massachusetts led the nation with a law authorizing public inspection of milk. Boston promptly appointed an inspector of dairies, the first anywhere, and forbade feeding distillery slops (waste grain) to dairy cattle. Rhode Island, New Hampshire, and Maine followed. Five years later Massachusetts forbade the watering of milk, a practice previously not uncommon, and required all cities to set up milk inspection. Then in 1869 it led again by establishing the nation's pioneer Department of Public Health.[6] From the current farm viewpoint these actions affected chiefly the production and sale of whole milk, but they were the seed for an ever-expanding policy of public concern with food and health.

At the moment most of New England's milk went into farm-produced butter and cheese, 25,000 tons annually of butter alone as the decade came in. The war years had varied effects. Though Vermont cows usually got no grain except corn meal, sometimes mixed with oats, that state's butter production went up by almost two million pounds: the rest of New England remained static or lost ground. In all six states the cheese total dropped: in New Hampshire and Massachusetts the decline was tremendous.

Vermonters showed their concern for the future: assembled at Montpelier in 1869, they organized the nation's first state dairy association (none too soon, for railroads had begun to bring in Midwest butter). Interest grew in respect to breeding for production. Jersey cattle, already on trial in southern New England, commenced to gain favor among Maine and Vermont stockmen. When in 1868 George Waring of Ogden Farm, Newport, Rhode Island, arranged a meeting of Jersey breed fanciers at Farmington, Connecticut, the American Jersey Cattle Club was born and its herd register established.[7] Maine Jersey fanciers followed in 1870 with the Winthrop Jersey Association. High-grade Guernseys and the first Brown Swiss were among other promising cattle imports. Undeterred by his experience with pleuropneumonia, Winthrop Chenery of Belmont continued his interest in Holsteins. Shorthorns were pushing north. In 1866 a group of twenty farmers about Springfield, Vermont, clubbed together to buy a purebred bull. Meanwhile in Maine, Herefords gained over Shorthorns. Despite such advances, by 1870 the number of milch cows reported for New England, 642,591, was less by 37,000 than it had been a decade before. Only Vermont had increased its cow numbers; Connecticut held steady, all the others dropped. Where possible, dairy farmers were shifting from butter and cheese to whole milk. By 1864 milk trains over the Worcester, Fitchburg, and Lowell railroads were bringing over 24 million quarts annually into Boston, a foretaste of greater changes ahead.[8]

Two of New England's staples, potatoes and onions, found hungry mar-

(a)

(b)

(c)

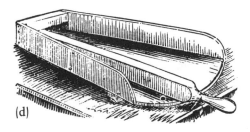

(d)

33. Implements for the farm wife's buttermaking: (a) cylindrical churn; (b) dash churn; (c) cylindrical butter worker: (d) lever butter worker. *Mapes*, Illustrated Catalogue *(1881)*.

kets during the war years. Onions reached a top of $10.00 a barrel on the New York market. Southport, Connecticut, alone is said to have grown 100,000 barrels during the war. One vessel from that port, the *White Rock*, carried 1,100 to 1,200 barrels a trip to New York. Several others sailed each week carrying, along with the onions, pork, apples, and grain. Danvers, Massachusetts, was a big onion producer, and in the Connecticut Valley, Sunderland and Deerfield took up the crop.[9] By use of heavy dressings of fish manure, pig manure, kelp, and mussel-bed, except in the excessively dry year of 1864, yields in all these areas were generally good.

Responding to wartime demand, Connecticut increased its potato harvest by half in the war decade; Maine and Rhode Island each by a fifth. Bangor, Maine, is reported to have shipped out 300,000 bushels yearly in this period. If census figures are to be believed, however, the New England crop went up in total only about one eighth. In the 1870 census all New England was reported as producing close to 24 million bushels, over two thirds in the three northern states, where many went into starch. As early as 1833 a Maine inventor had patented a potato-digger,[10] but it was to be 1890 before any digger assumed importance.

When the war cut off the North's supply of cotton, the cities with cotton mills languished, while woolen mills and wool growers cashed in. Aside from civilian clothing needs, the army required immense numbers of uniforms and blankets. The yardage of woven wool cloth more than doubled, and the price of wool jumped. Sheep numbers had dropped substantially during the two previous decades, but in the three northern states careful attention to breeding had held the decline of the wool clip to a mere 10 percent. Now demand became for a time acute. Only in Maine, however, did the 1870 census report show an increase in total clip. The war did not prevent the exhibit at Hamburg, Germany, in 1863, by George Campbell of Vermont of a dozen fine Merinos. In competition with 1,761 European entries, these Vermont sheep captured two first prizes. Campbell's ewes and rams had proved superior in weight and length of fleece to some of Europe's best, and later sold for a total of $5,000.[11]

As demands encouraged wool growers in the West to expand, they often turned to New England for superior breeding stock. Prices rose, and the best local rams were quoted in thousands of dollars. A short period of prosperity ensued, but increases in the numbers of western flocks and the return of cotton to the markets following the war's end coincided to prevent permanent prosperity for sheepmen. Nevertheless sheep lingered on northern New England hillsides until long after, when undisciplined dogs became prevalent. New England diners retained a fondness for roast lamb, so that Maine and Berkshire Hills flock owners, who had turned early to mutton breeds, held out well toward the century's end—their animals of much greater value than those which composed the fine wooled flocks of their fathers. In 1890 Franklin County in the Bay State's hills, with only 11,000 sheep, raised 8,000 lambs, valued at $4.50 each.[12] As western stock flooded in, sales of sheep at Brighton grew from 250,597 animals in 1863 to 524,069 in 1885.

During the war decade, hog numbers, as reported by the census, slumped by a quarter—from 326,176 in the 1860 report to 241,000 in 1870—only to rise beyond the 1860 figure by 1880 and to increase further by 1890. Aside from the fact that the 1869 census count is suspect, the later increase may have reflected the practice of using cheap western corn to fatten native pork. It also coincided with the rise in local butter and cheese making, with surplus skim milk and whey going to the hogs. The change, however, was of small significance, for with the growth of Boston packing plants, the flood of western hogs increased. Local hog growing had only a limited future, even though by 1886 the Brighton Market handled more than ten times the number of hogs sold there in 1863.[13]

The wartime leap in production of cigar tobacco was spectacular. The crop pushed up the Connecticut Valley even into New Hampshire and Vermont. New England yields per acre were the highest in the nation, and its leaf brought the top price. As cigar smoking gained wartime popularity, production grew from 9¼ million pounds in 1860 to over 15¾ million in 1870. The largest proportionate increase was in Massachusetts, where the crop more than doubled. Hatfield, with only two acres in 1850, grew between seven and eight hundred when the 1869 census was taken. Crop value in 1865 ran from $275 to $405 per acre, and war prices lifted many a farm mortgage; yet there was opposition on moral grounds to using New England's best land for a crop that lacked food value.[14]

Hop growing ceased to be of importance in Massachusetts, its former stronghold. Between 1860 and 1870, if census figures are to be believed, Maine trebled its small crop. Vermont, the largest producer of this period, which had more than doubled between 1850 and 1860, dropped from 638,677 pounds to 527,927 in 1870; yet for some years production in that state was considerable. The census taken in 1869 is the last where hops appear to be significant in New England. New York and the West took over the crop.

That questionable 1870 census report indicated a substantial decrease from 1860 in corn production in all states except Vermont; there it

showed a small increase. In average yield, New Hampshire led the Union
with 40.8 bushels per acre. Popular field corn varieties now included
New England Eight-Rowed, King Philip, Dutton (a high-producing Vermont strain selected by Salmon Dutton of Cavendish), Rhode Island Premium, and Northern White Flint. Some corn was being sown in drills
and the stalks used for summer feed. The practice increased of gathering
the mature stalks into standing bundles or stooks instead of lopping the
tops above the ear.[15]

In the 1870 census all small grain harvests were reported down from
ten years earlier, with rye the heaviest loser. Vermont, which had a slight
gain in its small wheat harvest, was an exception.

The value of market-garden vegetables showed substantial growth in
the war decade. Between the 1860 and the 1870 census reports the Mas-

34. Sheep dog, shepherd, and flock, Massachusetts, 1880's. *Society for
the Preservation of New England Antiquities.*

35. Braiding next year's seed corn into long strings, called "traces": 1880's. *Society for the Preservation of New England Antiquities.*

sachusetts total increased from $1,397,000 to almost $2,000,000, Connecticut's from a third of a million to almost $600,000, while Rhode Island's more than doubled, from $140,000 to $316,000. Even considering wartime inflation, there were substantial gains.

By this time strawberries were grown in quantity near the larger cities. Providence was one such market center. Nearby Dighton had been growing some berries; but with the opening in 1866 of the Dighton and Somerset Railroad to Providence local farmers increased production. By 1881 the town was picking 10,000 bushels a year. At first the popular variety in Dighton was Old Virginia. By 1875 Massachusetts was credited with marketing 1,156,801 quarts, valued at about 20 cents a quart. Earlier, the berries had grown on raised beds, but level, matted rows now took over.[16]

In the Boston suburban area yields of 4,000 quarts or more per acre, packed in the wood veneer quart box which that market favored, were not unusual. In the 1870 report of the U.S. Commissioner of Agriculture a Maine grower near Bangor was cited for producing on 20 square rods 590 quarts of the popular Wilson variety. These sold for 21 cents a quart, a high price for the time. A favorite New England berry was Cutter's Seedling.

Maine's apple trees in 1860 bore a half million dollar crop. In Massachusetts the value of tree fruits of all kinds came to $925,000. In apples the next decade showed little change, but by 1875 Massachusetts reported a crop of about 3⅓ million bushels of tree fruits of all sorts, worth over 1½ millions. New England's apple exports to England were building up, and would soon become a big market factor.

Amid all the upheaval of the war, the shortage of labor, the inflation of the currency, and the demands of the army, there was no radical alteration in New England's type of farming. At its end, though many farmers had some more or less profitable specialty, the general farm, with several strings to its not very long bow, continued to be the most common type. By the time of the 1870 census report, however, some thousands of the poorer farms had gone out of production. In three New England states alone over 400,000 acres were dropped from the category of improved land.

31. Discouragement

THE THIRTY YEARS that followed 1870, including as they did the panic of 1873, seem to have been the most difficult that New England farmers had faced since Shays's Rebellion. "Decades of almost unrelieved gloom," a writer on Connecticut calls them.[1] Prices of many staples, especially grain, were in almost continuous decline from peaks reached at the war's end, as cheap western grain, helped by railroad rate cuts, flooded in. By 1895 the quoted price for wheat at New York had dropped 60 percent. Never again except under wartime necessity would it be practical to grow wheat in New England. By 1876 the corn harvested in a town like Rochester, New Hampshire, was only a little over half what its farmers had husked a quarter-century earlier, and small grains had all but disappeared there. Between 1870 and 1890 farm valuations in Vermont receded from 135 to 100 million, while in Maine cattle numbers lessened one eighth from 1870 to 1890, and dropped one fifth more in the next decade.

New England's wool shearings decreased one sixth between 1870 and 1880. By 1900 they were only two thirds those of 1870 and never again reached a total of real importance. Cheap western horses made it impractical for Vermont and Maine breeders to cater to any market except that for race horses; and some of the best Maine beef breeders found it expedient to leave for the prairies with their herds.

In the 70's and 80's all states lost in number of "census farms." In the 1900 census report Massachusetts enumerators came up with a 9 to 10 percent gain and New Hampshire and Vermont showed slight increases. Yet the gain was of small significance, for between the 1880 and 1900 tallies, New Hampshire's farms had dropped by three fifths and Vermont's by half. Connecticut's cleared land reached its peak at the war's beginning, fell slowly till 1870, and receded fast thereafter. On Maine farms the woodlot had been relied on for cash income. When the last of it had been cut and sold, the farm owner had to get a job or move.

In 1890 New Hampshire's Commissioner of Agriculture reported 1,440 vacant or abandoned farms; Massachusetts' Commissioner, 1,576 in 1895. From 1870 on, fewer than two thirds of Vermont's natives were left to call that state home. It was the young in particular who took off. In 1871 at Northfield, Massachusetts, a group of ex-soldiers organized, sent a scout to spy out land in the New West, and planned to move as a body to settle there.

At home, as writer Rollin Lynde Hartt put it just as the century ended, "Steadily the river valleys, rich in water power, are robbing the uplands of their population. The people of New England are running down hill, Massachusetts has built the factory and mortgaged the farm. . . . Says Noah, 'All the spunkiest ones have up and got out.'" "Sweet Auburn," the town where Hartt was born, he considered now a skim-milk community. Tenancy increased in every New England state between 1880 and 1900, though it always remained of small proportions except in Rhode Island (19 percent there in 1899).[2]

Why indeed should a young man waste energy on a hill farm, say in the Sunapee region up half a mile from sea level with 90 days at the most for corn to mature between frosts, when as a peddler or soldier he had known the six-month season of the South or could obtain cheaply a virgin farm in the West? As a Vermonter who had long lived in the West pointed out in 1878, however, the proportion of unsuccessful farmers was quite as great in Illinois as in Vermont, and Governor Hoard of Wisconsin observed that the abandonment problem was every bit as serious in his state as in New England.[3]

One burden on farms in this postwar period was taxation. At the very time when farm prices were dropping, taxes were biting harder. A 1933 Maine study shows that the rate of taxation of farm property there reached its height for the whole nineteenth century in prosperous 1865, at .015. Though it dropped the next year to .0075, it continued to hover between .006 in 1870, .005 in 1880, and .004 in 1884, contrasted with prewar rates of only .002 and .003. Finally, after 1885, the rate dropped to .00275 for most of the rest of the century.[4]

At agricultural banquets captains of industry returning to the communities of their birth moaned over the farm situation, and city publicists shed tears in printers ink in current periodicals. Yet with sheep herding unprofitable and cattle prices low, decade by decade the poorer, stonier, frostier hill farms went relentlessly back to the woodland for which nature designed them. Houses that never would have been started had their builders known what lay west of the Hudson, burned or rotted, and back roads gradually filled with briers till timber took over. As the historian of Peterborough, New Hampshire, where many farms were tenantless, wrote in 1876: "We know not how these lands are to be recruited as long as the agricultural products of the West can be brought to us by a cheap transportation."[5]

Not everyone rushed to the wailing wall. In the 1870 report of the U.S.

Commissioner of Agriculture, a correspondent in the Warner, New Hampshire, area, much further north in that same state, reported that there the majority of farmers made a good living, buildings were good, and "some accumulate very respectable fortunes."⁶ Levi P. Warren of Sunderland, Massachusetts, in the Connecticut Valley, failed to share the usual alarm. Depopulation, he thought in the spring of 1871, was the result of progress in the art and science of agriculture. He saw "a youth of fourteen accomplish as much with a mower as a number of strong robust men formerly in the same time with scythes"; while the youth's younger brother ran the tedder and one younger still drove the hay rake. For the latter two, at any rate, it was a pastime.⁷

The statement held true also in regard to sowing seed for the Valley's crop of onions. Once this had been a backbreaking job lasting weeks, he said; now with a seeding machine a man could do two to three acres in a day. The time and effort once needed to get the crops to market over the road is cut, he noted; the railroad does it. If all those who used to be needed for farming had continued in it, the markets would be glutted. As to abandoned land, another farmer, just before the war, had pointed out that sterile land is "better left to the growth of wood." Let the poor lands go, and put time and manure on what will really produce—that seemed common sense to many.⁸

In any case, as Lewis Stilwell has admirably expressed it, New England farmers, Vermonters in particular, were never the plodding European peasant type that certain modern writers appear to believe they should have been, tied to the land; but a "climbing and creative stock."⁹ In their new locations many with mechanical ability became craftsmen, some, such as Theodore N. Vail, heads of great new industries. More became teachers, college presidents, politicians; Hiram Powers was a sculptor. Connecticut-born Isaac Crary fathered Michigan's agricultural college, pioneer of the state university movement. New Englanders set the tone in large part for that state and for Wisconsin, Minnesota, and Kansas, as Lois Mathews points out. Emigrants with experience in the deep woods, Frederick Turner shows, harvested the pine belt of the northern Middle West, and sometimes became millionaires. Luther Burbank, born on the old Burbank Farm in Lancaster, Massachusetts, and doing well as a market gardener in nearby Lunenberg, set out for California to garner fame as a plant breeder.¹⁰

"The greatest crop raised hitherto on these farms," wrote George Loring in reply to Timothy Titcomb's prophecy of doom in the *Atlantic Monthly*, "is a host of active, thriving busy men in professions, business, commerce." In 1896 another writer concluded: "The average boy looking for something to do, sees about four openings in other directions to one in agriculture," and picks one of the four.[11]

Girls left as well as boys, and often beginning as schoolteachers, took their part in civilizing the new settlements. The historian of Guilford, Connecticut, quotes a settler who married one such: "Many a fireside in distant states has been graced and made happy by one of the daughters of Guilford, who carried with them the rich grace of truth, gentleness and Christian character."[12] Such young people not seldom helped parents at home to pay off a bothersome mortgage, very likely assumed in part for their education. Later they might return to endow a library in the home village or present a park or public building.

What about those who remained? A substantial number of observers differ from the opinion commonly expressed (for example, by Percy Bidwell) that it was the best, most energetic persons who left. Van Wyck Brooks thinks that the stay-at-homes "were much more real than the pioneers, and their lives . . . more interesting . . . [They were] superior types." The stayers were apt to be the more prosperous, with too much to lose by pulling up stakes. Stuart Holbrook's grandfather came to the conclusion that it wasn't necessarily the abler or more intelligent who migrated; the restlessness came from "something in the blood." Contrariwise, Page Smith, in a recent study, concludes that it was the most conservative who left.[13]

Harold Wilson decides that "the inheritance of fertile and well-located farms served to retain . . . many men and women of ability and initiative."[14] In such a judgment anyone familiar with rural life as demonstrated in the twentieth century must find great merit. Where the best were eventually forced to give up, however, the country village was left poor indeed; with inadequate leadership, capital, and, in some instances, a village community almost depopulated.

One loss to the country town that was never made up is seldom appreciated, even today. This was the constant drain of wealth in the form of taxes assessed for schools, and of contributions for country churches. This was money lost, invested in the abilities and character of those very young people whose talents went to build new cities and new states elsewhere.[15] Another setback was the curtailment of town appropriations as resources diminished, resulting in poorer care for back roads, the closing of outlying schools, and general loss of confidence.

John Black calls attention to one point often overlooked, however.[16] Very little land in New England was actually abandoned. Some neighbor bought the old fields and added them to his cow pasture or woodland holdings. It was cultivation that ceased, not ownership, when the land reverted to nature. As a visiting Scot had observed in the decade before the war: "It is nonsense to talk of the soil being exhausted. There was never anything to exhaust." On many a rocky hillside, when the seeds of pine or birch sifted into old fields, nature was quietly returning the soil to its highest use, natural and economic.

At least one New Englander took action to offset the emigration: Wilbur W. Thomas, a Maine native, consul at Gothenburg, Sweden. With the backing of Maine's government, beginning in 1870, he brought in 600 hardworking Swedish farmer families. In three years they cleared 22,000 acres of prime Aroostook land and established the prosperous town of New Sweden.

32. Adapt or Perish

THERE WAS a second side to the coin. Untoward developments helped bring into play the capacity for adaptation to circumstances that had always distinguished New England's country people.

In the years after the war, from natural increase and the flood of immigrants, New England's population count shot up from just under 3½ million in 1870 to a total of 4,700,000 by 1890, a boost of over a third in two decades. Except for a 0.1 percent loss in Vermont in the 1890 census report, quite possibly due to a miscount, every state made at least a small gain each decade.

Of the immigrants whose numbers bulked heavily in the addition, most stayed in the tenements of cities and mill towns to earn cash wages and become consumers of food rather than producers. For with the help of these newcomers New England was making more than half of the nation's boots and shoes, a large proportion of its textiles and textile machinery, and manufactured goods of many other sorts. It also became more and more a center for banking and insurance, and at the same time a market for the best in food, with money to buy it. Its flour and much of its beef and pork might come from the West, but milk, butter, eggs, poultry, vegetables, and fruit came chiefly from local farms. Growing population spelled farm opportunity, and the local farmers grasped it.

To the up-country farmer looking for a product to replace the wheat, sheep, or fat cattle that the West now produced more cheaply, nothing could appeal more strongly than the hungry dairy-products markets of Boston, Providence, and the Connecticut cities, with their concentrations of people. Even with the new Hoosac Tunnel route opened in 1875, the cost and difficulty of transportation from the West of milk, butter, even cheese provided an umbrella to protect nearby producers. New Englanders were used to handling cattle; they had pasture and hay fields.

The demand for fresh milk in particular was growing. Within driving distance of the cities local farms had long been selling it. Now hundreds more situated within a few hours by rail were added to the "milkshed," as the fresh milk area came to be called. By 1864 nearly 25 million quarts of milk annually came by rail into Boston alone. Between 1870 and 1880 Massachusetts dairymen almost doubled the amount of milk they sent to market. Further out, butter buyers took the farm wife's production:

and where transportation was even more distant, she made cheese. By 1880, every New England state except New Hampshire reported an increase in milch cows, 66,426 of them, almost 10 percent, added in twenty years.

In these same two decades rail service made it practical also to increase butter production by more than one fourth. The New England total of farm-churned butter rose to 65,453,000 pounds. In the 1880 census even small Rhode Island was credited with over a million pounds of farm-made butter. Much of it was put up in five and ten pound boxes or crocks.

Butter, especially if well made, was a sure means of getting cash or at least credit at the country store or through a commission merchant. But farm-churned butter was not always of high quality. By 1870 excellent Midwest butter, sometimes shipped on by emigrant New Englanders, began to appear on eastern markets. It was the product of Iowa, Illinois, and Wisconsin creameries and took prizes at exhibitions; because of superior quality the best sold at as much as a 10 percent premium over local butter. Yet to the end of the century, the expanding markets absorbed all, both local and imported.[1]

Creameries were soon organized in New England also. They assembled the milk of a whole neighborhood, turned it into butter (or cheese), and sold the product. The farmer was paid for the fat or solids, and the skim milk or whey went back with him to feed his calves and swine.

Advances in related fields held promise for the dairy business. In 1881 the Mechanical Refrigerating Company opened in Boston the nation's earliest mechanical refrigeration plant. That same year the Maine Central Railroad started refrigerator service, Bangor to Boston. By 1884 use of the newly invented De Laval centrifugal machine began in Vermont. This separated the cream content of milk mechanically. Setting milk overnight in pans for the cream to rise and the skimming that followed were no longer necessary. The proportion of cream secured was greater, also. Soon all dairy plants used it. By 1890 a St. Albans, Vermont, butter factory was making two million pounds a year. In New Hampshire 40 cooperative creameries made three million pounds. Only one cloud shadowed butter's future: by 1888 Boston wholesalers were handling five and a half million pounds of oleomargarine, and some of it was sold as butter.[2]

While butter-making increased, farm cheese production dropped by three fourths between 1860 and 1880. In part this may have been due to growth of local cheese factories (the first one had opened in war time), which reduced farm cheese making, or it may have represented a shift to butter or selling whole milk. In any case the home cheese vat was on the way out. Cheese factories were often small, at first usually cooperatively owned, and not always capably managed. Together with the butter plants they did, however, relieve farm women of that hard labor in the dairy which, added to other duties, had often been too much for their health. As a result of these shifts in practice at least one country industry prospered, the making of butter tubs and cheese boxes. Farm pigs also benefited. In the 1890 census report, Vermont, Maine, and Massachusetts swine population reached its highest point in forty years.

While consumption of fresh milk gained, swifter rail transport and increasing use of ice soon made it possible to draw fresh milk from greater distances. Massachusetts farmers shipped cityward 61 million quarts in 1870; a decade later they had almost doubled it. In New Hampshire one river meadow town, Milford, sent down 880,000 quarts a year to the big city. In 1890 Bellows Falls made the first shipment of fresh Vermont milk to Boston. By 1895 that city was getting milk by rail from an area spread out like the fingers of a hand: from Vermont and New Hampshire; from Willimantic in northeast Connecticut; from Charlemont, Massachusetts, at the edge of the Berkshires on the Hoosac Tunnel route; via the Central Massachusetts Railroad from Northampton, in the Connecticut Valley; as well as from many nearer stations on each rail line. Besides supplying local New England markets, some Connecticut and Berkshire milk went to New York City.[3] Then in 1887 (the very year that the ice-cream soda was introduced), Maine's Turner Center Creamery began to ship iced fresh cream by rail. Meanwhile, the population of New England's largest city had grown from 177,840 in 1860, to 560,892 in 1900.

One notable effect of milk-shed extension was the incentive for farmers along rail routes to build larger barns, which held the increased numbers of milkers that an assured market made possible and stored the hay needed to keep them through the winter. Even before the fresh milk era, an occasional farm might tie up 60 cows; but with whole milk shipment, large herds became practical in many places.[4] So the decades following the Civil War saw the erection of numbers of the tall, combined hay and stock barns which became a characteristic of New England's countryside. In the northern tier of states where winter was hard, a milk room, wagon shed, and wood shed would tie the barn to the farmhouse. Doors opening between provided an inside passageway, and the whole sheltered the barnyard from the north wind.

While farmers thus added cows to increase New England's milk supply, city dealers were accused of extending it still further from their water taps; also of skimming off cream then recoloring what remained with caramel; and of treating milk with boracic acid to make it keep longer.[5]

Such practices householders did not always mind, but in this decade Massachusetts passed stringent control legislation, and in 1891 made illegal another abuse, the sale of oleomargarine as butter.

An important change was taking place in the feeding of cattle. This was the chopping of green corn, stalks and all, or green clover into ensilage to provide succulent feed all winter. The chopped-up fodder was stored in silos, where it fermented but did not spoil. The first ensilage in America has been variously claimed to have been made in Maryland, New York, and Illinois in 1876, but two local silos were described in the Vermont Agricultural Report of 1869–70, and the subject was at least discussed at a meeting in 1875 of New Hampshire's State Board of Agriculture. J. M. Bailey of Billerica, Massachusetts, had a silo before 1880. By 1881 there were said to be 50 silos in New Hampshire (one of them 20 × 20 × 12½ feet), a larger number in Vermont and Massachusetts. By 1888 Vermont claimed to have 100, while farmers all over New England experimented with the new method. Originally silos were square, their walls made of stone, and were sometimes wholly or partly below ground. Occasionally a barn still contains one of the masonry silos of this period. In 1887 "the silo system" had been termed "best adapted to high-priced lands and so-called high farming." Yet in that very year a Vermont professor, speaking to Rhode Island farmers, advocated them for general use. He advised building them of the less expensive wood rather than stone.[6] Succeeding decades were to see circular wooden construction become most common, and the silo brought to nearly every practical dairy farm.

Excitement and great uneasiness developed in 1880 with regard to tuberculosis in cattle. Isolated cases of tubercular cattle had been found earlier in several Massachusetts towns. Now the selectmen of Grafton, south of Worcester, called to the attention of the state's Cattle Commission the unhealthy condition of a local herd. It was housed in a tight, unventilated barn. One animal had died, two were emaciated, several coughing. When the Commission had one of the sickest animals slaughtered, its lungs were found to be almost solid with tubercles.[7]

This happening was especially unsettling because for human tuberculosis, "consumption," which had become very prevalent in New England, on farms as well as in cities, no certain cure was known. Villemin in Paris in 1865 had proved that tuberculosis could be transmitted by inoculation, but not till 1882 did Robert Koch find that among humans the bacillus was spread by sputum. Yet leading American physicians long remained skeptical of the bacillus explanation for the disease. A stay at a sanitarium at some elevated spot in rural surroundings appeared the most practical expedient.[8]

In 1885 Frank S. Billings, a Boston veterinary surgeon, alarmed the Massachusetts Board of Agriculture by reporting how widespread the disease had become among the state's cattle. He recommended public control at Brighton and other abattoirs and prohibition of the sale of meat and milk from diseased animals. The following year the Board besought the legislature to ask Congress for federal controls. Within two years the Board was told that one fourth of all cattle in eastern Massachusetts were infected.[9] To add to public alarm, pleuropneumonia had reappeared in cattle brought from the West. Foot-and-mouth disease in 1884 had been discovered in Maine but had been stamped out there. That same year the United States Congress took note of the prevalence of animal diseases and added a Bureau of Animal Industry to the Department of Agriculture, two years later authorizing payment of indemnity to owners of stock condemned for disease and slaughtered by official order. Meanwhile in 1885 a number of animals in Maine's state college herd were found to be infected with tuberculosis. Amid wide public agitation and criticism, the entire herd was slaughtered.[10]

Worried at the danger represented by the constant uncontrolled influx to the great cattle mart at Brighton of animals from many directions, the Massachusetts legislature passed a law requiring inspection of all cattle entering the state. Going further in 1892, it directed all towns to inspect their local cattle and to slaughter suspected animals, and authorized compensation to the owner for the occasional animal found, after slaughter, to have been free from disease. Town officials were very slow to act and had to be prodded again and again. That year Rhode Island destroyed 207 cattle, all but 5 diseased, yet the milk from these cows was sold up to the day of slaughter! Unprincipled butchers were even said to collect diseased cattle in the northern states and ship them to Massachusetts markets to be killed for beef.

Lacking adequate federal control, all New England states now set up quarantines. One prompt result was that cattle from the West suspected of being diseased were diverted from New England to New York, which had no inspection law.

In 1890 Dr. Koch found that by testing suspected animals with a bacillus extract, the presence of tuberculosis could be determined with reasonable accuracy. Tightening control, in 1894 Massachusetts adopted this tuberculin test, licensed slaughterers, and began branding cattle pronounced tubercular. The same year Vermont began inspection. Nevertheless it was still only at the owner's request that cattle were tested. Of 3,325 inspected in Massachusetts in 1895, 26 percent proved diseased; of 1,639 quarantined by local inspectors, 802 were condemned. Up to this time, of 26,958 in all examined by the Massachusetts Board of Cattle Commissioners and given the tuberculin test, 4,389 had been condemned. With milk a popular food, the number of milch cows in New England had been rising steadily; 75,345 were added between 1880 and 1890 alone. Now the increasing tuberculosis agitation cast a cloud over the future of the dairy business. By 1895 one weakness in tuberculosis control was in part remedied: all states except Vermont provided some compensation to owners of animals condemned. However, the futility of relying on physical inspection alone became clearer when the herd of 33 at an experiment station was tested. The entire herd, the report said, seemed to be in prime condition except for two; but under the tuberculin test 21 more reacted. Where was all this to end? [11]

Even though infection in the three northern states was much less than in the southern tier, in 1895 New England's cattle commissions jointly decided to require inspection for all interstate shipments. Meanwhile, across the long three-state border, New York was still without controls against diseased animals. Its state veterinary association asserted that the common practice there was to test cattle arriving from the West, send sound animals into New England, and sell the reactors in New York State. Much criticism appeared in the farm press, however, to the effect that the tuberculin test was proving inaccurate. Upon slaughter some condemned animals showed no sign of the disease; others passed as healthy might be found full of tubercles. In 1897 a special committee of the Massachusetts legislature was appointed to check on the testing of 140 cows in the Lowell area, 138 of which reacted to the test. Its report questioned the test's reliability and the dangers to health involved. Already Massachusetts was spending a quarter-million yearly, with no end in sight. At times legislatures refused appropriations for the work. Connecticut in 1897 repealed all laws except one forbidding the sale of milk from an infected animal. Two years later, half the herd at the state college was found to be tuberculous. Thus the century ended. Progress had been made, but still much confusion and difference of opinion remained. As long as physicians continued to doubt that bovine tuberculosis could affect humans, full control was a long way ahead. Meanwhile, many children and others on farms and elsewhere were to suffer. [12]

Paralleling the growth of dairy farming came an upsurge in interest in poultry. Poultry raising was no longer the pursuit of gentleman fanciers, interested as they continued to be, or solely a matter of barnyard flocks, cared for by farm wives, boys, and girls. Enthusiastic poultrymen experimented with improved housing, ventilation, and feeding; with new types of birds; with methods of selection and breeding. All this was preparation for the poultry leadership New Englanders were to show in the succeeding century. For several decades after the war, as cereal prices kept slipping, the relative cheapness of shipped-in western grain for feed offered a distinct advantage to close-to-market producers of both eggs and meat. New Englanders responded by increasing farm flocks and developing specialized poultry farms. The new incubators helped to make larger flocks practical.

As a single local instance of poultry's increasing status, Waldoboro, Maine, farmers in the year ending April 1, 1874, shipped by rail to Boston 1,600 boxes of 125 dozen eggs each, as well as 200 boxes that went by steamer. Poultrymen there were well started on what was to continue for a century an important local enterprise.[13] They were not alone. In the 1880 federal census report, the first for poultry separately, the six New England states held the country's six top positions in egg yield, Maine in the lead. New England's egg output was almost 7 dozen per bird, against a national average of 4½ dozen. (This figure in the twentieth century would appear small indeed. For 1925–29 the New England average was to be 11½ dozen, for 1945–49 almost 16½ dozen; both totals surpassed those of every other section of the nation except the Pacific states.)[14]

Between the 1880 and the 1900 censuses the numbers of New England's "chickens" (the census term) and eggs rose far faster than its human population: an increase of over 60 percent for the birds, 100 percent in eggs. In every state, bird numbers and egg production increased. Rhode Island and New Hampshire each doubled its bird population and more than doubled its egg total. Massachusetts and Maine, the two largest producers, were not far behind. The figures reflected not only increased demand but also breeding for egg production and the growing use of incubation to get early layers. By 1885 in Massachusetts alone, between 35,000 and 40,000 people, on a large or small scale, were said to be in the poultry game. That year eggs brought them $1,600,000; within twenty years an additional million dollars was added. By the time of the 1900 census, New England's hens were laying more than 52,000,000 dozen eggs annually. This figured out as nine dozen apiece or better for every man, woman, and child in the six states and was not far from an egg every third day for each New England inhabitant. At the farm these eggs were worth $9,000,000, nearly the same value as the whole New England apple crop.

Apart from eggs, some poultry keepers made a business of fattening chickens for roasting. Vermont and southern Rhode Island were noted for fat turkeys, and Plymouth County grew Pekin ducks for Boston hotels. South County, Rhode Island, still fancied geese. Roast duckling was becoming fashionable. One Bristol County poultryman sent 5,000 ducks to market each year at the age of eight weeks (and had 2,000 white Wyandotte and Plymouth Rock chicks besides). Another duck grower in southeast Massachusetts claimed in 1897 to have sold 50,000 duck eggs for hatching. He kept 2,500 birds for breeding, scattering his flocks over greensward for health. With the aid of the manure the birds made in their winter housing, he grew carrots and hay for the next season, and these helped to supply food and keep healthy fifty to sixty horses that he boarded. An ingenious farmer could make circumstances serve him.[15]

Here and there poultrymen began to raise chicks for sale. Rhode Island's largest breeder in 1899 claimed to house 4,000 layers and breeders, all scattered in a hundred colony houses. He hatched and sold thousands of chicks each year, as well as 1,500 to 2,000 goslings.[16] The ordinary poultry keeper was like the neighboring hen man who raised 600 layers and 1,000 incubated chicks. He found that feeding and housing the flock and retailing the eggs gave him all he could do, with a little help needed at times, and provided him a satisfactory income. This was termed, in 1898, a large and successful Rhode Island poultry farm.[17] The great majority of poultry, however, were still to be found in small farm flocks. The Plymouth Rock, originated in New England and developed into two main strains, Barred and White, was the most popular type, but the Rhode Island Red and several other breeds each had its advocates.

These closing years of the century saw also the beginning of publicly sponsored experimental work in poultry. In 1886 Rhode Islanders formed a state poultry association. By 1890 the new Rhode Island Agricultural College set to work at scientific development of the Rhode Island Red. In 1898 it offered the nation's first college course in poultry husbandry, which attracted students from as far as Illinois and Nebraska.[18]

33. How the Gardens Grew

Beckoned by a continually rising population, vegetable growers expanded. There were occasional setbacks. Potato production, plagued by disease and competition, scarcely held its own from 1870 to 1880. To make matters worse, the Colorado beetle arrived. As a result, by 1890 the harvest showed a big dip in every state, even Maine. By 1900, however, it had rebounded strongly; Maine in particular reported an increase. The Bangor & Aroostook Railroad was opened in 1894 to Houlton, then to Caribou and Fort Fairfield. It brought an immediate boom to Aroostook County. Though Aroostook's summer was short, it was one of New England's most fertile spots. On its fresh limestone soils with their weekly rains potato acreage leaped forward, rising in that decade from 16,641 to almost 42,000 acres. Newly designed and increasingly effective sprayers and diggers assisted by commercial fertilizer helped the "Empire of Aroostook" to produce potatoes on a scale and of a quality that opened markets down and around the coast as far as Texas.[1] The potato was one of New England's important exports. In the 1890 census report Maine topped the nation with an average yield of 300 bushels per acre, a little beyond Ohio's. New Hampshire, in third place, averaged 240 bushels; Massachusetts, fifth, reported 233. New Hampshire's leading potato towns were for a long time in the north, the starch-factory area.

New varieties helped. In 1876 J. J. H. Gregory, a Marblehead seedsman, announced the breeding by a Massachusetts youth of the new Burbank's Seedling, which was later to become the ancestor of the Idaho baking potato. In 1885 three Vermont growers, Brownell, Rand, and Alexander, bred a new variety, which was to become famous. They called it "Green Mountain"; it was destined for almost as wide cultivation and acclaim as that state's Early Rose of two decades earlier, and became the special favorite of Aroostook County.[2]

New England's second most important export vegetable, the onion, was undergoing certain shifts in location. Danvers and Peabody on the Massachusetts coast, despite insects and disease, continued to get heavy yields and to enjoy the advantage of the Boston market. Barnstable is no longer mentioned. Bristol, Rhode Island, had lost its overseas trade but continued to grow onions for Providence, now its market. In the decades just after the war, the Wethersfield and Southport, Connecticut, areas were at their height, growing 500–900 bushels per acre, and 80,000 to 100,000 barrels annually, to supply New York and more distant markets. To do this, growers imported New York City horse manure to supplement local supplies and seaweed. Prices fell, and disease increased there, but until the end of the century Southport was New England's leading producer.

Up the Great Valley in Massachusetts, Deerfield, Sunderland, Hadley, and Whately farmers began to expand in onion-growing. For labor, recruiters brought in hundreds of hard-working, aspiring Polish families to take over the stooping monotonous field work. Eventually the Poles were to acquire ownership of many of the farms, and handle merchandising of the crop.[3] In 1900 the federal census credited Connecticut with 422,000 bushels of onions, Massachusetts with 748,000, and Rhode Island with 116,000, over 1¼ million bushels in all New England. The yellow Danvers Globe was the favorite.

A third export specialty was canned sweet corn and other canned vegetables. Maine canners, selling countrywide, annually contracted for heavy acreages of corn, beans, and soup vegetables: 12,500 acres in 1882 for seventy-one factories. In the year preceding they had processed a pack of 11,350,000 cans of sweet corn alone. Canners provided a market for nearly $300,000 worth of Maine's dry beans also. Toward the end of the century, a half-dozen Vermont factories canned the corn from five to six thousand acres.[4]

The most striking change in vegetable growing was in the rapid strides made by market gardeners near cities. Their production of fresh vegetables constantly increased. (The Census Bureau's inattention to local deviations from nationwide crop categories prevents federal figures from reflecting this fully.)

Concord, Massachusetts, farmers had begun in the 1850's to fill their sandy plains with asparagus roots. By 1874, 35 or more large growers together with numerous smaller ones were in the business. Within a decade they produced nearly 75,000 bunches, half the Massachusetts crop, with an income of $200 to $300 per acre. Cucumbers and rhubarb were new Concord crops, grown under glass. One farm sold 25,000 cucumbers a year, together with two indoor crops of fresh rhubarb.[5] Pickle factories, opened in Cranston, Rhode Island, Lincoln, Massachusetts, and the Deerfield area, together with some in Vermont and New Hampshire, offered an outlet for what one grower called "as profitable a crop as I ever raised."[6]

Irrigation of upland meadows by sloping furrows from springs above is mentioned in Rhode Island in 1839. Irrigation to keep summer vegetables constantly growing goes back to Arlington, Massachusetts, at least to 1873, perhaps beyond. By 1877 a number of growers around Boston were using large-size hose and hand watering for cabbage, lettuce, celery, and cauliflower. In 1883 one grower declared water as essential for success for growing vegetables as for washing them. In Rhode Island the Budlong family enterprise at Cranston irrigated 180 acres of cucumbers. Most of these, along with horseradish, cauliflower, and small onions, 50,000 bushels a year in all, went into the firm's pickle products. By 1886 at least one strawberry grower near Providence and others near Boston used water to get full production from that crop. Some gardeners built windmills with elevated tanks, others provided artesian wells and steam pumps. Market gardening of such a type called for substantial capital, full equipment, and heavy manuring. Suburban land is "taxed highly and costs us very dear," one said. Dear also was the city horse manure that made the soil productive. But it all paid. Their highly tilled fields sometimes yielded a thousand dollars worth per acre of vegetables and small fruits.[7]

The "Boston hotbed," covered with glass sashes to force crops, was one productive resource. As long before as February 9, 1753, Reverend Edward Holyoke in his Salem diary had told of planting gourds, cucumbers, and lettuce in his hotbed; and well before the Revolution Boston newspapers advertised glass sash for them. The sides were thick plank staked up parallel and banked outside, the bed running east and west, with a slight slope south to catch the sun. A foot or more of the soil between was dug out and the excavation filled with steaming, fermenting horse manure, bought at a high price, up to a dollar per sash, from large city stables. A few inches of fine soil were filled in on it so as to leave a foot of air space, then the sash were laid across the planks. The sun warmed the soil by day and straw mats over the sash held in the manure's heat by night. Shielded by windbreak fencing, the market gardener's beds might run to hundreds of feet in length. In them gardeners grew vegetables such as lettuce, radishes, cucumbers, and greens to market size. To gain the early market they also started thousands of seedlings for transplanting to sunny outside slopes.

Real greenhouses had till the nineteenth century been the province of wealthy amateurs to force grapes and tropical fruits and flowers; but by 1839 at least one Arlington market gardener had a greenhouse in use to start early plants for transplanting outside.[8]

Marketing of greenstuffs and roots was simplified and standardized by the development at Boston of a uniform reusable package. The square, flat Boston bushel box took the place of the barrel and the nondescript bag that long remained in use elsewhere in the country. Its open face encouraged more honest, uniform, and attractive packing. Holding eighteen heads of lettuce or two dozen bunches of beets or carrots, it helped New England produce to ship well. Thus it became popular with buyers in New York and elsewhere, and contributed to the development of a considerable outside trade. Toward the end of the century a winter visitor to Florida complained that the only vegetables offered in stores there were shipped down from Boston![9]

Increasingly, greenhouse men saw opportunities in growing flowers for sale as well as vegetables. Between the 1880 and the 1890 census reports the number of florists rose substantially in all the states. To provide better sales facilities, Boston area growers in 1892 organized the Boston Flower Exchange and set up their own market place. The Massachusetts state census of 1895 gave a half million value to its commercial flowers. In Connecticut by 1900 the U.S. census reported almost as much, and the Massachusetts value by then was up to $1,639,000. Along with the flowers, growers built up a substantial sale in started plants.

Gardeners found small fruits excellent companions to vegetables. As markets expanded and better varieties were brought out, strawberry production became increasingly important. The Wilson was popular and the large and delicious Marshall, originated in Marshfield, Massachusetts, was acclaimed in 1890. By that time Concord and the Dighton area east of Providence had become considerable centers of production. Yet as early as 1878, Concord had been able to count 100 or more growers and over 50 acres of berries, the leading producer marketing 25,000 quart boxes. In 1885 for the whole state of Massachusetts the total reached 4,000,000 quarts with a value of $400,000, twenty times the crop reported two decades before. Connecticut also was marketing large crops. Ledyard, in the New London area, was one production center, single farms there selling up to 6,000 baskets; while in 1900 one New Haven market gardener picked 50,000 quarts.

Cranberry growing gained favor steadily also, helped by the recently invented cranberry scoop. In its most prosperous year, 1895, growers harvested a crop of 150,000 barrels, worth an estimated million dollars.[10] By the end of the century, Cape Cod had invested $1,400,000 in bogs that totaled 3,500 acres, many of the owners men who had previously followed the sea; Plymouth County next door, however, was the crop's center. An acre of well-made bog, fruiting properly and served with adequate water, might be worth $1000. Severe troubles, unfortunately, lay ahead for this fruit.

A modest development took place in grapes. Moore's Early was a new
(1871) Massachusetts variety. One Worcester County fruit town, in 1885,
reported 20,000 vines with a yield of 128,000 pounds, while the whole
state produced almost 3,000,000, half of them hothouse grown.

The invention in 1852 by Rev. L. L. Langstreth of Pennsylvania of the
moveable-frame hive became the foundation for all future bee-keeping.
Five years later he was living in Greenfield, Massachusetts. Aside from
producing honey the bees were the means of fertilizing apples and other
fruit blooms. As greenhouse men and market gardeners turned to growing cucumbers, bees being indispensable for their crop also, they hired
bee colonies from apiarists. Though bees were never destined to great
numbers in New England, they had enthusiastic devotees in all its states.
By 1876 James Wood, an apiarist in Prescott, Massachusetts, had gained a
national reputation as a breeder of pure Italian queens. Total value of
bees in 1900 was $206,000; Maine and Vermont were the leaders.

The gravel hills of southern Maine, southern New Hampshire, Connecticut, western Rhode Island, Massachusetts, and parts of Vermont, set
largely with orchards of Baldwins, Russets, and Greenings, produced
crisp tasty apples that not only New England but Old England welcomed.
"The foreign market for our fruit is as well established as for our wheat,"
Colonel Wilder, leading horticulturist, commented in 1876. The price off
the steamer at Liverpool in 1878 was a pound sterling per barrel. The year
1880, with its big apple crop, saw especially huge shipments go abroad.
Steamers with Maine apples left Portland every week. In 1896 almost a
million barrels went across from Boston. As time went on, Maine orchardists turned considerably (and mistakenly) to the huge, handsome
Ben Davis as an export variety; although easily raised, it was of inferior
quality. In the rest of New England, Baldwins and Russets remained
popular.

Immense quantities of apples, especially those from minor orchards on
general farms, went into cider and vinegar, or to canners and evaporators
who prepared dried apples for the hotel and grocery trade as well as for
export "to the remotest nations." Gloucester's fishing fleet alone, to feed
its 4,300 fishermen, made 37 tons of dried apples into pies and apple
sauce in the course of a year. Farm families continued to slice and dry
apples on strings in the kitchen around the fire, a tedious job.[11]

Every state was interested in apple growing. Between 1890 and 1900
New Hampshire's orchards shrank somewhat, while Massachusetts was
doubling its production. In 1900 Maine had over four million apple trees.
Vermont developed profitable orchards about Lake Champlain and in its

southern section but did not become an important apple state. Even in small Rhode Island the crop was considerable. Nevertheless one observer claimed that a large proportion of New England orchards made a sorry picture of disease and neglect.

Not only apples but pears, peaches, quinces, cherries, and currants continued to be of market importance. New England's first large commercial peach orchard was the work of J. H. Hale. His plantings at South Glastonbury and those of other growers in that area were said to number three million trees and made Connecticut for several decades New England's peach state. Hale gave to horticulture the excellent peach variety that bears his name. Except in years of extreme cold, peaches became a market crop well north in New England. In 1898 Wilbraham, east of Springfield, had an orchard of 3,000 trees. A fertile hill fruit town such as Harvard, Massachusetts, could claim 13,743 peach trees, a number substantial even when compared with its 27,717 apple trees. But winterkilling, disease, and increasing rail shipments from the South and New York eventually limited New England's production. Along with peaches, many a hilly acre, especially in Connecticut, was set to Luther Burbank's new hybrid Japanese plums.[12] Burbank had started his horticultural career on a farm in Lunenburg, Massachusetts, then transferred to California.

Cigar tobacco was for the rest of the century the leading money crop of the Connecticut Valley. The fields extended north into southern New Hampshire and Vermont, and into Connecticut's Housatonic Valley. Volatile prices and poor seasons weeded out soils and growers unsuited to the crop; but as cigars grew more popular, Connecticut's production increased from 8,328,000 pounds, the 1870 census figure, to over 14,000,000 at the next report. In Massachusetts the single town of Whately in 1870 produced leaf of an estimated value of $275,000, but production in the state as a whole dropped back almost 2,000,000 pounds in the next decade. In the 1880 census report the value of its entire 5,369,000-pound pack was given as just under $700,000 but was only half that received at the war's end.

One important cause of tobacco trouble was that manufacturers discovered on the island of Sumatra in the East Indies a superior light-colored wrapper tobacco leaf that they could import cheaply. Tobacco leaf sells by the pound. Two pounds of the excellent Sumatra leaf would furnish the outside wrappers for a thousand cigars. To wrap that number in Connecticut Valley leaf required four pounds or more. Dismayed at loss of their market the local farmers in 1883 organized a Connecticut

Valley Tobacco Growers Association. They persuaded Congress to enact a tariff of $2.00 per pound. From 1890 on, this slowed importation and helped the local market.

Then the new state experiment stations went to work on tobacco. Charles Goessman at the Massachusetts station studied and advised on soil conditions, which varied widely. In 1900 Connecticut investigated the possibility of growing fine leaf under artificial shade, making studies that were to save the growing of wrapper tobacco for New England for another half century. Invention of a transplanting machine in the 1880's was a step toward efficient and more profitable production. To meet one hazard of the business the growers themselves formed the Tobacco Growers Mutual Insurance Company, which issued the nation's first hail insurance policy.[13]

General farmers continued to raise some small grain, even wheat, but as horses replaced oxen both on farms and in cities, oats gained favor. Vermont led in 1880, raising 3,742,282 bushels. By 1890 Maine, which reported 2,265,595 in the 1880 census, had boosted production to 3,668,909; Vermont stayed nearly even. By 1900, however, all states save Maine showed a decline in oats. Except that its straw was salable, rye was no longer important anywhere, and barley only in Maine and Vermont. Buckwheat had seldom been popular except in Maine. There its production continued, especially among the Aroostook French.

Production of New England's most widespread crop, hay, remained important throughout the century's final decades. Nearly every state made a modest gain of 10 to 20 percent, the largest in Maine. This may have reflected, in part, the increase in dairying, in part, the increasing city demand for hay and its ready transport by either rail or water. Durham, New Hampshire, for example, sent 1,500 tons of hay annually to Boston. The Belfast, Maine, area shipped large quantities by sea, some of it for cows kept in crowded city and suburban dairies. Day calls attention to another money crop, a substantial production in eastern Maine of clover seed for sale.[14]

Maple products had for a century been the year's first harvest for thousands of upland farmers, especially in Vermont, New Hampshire, and western Massachusetts and Connecticut. A farmer might tap from 1,000 to 1,500 trees. The maple orchard supplied farm families with sweets, making purchase of cane sugar unnecessary. Maple sugar had been sold in competition with cane, at first for a lower price. During the Civil War, with cane sugar cut off, maple gained popularity and reached higher prices. Vermont was the leading producer, reporting almost 9 million pounds in 1870, increasing to 11¼ million in 1880, and to over 14 million in 1890, about one fourth of the nation's supply. New Hampshire's totals ran from just under 2 million to 2¾ million pounds; several of its towns harvested 40,000 to 80,000 pounds, Acworth setting the pace. The town of Sandisfield, the leading Massachusetts producer, made 200,000 pounds in 1855, and continued substantial crops for years.

By the end of the century there was a change in popular demand. More and more maple was sold each decade as syrup, Vermont alone producing 160,000 gallons in 1900. Passage of the Pure Food Act in 1906 strengthened its position, choking off the common practice by food distributors of adulterating maple with glucose.[15] By 1910 the value of Vermont's harvest was to pass a million dollars; by 1920, 3½ millions, as maple syrup came to be generally appreciated as a table delicacy. Though the crop required much hard work—and sometimes in years when sap flowed poorly was a disappointment—maple producers were a welcome source of cash for thousands of hill farmers.

The decade of the Civil War marked New England's high point for cultivated land and the low point for its forest cover. Connecticut in 1870 was three fourths "improved land"; Massachusetts, Vermont, and New Hampshire roughly two thirds. Even Maine reached its highest point of clearance in 1880. The "improvement," nevertheless, may often have been only that the wood was cut off and cattle turned in to browse on the herbage.

During the sixties for more and more factories and railways coal took over as fuel, yet Civil War demands boosted prices of cordwood. A growing population still used great quantities of wood to cook and keep warm. Iron forging, glass making, and other industries demanded immense supplies of charcoal and cordwood. At Lancaster, New Hampshire, in 1874, wood brought more income than potatoes and half as much again as butter. Where the local market was good, farm woodlots might be cut every 15 or 20 years. Trees were sometimes sold standing, by auction in eighth-acre lots. Lumber mills were as busy as ever.

Altogether in each of the larger states, the woods in 1870 added from one to one and three fourths million dollars to rural income and one fourth million even in Rhode Island. At the same time they supplied material for important local wood manufactories, tanneries, shipbuilders, and farm use.

Steadily, as people left the hills, young forest began to take over. Petersham, Massachusetts, for example, saw its woodlands almost double between 1865 and 1885, and double again by 1905, when trees again cov-

ered 55 percent of the town's area.[16] Such changes did not inevitably decrease cultivated land. While poor areas of the farm were allowed to return to woods, tillage might even increase.

One discouraging development for the forest was the accidental introduction into New England from Europe in 1868 of the gypsy moth. A decade later this pest came to public notice with widespread defoliation of
forest and shade trees in eastern Massachusetts. From there, carried by
the winds, the moths spread rapidly. In 1897 appeared the brown-tail
moth, to add to the destruction. Great areas of woodland and thousands
of street trees were ruined and cut down. After the value of lead arsenate
as a spray was discovered in 1892, reasonable control was established. Bi-
ological controls eventually displaced spraying, but no permanent remedy has yet been found.

As an offset, hundreds of village improvement societies all over the six
states were busy lining principal highways with elms, maples, and oaks.
State legislatures passed new acts for protection of street trees and required the election of tree wardens. In 1900 Yale established its famed
School of Forestry, and the practice of forestry became a profession.

34. Any Way to Make a Dollar

DURING THESE difficult transition decades a new source of income for country people became important: the summer visitor. To Newport, Rhode Island, the summer guest had long been an old story. Planters from the West Indies and the Carolinas and visitors from humid Philadelphia had been going there for the warm months since decades before the Revolution. Some lodged with townspeople: some, after a time, drawn by the equable climate and the considerable social life, bought property. Under the new nation Newport came into favor again. Across Narragansett Bay, Westerly's first summer hotel dated from 1840, and after the war, cottages multiplied at Watch Hill and Weekapaug. Narragansett Pier by 1890 was becoming a cottage city like Newport.

The White Mountains too attracted visitors. By the middle of the century the Glen House at Mt. Washington's base could accommodate 350 persons. Jackson with two hotels was popular. At Gorham the railroad built a large hotel. By 1875 the value of Bethlehem's tourist trade, $160,000, considerably exceeded that of its soil productions. The "large influx" of visitors afforded a "fine opportunity to market surplus produce at advance rates." Franconia, equally popular, counted three hotels and eight large boarding houses, and almost every house took guests; while Conway's 2,000 permanent summer guests and thousands of visitors, like Bethlehem's, left considerably more money than was derived from its traditional crops. Lake Champlain's southern end became a fashionable resort in the middle of the century, and the Green Mountains, even before the Civil War, were beckoning visitors. Brattleboro had its first summer hotel in 1845. Newport on Memphramagog had a hotel and an iron lake steamer in 1870; and at Sheldon, mineral springs attracted many.[1] Woodstock's famous Inn dates from 1892.

On Lake Winnepesaukee, by 1870 it was reported that "The inhabitants are generally engaged in farming and keeping summer boarders." Wolfeboro's summer visitors were worth $125,000 to that community. Center Harbor entertained 600 summer guests in 1875, in addition to transients by the thousands. Around New London, summer people began to arrive in the 1880's. They continued to come, for long stays, right up through the end of the century. Some boarded (1,200 registered in 1900); others bought property. The Monadnock region had been popular since long before the Civil War. Farmers near Dublin Lake were taking boarders by 1840. Organized camping is said to have had its inception at Squam Lake in 1888, and the original ski club was born at Berlin in 1900. On the larger lakes "elegant steamboats" added to the attractions. Massabesic, near Manchester, its shores dotted with cottages, in 1893 boasted four steamers. On the coast at Hampton almost every house had a few boarders by 1875, and there was said to be a home market there for all the farmers' surplus.[2]

In Maine the Ricker family had been entertaining guests at Sabbathday Lake since 1794. By the 1840's their Poland Spring water had attained a reputation that brought increasing numbers of guests. Moosehead Lake got its first excursion steamer in 1836. On the coast, Old Orchard Beach about 1840 developed entertainment facilities. A large three-story hotel opened in the Portland, Maine, area in 1849, followed by numerous others. Bar Harbor began to attract about the same time, but it was later in the century before it gained society recognition. At Cape Elizabeth the first summer hotel dated from 1875.

Lenox and Stockbridge, Massachusetts, drew the wealthy and fashionable of New York decades before the Civil War; while Connecticut's Sound and lakes and Massachusetts' shore resorts attracted artists and sojourners long before the century's end. By 1870 Princeton, beside Mt. Wachusett, had a half dozen hotels besides farm boarding houses.

This increasing influx of visitors brought many an up-country farm family a lucrative market for milk (cream especially), eggs, vegetables, and farm cooking, and a welcome income also from surplus rooms in the farm dwelling. The hotel trade bought supplies largely from city dealers, yet even so, formed an important outlet for market gardeners, growers of small fruits, and dairymen, though they might be one or two hundred miles away. New Hampshire claimed 1,400 summer hotels and boarding houses by 1890, "annually filled to overflowing." A Vermont report said, regarding cream, "We shall be strangely blind, if we fail to . . . cater to this new demand which has come to our very doors."[3]

The time for summer people to take over abandoned farms was still largely ahead, but already, though not always welcomed, they formed an important stabilizing factor, increasing farm and community income for many a hill and shore town, and, equally important, stirring the social and intellectual life of neighborhoods that were losing population and might be inclined to lethargy.[4] Governor Nahum J. Bachelder was to say in 1905 that for New Hampshire, the summer business was worth as much as the state's hay crop—three million dollars. Some resented the intrusion, but in general farm people benefited from both, not only in New Hampshire but in every New England state.

35. Agriculture Organizes

WIDESPREAD ORGANIZATION, both governmental and voluntary, characterized agriculture during the last half of the nineteenth century. Partly this was the result of economic pressures, partly it arose from an urge to improve animals, crops, methods of production and sale, and community life as well.

The Civil War was one year along when President Lincoln signed the act creating the United States Department of Agriculture. In 1889 its Commissioner was made a member of the cabinet. Meanwhile, the Bureau of Animal Industry had been set up in 1884 and several other bureaus and divisions added, including by 1888 the Office of Experiment Stations. In 1890 the Weather Bureau was transferred to Agriculture.

In certain respects organization by New England state governments preceded federal legislation. One timely step had been the creation of cattle commissions to meet the pleuropneumonia crisis. This had made possible also Maine's successful confinement of a foot-and-mouth disease outbreak in 1884. Massachusetts next set up a Dairy Bureau in 1892.

Official state organization on behalf of agriculture had begun even earlier. Massachusetts formed a State Board of Agriculture in 1852; Maine (after a short-lived earlier attempt) followed in 1856; Connecticut, in 1866; New Hampshire, 1870; Vermont, 1872; and Rhode Island, 1892. These boards were usually composed of one representative from each of the state's county or regional agricultural societies, in some cases with other state officials or appointees added. They met at the state capital, and from time to time in other central locations. Prominent speakers, persons of agricultural and scientific attainment, presented papers on timely subjects, often before a considerable audience besides board members. These papers and discussions—example, William S. Clark's articles on "The Circulation of Sap in Plants" and "Observations on the Phenomena of Plant Life"—received wide publicity. They were customarily gathered by the board's paid secretary and printed in an annual volume, distributed in some states by the thousands. The secretaries of the state boards, devoted men such as Stephen L. Goodale of Maine, Theodore S. Gold of Connecticut, and Charles L. Flint of Massachusetts, also wrote important contributions of their own.

The boards made grants from public funds to local groups for holding agricultural exhibitions where the best in stock, crops, and home products were entered in competition. They encouraged county societies to set up Farmers' Institutes. These offered winter courses of lectures, often lasting several days, at which staff members from agricultural colleges and experiment stations, farm publication editors, and visiting notables were instructors. Attendance was general, and, as Day makes clear for Maine, the institutes opened the scientific and theoretical aspects of agriculture to ordinary farm people under circumstances such that they could learn, yet feel at ease.

Through the century's closing decades the state governments also gave increasing financial support to their agricultural colleges, though not infrequently against apathy and opposition. Connecticut added an agricultural school at Storrs, which in 1893 became a college.

These efforts were effective, as W. H. Jordan of Geneva, New York, commented in 1898: "What a vast amount of scientific, well-organized, useful facts and principles have been assimilated by New England agriculture during the past 25 years." "The college," he said, "has been the local interpreter of the lessons of modern science."[1]

Connecticut in 1875 became the first state in the country to appropriate public funds for an agricultural experiment station, "to be used in employing competent scientific men," as the act provided. It opened at Wesleyan's Middletown campus with Wilbur O. Atwater as director, and two years later moved to New Haven, where Samuel W. Johnson was appointed to head it. Wholly financed by the state after its first year, by 1877 it was issuing analysis reports that exposed shady practices in the booming commercial fertilizer industry, was beginning tests of seeds offered for sale, and soon started testing 1500 varieties of grasses. In 1881–82 Atwater and Charles D. Woods provided, and in 1889 published, what is believed to be the earliest proof of the assimilation of nitrogen from the air by clover.

Massachusetts, its Agricultural College already versed in scientific experimentation, funded its station in 1882, Maine, in 1885; New Hampshire and Vermont, in 1886. With the passage of the Hatch Act by Congress in 1887, federal finance and organized support came to the aid of all the stations.

Connecticut's stations soon went deep into studies of human and animal nutrition. Among important results, this pioneering led to the development of diabetic foods. At Amherst, Massachusetts, Professor Charles H. Fernald began his notable work in entomology, while Professor Charles A. Goessman was specializing in soil fertility, plant growth, sugar-beet and tobacco-crop research. Rhode Island in 1890 began its work on poultry. Maine in 1891 came up with a recommendation for Bordeaux mixture for apple scab and worked on field crops, feeds, and egg fertility; New Hampshire, on milk quality and fertilizers; Vermont, on wool, milk, and potatoes. The contributions of New England stations to the nation's and the world's well-being have been notable indeed, and those of the entire nation of a value incalculable.[2]

Meanwhile, Harvard University, aided by a bequest from James Arnold of New Bedford, established on the site of its Bussey Farm its famed Arnold Arboretum and soon began to assemble the most comprehensive tree and shrub collection of the western world. Professor Storrs in 1887 published there *Chemistry and Its Relation to Agriculture* and put out the country's first experiment station bulletin. Harvard scientists Dr. Theobald Smith and Dr. Daniel Salmon offered new and valuable information on the cause and prevention of hog cholera.

In the dairy field, organization took two paths, one the formation of breed associations and state stockmen's groups, the other the development of local enterprises, many of them cooperative, to manufacture butter and cheese and to collect cream for shipment.

Vermont farmers honored their calling by organizing in 1869 at Montpelier the country's first dairy association. Maine followed in 1874, and Connecticut, in 1882. Breeders of individual types of cattle gathered also in associations. Several of these had their birth in New England but became national in scope. Their purpose was to improve dairy blood lines and keep records of purebred and superior animals and their progeny.

From the home of its secretary at South Wilbraham, Massachusetts, the Association of Breeders of Thorough-Bred Neat Stock in 1863 published the earliest American Devon herd book. This included pedigrees of 501 Devons, from 58 breeders in 15 states. A second volume followed five years later. At Farmington, Connecticut, in 1868, Jerseymen set up the American Jersey Cattle Club; two years later at Winthrop, Maine, what was to become the Maine State Jersey Cattle Club was formed. W. W. Chenery of Belmont, Massachusetts, in 1871 took the lead in organizing the Association of Breeders of Thoroughbred Holstein Cattle. In 1885 this was to unite with a Friesian group to become the Holstein-Friesian Association of America. Next, in 1875, came the American Ayrshire Breeders' Association. This group, reorganized in 1886, still has headquarters at Brandon, Vermont. In 1877 the American Guernsey Cattle Club was founded in Massachusetts and its herd register set up. The breed's national headquarters remains in New England, at Peterborough, New Hampshire. The Brown Swiss Cattle Breeders' Association followed, formed at Worcester in 1880.[3]

Up to this time the milk from a farmer's dairy cows had been turned into butter chiefly at home. The census report of 1880 marked the high point for butter made on farms, as that of 1850 had for cheese. But Midwest butter of excellent, uniform quality had for a decade or so begun to top New England markets. Eastern farmers soon concluded that combining their butter-making efforts should yield better results than a multitude of small operations.

Cheese factories had been established during the Civil War. Maine's first started at Sandy River in 1872. What is said to have been the first New England butter creamery opened in 1879 at Shelburne in Vermont's Champlain Valley. The following year, at Hatfield in Massachusetts' Connecticut Valley, local farmers united to set up a cooperative butter factory, and across the river in Easthampton another began in 1881. Maine farmers sent a scout to observe, and in 1883 opened that state's first cooperatives at Wales, Winthrop, New Gloucester, and Machias. Turner Center, destined to become best known of all, began business the next February.[4] Soon, in addition to butter, this plant was selling the sweet cream for which it was to become famous. Some creameries proved too small to be efficient, but Maine's butter production kept growing through 1900. The other states gradually turned more to the sale of whole milk.

Individuals with capital also opened commercial creameries, some of them growing to large size. By the 1900's in each of the butter-making states the number of independent creameries equaled the total of cooperatives.

Some local plants achieved a good deal of success. The Franklin County, Vermont, creamery, served 1,200 farmers milking 16,000 cows, made 2¾ million pounds of butter in a single year. By 1890 it was claimed to be the largest butter manufacturer anywhere. A cooperative creamery in the Quinebaug Valley at the Massachusetts-Connecticut line, formed in 1887, supplied Boston's Adams House, Parker House, and Young's Hotel for years, as well as the famous S. S. Pierce grocery firm. It claimed to be the most prosperous in New England.[5]

In the field of whole milk, effective organization was not to come till later. An Old Colony Milk Producers Association in Plymouth County is recorded in 1877. In the 1891 report of the Massachusetts Board of Agriculture a speaker credited a Milk Producer's Union with gaining a cent on the price of milk. The successful Springfield Cooperative Milk Association handled about 8,000 quarts daily before the close of the century. But not till the organization of the New England Milk Producer's Association in 1917 was there to be an effective counterweight to the power of the

Boston milk dealers, five of whom gradually concentrated control of the retail milk business of that area and dictated prices paid farmers and the territory from which milk was imported. In the New York milkshed, which came to include western Connecticut and a part of Massachusetts, conditions were chaotic. The Five States Milk Producers Association, organized in 1898, strove with small success to surmount them.

Organization went on in other branches of agriculture. Orchardists began with the Connecticut Pomological Society in 1871, the Maine State Pomological Society in 1873, and the Massachusetts Fruit Growers' Association in 1895. All are still active.

In poultry husbandry the Boston Poultry Show continued its successful annual exhibitions. The American Poultry Association dated from 1873. Maine and Rhode Island poultrymen had organized by 1886.

A New England Tobacco Association gathered members in 1883 to fight for tariff protection, but it was shortlived. Eighteen eighty-six saw the formation of the Boston Market Gardeners Association, the earliest body in the country in the field of vegetable growing. Eighty years later it was to evolve into the New England Vegetable Growers Association. The seed growers of Connecticut and their competitors of other areas got together at Hartford in 1892 to form the American Seed Trade Association. The Society of American Florists was organized in 1885, and in the depression year of 1894 the Boston Flower Exchange set up business in the basement of the Park Street Church. In 1894 forty-four citizens of Windsor, Connecticut, and nearby towns set up a vegetable cannery that in two seasons put up 20,000 cases of tomatoes, 1,200 barrels of ketchup, 15,000 cases of squash, and large amounts of bottled juices. Under various managements this cannery was to last beyond World War I.

Community farmers' clubs, which before the war had enjoyed a slow growth, now spread widely. Sometimes, as at Industry, Maine, mechanics were also members. These held frequent meetings and discussions, often assembled their own libraries, and held exhibitions of local products. Besides their agricultural value, as Jarvis M. Morse points out, they quickened social life in country communities and softened jealousies and bickerings. From discussions at "the wide-awake club" in Woodstock, Connecticut, a local history states, new interest in farming arose and this club led its members to improvement on traditional practices. Greens Farms Club, organized in the winter of 1860, was known for 50 years for its progressiveness. It was the Belmont, Massachusetts, club that introduced the strawberry festival custom. Between 1860 and 1875 Maine alone counted as many as 75 such local farmers' clubs. They flourished in farming communities in the other states, some into the next century. In more than one town the Farmers' Club became for decades the leading community organization. Harvest clubs that included both sexes became leaders in the Connecticut Valley. There, in 1898, the Hampden County club was discussing immigration and the future of the Philippines.[6]

Important in the impression that it made on rural living as well as on agriculture as a means of livelihood was the rise during the last quarter of the century of the Grange. Oliver Kelley of Washington conceived of a new secret order, distinctively rural, to include both men and women.[7] The time was ripe and the movement widened to include all the northern states. At the beginning the idea spread slowly. The first local grange organized in New England is said to have been that at St. Johnsbury, in northeastern Vermont, formed July 1, 1871; its State Grange was formed exactly a year later. In 1873 Massachusetts, Maine, and New Hampshire followed with State Granges; Connecticut did the same in 1874, and Rhode Island in 1889.

These early organizing steps began just as the great panic and depression of 1873 gripped the nation. Amid the general disaster farm people felt the need of a powerful, effective instrument to protect themselves and their interests. Soon the growth of the new Grange order became electric. Important political effects resulted nationally, among them control of railway transportation through the Interstate Commerce Commission.

The comparative stability and wealth of New England, the lighter burden of mortgage debt on its farms, and their closeness to market spared the farm people of these six states the worst effects of the depression and the political extremism that convulsed the West. The New England granges did act in both political and economic fields. However, both the original mushroom growth of the order and the downward plunge in membership that succeeded it when economic hopes were not realized were less spectacular in New England than in newer states lacking industry and far from market.

For a decade or two the Grange's future looked uncertain. But the New England Grange movement took root; membership stabilized, then began a steady increase. By 1897 populous Worcester County, Massachusetts, for example, could list fifty local granges with 4,889 members. Some of the organization's newly developed cooperative ventures failed. Others, however, including successful insurance companies and community stores, weathered all difficulties and settled down to long and useful lives. For their members and other country people these enterprises often made substantial savings.[8]

More important than their business aspect, however, was the value of the local and county granges as rural social centers. Something on the lines of the old Lyceum and farmers' clubs, they served as a focus for education, for excellence in handicrafts and gardening, and as a means of community betterment. The Grange was powerful in support of agricultural education and active in sponsoring local fairs and exhibitions of farm products and handicrafts.

County pomonas and state granges often became ladders to political preferment, a development not necessarily unfortunate in its results. In states in other parts of the country the Grange mushroomed, then almost vanished. In New England, which came to be called the Gibraltar of the order, it took root and became an important and helpful rural influence.

36. The Farm Wife

OFTEN IN THIS PERIOD and the opening decades of the 1900's the special burdens of the times fell disproportionately on the farm woman. If income was low or a mortgage payment had to be met, it was likely that to her ordinary responsibilities she added more poultry raising or increased butter making. If, in the effort to find a livelihood, the farm advertised for summer visitors, as many did, she toiled through the hot months to serve them fresh biscuits and strawberry shortcake, while she coped with mountains of washing.

Home canning in glass jars had come in; so the housewife could now vary the family's winter diet and make the garden last through the year. Yet this added extra hot hours of canning to her summer schedule. On a dairy farm in haying time, or where, near a city, the farmer turned to vegetables, these months might mean the extra burden of immigrant helpers also to be housed and fed. As countryman Robert Frost recognizes in his poem "A Servant to Servants," such a cross was quietly borne, and not seldom the farm woman added a blessing. Whittier had described the quiet, saintly country woman of his time in "The Friend's Burial." Frost, in his "Death of the Hired Man," was to portray again her gentle influence.

The housewife did get relief, helped by several inventions. The iron cookstove was far better than the fireplace and brick oven, not only for preparing meals but for providing comfort in the kitchen in winter. To complement the stove came the ice chest, often kept cold by ice from a pond on the farm, and with it the ice-cream freezer, which a son was always ready to turn. Tinware, china, and washboards also became commonplace.

In more and more farmhouses running spring water or at least a pump from the well lightened woman's kitchen work and washing, and an iron or soapstone sink and set tubs received the water. The men piped in water from the spring or above the well erected a self-governing windmill. Near cities, prosperous farmers put in bathrooms. To help the woman in another branch of her duties, Elias Howe, Jr.—a Spencer, Massachusetts, farmer—had patented the lock-stitch sewing machine, and on a Sterling farm in that state Ebenezer Butterick originated Butterick dress patterns. The spinning wheel could now gather cobwebs in the attic, while ma-

36. Ice to cool summer's produce. Spy Pond, Arlington, Mass. Ballou's Pictorial Drawing Room Companion (1854).

chine-made sewing thread, pins and needles, cottons, and dress goods came within the means of almost all. Speaking in 1895 before Vermont's State Board of Agriculture on "Farm Life in the Vermont Hills," Mrs. Ellen C. Stearns dwelt on some of these changes: the coming of the big cookstove, the sewing machine, the conveniences for dairy work: "a hundred things," she said, "for use or beauty that our grandmothers never dreamed of." Moreover, as contemporary writers point out, the use of haying and other machines cut sharply the number of harvest hands the farm wife had to feed.[1]

So it was not altogether true, as one ministerial observer charged in 1889, that the introduction of machinery had done nothing to take the strain off the farmer's wife. Nevertheless, despite the improved lot of farm women, daughters were still leaving the old homestead. In 1896 Harriet M. Rice told the Vermont Board of Agriculture why. The daughter, she said, wants to be independent. "If she has a letter to mail she doesn't have to ask Pa for . . . two cents. She doesn't want to be obliged to

tease for a new dress . . . hat . . . or shoes." Fortunately, either many fathers were less grudging, or many daughters more dutiful, for Vermont
farm houses never ceased to remain farm homes.[2]

Where a farm was doing well, the wife's duties could also be lightened
by hiring at small wages one of the Irish, Swedish, or Polish girls that
every steamer brought; or a smart country girl from Nova Scotia. This
was a frequent arrangement beneficial to both parties. If immigration created problems, in this respect at least it appeared a benefit. In any case its
effects on New England as a whole during the century's second half, and
particularly on the southern tier of states, were profound. Yet in the
country districts, except for a remarkable increase in food demand, in
only a few localities did farms see great changes arise from it. Lacking
capital, most of the newcomers herded in cities or manufacturing towns
where they could get wage jobs.

Among exceptions were the Polish who were drawn into the labor
shortage of the Connecticut Valley as tobacco and onion growers increased acreage. A modest number of French Canadians, attracted by the
broom trade, had filtered in earlier. In the 1880's enterprising recruiters
began to bring Slavs into the tobacco towns from New York where they
had landed. Though the immigrants distressed local people by over-
crowding to save money, also because the women neglected the house for
the fields, they proved hard workers.[3]

On the large market gardens in city suburbs and on small-fruit and asparagus farms, Irish immigrants filled the labor forces, living usually in
quarters provided by the farmer. Eventually, however, many of them also
would get farms of their own, though not in the proportion of the land-
loving Polish. But the great bulk of small farms continued to get along
with family labor and, if needed, the help of the proverbial "hired man."
He was often as competent as the farm owner, sometimes more so. His
advice was worthy of respect. If single, he lived with the family as one of
them. Sometimes for years, in case of accident, death, or widowhood, he
held the farm and family together.

In an 1897 *Atlantic Monthly* article Alvan F. Sanborn describes a country community that he calls "Indian Ridge." It is a town of thrifty farms,
with little wealth but scarcely any real poverty. Food, dress, and home
furnishings are all of the simplest, yet the town has forty miles of good
roads, and adequate public buildings and schools. A church with an able
minister plays a prominent part in the well-being of the place, and there
is a lively country store where local sages foregather. Some inhabitants
work in mills, farming a little on the side. The young people staff the canning factory in season. The village takes pride in former residents who

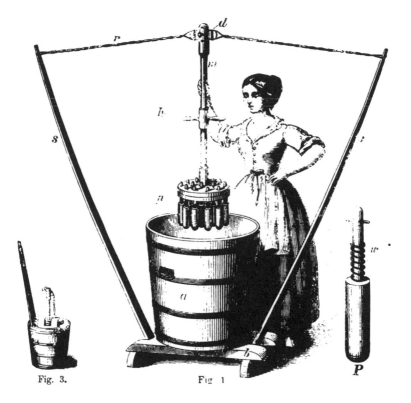

Fig. 3.   Fig. 1   P

DESCRIPTION.—Fig. 410 shows the implement set up and in operation. *a* is the tub, 26 inches high, and 24 inches in diameter at the top, and 21 inches at the bottom.   The tub stands upon the base-board, *b*.   The pounder, *c*, is made up of a series of 16 smaller pounders or pestles, *p*.   One of them is shown enlarged at *P*. These pass loosely through *c*, being held from dropping out by small brass pins. A strong spiral brass spring, *w*, keeps them down as far as the spring across the top will permit.   It will readily be seen that when brought down forcibly upon clothing in the tub, the small pestles or pounders will yield, by compressing the springs, *w*.

37. The "Metropolitan Washing Machine." *Mapes*, Illustrated Catalogue *(1861)*.

have gone elsewhere and done well. The place has its faults, Sanborn admits, but life in Indian Ridge is by no means the utterly empty affair that existence in a farming village is popularly supposed to be.[4]

Without for a moment ignoring the many villages, in the hills especially, where the spark of life glowed now but dimly, Sanborn's appears a realistic description of hundreds of farming communities across all six New England states as the nineteenth century drew toward its end; and from them were still appearing distinguished persons, such as the Concord sculptor Daniel Chester French, whom his daughter described as always a farmer at heart.

VI. A FOURTH CENTURY

37. Seven Million to Be Fed

A S NEW ENGLAND'S farming in 1900 entered the final two decades of its third century of history, the key factor continued to be its ever-expanding local market. No longer was its market only the distant West Indies and the Southern river towns of the previous century's beginnings, but also, now, the 7,400,000 people within its own perimeter, augmented by millions more only 200 miles away. The region's farmers could not afford to grow much bread grain, or fatten stock, but for the fresh milk, fruits, vegetables, eggs, and other high-value produce which the well-paid populace that surrounded its farms demanded, distance and transportation costs would for another generation afford New England a protective shield.

Sensing this, the Yankee farmer built larger barns for cattle and hay; silos for corn fodder; storages for potatoes, tobacco, and onions; greenhouses for vegetables and flowers. He paid out cash for fertilizers and in general so conducted his operations as to make life on the farm not only endurable but in the majority of cases comfortable. Poor hill farms, it is true, went begging for a few years yet, and woodland continually encroached on pastures, but good farmers resisted stubbornly, and those well located for community life and transportation increased production.

A favorite conception of the New England farmer has been of a person of rock-ribbed independence, beholden to nobody, neither seeking nor receiving favors from government or any other source. If this had ever been true, the wall of self-sufficiency was breached in the Civil War, with establishment of the Department of Agriculture at Washington and authorization of the nationwide system of agriculture education and research. In all this improvement New England was alert to share. By the end of the century dividends from these ventures were clearly manifest in advances in agriculture and chemistry which benefited the entire nation.

The first move has already been described, the landmark Morrill Act passed in the midst of civil war, affording federal funds to educate boys in agricultural and mechanic arts. By 1888 every New England state had taken advantage of the act to set up a college of agriculture. From time to time these ran into indifference or active opposition, yet their momentum increased as the years passed. It even spilled over to a foreign nation, for Japan called on the experience of the Massachusetts college to establish a similar system. In 1876 President William S. Clark organized the college at Sapporo, in Hokkaido, the northern island, since become a great university and one of the most important education centers of the Japanese nation. His name is still held in high respect in Japan. In New England itself, by the end of the nineteenth century, ever larger groups of serious students were graduating from each of its six agricultural colleges. Many went on to take posts of leadership not only in New England, but in education and in such new fields as entomology and agricultural chemistry, all across the nation and in other countries.

One path that beckoned these graduates led to the second landmark institution, the agricultural experiment station, born at Middletown and New Haven. A gift of $1,000 by Professor Levi Stockbridge initiated the Massachusetts station in 1878, the first public appropriation being made five years later. In 1887 the Hatch Act provided national funds and supervision for the support of such stations in each state of the republic. The Adams Act which was to follow in 1906 increased federal financing.

Connecticut's Storrs station inaugurated its famous egg-laying contest in 1911. After pioneering in the nature of vegetable proteins, in 1913 came the discovery by Thomas B. Osborne and L. B. Mendel of Vitamin A; and identification of the amino acids and of two more vitamins in foodstuffs followed. Donald F. Jones, Edward M. East, Herbert K. Hayes, and others worked out the principles underlying the double-cross hybridization of corn, destined so tremendously to increase the corn crops of the nation and the world. Jones' theory of genetics was published in a Connecticut station bulletin in 1918, and the first cross-bred seed was made available in 1921.[1]

The Rhode Island station emphasized the need of New England's sour soils for lime, and fixed the desirable qualities of the Rhode Island Red as a poultry breed. In 1908 its researchers determined that the fatal blackhead in young turkeys was a coccidial disease spread by sparrows and other wild birds.[2]

While this went on, Massachusetts was busy on egg genetics; and in 1905 began work on cranberry pests that resulted in 1910 in the cranberry experiment station at Wareham. In 1916, through the influence of the Boston Market Gardeners Association, the state set up at Lexington the nation's first experiment station for vegetable growing, a move that was to result in important improvements in varieties and in insect and disease control. The Amherst station continued to study tobacco and onion diseases. Meanwhile at Concord with the help of the federal

Department of Agriculture, skilled farmers brought forth two disease-resistant asparagus strains, Martha and Mary Washington, on which that vegetable's nationwide future was to be built.

In 1913 the Maine experiment station, which had originated a trapnest and an open-front house for poultry, began to investigate breeding and feeding problems in cattle and poultry, and studied apple insects. The legislature appropriated funds to buy "Highmoor Farm," where both potato and apple experiments were to yield important fruit.

New Hampshire's station began a variety of investigations. Enthusiastic young scientists tried such crops as beans and sweet corn under glass, made variety tests of potatoes, delved into soils, studied the life of the forest caterpillar, and went after that enemy of apples, the codling moth. In the poultry field its staff developed the Barred Plymouth Rock, destined to serve as the foundation for an ever-expanding broiler business.

Vermont investigators naturally kept a close eye on milk and cream problems; worked on that animal closely allied to dairy manufactures, the hog; and emphasized truthful branding of seeds. All the stations had as regular useful chores the analysis of fertilizers, feeds, and seeds sold within their borders, in addition to the prevention of fraud.

The value of such experimental work, its results often published in scientific journals, went far beyond any dividends to agriculture itself. The Connecticut station's studies in dietary nutrition, digestion, and metabolism, for example, were of worldwide importance. Its exposures of false claims in labeling concoctions offered for human use (392 misbrandings, adulterations, and failures to meet quantities out of 1,369 samples in the 1916 report alone) helped bring honesty into the food and drug business.[3]

The problems of the country's tremendous growth in population and production seemed to call more and more for the intervention of government in agriculture and rural affairs, if not for the benefit of rural people themselves, in the interest of the physical and economic health of the nation. President Theodore Roosevelt's White House Conservation Conference in 1908 opened to the nation an enlarged conception of its duty to its basic resource, the land itself, to the abuses of soil and forest that had become a thoughtless habit, and to the obligation to preserve the nation's natural heritage. The disclosure of fraud and disregard of health that resulted in the Pure Food and Drug Act and the Meat Inspection Act of 1906 helped rivet public attention on food and the necessity for its healthful production and distribution. In New England, with its heavy burden of tuberculosis in both humans and livestock, Dr. Theobald Smith's reports on the transmissability of hog cholera and tuberculosis

between animals and man offered examples of farm problems with ramifications so wide that only sustained and expensive public action could
solve them.[4]

The century's second decade saw the Congress enact two more major
pieces of agricultural legislation: (1) the Smith-Lever Act, to become the
foundation of the county extension system—agricultural advice, home
economic instruction, and 4-H clubs; (2) the Federal Farm Loan Act, on
which a far-ranging structure of rural credit was to be erected. This decade's legislation included also in 1911 a federal insecticide law; in 1912,
establishment of nationwide parcel post; and the Smith-Hughes Act for
vocational agricultural training. In addition, the Department of Agriculture was authorized to set up a market-reporting service and a Bureau of
Roads.

Of all these, establishment of the agricultural extension services by
the agricultural colleges had the most immediate import for farm families, and the greatest influence on farm production. This was particularly
true in areas such as New England, where farm people had a good general
education and some experience in organization.

Extension teaching of a sort by the colleges had been going on for years,
as President Kenyon L. Butterfield of the Rhode Island college pointed
out in 1905. Correspondence courses reached farmers too old or too busy
to study at college, and helped young farmers not able to spare four years
of college residence. Farmers' winter institutes took instruction to the
snowbound town halls of New Hampshire. About 1900 the Rhode Island
college organized a "Nature Guard" of boys and girls, forerunner of the
4-H Club movement. Summer field meetings were in vogue, and agricultural professors addressed farmers' clubs and pomona granges in all
states. By 1913 J. L. Hills, seeking state aid, could truthfully tell Vermont
dairymen, not keen to spend the state's money, "The agricultural college,
experiment station, and the national Department of Agriculture are the
main purveyors of direct information and instruction."[5]

To Vermont's Bennington, Windsor, and Caledonia counties goes the
honor of appointing in 1911 the first county agricultural or farm demonstration agents in New England, a step forward shared for the rest of the
nation with Broome County, New York. Four Maine counties, with a
grant from the General Education Board, a Rockefeller foundation, followed in 1912 to 1914.[6] By 1915 Connecticut could show a county agent
in each of its six counties. Meanwhile, in 1914 the federal Smith-Lever
Act had authorized federal support of state and county agricultural extension work.

Soon agricultural agents were joined by home demonstration agents, to assist countrywomen in their domestic sphere. Work with farm boys and girls began in Maine in 1913 and in Vermont the following year. By 1918 Vermont had enrolled 3,800 enthusiastic youngsters in 152 towns into calf, lamb, garden, and similar clubs. If these educational experiments were to have a continuing impact, it became plain that country people themselves must participate in management. So organizations called county farm bureaus appeared, sponsored not only by farm people but others interested in rural affairs, to set direction and provide financial aid for the work of the county extension agents. Membership included both men and women; general farmers, gentlemen farmers, and leaders in the specialized farm fields that were more and more becoming separate branches of agriculture. The college-trained young men and women who took county agent positions had a true missionary spirit. No day was too long. They might be chief attractions at an evening meeting in a far corner of the county, yet be on call at the office by eight next morning to give advice on a sick cow; and woe to the agent not at hand ready to respond! Their state extension directors were men such as Joseph Carrigan of Vermont, Arthur Deering of Maine, John Kendall of New Hampshire, Willard Munson of Massachusetts, and other leaders of vision—their goal a healthy, vigorous, well-informed countryside.

Private organizations in New England's specialized farm fields went on also. One more national breed association had its birthplace there—the American Devon Cattle Club, formed in 1918 at Agawam, Massachusetts. In dairying, though many farmers and small dealers had their own milk routes, control of the Boston and New York milk markets had gradually become concentrated in the hands of a few large dealers. These decided both the price to consumers and the return to producers. If opposed, they secured supplies by extending the "milk shed" or supply zone further up country. Tactics that farmers thought oppressive in 1910 brought on a "Boston Milk War," led for the farmers by the newly formed Boston Cooperative Milk Producers Union. In the following year the dealers succeeded in having the courts declare the Union an illegal combination in restraint of trade. One factor favoring the dealer was the gradual introduction of pasteurization, a process requiring capital and expensive equipment.

Undiscouraged, New Hampshireman Richard Pattee traveled farm to farm and town to town in that state, Vermont, and Massachusetts, convincing dairymen of the necessity for a legal bargaining association powerful enough to secure fair wholesale prices for their production. The resulting New England Milk Producer's Association reached a membership of 20,000 in 1920, and became for the next half century the strongest influence for the farmers at the bargaining table.[7] It formed an alliance with Maine's well-managed Turner Center Creamery. The Creamery pioneered in offering premium payments for off-season milk, a move designed to reduce the demoralizing spring flood of milk and increase the winter supply. Under the management of Edward L. Bradford, Turner Center grew to have twenty-three receiving stations, a headquarters plant, and distributing stations in Massachusetts and Rhode Island; do a business close to five million dollars a year; and own property worth nearly half that figure. Meanwhile, by 1920 in Vermont five cooperative creameries had federated.

Farmers were working into other cooperative ventures. In addition to Grange stores and insurance companies, as well as cooperative butter plants, by 1920 a half dozen farmers' exchanges in New Hampshire were buying farm supplies for members. Four canning cooperatives in Maine by 1922 canned half the blueberry crop. The Flower Exchange in Boston continued to afford its members an effective outlet for flowers. But the Eastern States Farmers Exchange and similar groups that were to systematize the wholesale purchase of farm supplies were still ahead.

Dairying now had become the most important branch of New England agriculture. With the advent of the Babcock test to determine butterfat content of milk, it was possible to contrast the fat yield of individual cows and of different breeds of cattle. Testing, however, proved economical only when a substantial number of dairy animals warranted a full-time tester. The country's first cow-test association is said to have been formed in Michigan in 1905. Waterford, Maine, dairymen took up the plan in 1907. Windsor, Vermont, in 1909, formed a dairy herd improvement association, followed in 1911 by one in Massachusetts.[8]

Constant improvement continued in making and handling milk. Pasteurization had no sooner begun to make milk safe from typhoid and tuberculosis germs than a Torrington, Connecticut, creamery in 1915 by accident discovered how milk could be homogenized. The easily cleaned glass delivery bottle superseded the tin quart can; and in 1921 the first shipment of milk bottled in the country for retail delivery left Vermont's Bellows Falls Creamery for a Boston grocery chain. An agreement made under the spur of Food Administrator Herbert Hoover kept the market price stable during the war years.

Though New England's dairy cow total remained between eight and nine hundred thousand all through this period, except for a temporary rise during the war, the proportion of milk that went into butter and cheese (especially the latter) shrank. By contrast, sales of fresh milk grew almost continuously. By 1920 the large Connecticut cities alone consumed about 350,000 quarts a day.

Milksheds expanded. It became uneconomical for each individual farmer to carry his milk to the railway station. Instead dealers arranged for teamsters, later truckmen, to pick up the 8½ quart cans at farm roadside points. As a result even farmers with as few as a half dozen cows could market milk.

Control of tuberculosis remained a vexing problem for farmers and public alike. In 1917, with the cooperation of the United States Livestock Sanitary Association, the federal Bureau of Animal Industry inaugurated a program of accrediting entire herds, later entire counties, as free from tuberculosis, a promising forward step. The first area of the nation accredited as completely free from bovine tuberculosis in its dairy cows was the District of Columbia. Tuberculin testing had been going on there since 1906; its first entire herd was accredited in 1918. The next year Congress appropriated a half-million dollars to partly indemnify owners of cattle slaughtered as diseased. In New England, Vermont took the lead in accreditation, followed by Maine, Connecticut, and New Hampshire. In the northern states, which bred their own cattle, the disease affected a much smaller proportion than in Massachusetts and Rhode Island, supplied with cows largely by the great Brighton market, where the situation was worst. By 1920, 2,161 Vermont herds containing 38,839 cattle were under supervision, of which 1,343 herds with 16,082 cattle had been found free of the disease.[9] Only Minnesota (with five times the total cattle population) was ahead of Vermont in animals tested.

The long and extremely costly battle to wipe out the tuberculosis scourge nationwide had opened. It would involve the slaughter of cows by the scores of thousands, purebreds and grades alike, and last a whole generation. Sometimes the struggle meant destruction of a famous herd, built up through a lifetime—a bitter tragedy and perhaps financial ruin to the farmer. It involved public appropriations enormous for the time, and seemingly without end. In the long run, however, success in the fight was to prove a tremendous benefit to both the health of the great consuming public and to the dairy industry itself.

During the gradual shift from making butter and cheese to marketing whole milk, the number of New England's dairy cows reached almost a million in 1905, then dropped slightly. Generally speaking, however, any numbers the three southern states and New Hampshire lost, Vermont and Maine gained. During these years, breed associations were gathering prestige and experience. Gradual increases in production per cow resulted as the Babcock test came into general use and herd improvement

associations made records of production reliable. However, like other
pioneer efforts in agriculture, the early associations suffered severely
after 1916 because of World War I restrictions and dislocations. No great
change took place in feeding cows, except that the urge to make winter
milk tended to increase the purchase of grain from the West, while silos
for the storage and fermentation of corn fodder and other green crops continually grew in favor. By 1921 Vermont could count 9,445 silos, one to
every 30 cows. In all states, as Clarence Day truly says of Maine, the silo
became the visible badge of the good dairyman. Yet the capital expense
involved in such improvements tended to discourage and weed out the
small general farmer. He continued to depend on hay, which in most
towns still surpassed every other farm crop in value. Meanwhile, many a
farmer who turned to fruit or vegetables continued to keep a family cow
or two, for daily milk and Sunday ice cream.

Other than the dairy cow, large animals on New England farms receded
in importance. Oxen grew steadily fewer. Horses took their place, but of
these more and more came from the West, bred and raised cheaply there.
For New England, except on professional stud farms which bred race
horses or saddle horses, they had become farm tools rather than farm
products.

What with dog devastation, Western competition, and imports of foreign wool, the number of sheep dropped also. Despite improved breeding,
Vermont's wool clip in 1920 was but one eighth of its 1850 total: it had
dropped by two thirds in two decades. Maine, growing sheep with an eye
largely for the spring lamb market, led the six states in wool clip in the
1920 census figures; but the 665,453 pounds produced was less than half
the figure reported in 1900. Farmers could do better making milk.

Swine numbers, never great in New England, had varied but slightly in
sixty years. They held their average of two per farm only by virtue of the
large herds maintained to fatten on city garbage and the farm porkers
kept on dairy and kitchen wastes, the latter usually butchered at home.
Though a cholera serum had been developed in 1905, disease continued
to cause severe losses.

Hay was still the most widespread farm crop, but tonnage dropped
after 1900 except in Maine and Vermont. Most was consumed right on
the farm. A town such as Gorham, Maine, west of Portland, however,
could ship out 5,000 tons in 1903 to feed city horses and help cash
income.[10]

Indian corn production had substantially decreased in New England as
a whole, yet held its own surprisingly in the area's three southern states.

Partly as a result of the World War, Connecticut's 1919 crop of over two million bushels equaled that of 1860. Massachusetts' corn harvest had dropped only one fourth in sixty years; Rhode Island's, one third. Although the northern states turned more to sweet corn for canneries and fodder corn for cattle, 1910 saw at Worcester what was termed a "magnificent display" of field corn at a New England Corn Exhibit.

Maine and Vermont still grew a considerable amount of oats. Aroostook County with its short season kept on with oats (4,500 acres in Presque Isle in 1936) and buckwheat as rest crops from potatoes. Except for a spurt of wheat grown in wartime for poultry feed, all other grains, by the end of New England's third century of farming, had become minor factors.

Tree fruits, especially apples, continued largely to be the product of general farms, though orchardists with a thousand or more trees were becoming common. Orchard pests were not yet such a problem that spraying was an absolute necessity, and the great freeze of 1933–34 was still ahead. Uniformly graded and packed fancy apples from the new Northwest were topping New England's markets; but ordinary apples, poured into flour barrels and old bushel boxes and well topped out, were still readily salable. The poorest went into cider or dried apples (delicious in pies), stocked by every grocer. Maine was now the leading apple state, its crop running from a million to a million and a quarter barrels a year; Massachusetts was next; and New Hampshire and Connecticut about even in their production. In 1904 the central New Hampshire town of Bristol shipped out 10,000 barrels. Yet New England's total crop did not equal that of the Empire State of New York. Professional orchardists, allied in state pomological societies, began to plant trees in blocks and to use sprays recommended by the state experiment stations. They were destined in the next few decades to take over New England's apple production and the cream of the market. These men backed new state inspection laws for nursery stock, designed to keep out a horde of pests and diseases that imported trees and plants might bring in. Some of the very worst of these pests, alas—gypsy and brown-tail moths, railroad worm, codling moth, and San Jose scale—were already established and spreading.

Commercial peach growing, along with Japanese plums, had in the late 1800's begun to cut a substantial figure, especially in Connecticut. It boomed in the next decade. By 1896 there were said to be a million and a half peach trees in that state, with returns of two to five hundred dollars per acre received for superior local fruit. Their number doubled by 1900.

In 1901 Connecticut's crop was said to be worth as much as two million dollars. A severe winter in 1917–18, however, killed trees on hundreds of acres and gave local enthusiasm a crushing setback.[11]

Urged on only by his deep interest in plants, a Belchertown, Massachusetts farmer, Everett Howard, with his son, was seeding and breeding strawberries and flowers on his rocky 35-acre farm. In 1908 the firm introduced the Dighton berry, named for a leading strawberry town in southeast Massachusetts. Already in 1906 they had fruited another new berry, to which they gave the number "17." Besides yielding bountifully, it had the great advantage of being virus-free. Plants sent to a midwestern state experiment station for trial caught the attention of a local nurseryman there. In the absence of a plant copyright law the new variety was introduced as "Premier" by midwestern firms, so that the true originator received little financial benefit. However, Mr. Howard's son was eventually able to prove that his firm was the source of what became for decades the country's most valuable strawberry, the "Howard 17" or "Premier."[12]

Commercial strawberry growing in New England attained its height at the opening of the twentieth century, when receipts for the berries sold reached ten million dollars, only a million less than the value of New England's fifty-two million dozen eggs. Concord, Dighton, and Falmouth in Massachusetts, Cape Elizabeth in Maine, and some Rhode Island and Connecticut towns continued for several decades to grow large acreages of the berries and to hold part of the market in the face of a flood of berries crowding in from other regions by rail and coastwise boat. Two hundred Portuguese growers in Falmouth, Massachusetts, with the help of the state's Department of Agriculture, made a name in the market for their 600,000 quarts of berries annually by buying supplies, grading carefully, and selling together.[13]

Further north, fresh Maine and New Hampshire blueberries went to market in round veneer boxes packed in crates. Blueberry growing expanded beyond Maine's Washington County, and packing plants to handle the crop appeared in the new areas. Harvesting the berries and growing dry beans for the canners helped many a family in eastern Maine to piece out a living. Maine canned blueberries sold coast to coast, now meeting competition from those of other sections but still the largest crop in any state. In 1922 Washington County harvested 184,050 bushels, giving employment to 541 persons just to process them.[14] A portent of things to come was a first exhibit in 1913 at the Massachusetts Horticultural Society of cultivated blueberries.

The Massachusetts cranberry crop reached 575,000 barrels in the heavy year of 1893, and 600,000 in 1899. It ran at about 400,000 to 500,000 in the early 1900's, while experiments in disease control and bog management went forward. One important result of these investigations was the discovery by Dr. H. J. Franklin, head of the Wareham Experiment Station, of a way to forecast a threatened frost by noon of the preceding day. For this innovation in 1920 he received the gold medal of the Massachusetts Horticultural Society. This station also developed controls for the disease known as "false blossom," believed to have been imported from Wisconsin.[15] Meanwhile in 1912, Ocean Spray began the commercial canning of cranberry sauce, opening a valuable new outlet for that fruit.

38. An Artful Adjustment

A S THE NINETEENTH CENTURY turned into the twentieth, vegetable growing increased by leaps and bounds. Maine's average
yield per acre of potatoes soon surpassed that of any other state in the
nation. Its production of 9,813,748 bushels in 1899, two thirds of them
from Aroostook's 42,000 acres, was tripled a decade later. Meanwhile,
the crop of every other New England state except Vermont declined. The
exigencies of World War I reduced the harvest; yet in 1919 Maine still
reached the enormous yield of 25,531,470 bushels. During this very period, however, farms in some of Maine's older towns were being abandoned and cultivated land reverted to forest.

Aroostook's sixty starch factories took part of the potato crop, in years
of low prices especially; yet Maine's market, reached by cheap ocean
freight, included the entire Atlantic coast. Wherever shipping costs
permitted, its potatoes went inland as well. It was a chancy business,
income dependent on price and weather. Aroostook farmers gained a
reputation as gamblers, trusting in good years to overcome the losses
and debts of the bad. Yet as a whole the county prospered and gained
population.

Southern and western farmers came to value Maine potatoes for seed.
They found that Maine seed yielded better than their own. This reputation had its dangers, for some Maine tubers carried an imported disease,
powdery scab, as well as other troubles. The appearance of potatoes, sold
for seed by commercial brokers, might offer few clues as to infection or
inheritance, and disappointment sometimes resulted. To prevent loss of
Maine's seed market scientists were called in from the recently formed
Bureau of Plant Industry at Washington. They suggested establishing (1)
standards of excellence for potatoes sold for seed and (2) a guarantee of
practical freedom from disease. They proposed inspection for disease in
the field even before harvest, and attachment of an official government
statement as to quality. Maine people listened and acted. Henceforth a
blue tag on the bag would certify that Maine's Department of Agriculture
had inspected the seed and approved it as safe to plant.

The seed from the first few hundred acres inspected and certified soon
built a reputation. Bags marked with the blue tag began to command a
commensurate premium. All these measures were costly, but by pioneer-

ing such certified seed Maine opened a new era in potato growing. More and more growers joined the campaign; succeeding decades brought ever higher standards. The innovation spread to Vermont, which by 1922 was certifying 110,600 bushels from 553 acres, then to other states and to the Canadian provinces. For Maine the result was ever greater competition, but the state held its own. Thus New England had pioneered another agricultural advance, of the highest value to the food supply of the whole nation.[1]

As potatoes were to Aroostook, cigar tobacco was to the Connecticut and Housatonic valleys. The threat from Sumatra's high-grade leaf had to be overcome, and it was, by the Connecticut Experiment Station in cooperation with the U.S. Department of Agriculture. In 1901 scientists proved that for use as wrappers on the outside of cigars local leaf grown under the shade of cotton cheesecloth tents could equal the imported leaf in quality, even excel it. Cigar manufacturers were enthusiastic at the samples submitted. Congress granted tariff protection. From a modest beginning of a few acres, plantings of shade-grown tobacco mushroomed. By 1910 the yield had reached 1,800,000 pounds; by 1923, 8,600,000. Two thirds of the shade crop was grown in Connecticut. Overproduction and other difficulties ensued, yet shade-tobacco growing continued to be a prosperous minor branch of New England agriculture. Partly because of the heavy capital involved, production of this specialized type became largely the field of corporations and cigar manufacturers rather than of individual farmers. Yet it provided work and helped local income.[2]

Cigar sales kept rising. The ordinary Valley outdoor grower, despite disappointing years, kept boosting his production of the broad and Havana-seed leaf. Beneath the light-colored, expensive shade-grown cigar wrapper, the best of these types formed the second layer, "the binder," which held together the lower quality "filler."

Farmers fed their tobacco fields lavishly with stable manure (in 1906 they imported a thousand cars from Boston and New York) and with cottonseed meal, ground bone, potash, and lime. The soil responded with excellent crops, much of the production high-grade tobacco.

Harvest came in August. Workers cut the plants at the base and hung them on portable frames. A low wagon bore these frames to long, side-ventilated barns for curing. In four to six weeks during some short period of "tobacco damp" when they were pliable, the tobacco was taken down and borne to warehouses for sorting, packing, and fermentation. Every step required skill and judgment. Only a handful of soils elsewhere in the nation could produce cigar leaf of a quality to compare with that grown in the Connecticut and Housatonic valleys.

Prices fluctuated widely from year to year according to economic conditions, weather, and size and quality of crop, but between 1900 and 1920 production in both Connecticut and Massachusetts doubled. It was not uncommon for tobacco farmers to become wealthy, especially in the war years; and the whole countryside prospered with them. In 1920 Hartford was the leading tobacco county in the nation. Depression was soon to deal tobacco farmers some sad blows, but for a time the goose hung high.

The light loams of the Valley, highly fertilized and carefully tilled, were as well suited for onions as for tobacco. Polish immigrant families imported to grow the tobacco crop proved equally adept in onion fields. In 1900 Connecticut still grew over 400,000 bushels of onions; but by that time the Massachusetts area, centered about South Deerfield on both sides of the Connecticut River bridge, had nearly doubled Connecticut's production figure to become onion headquarters for the next two generations. By 1910 the single town of Hatfield was shipping out 500 to 600 carloads yearly. The highest yield came in 1920, with a 450 bushel per acre average for Massachusetts (including the fields of the Danvers market gardeners on the Essex County coast); but a yield of only 280 bushels in 1921 brought the growers almost twice as much money. The value of the Massachusetts onion crop, $748,309 in 1899, with war's inflation increased to $1,913,000 in 1923, the income from 3,360 acres.[3]

Outfitted in straw hats and blue jeans, and in bare feet, boys and girls of Polish families did the kneeling jobs in the onion fields. Through hot summer days they planted the sets and later weeded the seeded rows, while their elders with horse-hoes took care of the tobacco and cut the hay. Little by little these families accumulated money, bought farms, and at length came to own much of the best land in the tobacco-onion towns of Hatfield, Hadley, Whately, (North) Amherst, Sunderland, and Deerfield. A few of the most enterprising became onion brokers, supply dealers, and respected businessmen in other lines. In time both in Massachusetts and Connecticut, farmers bearing Polish surnames were elected selectmen and school committeemen.[4]

Other immigrants were progressing. In central New England, Finns began to take over the inexpensive, gravelly hill farms of Worcester County, Massachusetts, and southern New Hampshire. They raised berries and poultry. Bringing with them European cooperative ideas, in 1907 they established the United Cooperative Society of Maynard and the United Farmers at Fitchburg to do their buying and selling. In southern Worcester County, on better soil, a group of Holland dairymen and mechanics bought farms. Norwegians and Swedes concentrated in the Concord

River Valley to raise berries and asparagus. Italian workers were making their start in suburban market gardens and florists' greenhouses in Rhode Island, Connecticut, and Massachusetts. Portuguese had long been taking up dairy and vegetable farms in eastern Rhode Island and southeastern Massachusetts. In Grand Isle County, Vermont, and Aroostook County, Maine, it was French Canadian farmers who became numerous. One Aroostook town was very properly named New Sweden. In the southern Berkshires a Jewish colony from New York City tried their hand at farming. From all these manifold European strains many proved good farmers and citizens, in time taking their places with descendants of earlier comers in all the enterprises of the countryside.

Growing fresh vegetables was increasingly such an enterprise. By the time of the Twelfth Census report in 1900, over one third of Rhode Island's farm income came from vegetables; for Massachusetts and Maine, with potatoes included, the proportion was one fourth, and for Connecticut almost one fifth. Yet vegetables used only a little over one acre in fifteen. The largest acreage by far was within twenty miles of Boston. For crop value per acre, Massachusetts, Rhode Island, Connecticut, and New Hampshire led all states of the nation.[5]

Market gardeners in these areas had become highly skilled, their experience often running back in families for several generations. Glass-grown crops reached large proportions. The earlier, simple, wood-frame greenhouses had developed into rows of capacious steel and glass structures, heated by steam. Under heavy manuring and irrigation, greenhousemen harvested as many as four crops of lettuce during the colder months. A more common practice was a fall crop of tomatoes, then two crops of lettuce in midwinter, followed with the returning sun by another of tomatoes or cucumbers. North Leominster and Baldwinsville on the Hoosac Tunnel route were heavy shippers of cucumbers. New England's high-quality greenhouse products topped the market in New York and other centers.

Out-of-doors, market gardeners generously fertilized their fields with manure and chemicals, and made them yield two, three, even four crops a year by intercropping lettuce, spinach, radishes, and beans among long-season crops. Cabbages, carrots, beets, and parsnips followed lettuce and quick-growing leaf vegetables. Marshy land proved excellent for celery, a Boston specialty known far and wide for quality. One unwelcome visitor wsa discovered near Boston in 1917, the European corn borer. This insect damaged first the locally popular sweet corn, but was destined to become a menace also to the nation's immense field corn production. Vegetable

38. Corn and pumpkins have fed New England through three centuries.
Food Marketing in New England *(1955)*.

prices fluctuated according to supply and demand as well as with the general economy, but vegetable market transactions were universally for cash, a great advantage to farmers. Pickle factories, processing cucumbers, onions, and specialties flourished in the central Connecticut Valley even into Vermont, with local farmers growing for picklers under contract.

Numerous greenhousemen had turned to growing commercial flowers, at first hardy violets, pansies, and sweet peas, then, with more reliable heating, more tender varieties. By 1937 the Budlong Farm at Cranston, Rhode Island, with thirteen acres under glass, each day cut 18,000 roses, mostly White Killarney.[6] Enterprising growers originated new varieties and before long made New England the nation's headquarters for carnations. At Cromwell, Connecticut, a Swedish newcomer, product of thorough training in European methods, had put up his first greenhouse in 1872. By the century's end the A. N. Pierson "Cromwell Gardens" had ten acres under glass, with 25 greenhouses in roses alone; four in carnations with 35,000 plants; and 2,400,000 lilies of the valley (a then popular wedding flower); with other plants in proportion. By 1920 Cromwell Gardens had achieved national notice for its hardy chrysanthemums. Thus New England's greenhouse flowers found markets all over the East.

Irrigation, both for glass and for field vegetables, had become common in the high-priced market garden districts. There were now automatic sprinklers fed by municipal systems, under pressure, or by water pumped from private ponds and wells—sometimes both.

In 1910 Hartford provided space for a local produce market. Not long afterward, organized Boston market gardeners defeated an attempt to limit their centuries-old right to sell produce in the market streets about Faneuil Hall. The nation's Department of Agriculture set up an Office of Markets in 1917. Market gardeners about Providence in 1918 formed the Providence Farmers Exchange. New Hampshire was the earliest state to begin publishing prices for farm produce, and to search out markets locally. In 1919 Boston's first daily produce report was inaugurated, a valuable summary of supplies and prices. Two years later the Massachusetts legislature was persuaded to adopt a standard for the wooden bushel-box in which most fresh produce there and in other New England centers went to market.[7]

Connecticut continued to be an important headquarters for vegetable seeds, especially sweet corn and onion seed. When diseases discouraged local growers, the state's enterprising seedsmen served their customers with seed grown on new land in the Far West.

In central and western Maine, sweet corn for the canners remained a leading crop. Annual plantings ran 11,000 acres or more, and the pack filled over 20,000,000 cans. Beans for the baked bean trade, green peas, squash for bakeries, and apples helped to keep seventy factories busy. Growing and processing these crops brought income to hundreds of farm families, while the vines and waste afforded fodder for their stock.[8]

39. Close of the Third Century

NUMEROUS FACTORS, both on farms and off, made the final decades of New England's third century of farming a time of flux, the end of old ways and the opening of new.

World War I proved one of the most potent. Because of the immense destruction of ships and cargoes by submarines, one of the nation's prime objectives had to be feeding England as well as its own armies in France. Western grain, which normally nourished New England's people and livestock, had to be sent overseas. Shipments to Europe were three times the usual. As far as possible home-grown food and feed had to fill the gap. Home canning of vegetables boomed; but to can fruit, sugar was lacking, so rhubarb and some fruit went to waste. If poultry were to eat grain, New England farms had to raise much of it. Indian corn became again a mainstay crop. Some farmers went back to wheat, and it did well. As in the Civil War, with labor short, farmers found labor-saving devices indispensable. All young men 21 to 30 had to register, though where need was shown, young farmers could be deferred to help in food production.

War dislocations made essential a degree of national economic control never before conceived of. Daylight saving became mandatory, and gasoline-less days cut automobile use. Florists had to curtail as coal became too precious to grow winter flowers. Under such rigorous conditions of public planning, the newly established system of county agricultural and home demonstration agents, trained to advise and now forced to lead, proved of tremendous worth. These new professionals established themselves solidly in the esteem of farm people and the public.

Only temporarily slowed by the war, innovations continued to revolutionize country life and habits. Henry Ford had introduced his Model T automobile in 1908, and in 1916 the Goodyear Company had developed the pneumatic truck tire. Though use of the tire had to await the end of the war, both Ford's economical automobile and the pneumatic tire were to prove of immense value to farm people. By 1920 one Vermont farm in four had an automobile; a decade later the ratio was two out of three. (The farm tractor was still in its infancy.) Telephone wires lined village roads, often pushing far out through the country. Occasionally the farmers of a town organized their own company and gradually extended its service.

In 1920, even in the rural state of Vermont, one farm family in ten had electricity, at first for light only.[1] Its use was to triple in the next decade. Later came welcome assistance to many an overworked farm woman as the current made possible reliable refrigeration for both kitchen and dairy. A gasoline engine was likely to saw up the stove wood. One labor-saving appliance after another followed. Clarence Birdseye's discovery of how to process frozen foods was just ahead—to come in 1924.

With state, then federal appropriations, main roads vastly improved. By 1905 Massachusetts was appropriating almost a half million dollars in state aid. New Hampshire was voting $10,000 for a highway map. In 1916 the federal government had set up in the Department of Agriculture a Bureau of Public Roads and authorized aid to the states in building rural post roads. Gradually, for farm-to-market roads, well-drained crushed stone surfaces began to take the place of mud and gravel. It would be another generation before stone fill and "tarvia" would make the ordinary country road passable in mud time, but these beginnings were important.

With better roads and the use of automobiles and trucks increasing, the village general store gradually lost importance as an outlet for farm produce and became merely a source of necessary supplies. Farmers turned to more efficient outlets. The introduction of parcel post in 1912 and the organization of more adequate sources of credit both helped the decline of the village merchant.

With each succeeding decade the number of New England farms listed by census takers diminished. For example, Rhode Island's "census farms" dropped from 5,292 in 1909 to 4,083 in 1919, and the number mortgaged fell even more precipitously. For New England as a whole the reduction in twenty years amounted to 35,324, more than the total of all farms counted in Vermont at the 1899 enumeration. Many a farm continued to be occupied chiefly because its buildings were good: its fields went largely unused, except perhaps that the hay was cut by a neighbor. By contrast, in the nineteenth century's first decade New England's total population grew over 17 percent and almost 13 percent again in the second, the size of the local farm market continually expanding. This growth, and the higher prices for farm products that often looked tempting, attracted shipments of farm produce from every quarter of the nation and from Canada. Competition increased year after year. More and more it forced the poorly located, ill-conducted, now economically unjustified general farm to drop out. The better situated, better managed farms, however, concentrated on products in special demand, and prospered. From replies by farmers to a questionnaire, one of the able new county agents in the Connecticut Valley in 1920 reached the following conclusions: of 21 dairy farms, 15 were profitable; of 7 onion farms, 5 paid; of 5 tobacco farms, 4; of 5 poultry farms, 4; of 3 potato farms, 2 paid; and of 2 each in sheep and maple sugar enterprises, both did well. His prize farm exhibit was 13 apple growers; only one considered his business unsuccessful. Large and medium-sized farms did best, he found. Among the small ones, almost half considered farming a losing game.[2]

Enterprising farmers on good farms, in many cases members of dairy, fruit, vegetable, and similar associations, found in the county extension system an inviting rallying point. Rapid growth of a new and parallel organization, the county Farm Bureau, was a natural consequence. Bureau membership soon came to include most practical farmers in every branch of agriculture.

Once organized by counties, these sensed their need for making known their views on the great public issues arising from the war and the depression that promptly succeeded it. Conventions of county delegates speedily organized state Farm Bureau federations. These in 1920 launched the American Farm Bureau Federation.[3] With memberships of many thousands in each state, and supported by more adequate finance than any previous farm organizations, these national and state groups became for the next three generations powerful factors in deciding public questions. They developed leaders of commanding ability who attained national respect. Among such were "Uncle George" Putnam, president for over a quarter-century of the New Hampshire Farm Bureau Federation, and Arthur Packard, who headed the Vermont organization for an equal period. They employed staff to investigate farm problems and seek practical solutions, often by new legislation. They raised capital to provide cooperative sales, insurance, and purchasing facilities of many types. The American Farm Bureau Federation took its place as one of the most influential of the nation's business organizations. Local county Farm Bureaus gave needed support and balance to the system of agricultural education and experiment, and helped agriculture overcome the war's dislocations and readjust into a modern business.

Meanwhile, many more small farmers who in the nineteenth century had taken in shoe parts or hat-making to add income, went to work full time in a local mill or factory. The farm, however, now down to a single cow and garden, and chiefly a home, remained a valued recourse when the mill work slacked in the 1921 depression. Like small farms, small country industries were casualties of economic change, leaving fewer openings for part-time labor, long a small farmer's resource.

One offset to economic dislocations was continued rapid growth in "summer business" in every state, especially New Hampshire. That state offered an excellent example of what a wide-awake government can do to meet economic dislocations. Empty farms blessed with decent buildings and sites passed continually into the possession of summer visitors from the cities, persons who had begun as boarders and to whom a country home of their own appealed. The popular "Old Home Week" movement inaugurated in 1899 by Governor Rollins helped; the 4,000 copies of the state's *New Hampshire Farms for Summer Homes*, issued annually from 1902 on, sent visitors scouring the countryside for the bargains. President Theodore Roosevelt's Country Life Commission of 1908 added momentum.

The summer vacation boom brought visitors by the thousands. In 1920 New Hampshire counted summer hotels in 59 towns. One town of only 100 people in 1918 entertained 3,000 guests; another of 300 claimed to put up 10,000 visitors. Cornish was described as a little New York; Washington people congregated at Springfield; Montclair visitors at Littleton; St. Louis folks in Cheshire County. Bostonians had for decades found the Monadnock region enticing. Eastman's cheap Kodak was called an incentive. A state report asserted that the economic lift from this development had doubled assessed values in many towns. Literally hundreds of farmers were said to pay off mortgages and accumulate property by taking advantage of a two-to-three-month market right at hand, "better than Boston for everything that their town could produce."

A Vermont farmer described how through these two decades, with two or three helpers, he had gardened for 80 to 90 guests. Vegetables were what they wanted. He couldn't give them asparagus too often—until peas arrived! Princeton, Massachusetts, beside Wachusett Mountain, gloried in the buildings erected by summer residents on discontinued farms. On the Maine, Connecticut, and Rhode Island shores, demand for cottages mounted. Their occupants, often distinguished persons, were reported to pay well for fruits, vegetables, and dairy and poultry products. All this helped rural New England adjust to a new economic era, and sparked local improvements. "A town cannot be found that has not felt its quickening influence," was an official New Hampshire comment.[4]

A new government-sponsored system of farm credit eased the readjustments that followed the war. Because of the wide distribution of mutual savings banks, which farmers had often helped form, New England's farmers had long been better served as to mortgage credit than those of most parts of the nation. Yet as a result of the difficulties that marked the closing years of the nineteenth century, farm mortgages had fallen out of favor. Hence, organization in 1917 of the Federal Land Bank at Springfield to provide farm credit for farmers of New England and New York came as an important stabilizing factor for farm enterprise. That same year saw the Eastern States Exposition launched in Springfield to begin a fruitful career of exhibitions and prizes for the next half century and longer.

So as a whole, and sometimes painfully, New England farming adjusted. Backwoods and hilltop farm buildings, especially unused barns, were burning, decaying, slumping into cellars; on the contrary, good dairy, fruit, and garden farms, especially near transportation, exhibited an outlook quite different. Substantial farm dwellings, thousands of them, well clapboarded and painted white or buff with lead and oil, bordered country roads in every state. On their south sides or in front rose great elms and maples to cool the dwelling in summer and shade the well-kept lawn. The New England farmer was often accused of being tight-fisted and insensitive to aesthetic considerations; yet there stood the ample, comfortable farmstead, an obvious refutation too often taken for granted by all because so common.

Outbuildings, too, were often good. Dairymen needing shelter for increasing numbers of cattle and the hay to keep them through the winter had built sturdy barns, a hundred feet long or more, with wide doors opening at each end for the haywagon to enter and leave, and smaller side doors for cattle. Ordinarily they stood on stone wall foundations, enclosing a manure cellar and hogpen, perhaps floored with cement.

Though siding might be only wide vertical boards, more often both walls and roof were shingled, walls even painted. A cupola for hay ventilation crowned the whole. North of the Massachusetts line, house and barn were likely to be connected by a shed or two, offering a covered walkway for bad weather and providing a sheltered yard for family and stock. Everything reflected characteristic adaptation to climate and circumstances.

Thus the year 1921 approached, and with it the beginning of the fourth century of New England farming. Like the year which saw the long-ago Pilgrim fathers harvest their first crop, the outlook had its features both of hope and of difficulty.

40. The Earth Remains

THIS ACCOUNT of three centuries began with an excursion into pre-history and a description of the locality now titled New England according to the impressions of the first comers. It may appropriately end with a review of how soil and landscape had fared in the course of three hundred years and how the character of New England stood as a new generation inherited it.

Contrary to often repeated assertions, it has been shown that the land the first immigrants entered from overseas was not a gloomy, unending primeval forest, alive with wild beasts, some of them ferocious. It was instead an inhabited land, adapted in the course of centuries to the uses of an intelligent, capable branch of the human race.

From the westernmost limit of the Connecticut shore in what is now New England to the Saco River on the Maine coast, level treeless salt marsh fringed much of the shore. Fresh meadows bordered the edges of the great rivers and several of their interior tributaries.

Alongside the numerous sheltered harbors, bays, and estuaries and on offshore islands the native inhabitants had cleared substantial areas to provide village sites, and fields for their crops. They had cut the neighboring trees for firewood. Most of the early explorers of the coast who have left records—Verrazano, Champlain, John Smith, George Waymouth, Van der Donck, De Vries—were as much impressed by the open spaces that they found near the shore and up the great rivers, even the Kennebec in Maine, as with the noble forest trees that they also describe. These open plains and uplands, cleared by their Indian inhabitants, were the chief factor that made it possible for the Pilgrims to exist at Plymouth, for the Puritans to settle down comfortably about Boston Harbor and Massachusetts Bay, and for certain dissident or uneasy groups among them to colonize the southern Connecticut Valley, the shores of Narragansett Bay, and coastal New Hampshire.

Not even in the interior was unending woodland the rule. To the Indian village sites and cultivated fields that the settlers found alongside many interior ponds and tributaries scores of local historians attest. Villages dotted the territory occupied by the inland Nipmuck, Pocumtuck, Pennacook, Abenaki, and similar tribes. Besides village sites and cultivated fields every tribe had its own carefully delineated hunting grounds.

For example, the Wampanoags, Massasoit's people, hunted in what are now Rehoboth and Raynham. In Connecticut the Naugatuck Valley and the Litchfield hills were hunting grounds, and in central Massachusetts so were the Brimfield-Monson neighborhood and the Ware River Valley. Such areas had been kept free of large timber by Indian fires. The purposes were at least threefold. First, the deer herd and the bears served the natives in place of livestock as a prime source of meat, clothing, and wigwam covering. Such game animals are not habitants of the deep forest, but increase where in the seasons following a fire, herbage is tender and easy to browse or penetrate. Besides providing a source of meat and skins, these scorched clearings served a second purpose: burning them over brought successive years of raspberries, blueberries, strawberries, and later black cherries, all important food for the natives (and for game). A third motive for periodic burning, the colonial writer Edward Johnson states, was to clear underbrush so as to make travel and hunting easier. Anyone who has ever fought a way through masses of laurel, bullvine, or ground juniper can appreciate the importance of this aspect.

Spring fires, however, ordinarily left undamaged the extensive swales where cedars, maples, and often some pine grew thick, and the miles-long plains where mature pine soared. Fallen leaves burned but oaks and nutbearing trees, sources of food for both men and game, remained unharmed.

By modern standards, however, at the time of white settlement population was light. Even the better inhabited southern portions of New England were thinly peopled. Northern New England—except for parts of the Champlain, Connecticut, and Merrimack, and certain Maine valleys—was almost total wilderness.

It is easy to exaggerate the immediate effects on such a landscape of the coming of the English. Keep in mind, for one detail, that handling an axe was a skill unknown to most of the newcomers. Recall also that for the first half century and more the chief goal in farming at Massachusetts Bay was livestock and its products. Grain was grown mostly for family food. For cattle the scythe, not the axe, was the primary implement, and the natural salt and fresh marshes of coast and river, not cultivated fields, the source of feed. Besides cattle the other important domestic animals at first were hogs and goats. These made the woods and native vegetation their feeding ground.

So, at first, tillage to grow bread grain and roots for human food was confined largely to long-cultivated former Indian fields. Forest cutting was chiefly for housing and shipbuilding, until export demand made it profitable to cut and merchandise lumber, spars, and staves. Moreover, the English set up their villages largely on Indian sites, some of them left vacant by fatal epidemics, others deeded to the colonists by the original possessors.

The landscape, therefore, would for decades show few totally new clearings. English dwellings, laid out on village plans, had indeed taken the place of dome-shaped Indian wigwams. Fences, occasionally a wall, surrounded the old fields. Apple trees now blossomed in spring. Nevertheless, noticeable changes in the landscape were few and to be found almost entirely near salt water and on the open lands of inland valleys. In only one area, along the Piscataqua River where New Hampshire and Maine now meet, was there in the first half century lumbering on a scale sufficient to alter substantially the existing ecology.

One change in natural surroundings, however, deadly serious to the farming colonists yet easy for moderns to forget, resulted from the coming of the cattle, hogs, sheep, and poultry of the colonists. There appears to have been an alarming increase in predatory wild animals and birds. Town records are full of measures against wolves and bears, which, finding domesticated European livestock greatly to their liking and easy to hunt, rapidly multiplied. One consequence was the designation of numerous insular spots off the coast as "hog islands" and "calf pastures," valuable because safe from predators. From the air, crows, blackbirds, and passenger pigeons plundered the new cereal crops of the English. Unlike maize, these grains had no tough protective husk. Frequent votes of bounties in town records attest their damage. Thus matters continued for nearly a half century.

The end of King Philip's War, in 1676, opened large additional tracts of confiscated Indian lands to white settlement. However, the French and Indian wars that began only fifteen years later ushered in six decades of intermittent but deadly raids on outlying New England villages and blocked English expansion elsewhere. Northern Worcester County at this period was called a howling wilderness, a dreary waste. In the quarter-century of 1700–25, fewer than twenty new towns were incorporated by Massachusetts. Up to 1750 any growth was chiefly a filling-in of territory, new parishes formed from or near older ones, mostly in the settled parts of the provinces. Meanwhile, in Maine, New Hampshire, and the upper Connecticut Valley, what had promised to become flourishing villages lay burnt—deserted and reverting to nature. Connecticut and Rhode Island alone were for the most part physically unscathed.

Yet within reach of the coast, timber was being constantly felled. Despite wars, shipbuilding and export went forward. Almost every cargo included shingles, staves, and hoops. White pines, oaks, and cedars were cut increasingly; pitch pines were bled.

In the older towns much cultivated land had already been depleted. Growing small grain year after year led to gullies in the upland. As forest decreased and wolves and wildcats were exterminated, sheep more and more took over the cleared pastures. New England's population was growing, its forest receding, its landscape opening.

Lower Cape Cod was cutting its forests and found sand dunes filling anchorages and burying salt marsh. To hold blowing sand, towns there were forced to control cutting and grazing, and to plant beach grass. River towns elsewhere took measures to ensure free passage of fish upstream for spawning to conserve this valuable resource. Jared Eliot of Connecticut warned in print that irreplaceable upland topsoil was washing down from unclothed grainfields, to muddy clear brooks. Massachusetts in 1743 legislated to restrain the firing of woodland, which destroyed fences, wasted soil fertility, and prevented reproduction of desirable timber. The first manifestations of what is today called conservation had been voiced.

Meanwhile, all through settled southern New England new features appeared on the land. Miles of stone wall laced the cleared pastures, orchards bloomed and fruited, neat dwellings filled villages, and to travelers the landscape appeared civilized. In 1760 a visitor likened Connecticut's fertile valley to one continuous town.

The year 1763, when the Treaty of Paris ended the French and Indian War, is a watershed in New England ecological history. Within the bounds of the older towns of Connecticut and Massachusetts the land was already fully distributed. Meanwhile a numerous third or fourth generation of native-born grew up. How were they to be accommodated? Once the treaty had removed the menace of Indian attack, the expansive forces burst old bounds. Connecticut's young people poured west into the Housatonic Valley and north up the Connecticut into Vermont. From Massachusetts' older towns settlers streamed into New Hampshire and the Berkshire Hills.

By 1775 the whole unsettled remainder of Connecticut had been divided into townships. In 1762 Massachusetts auctioned off its western wilderness for township sites. By the end of 1775 it had incorporated close to sixty new towns. New Hampshire in fifteen years set up a hundred new townships. Its own farmers pushed north as far as Lancaster and the Coos country. Some Massachusetts settlers found easy access to Maine by water and went east in swarms.

Unlike their forefathers, except for the few fortunate enough to find meadows or a very few spots where land had been Indian-cleared, all these newcomers had to chop their homesteads out of the forest. But by now the English were used to the axe. With skillful methods of preparation and good help, a whole acre of trees might fall in a single day. Then the next season, either with or without help of fire, the opening thus made became a sunlit corn or wheat field. When, a few years later, bread and housing for the family were secure, further clearing might result in merchantable potash, and provide English pasture grasses for cattle which could reach market on their own hooves. Moreover, salable wheat throve on the rich new soil, twenty to forty bushels to the acre.

But so for some years did bears and racoons, grateful to the settlers for sweet young corn ears. Deer cropped fruit-bearing trees. Wolves, bears, and wildcats from the adjoining forest found the newcomers' hogs and young stock to their taste. One Thetford, Vermont, farmer claimed to have killed three bears in his corn in a single night. It took time for the settlers to tame both the land and its native wild life.

These pioneers commonly built their towns and farmsteads on high land, avoiding damp places and valley plains darkened by white-pine stands. Hillsides offered the best pasturage also. About Lake Champlain and the Connecticut and Maine rivers on which the logs could be floated to mills for export, logging went on.

Thus for a full half-century after the American Revolution took the New England states into the new republic, the pattern continued. Then a transformation came to upland New England. The sheep craze began. By this time, predators were under control. Insects, disease, soil mining, and the Erie Canal had taken the profit out of wheat. Now tariff protection and a strong demand for fiber from the fast-expanding woolen industry made it profitable to breed by thousands the recently introduced Merino sheep. To provide pasture, Vermont and New Hampshire hills were cleared and grassed to their summits. Flock owners added farm to farm, until in the sheep towns, except in the roughest areas, accessible woods almost disappeared. The former occupants moved west. Sheep moved in.

It was in the same era that the through turnpikes cut across the landscape, then the canals and railways. Next came the gold rush and the opening of the prairies. All these forces enticed families from hill farms, many of them cleared less than a century but now lacking promise for the future. The Civil War brought even more displacements. In all New England except Maine and northern New Hampshire, land clearing had reached its zenith; Connecticut by 1860 was three fourths open land. In Massachusetts, in three of its westernmost counties, the proportion of land cleared was still greater. With 1,159 sawmills operating in 1865, Massachusetts harvested 140 million board feet of lumber. Each year left more thousands of its acres unclothed.

Still, even in 1851 Henry Thoreau, passing through first-settled Plymouth, reported forest that axe had never touched. In the Connecticut Valley the English traveler Johnston commented on what he called the less promising portions where, he said, "the Saxon woodsman" had only begun. The chopper had as yet scarcely entered northern Maine, except for Aroostook, and much of it was to remain permanently in forest.

Meanwhile, faint signs of a change in attitude toward the forest appeared. At Enfield, Connecticut, the Shaker colony in 1866 was planting a pine grove. George P. Marsh was in print protesting the destruction of the woods. More impelling, at the very time that Colebrook, New Hampshire, was burning peat, New England's factories and railroads were turning to mined coal. Soon its dwellings also would be heated by anthracite; the market for cordwood was gradually curtailed, and cutting immature woods for fuel would eventually sink to small proportions. The rage for sheep raising had tapered off. On mountainsides and rough lands nature was taking over once more. The gradual return to woodland often took the form of "pasture pine." Pine seeds sifted into the uncropped herbage to become solid acreages. These were eventually to yield a welcome and valuable box and board lumber harvest in the twentieth century, and here and there a popular picnic grove.

Besides the gradual return of the forest, more effective means of draining and utilizing land were altering the farm landscape. Swales that had once produced only cattails and bunch grass were now drained and leveled to become productive hay meadows. In southeast Massachusetts hundreds of acres of natural bog were ditched and leveled at great expense, then set with cranberry vines, to provide a marketable crop of increasing value.

On every active farm, however, some proportion of cultivated land, most often in corn, was always to be found. After a few years this gave way to grass, so that extensive soil washing became unusual. "You don't know the first meaning of the word erosion," an Ohio speaker told an audience of Connecticut farmers.

On the uplands the labors of a half dozen generations had cleared farm fields of rocks and concentrated them in unnumbered miles of stone wall that became a hallmark of the New England countryside. Apple trees by the thousands lined the walls or were enclosed within them, lending to the landscape both fragrance and fruitfulness. In the air Italian bees hummed all summer, enjoying both native blossoms and imported clovers. A wealth of small birds—robins, sparrows, swallows, bluebirds—had multiplied, to replace the wild turkeys and passenger pigeons that had welcomed the first explorers.

During the decades that followed the Civil War millions in added population had filled up New England cities and manufacturing towns, and suburbs had spread. Responding to the craving of their people for milk and butter, meadows, some of which had pastured sheep, now fed a million dairy cows. Wheat fields became hay fields. Corn more and more was cut green into silos rather than shocked. Deer were now protected by law, bears and wolves found only in the wildest places.

The herbage of lane and hayfield had subtly altered from colonial times. Clovers and timothy were now the rule. Buttercups, daisies, dandelions, burdocks, tansy, literally a thousand new field plants edged roadsides and filtered into meadows. Following in the white farmer's footsteps, they had increased until most persons thought them native. Overseas shrubs, the barberry, and the lilac had also managed to scatter widely. Meanwhile, ragweed and goldenrod, weeds that Indian farmers had fought, continued to find to their liking the vastly enlarged cornfields of their successors.

In further ways the landscape had been altered. Though the automobile had as yet by no means fully taken over, the network of highways had expanded tremendously. Roads reached almost every part of the six states. The greatest rivers no longer flowed unhindered, but at every considerable fall dams, interrupting their plunge, had created new lakes. Spawning fish could no longer reach their headwaters to reproduce. The effluent from paper mills, lumber mills, wool-cleaning plants, and cotton-print works polluted many streams. Yet in the great majority of smaller streams water still flowed free, often with less obstruction than in earlier days when every brook supported a series of useful local industries.

Despite all changes, in the face of the constant presence of seven and a half million humans living in the midst of one of the busiest workshops and playrooms of a mighty nation, the beginning of its fourth century, like its first, found New England's a beckoning landscape. Buildings and roads and people in reality covered but a small proportion of its surface. For the rest, three fourths was once more forest. About and between and amongst the whole lay the green and pleasant pattern of the farmlands. These filled most of its valleys and reached long fingers into its unnumbered hills.

After three centuries the soil was no better and no worse. Never, except in a few favored areas where forest mold, accumulated through

39. The original "homestall" granted 1636 to John Coolidge, the president's ancestor, at Mt. Auburn, near the Cambridge–Watertown line. Still being farmed in the 1880's, when this photograph was taken. *Society for the Preservation of New England Antiquities.*

thousands of years, offered a temporary illusion of riches had most of it been really fertile. The Pilgrims in 1621 had enriched the sandy Plymouth slopes with fish and harvested a grain that gave them reason for Thanksgiving. Their successors in 1921 were still forced to enrich the soil. It was corn that the Pilgrims had harvested. Their successors did the same, but in addition husbanded livestock and enjoyed the meat, milk, butter, and eggs that stock supply. The Pilgrim farmers gave thanks for bare necessities; nineteenth-century farmers grew potatoes, vegetables, fruits, tobacco, and flowers, and offered them for sale, to supply their other needs. Such crop alterations, as John Black has pointed out, were not haphazard developments but deliberate selections on the part of the farm people. Thus, despite the economic depression that marked 1921, the three-hundredth year of New England agriculture, the modern farmer, like the first, could appropriately celebrate Thanksgiving.

Alongside descendants of Pilgrims, Puritans, and Indians, New England farms now offered home and livelihood to numerous families of Nova Scotian, French, German, Irish, Italian, Polish, Lithuanian, Scandinavian, Scottish, Portuguese, and other blood. Yet the requisites for survival and success continued virtually unaltered. After three centuries, farm prosperity and contentment remained the fruit of intelligence and industry.

One other condition remained unchanged. In this new generation the promise for the future still beckoned chiefly such men and women as look to the soil for life as well as for a living. Among them was one of the century's most discerning poets, Robert Frost. Also among them, despite the vicissitudes of the passing years, were hundreds of families in each state who still possessed and found a livelihood on farms that their ancestors had originally acquired from the Indians or hewn out of the green forest. It was a record of continuity of enterprise unmatched in any other calling. Beyond all that, New England's farms continued to nurture men and women of a quality capable of reaching the highest distinction in the professional, business, artistic, and political life of the nation. In just two years beyond the three-hundredth anniversary of the first stirring of Plymouth soil, one of these, born on a farm in the Plymouth in Vermont, would receive there from his father the oath of President of the United States. His blood and surname would be those of the John Coolidge who in 1636 received the allotment of a "homestall of twelve acres" and "Lott 1" with thirty acres in Watertown, in the new colony of Massachusetts Bay. He would come of a family to whom some New England farm had ever since been home and occupation.

The path had been a long, deep furrow.

Notes

PART I. THE ROOTS

1. New England's First Farmers

1. Alvin M. Josephy, Jr., *The Indian Heritage of America* (New York: Knopf, 1968), p. 83. Douglas S. Byers, "Radio Carbon Dates from Bull Brook," Massachusetts Archaeological Society *Bulletin*, 20 (1959), 33. William S. Fowler, *Ten Thousands Years in America* (New York: Vantage, 1957), p. 109. Walton F. Galinat, *Plant Habit and Adaptation of Corn*, Bulletin 565, University of Massachusetts Experiment Station (Waltham, 1967), p. 4.

2. Roger Williams, *An Helpe to the Native Language of That Part of America Called New-England* ("Williams' Key,") (Providence: Narragansett Club, 1866), p. 144.

3. Galinat, *Plant Habit of Corn*, p. 5.

4. John Winthrop, *The History of New England, 1630–1649*, ed. James Savage (Boston, 1825), 1 : 147.

5. I have enlarged on certain aspects of Indian agriculture and food economy in the following: Howard S. Russell, "New England Indian Agriculture," Massachusetts Archaeological Society *Bulletin*, 22 (1961), 58–61; ibid., "How Aboriginal Farmers Stored Food," 23 (1962), 47–49; and ibid., "New England Agriculture from Champlain and Others," 31 (1969–70), 11–16.

6. For light on the Pilgrims' agricultural experience the following works, supplementing their own accounts, are helpful (listed alphabetically by author): Charles M. Andrews, *The Colonial Period of American History* (New Haven: Yale University Press, 1934–38), 1 : 291; Edward Arber, *The Story of the Pilgrim Fathers, 1606–1623* (Boston, 1897), pp. 58–164; Warren O. Ault, "Open Field Husbandry and the Village Community," American Philosophical Society *Transactions*, n. s. 55, pt. 7 (1965), 11; Charles E. Banks, *The English Ancestry and Homes of the Pilgrim Fathers* (New York: Grafton Press, 1929), pp. 25, 33, 37, 99, 116, 127; John A. Boyle, *The English in America* (London, 1887), 1 : 45; Martin S. Briggs, *Homes of the Pilgrim Fathers in England and America* (London: Oxford University Press, 1932), pp. 29, 30; John M. Brown, *The Pilgrim Fathers of New England and Their Puritan Successors* (New York, 1895), pp. 69, 126; Henry M. and Morton Dexter, *The England and Holland of the Pilgrims* (Boston: Houghton Mifflin, 1905), pp. 379, 390; Darrett B. Rutman, *Husbandmen of Plymouth: Farms and Villages in the Old Colony, 1620–1692* (Boston: Beacon Press, 1967), p. 4; Roland G. Usher, *The Pilgrims and Their History* (New York: Macmillan, 1918), pp. 10, 35, 63, 69, 75.

7. William Bradford, *Bradford's History "Of Plimoth Plantation": From the Original Manuscript* (Boston, 1898), p. 18.

8. Usher, *The Pilgrims*, p. 75.

9. Usher, *The Pilgrims*, p. 91. Bradford, *"Of Plimoth Plantation,"* p. 121. *Mourt's Relation*, ed. Henry M. Dexter (Boston, 1865), p. 132. Fulmer Mood,

"John Winthrop, Jr. on Indian Corn," *New England Quarterly*, 10 (1937), 125. How Squanto and the southern New England Indians may have acquired the practice of fertilizing cornhills with herring is a matter of dispute. I believe that the straightforward assertions of the colonial writers are to be taken at face value. Any other conclusion ignores too many agricultural and historical realities.

2. Massachusetts Bay

1. Winsor, *Narrative and Critical History of America*, 8 vols. (Boston, 1880–81), 3:31, 326. Frances Rose-Troup, *Roger Conant and the Early Settlements on the North Shore of Massachusetts* (n.p.: Roger Conant Family Association, 1926), pp. 11, 12. Herbert L. Osgood, *The American Colonies in the Seventeenth Century* (New York: Macmillan, 1904–07), 1:129. Clifford K. Shipton, *Roger Conant: A Founder of Massachusetts* (Cambridge: Harvard University Press, 1944), pp. 62, 65.

2. Francis Higginson, "New-England's Plantation," in Alexander Young, ed., *Chronicles of the First Planters of the Colony of Massachusetts Bay in New England, 1623–1636* (Boston: Little, Brown, 1846), p. 259. Rose-Troup, *Conant and the Early Settlements*, pp. 11, 12.

3. Nathaniel B. Shurtleff, ed., *Records of the Governor and Company of Massachusetts Bay in New England* (Boston, 1853–54), 1:24–40. Young, *Chronicles*, p. 14.

4. Young, *Chronicles*, pp. 246, 247. James D. Phillips, *Salem in the Seventeenth Century* (Boston: Houghton Mifflin, 1933), p. 72.

5. The views expressed result from study of many sources, including Charles E. Banks, "English Sources of Emigration to the New England Colonies in the Seventeenth Century," Massachusetts Historical Society *Proceedings*, 60 (1926–27), 366–72; Banks, *The Winthrop Fleet of 1630* (Boston: Houghton Mifflin, 1930); Banks, *The Planters of the Commonwealth* (Boston: Houghton Mifflin, 1930), preface, pp. viii, 12–14, 30, 31; Allen French, *Charles I and the Puritan Upheaval* (Boston: Houghton Mifflin, 1955), pp. 342, 362, 375; Richard Frothingham, *History of Charlestown, Massachusetts* (Boston, 1852), pp. 22, 78 (and numerous other local histories); Charles M. Andrews, *The Colonial Period of American History*, 4 vols. (New Haven: Yale University Press, 1934–38), 1:496ff.

6. Among works on contemporary English agriculture helpful toward understanding the background of New England's agriculture are Warren O. Ault, "Open Field Husbandry and the Village Community: A Study of Agrarian By-Laws in Medieval England," American Philosophical Society *Transactions*, n. s. 55, pt. 7 (Philadelphia, 1965), 1–102; Carl Bridenbaugh, *Vexed and Troubled Englishmen* (New York: Oxford University Press, 1968); George G. Coulton, *The Medieval Village* (Cambridge, England: Cambridge University Press, 1925); H. C. Darby, ed., *An Historical Geography of England before 1800* (Cambridge, England: Cambridge University Press, 1936); Thomas Davis, *A General View of the Agriculture of the County of Wiltshire* (London, 1794); George L. Gomme, *The Village Community* (New York, 1890); H. P. R. Finberg, ed., *The Agrarian History of England and Wales*, vols. 1, 4 (Cambridge, England: Cambridge University Press, 1972, 1967); Norman S. B. Gras and Ethel Culbert, *The Economic and Social History of an English Village* (Cambridge: Harvard University Press, 1930); Howard L. Gray, *English Field Systems* (Cambridge: Harvard University Press, 1915); Herbert Hall, "The Romance of Marshland Farming," *Contemporary Review* (June, 1933); John

Hatcher, *Rural Economy and Society in the Duchy of Cornwall, 1300–1500* (Cambridge, England: Cambridge University Press, 1970); W. G. Hoskins, *The Midland Peasant* (London: Macmillan, 1957); Frederick W. Maitland, *Township and Borough* (Cambridge, England: Cambridge University Press, 1898); John Norden, *Essex Described* (London, 1840); Wallace Notestein, *The English People on the Eve of Colonization, 1603–1630* (New York: Harper and Row, 1954); Rowland E. Prothero, *English Farming, Past and Present* (London, 1912); Michael Robbins, *Ancient Middlesex* (London, 1953); Frederick Seebohm, *The English Village Community*, 4th ed. (London, 1890); Mabel E. Seebohm, *The Evolution of the English Farm* (Cambridge: Harvard University Press, 1927); Robert Trow-Smith, *A History of British Livestock Husbandry to 1700* (London: Routledge and Kegan Paul, 1957); Thomas Westcote, *A View of Devonshire* (1630) (Exeter, England, 1845).

3. Stirring the Soil

1. Richard J. Frothingham, *History of Charlestown* (Boston, 1852), pp. 19, 20.

2. Alexander Young, ed., *Chronicles of the First Planters of the Colony of Massachusetts Bay in New England, 1628–1686* (Boston, 1846), pp. 396, 404. Cambridge, Mass., *Proprietors' Records of the Town* (Cambridge, 1896), pp. 2, 6, 7, 8, 16. Nathaniel B. Shurtleff, ed., *Records of the Governor and Company of Massachusetts Bay in New England, 1628–1686* (Boston, 1853–54), 1:388.

3. Edward Johnson, *Wonder Working Providence of Sion's Saviour in New England* (London, 1654), ed. William F. Poole (Andover, 1867), pp. 56, 83. John White, "The Planter's Plea," in *The Founding of Massachusetts* (Boston: Massachusetts Historical Society, 1930), pp. 138–201.

4. James D. Phillips, *Salem in the Seventeenth Century* (Boston: Houghton Mifflin, 1933), p. 93. Thomas Lechford, *Plaine Dealing or News from New England*, 1642, reprint ed. J. H. Trumbull (Boston, 1867), p. 109. John Underhill, *News from America* (London, 1638), ed. Charles Orr (Cleveland, 1897), p. 65.

5. William B. Weeden, *Economic and Social History of New England, 1620–1789* (Boston: Houghton Mifflin, 1890), 1:331. Sylvester Judd, *History of Hadley, Massachusetts*, new ed. (Springfield, 1905), p. 354.

6. Fulmer Mood, "John Winthrop, Jr. on Indian Corn," *New England Quarterly*, 10 (1937), 128. Jasper Dankers and Peter Sluyter, "Journal of a Voyage to New York in 1679–80," Long Island Historical Society *Memoirs* (Brooklyn, 1867), 1:394. Edmund Browne, "Report on Massachusetts," Colonial Society of Massachusetts *Transactions*, 8 (1900), 77.

7. Johnson, *Wonder Working Providence*, pp. 56, 120. Mood, "John Winthrop, Jr.," p. 127. Joseph B. Felt, *Annals of Salem* (Salem, 1845), 1:243.

8. Edmund S. Morgan, "Masters and Servants in Early New England," *More Books*, 17, no. 7 (Boston Public Library, 1942), p. 311. Gerald Johnson, *Our English Heritage* (Philadelphia: Lippincott, 1949), p. 57.

9. Shurtleff, *Bay Colony Records*, 2:181.

10. Thomas Wiggin letter, quoted by Willard H. Clark, *History of Winthrop, Massachusetts* (Winthrop, 1952), p. 50. James D. Knowles, *Memoir of Roger Williams* (Boston, 1834), p. 119.

11. John Josselyn, *An Account of Two Voyages to New England* (London, 1674/5), p. 182.

12. Mildred Campbell, "Social Origins of Some Americans," in James M. Smith, ed., *Seventeenth Century America* (Chapel Hill: University of North Carolina

Press, 1959), p. 73. Alice Clark, *The Working Life of Women in the Seventeenth Century* (London, 1919), p. 46.

4. Distance Beckons the Uneasy

1. For motives and methods leading to new settlements, see Archer B. Hulbert, *Soil: Its Influence on the History of the United States* (New Haven: Yale University Press, 1930), pp. 105ff; Charles M. Andrews, *The River Towns of Connecticut* (Baltimore: Johns Hopkins, 1889), pp. 30, 78; George L. Haskins, *Law and Authority in Early Massachusetts* (New York: Macmillan, 1960), pp. 48–77; and Lois Mathews, *The Expansion of New England* (Boston, 1909), pp. 1–36.

2. William Bradford, *Bradford's History "Of Plimoth Plantation": From the Original Manuscript* (Boston, 1898), pp. 361–63. Frederic W. Cook, ed., *Historical Data Relating to Counties, Cities and Towns* (Boston, 1948).

3. Justin Winsor, ed., *Narrative and Critical History of America*, 8 vols. (Cambridge, Mass., 1884–89), 3:326. Byron Fairchild, *Messrs. William Pepperell, Merchants at Piscataqua* (Ithaca, N.Y.: Cornell University Press, 1954), p. 65. Wilbur Spencer, *Pioneers of Maine Rivers* (Portland, 1930), p. 65.

4. Ralph May, *Early Portsmouth History* (Boston: Goodspeed, 1926), p. 99.

5. John A. Boyle, *The English in America* (London, 1887), 1:275. Spencer, *Pioneers*, pp. 86, 128, 131. Edwin Sanborn, *History of New Hampshire . . . to 1874* (Manchester, 1875), p. 40. Clarence A. Day, *A History of Maine Agriculture, 1604–1860*, University of Maine *Bulletin* 56 (1954), p. 10.

6. Edwin A. Charlton, *New Hampshire as It Is* (Claremont, 1857), pp. 19, 37.

7. Day, *Maine Agriculture*, pp. 10, 11. Spencer, *Pioneers*, p. 47.

8. Justin Winsor, ed., *Memorial History of Boston, 1630–1880* (Boston, 1880), 1:84.

9. Samuel G. Arnold, *History of the State of Rhode Island and Providence Plantations* (New York, 1859), p. 98.

10. James D. Knowles, *Memoir of Roger Williams* (Boston, 1834), pp. 102, 119.

11. J. Russell Bartlett, *Letters of Roger Williams* (Providence: Narragansett Club Publications, 1874), pp. 71, 85.

12. Peter J. Coleman, *The Transformation of Rhode Island . . . 1790 to 1860* (Providence: Brown University Press, 1963), p. 5. W. L. Watson, "A Short History of Jamestown . . . Rhode Island," Rhode Island Historical Society *Collections*, 26 (1933), 42.

13. Daniel Howard, *A New History of Old Windsor, Connecticut* (Windsor, 1935), pp. 7–14. John Winthrop, *The History of New England, 1630–1649*, ed. James Savage (Boston, 1825), 2:132, 184. Louis B. Mason, *The Life and Times of Major John Mason of Connecticut, 1600–1672* (New York: Putnam, 1935), p. 78.

14. Walter Hard, *The Connecticut* (New York: Holt, Rinehart, 1947), p. 55. William DeLove, *The Colonial History of Hartford* (Hartford, 1914), p. 156.

15. John G. Palfrey, *History of New England* (Boston, 1858–90), 1:534. Mathews, *Expansion*, pp. 14–30. Winsor, *Narrative*, 3:332. Charles H. Walcott, *Concord in the Colonial Period* (Boston, 1884), p. 35.

16. John W. Oliver, *History of American Technology* (New York, 1956), p. 41.

5. To Market, to Market

1. William Bradford, "A Description and Historical Account of New England in Verse," Massachusetts Historical Society *Collections* 3 (1794), 78. John Winthrop,

The History of New England, 1630–1649, ed. James Savage (Boston, 1825), 2:21, 31. Edward Johnson, *Wonder Working Providence of Sion's Saviour in New England* (London, 1654), ed. William F. Poole (Andover, 1867), p. 172. Marion H. Gottfried, "The First Depression in Massachusetts," *New England Quarterly,* 9, no. 4 (1936), 655. William Hubbard, "General History of New England," Massachusetts Historical Society *Collections,* 2nd ser., 5 (1815), 140.

2. Alan Everitt, "The Marketing of Agricultural Produce," in Joan Thirsk, ed., *The Agrarian History of England and Wales,* vol. 4 (Cambridge, England: Cambridge University Press, 1967), pp. 466–591.

3. Winthrop, *History,* 2:31.

4. Samuel Maverick, *A Briefe Description of New England . . . From a Manuscript Written in 1660,* ed. John W. Dean (Boston, 1885), p. 26. Bernard Bailyn, *The New England Merchants in the Seventeenth Century* (Cambridge: Harvard University Press, 1955), pp. 96–100. *Essex County Probate Records* (Salem: Essex Institute, 1916), 1 (1633–44); 2 (1665–74). *Suffolk County Estates, 1675–1696.*

5. Thomas Minor, *Diary, 1653–1684* (New London, 1899), p. 90.

6. J. Franklin Jameson, ed., *Narratives of New Netherland, 1609–1664* (New York, 1909), p. 423. Amelia Forbes Emerson, *Early History of Naushon Island* (privately printed, 1935), p. 197.

7. Everett S. Stackpole, *History of New Hampshire* (New York: American Historical Society, 1916), 1:128. Ralph May, *Early Portsmouth History* (Boston: Goodspeed, 1926), p. 169. William M. Carleton, "Masts and the King's Navy," *New England Quarterly,* 12 (1939), pp. 4–18. Bailyn, *Merchants,* p. 100.

8. First Ironworks Association, *The Saugus Restoration* (Saugus, Mass., 1951). Samuel E. Morison, *Builders of the Bay Colony* (Boston: Houghton Mifflin, 1930), p. 279.

6. Patterns from Home

1. For the Colony charter, its transfer to Massachusetts Bay, and the government of the early colonies, these works are useful: Charles M. Andrews, *The Colonial Period of American History* (New Haven: Yale University Press, 1934–38), vol. 1, chaps. 17, 18; Samuel E. Morison, *The Oxford History of the American People* (New York: Oxford University Press, 1965), pp. 65–67; and George L. Haskins, *Law and Authority in Early Massachusetts* (New York: Macmillan, 1960), pp. 10–20.

2. Nathaniel B. Shurtleff, ed., *Records of the Governor and Company of Massachusetts Bay in New England, 1620–92,* 5 vols. (Boston, 1853–54), 1:157. Lemuel Shattuck, *History of the Town of Concord . . . to 1832* (Concord, 1835), p. 3. Townsend Scudder, *Concord, American Town* (Boston: Little, Brown, 1947), pp. 4–8. C. H. Walcott, *Concord in the Colonial Period* (Boston, 1884), p. 17.

3. Among the works on the development of town government, the following, with the colony records, are enlightening: Roy Hidemichi Akagi, *Town Proprietors of the New England Colonies* (Philadelphia: University of Pennsylvania Press, 1924); Charles M. Andrews, *The River Towns of Connecticut* (Baltimore: Johns Hopkins, 1889); H. R. R. Finberg, *The Agrarian History of England and Wales,* vol. 1 (London: Cambridge University Press, 1972); Anthony N. B. Garvan, *Architecture and Town Planning in Colonial Connecticut* (New Haven: Yale University Press, 1951); George L. Gomme, *The Village Community* (New York, 1890); George E. Howard, *An Introduction to the Local Constitutional History of the*

United States (Baltimore: Johns Hopkins, 1889), vol. 1; George L. Langdon, Jr., *Pilgrim Colony: A History of New Plymouth, 1620–1691* (New Haven, 1966); Frederick W. Maitland, *Township and Borough* (Cambridge, England: Cambridge University Press, 1898); Edna Scofield, "The Origin of Settlement Patterns in New England," *Geographical Review*, 28 (1938); and Michael Zuckerman, *Peaceable Kingdoms: New England Towns in the Eighteenth Century* (New York: Knopf, 1970). Among studies of early communities are Philip J. Greven, Jr., *Four Generations: Population, Land and Family in Colonial Andover, Massachusetts* (Ithaca, N.Y.: Cornell University Press, 1970); Sumner C. Powell, *Puritan Village: The Formation of a New England Town* (Middletown, Conn.: Wesleyan University Press, 1963); Kenneth A. Lockridge, *A New England Town: The First Hundred Years. Dedham, Massachusetts. 1636–1736* (New York: Norton, 1970).

4. Besides the lists above and the wealth of town histories, valuable viewpoints appear in the following: Herbert B. Adams, "The Germanic Origin of New England Towns," in vol. 1 of *Local Institutions* (Baltimore: Johns Hopkins, 1882); Richard Bushman, *From Puritan to Yankee: Character and the Social Order in Connecticut, 1690–1765* (Cambridge: Harvard University Press, 1967); John A. Boyle, *The English in America*, vol. 2, (London, 1887); Melville Egleston, *The Land System of the New England Colonies* (Baltimore: Johns Hopkins, 1886); William C. Foster, ed., "Early Attempts at Rhode Island History," Rhode Island Historical Society *Collections*, 7 (1885), 5–109; Wallace Notestein, *The English People on the Eve of Colonization, 1603–1690* (New York: Harper and Row, 1954); and Page Smith, *As a City upon a Hill: The Town in American History* (New York: Knopf, 1966).

5. *Colonial Laws of Massachusetts*, p. 35.

7. Settling In

1. Lucien R. Paige, *History of Cambridge, Massachusetts, 1630–1877* (Cambridge, 1877), p. 95n.

2. Edward Johnson, *Wonder Working Providence of Sion's Saviour in New England* (Andover, 1867), p. 84. Alexander Young, *Chronicles of the First Planters of the Colony of Massachusetts Bay in New England, 1630–1636* (Boston, 1841), p. 246. James M. Usher, *History of Medford* (Boston, 1886), p. 29.

3. Massachusetts Historical Society *Collections*, 4th ser., 6 (1863), 146–147. L. C. Corbett, et al., "Fruits and Vegetables," United States Department of Agriculture *1925 Yearbook*, p. 120.

4. John Winthrop, *The History of New England, 1630–1649*, ed. James Savage (Boston, 1825), 1:331n. Clifford K. Shipton, *Roger Conant: A Founder of Massachusetts* (Cambridge: Harvard University Press, 1944), p. 43.

5. Usher, *Medford*, p. 29.

6. Alice Lapham, *The Old Planters of Beverly in Massachusetts and the Thousand Acre Grant of 1635* (Cambridge: Riverside Press, 1930), p. 93.

7. Samuel G. Arnold, *History of the State of Rhode Island and Providence Plantations* (New York, 1859), pp. 98, 137.

8. Henry R. Stiles, *History and Genealogies of Ancient Windsor, Connecticut* (Albany, 1863), 1:478. Ulysses P. Hedrick, *History of Horticulture in America to 1860* (New York: Oxford University Press, 1950), p. 36. Thomas Minor, *Diary, 1653–1684* (New London, 1899), p. 57. Samuel Maverick, *A Briefe Description of*

New England . . . From a Manuscript Written in 1660, ed. John W. Dean (Boston, 1885), p. 217.

8. The Farm Family

1. George F. Dow, *Everyday Life in the Massachusetts Bay Colony* (Boston: Society for the Preservation of New England Antiquities, 1935), p. 98. Sherman A. Adams, revised by H. R. Stiles, *History of Ancient Wethersfield* (New York, 1904), p. 950. Frederick Freeman, *History of Cape Cod* (Boston, 1860–62), 1:185.
2. George P. Winship, ed., *Boston in 1682 and 1699: A Trip to New England by Edward Ward, and A Letter from New England by J. W.* (Providence, 1905). Benjamin Tompson, *New England's Crisis* (Club of Odd Volumes reprint, 1894), p. 6.
3. John Dunton, "Journal," Massachusetts Historical Society *Collections,* 2nd ser., 2 (1846), 120. Ann Hardy, "How to Boil Meat Successfully," *The Listener,* January 28, 1954.
4. Edmund Browne, "Report on Massachusetts," Colonial Society of Massachusetts *Transactions,* 7 (1900), 78.
5. John Josselyn, *New England's Rarities Discovered,* ed. Edward Tuckerman (Boston, 1865), p. 103. Dow, *Everyday Life,* pp. 42ff.
6. Dow, *Everyday Life,* p. 64. W. F. Woodward, *The Way Our People Lived* (New York: Dutton, 1945), p. 11. Adams, *Wethersfield,* p. 951.
7. Edward Johnson, *Wonder Working Providence of Sion's Saviour in New England* (Andover, 1867), p. 174.
8. *Essex County Probate Records* (Salem: Essex Institute, 1916); *Suffolk County Estates;* William DeLove, *The Colonial History of Hartford* (Hartford, 1914), p. 156; and similar local records.

PART II. WAR AND TRADE, 1675–1775

9. A Surplus to Sell

1. Edward Randolph, *Report to the Committee for Trade and Plantations,* October 12, 1676 (Boston: Prince Society Reprint, 1898), 2:248.
2. Robert Mason, quoted in Everett S. Stackpole, *History of New Hampshire* (New York: American Historical Society, 1916), 1:121. Victor S. Clark, *History of Manufactures in the United States, 1607–1860* (Washington, 1870), pp. 90–94.
3. William D. Miller, *The Narragansett Planters* (Worcester: American Antiquarian Society, 1934), pp. 160, 328. Peleg Sanford, *The Letter Book of Peleg Sanford of Newport, Merchant, 1666–1668* (Providence: Rhode Island Historical Society, 1928), p. 30. Frances M. Caulkins, *History of New London* (New London, Conn., 1852), pp. 232, 234ff. Roland M. Hooker, *Colonial Trade of Connecticut* (New Haven: Yale University Press, 1936), p. 13.
4. Sherman A. Adams, revised by H. R. Stiles, *History of Ancient Wethersfield* (New York, 1904), p. 541. For illuminating discussions of New England's agricultural commodities in foreign trade, see Bernard Bailyn, *The New England Merchants of the Seventeenth Century* (Cambridge, Mass., 1955), and William B. Weeden, *Economic and Social History of New England, 1620–1789* (Boston, 1890).
5. Edward Johnson, *Wonder Working Providence of Sion's Saviour in New England* (Andover, 1867), p. 208.
6. Joshua Hempstead of New London, *Diary, 1711–1758* (New London, 1901),

entry, June 26, 1724. Robert W. Howard, *The Horse in America* (New York: Fuller, 1965), p. 41. Caulkins, *New London*, p. 483. Thomas Allen, of New London, MS Account Books, American Antiquarian Society, Worcester.

7. Carl R. Woodward, "Rural Economy in Rhode Island," *Rhode Island History*, 5 (1946), 121.

8. Weeden, *Economic and Social History*, 1:376.

9. Allen, Account Books.

10. Hempstead, *Diary*, p. 83 and dates listed. William B. Weeden, *Early Rhode Island: A Social History of the People* (New York: Grafton Press, 1910), p. 320.

11. English Shipping Records Relating to Massachusetts Ports, 1756–1763, pt. 3, nos. 1144–1417, at Peabody Museum, Salem.

12. Belcher Papers, "To the Lords of Trade," Massachusetts Historical Society, pt. 1, p. 71. James Birket, *Some Cursory Remarks Made . . . in His Voyages to North America, 1750–51* (New Haven, 1896), pp. 11, 20, 24. Weeden, *Economic and Social History*, 2:503.

13. Clark, *Manufactures*, 1:82. *Commerce of Rhode Island, 1726–1800* (Boston, 1915), 1:486. Percy W. Bidwell and John I. Falconer, *History of Agriculture in the Northern United States, 1620–1860* (New York: Peter Smith, 1941), p. 98.

14. Charles E. Banks, *History of Martha's Vineyard* (Boston: Houghton Mifflin, 1911–25), 1:436. Daniel Ricketson, *History of New Bedford, Massachusetts. Including Westport, Dartmouth and Fairhaven* (New Bedford, 1858), p. 65. Carl Bridenbaugh, *Cities in the Wilderness: The First Century of Urban Life in America, 1625–1702* (New York: Ronald Press, 1938), p. 177. Timothy Pitkin, *A Statistical View of the Commerce of the United States . . .* (Hartford, 1816), p. 43.

15. Calculated from provisioning of Allen vessels out of New London, 1758–68: Allen, Account Books, November 9, 1768.

16. Edward P. Hamilton, *The French and Indian Wars* (New York: Doubleday, 1962), p. 109.

17. Bidwell and Falconer, *Agriculture*, p. 142.

18. Randolph, *Report*, p. 248. Daniel Neal, *History of New England to 1700* (London, 1720), 2:584; and Albert E. Van Duzen, *Connecticut* (New York: Random House, 1961), pp. 111, 114.

19. Amos E. Brown, *Faneuil Hall and Faneuil Hall Market* (Boston, 1900), pp. 66ff. Justin Winsor, ed., *Memorial History of Boston* (Boston, 1880–81), 1:232, 539ff.

20. Brown, *Faneuil Hall*, pp. 67, 69, 97–100. Karen J. Friedman, "Victualling Colonial Boston," *Agricultural History*, 44 (1973), 189–205.

10. Growth of the Land: Grass and Grain

1. William Hubbard, "A General History of New England," Massachusetts Historical Society *Collections*, 2nd ser., 5 (1848), 23.

2. Charles L. Flint, *A Hundred Years' Progress of American Agriculture*, Massachusetts Board of Agriculture, *1873 Report*, p. 21.

3. Thomas Minor, *Diary, 1653–1684* (New London, 1899). Solomon Lincoln, Jr., *History of Hingham* (Hingham, 1827), p. 83.

4. Grant Powers, *Historical Sketches of the Coos Country, 1754–1785* (Haverhill, N.H., 1847, reprint 1880), p. 74.

5. Massachusetts Historical Society *Proceedings*, vol. 4 (1858–60), p. 295.

6. William Douglass, *A Summary, Historical and Political, of the British Set-*

tlements in North America (Boston, 1755), 2:207; Lord Adam Gordon, "Journal," in Newton D. Mereness, ed., *Travels in the American Colonies* (New York: Macmillan, 1916), p. 451.

7. Thomas Anburey, *Travels through the Interior Parts of America* (London, 1789), 2:218.

8. Joshua Hempsted, *Diary* (New London, Conn., 1901), October 1711 and October 1723, 1724 entries. Berthold Laufer, "American Plant Migration," *Scientific Monthly*, 28 (1927), 239–51.

11. Growth of the Land: Vegetables and Fruits

1. John Winthrop, *The History of New England, 1630–1649*, ed. James Savage (Boston, 1825), entry of January 8, 1636. Clifton K. Shipton, *Roger Conant: A Founder of Massachusetts* (Cambridge: Harvard University Press, 1944), p. 76.

2. Edward L. Parker, *History of Londonderry, New Hampshire* (Boston, 1851), pp. 35–49. Clarence A. Day, *A History of Maine Agriculture, 1604–1860*, University of Maine Studies, no. 68 (Orono, 1954), p. 35. H. B. and Harvey Wright, *The Settlement and Story of Oakham, Massachusetts* (Oakham, 1947), 1:5ff. Liberty H. Bailey, *Cyclopedia of American Agriculture*, 5th ed., 4 vols. (New York: Macmillan, 1917), 2:520. Charles K. Bolton, *Scotch Irish Pioneers in Ulster and America* (Boston: Little, Brown, 1910), p. 200. Arthur L. Perry, *Origins of Williamstown* (Williamstown, Mass., 1900), pp. 81, 91. Mary T. Wilson, "Americans Learn to Grow the Irish Potato," *New England Quarterly*, 32 (1959), p. 334.

3. Edward H. Jenkins, *A History of Connecticut Agriculture* (New Haven, n.d.), p. 328. Thomas Allen, of New London, MS Account Books, American Antiquarian Society, Worcester, November 1759 entry.

4. James Birket, *Some Cursory Remarks Made . . . in His Voyage to North America, 1750–51* (New Haven, 1896), p. 11. Victor S. Clark, *History of Manufactures in the United States, 1607–1860* (Washington, rev. ed., 1870), 1:82.

5. Ezra Stiles, *Extracts from the Itineraries, 1755–84: With a Selection from His Correspondence*, ed. Franklin B. Dexter (New Haven: Yale University Press, 1916), p. 215.

6. Adrian F. McDonald, *The History of Tobacco Production in Connecticut* (New Haven: Yale University Press, 1936), pp. 4ff. Elizabeth Ramsey, *The History of Tobacco Culture in the Connecticut Valley* (Northampton, 1930), p. 114.

7. United States Department of the Interior, Census of 1880, vol. 3, *Manufactures of Tobacco*. Sherman A. Adams, revised by H. R. Stiles, *History of Ancient Weathersfield* (New York, 1904), pp. 623, 946.

8. William B. Weeden, *Early Rhode Island: A Social History of the People* (New York: Grafton Press, 1910), p. 321. James B. Hodges, *The Browns of Providence Plantation* (Cambridge: Harvard University Press, 1952), pp. 6, 23, 31, 249.

9. Wilfred H. Munro, *The History of Bristol, Rhode Island* (Providence, 1880), p. 337. Charles O. F. Thompson, *Sketches of Old Bristol* (Providence, 1942), p. 118. Adams, *Weathersfield*, pp. 615, 948.

10. Ulysses P. Hedrick, *A History of Horticulture in America* (New York: Oxford University Press, 1950), p. 42. A. J. Pieters, "Seed Selling, Seed Growing, and Seed Testing," United States Department of Agriculture *1899 Yearbook*, p. 550; *1925 Yearbook*, p. 325. Sylvester Judd, *History of Hadley, Massachusetts* (Springfield, 1905), p. 363.

11. George Dow, *Holyoke Diaries* (Salem: Essex Institute, 1911), pp. 7, 13, 20,

59. Anne Hulton, *Letters of a Loyalist Lady* (Cambridge, 1927), p. 34. Stiles, *Itineraries*, p. 217. John W. Hanson, *History of the Town of Danvers* (Danvers, 1848), p. 93.

12. Charles J. Taylor, *History of Great Barrington* (Great Barrington, Mass., 1882), p. 52.

13. Timothy Walker, *Diaries, 1730–1782*, New Hampshire Historical Society *Collections*, 9 (1889), 1764 entries. Lord Adam Gordon, "Journal," in Newton D. Mereness, ed., *Travels in the American Colonies* (New York: Macmillan, 1916), p. 451.

14. Percy W. Bidwell and John I. Falconer, *History of Agriculture in the Northern United States, 1620–1860* (New York: Peter Smith, 1941), p. 99. Henry S. Nourse, *History of the Town of Harvard* (Clinton, Mass., 1894), p. 99. George F. Daniels, *History of the Town of Oxford* (Oxford, Mass., 1892), p. 775.

15. Francis F. Drake, *The Town of Roxbury: Its Memorable Persons and Places* (Roxbury, 1878), p. 119. John Josselyn, *An Account of Two Voyages to New England* (London, 1670–75), p. 190. Samuel Maverick, *A Briefe Description of New England*, ed., John W. Dean (Boston, 1885), p. 27.

12. Growth of the Land: Livestock

1. Everett S. Stackpole, *History of New Hampshire* (New York: American Historical Society, 1916), 2:39.

2. Matthew Patten, of Bedford, N.H., *Diary, 1754–1788* (Concord: Rumford Press, 1903), p. 117.

3. Samuel Orcutt, *History of the Old Town of Derby, Connecticut, 1642–1880* (Springfield, 1880), p. 125. Ezekiel Read, Book of Accounts, 1712–1733, MSS in possession of the family of H. F. Tompson, Seekonk, Mass. Glenn Weaver, *Jonathan Trumbull, Connecticut's Merchant Magistrate* (Hartford: Connecticut Historical Society, 1956), pp. 14ff.

4. Edgar M. Bacon, *Narragansett Bay: Its Historic and Romantic Associations* (New York: Putnam, 1904), pp. 249, 283.

5. Elisha R. Potter, Jr., "The Early History of Narragansett," Rhode Island Historical Society *Collections*, 3 (1835), 111, 131.

6. James Birket, *Some Cursory Remarks Made . . . in His Voyage to North America* (New Haven, 1896), p. 13. A. P. Usher, "Colonial Business and Transportation" in Albert B. Hart, ed., *Commonwealth History of Massachusetts* (New York, 1928), 2:392.

7. William S. Pattee, *History of Old Braintree and Quincy* (Quincy, 1878), p. 550. Henry M. Burt, *The First Century of the History of Springfield* (Springfield, 1898), 2:442.

8. Ebenezer Parkman, *Diary*, ed. Harriette E. Forbes (Westborough, Mass.: Historical Society, 1899), p. 42. Benjamin Hall, *History of Eastern Vermont from Its Earliest Settlement to the Close of the 18th Century* (New York, 1858), p. 98. Federal Writers Project, *Connecticut* (Cambridge: Riverside Press, 1938), p. 469. Harry J. Carman, ed., *American Husbandry* (New York: Columbia University Press, 1934), p. 59.

9. Samuel Sewall, *Diary*, ed. Mark Van Doren (New York: Macy Massins, 1927), p. 17.

10. William Douglass, *A Summary, Historical and Political, of the British Settlements in North America* (Boston, 1755), 2:218.

11. Rev. Samuel Deane, *Extracts From Diary, 1761–1814*, ed. William Willis (Portland, Me., 1849), p. 240. Philip Padelford, ed., *Colonial Panorama 1755: Dr. Robert Honyman's Journal for March and April* (San Marino, Calif.: Huntington Library, 1939), p. 54.

12. Henry White, *Indian Battles, with Incidents in the Early History of New England* (New York, 1859), p. 349.

13. Joseph Green, *Diary, Historical Collections*, 2nd ser., 10 (Salem: Essex Institute, 1869), entry for August 31, 1711. John H. Lockwood, *Westfield and Its Historic Influences* (Westfield, 1922), 1:390.

14. Thaddeus W. Harris, *Insects of Massachusetts Injurious to Vegetation* (Cambridge, 1841), p. 136.

15. Timothy Dwight, *Travels in New England and New York, 1796–1815* (New Haven, 1821–22), 1:49. Grant Powers, *Historical Sketches of . . . Coos Country, 1745–1795* (Haverhill, N.H., 1880), pp. 153, 159.

13. Wealth from Forests

1. *Watertown Records, Comprising the First and Second Books of Town Proceedings* (Watertown, Mass., 1884), p. 14. Thomas F. Waters, *Ipswich in the Massachusetts Bay Colony, 1633–1700* (Ipswich, 1905–17), p. 66. Bernard C. Steiner, *History of the Plantation of Menunkatuck and of the Original Town of Guilford, Connecticut* (Baltimore, 1897), p. 181.

2. John J. Currier, *History of Newbury, Massachusetts, 1635–1902* (Boston, 1902), pp. 128, 129.

3. Clarence A. Day, *A History of Maine Agriculture, 1604–1860*, University of Maine Studies, no. 68, (Orono, 1954), p. 40. Frederick Freeman, *History of Cape Cod* (Boston, 1860–52), 2:112.

4. See enlightening discussions in: William M. Carleton, "Masts and the King's Navy," *New England Quarterly*, 12 (1939), 4–18; Joseph J. Malone, *Pine Trees and Politics: The Naval Stores and Forest Policy of New England, 1691–1775* (Seattle: University of Washington Press, 1964); Benjamin H. Hall, *History of Eastern Vermont from Its Earliest Settlement to the Close of the Eighteenth Century* (New York, 1858), p. 143; and local histories.

5. William B. Weeden, *Early Rhode Island: A Social History of the People* (New York: Grafton Press, 1910), 1:356.

6. Andrew Burnaby, *Travels Through the Middle Settlements of North America . . . 1759 and 1760*, 2nd ed. (London, 1775), p. 151.

7. J. E. A. Smith, *History of Pittsfield . . . 1734–1800* (Boston, 1869), p. 42.

14. The Ways and the Means

1. For development of new towns, an excellent monograph is Clifford K. Shipton, "The New England Frontier 1607–1763," *New England Quarterly*, 10 (1937), 25–36.

2. Everett S. Stackpole, *History of New Hampshire* (New York: American Historical Society, 1916), 1:350. Edward L. Parker, *History of Londonderry, New Hampshire* (Boston, 1851), pp. 97ff. Thomas Smith, *Extracts from Journals, 1719–1788*, ed. William Willis (Portland, Me., 1849), pp. 53, 143. Rising Lake Morrow, *Connecticut Influences in Western Massachusetts and Vermont* (New Haven: Yale University Press, 1936), pp. 10–14. Marcus Lee Hansen, *The Min-*

gling of the Canadian and American Peoples (New Haven: Yale University Press, 1940), 1 : 30–35.

3. Samuel Williams, *The Natural and Civil History of Vermont* (Walpole, N.H., 1794), p. 312.

4. Estate inventories such as those in *Essex County Probate Records* (Salem: Essex Institute, 1916) correct erroneous impressions.

5. Joshua Hempstead, *Diary* (New London, Conn.: New London Historical Society, 1901), entry of March 22, 1742.

6. Joseph Merrill, *History of Amesbury and Merrimac* (Haverhill, Mass., 1880), p. 237. Abbott L. Cummings, ed., *Rural Household Inventories, 1675–1778* (Boston: Society for the Preservation of New England Antiquities, 1964).

7. Warren R. Cochrane and George K. Wood, *History of Francestown, New Hampshire, 1759–1891* (Nashua, 1895), p. 381.

15. Life on the Farm

1. Quoted by Marshall B. Davidson, *Life in America* (Boston: Houghton Mifflin, 1951), p. 492.

2. Joseph Andrews, Journal, 1752–1787, Massachusetts Historical Society, Boston. Zaccheus Collins, Diary, 1726–69, Essex Institute, Salem, Mass.; Timothy Walker, *Diaries, 1730–1782*, New Hampshire Historical Society *Collections*, 9, (1889); Joshua Hempstead, *Diary* (New London, Conn.: New London Historical Society, 1901), for dates noted.

3. Clarence W. Bowen, *Woodstock: An Historical Sketch* (New York, 1886), p. 60. Ellen M. Raynor and Emma L. Petitclerc, *History of the Town of Cheshire* (Holyoke, 1885), p. 61.

4. Ebenezer Parkman, *Diary*, ed Harriette E. Forbes (Westborough, Mass.: Historical Society, 1899), p. 172.

5. Joseph Green, *Diary, Historical Collections*, 2nd ser., 10 (Salem: Essex Institute, 1869), and Walker, *Diary*, for dates mentioned. William D. Miller, *The Narragansett Planters* (Worcester: American Antiquarian Society, 1934), p. 22. Edgar M. Bacon, *Narragansett Bay: Its Historic and Romantic Associations* (New York: Putnam, 1904), p. 242. Samuel E. Morison, *The Oxford History of the American People* (New York: Oxford University Press, 1965), p. 149. Charles H. S. Davis, *History of Wallingford, Connecticut* (Meriden, Conn., 1870), p. 339.

6. Data for the following paragraphs on health come from diverse sources. Among the more informative, in addition to town and regional histories, are John B. Blake, *Public Health in the Town of Boston, 1630–1822* (Cambridge: Harvard University Press, 1959); Zabdiel Boylston, *An Historical Account of the Small Pox Inoculation in New England*, 2nd ed. (London, 1784); John Demos, *A Little Commonwealth: Family Life in Plymouth Colony* (New York: Oxford University Press, 1970); Philip J. Greven, Jr., *Four Generations . . . in Colonial Andover* (Ithaca, N.Y.: Cornell University Press, 1970), Gerald Johnson, *Our English Heritage* (Philadelphia: Lippincott, 1949), pp. 30ff.; and Nathaniel S. Shaler, "Physiography of North America," in Justin Winsor, ed., *Narrative and Critical History of America*, 8 vols. (Cambridge, Mass., 1884–89), 4 : x–xxi. The quotation is from Ralph D. Smith, ed., *History of Guilford, Connecticut* (Albany, 1877).

7. Josiah Paine, *History of Harwich, 1600–1800* (Rutland, Vt.: Tuttle, 1937), p. 118.

8. Benjamin Chase, *History of Old Chester, New Hampshire* (Auburn, N.H.,

1869), p. 425. Samuel Orcutt, *History of the Towns of New Milford and Bridge-water, Connecticut 1703–1882* (Hartford, 1882), p. 106.

9. Matthew Patten, *Diary 1754–1788* (Concord: Rumford Press, 1903), dates 1772ff. Ezekiel Read, of Seekonk, Mass., "Book of Accounts, 1712–33" in posses-sion of Harold F. Tompson family, Seekonk, Mass. William R. Bliss, *Colonial Times on Buzzards Bay* (Boston, 1888), p. 30.

10. Robert E. Brown, *Middle-Class Democracy and the Revolution in Massa-chusetts, 1691–1780* (Ithaca, N.Y.: Cornell University Press, 1955), pp. 14, 16, 18.

11. Edmund B. Barton, *Brief History of . . . Braintree, 1640–1940* (Braintree, 1940), p. 28.

12. Jackson T. Main, *The Social Structure of Revolutionary America* (Prince-ton, N.J.: Princeton University Press, 1965), p. 254.

13. Charles S. Thompson, *Evolution of the American Public Library, 1653–1876* (Washington D.C.: Scarecrow Press, 1952), p. 42. Louis B. Wright, *The Cul-tural Life of the American Colonies* (New York: Harper, 1957), p. 148.

14. George L. Kittredge, *The Old Farmer and His Almanack* (Boston: Ware and Co., 1904), pp. 59, 60. Joseph T. Buckingham, *Personal Memoirs* (Boston, 1852), 1:12.

15. Jared Eliot, *Essays upon Field Husbandry in New England* (Boston, 1760). Jared Eliot, *Essays upon Field Husbandry and Other Papers,* ed. Harry J. Carman, et al. (New York: A.M.S. Press, 1967).

16. Charles S. Grant, *Democracy in the Connecticut Frontier Town of Kent* (New York: Columbia University Press, 1961), pp. 135, 167.

17. Michael Zuckerman, *Peaceable Kingdoms: New England Frontier Towns in the Eighteenth Century* (New York: Knopf, 1970), pp. 200–17. Brown, *Middle-Class Democracy,* p. 93. David Hawke, *The Colonial Experience* (New York: Bobbs-Merrill, 1966), p. 474.

PART III. THE REVOLUTION AND ITS AFTERMATH, 1775–1825

16. Patriotic Fervor

1. It seems unnecessary to enter deeply into the political and constitutional as-pects of the crisis leading to the Revolution—already the subject of an immense body of historical investigation and description by distinguished scholars.

2. William Lincoln, *Journals of the Provincial Congress of Massachusetts in 1774 & 1775* (Boston, 1838), p. 317. Joseph Merrill, *History of Amesbury and Mer-rimac* (Haverhill, Mass, 1880), p. 254.

3. Benjamin L. Mirick, *History of Haverhill, Massachusetts* (Haverhill, 1832), p. 177.

4. Albert E. Van Duzen, *Connecticut* (New York: Random House, 1961), p. 158. Payne K. Kilbourne, *Sketches and Chronicles of the town of Litchfield, Connecti-cut* (Hartford, 1859), p. 120. I. W. Stuart, *Life of Jonathan Trumbull, Senior, Gover-nor of Connecticut,* 2nd ed. (Hartford, 1878), p. 468. Henry H. Vail, *Pomfret, Ver-mont,* ed. Emma C. White (Boston: Cockayne, 1930), p. 177.

5. Florence S. M. Crofut, *Guide to the History and Historic Sites of Connecti-cut* (New Haven: Yale University Press, 1937), 2:396. Henry R. Stiles, *History and Genealogies of Ancient Windsor, Connecticut* (Albany, 1833), p. 403.

6. Clarence A. Day, *A History of Maine Agriculture, 1604–1860,* University of Maine *Bulletin* 56 (1954), p. 62. Ralph V. Harlow, "Economic Conditions in Mas-sachusetts, 1775–1783," Colonial Society of Massachusetts *Transactions* 20

(1920), 179, 181. Oscar and Mary Handlin, *Commonwealth; A Study of the Role of Government in the American Economy: Massachusetts, 1774–1861* (New York: New York University Press, 1947), p. 11. J. E. A. Smith, *History of Pittsfield, Massachusetts, 1734–1800* (Boston, 1869), p. 471. David Willard, *History of Greenfield* (Greenfield, Mass., 1838), p. 63.

7. Samuel Lane, *A Journal for the Years 1739–1803*, ed. Charles L. Hanson (Concord, N.H.: Historical Society, 1937), p. 51. John W. Hanson, *History of the Town of Danvers to 1840* (Danvers, Mass., 1848), p. 97. Merrill Jensen, "The American Revolution and American Agriculture," *Agricultural History*, 43 (1969), 114–19.

8. Robert A. East, *Business Enterprise in the American Revolutionary Era* (New York: Columbia University Press, 1938), pp. 74–81. Van Duzen, *Connecticut*, p. 160. Harlow, "Economic Conditions," 182–84.

9. Samuel E. Morison, *Maritime History of Massachusetts* (Boston: Houghton Mifflin, 1921), p. 29. J. Franklin Jameson, *The American Revolution Considered as a Social Movement* (Boston: Beacon Press, reprinted 1963), pp. 61–64. Ebenezer Parkman, *Diary*, ed. Harriette E. Forbes (Westborough, Mass.: Historical Society, 1899), p. 79.

10. William R. Bliss, *Colonial Times on Buzzards Bay* (Cambridge, 1888), p. 140.

11. Merrill Jensen, *The New Nation: The United States during the Confederation* (New York: Knopf, 1950), pp. 238ff.

17. A New Century Approaches

1. Porter E. Sargent, *A Handbook of New England* (Boston, 1916), p. 62. Jedediah Morse, *The American Geography*, 2nd ed. (London, 1792), p. 145.

2. Assembled from Abbott L. Cummings, ed., *Rural Household Inventories 1675–1775* (Boston: Society for the Preservation of New England Antiquities, 1964).

3. James T. Adams, *Provincial Society 1690–1763* (New York: Macmillan, 1927), pp. 305ff.

4. George L. Kittredge, *The Old Farmer and His Almanack* (Boston: Ware and Co., 1904), p. 18.

5. Clarence A. Day, *A History of Maine Agriculture, 1604–1860*, University of Maine *Bulletin*, 56 (1954), p. 235.

6. Massachusetts Society for Promoting Agriculture, *Centennial Report* (1892), p. 7. William H. Child, *History of Cornish, New Hampshire* (Concord: Rumford Press, 1912), 1:214. Benjamin F. Mirick, *History of Haverhill, Massachusetts* (Haverhill, 1832), p. 184.

7. Frederick J. Wood, *Turnpikes of New England* (Boston: Marshall Jones, 1919), p. 35.

8. Noah Porter, Jr., *Historical Discourse in Commemoration of the Original Settlement of Farmington in 1640* (Hartford, 1841), p. 81. W. Winterbotham, *An Historical, Commercial, and Philosophical View of the United States of America* (New York, 1792), 2:163.

9. Quoted by Lyman Carrier, *The Beginnings of Agriculture in America* (New York: McGraw-Hill, 1923), p. 151.

10. Sarah L. Bailey, *Historical Sketches of Andover, Massachusetts* (Cambridge: Houghton Mifflin, 1880), p. 403.

11. Samuel Deane, *The New England Farmer or Georgical Dictionary*, 2nd ed. (Worcester, 1797), intro.

12. Day, *Maine Agriculture*, p. 83.

13. Jacques Pierre Brissot de Warville, *New Travels in the United States of America Performed in 1788*, 2nd ed. (London, 1794), p. 390.

14. Philip Padelford, ed., *Colonial Panorama 1775: Dr. Robert Honeyman's Journal for March and April* (San Marino, Calif.: Huntington Library, 1939), p. 49.

15. Peter Whitney, *History of the County of Worcester* (Worcester: Isaiah Thomas, 1793), p. 314.

16. See, for example, "The Account of the Emigration of Capt. William Allen from Martha's Vineyard to Maine," in William C. Hatch, *History of the Town of Industry, Maine* (Farmington, 1893), pp. 72–89.

18. Lines of Force

1. *Compendium, United States 10th Census*, June 1, 1880, revised ed. (Washington, 1885), pt. 1, pp. 4, 5.

2. Edward A. Kendall, *Travels through the Northern Parts of the United States in 1807–1808* (New York, 1809), 2:259, 3:28. John C. Pease and John M. Niles, *A Gazetteer of Connecticut and Rhode Island* (Hartford, 1819), pp. 13, 186, 196, 203, 246. Daniel W. Teller, *History of Ridgefield, Connecticut* (Danbury, 1878), p. 171.

3. George Howe, *Mount Hope: A New England Chronicle* (New York: Viking, 1959), p. 136.

4. Ralph Hall Brown, *Historical Geography of the United States* (New York: Harcourt, Brace, 1948), p. 156. James Stuart, *Three Years in North America* (Edinburgh, 1833), p. 310. Blanche E. Hazard, *Organization of the Boot and Shoe Industry in Massachusetts* (Cambridge: Harvard University Press, 1921), pp. 135, 138, 204–7. Rodolphus Dickinson, *A Geographical and Statistical Survey of Massachusetts* (Greenfield, 1813), pp. 68–75.

5. Richard J. Purcell, *Connecticut in Transition, 1775–1818*, new ed. (Middletown, Conn.: Wesleyan University Press, 1963), p. 83. Pease and Niles, *Gazetteer*, 13, 36, 183. Federal Writers Project, *Vermont* (Cambridge: Riverside Press, 1937), p. 30. Lewis D. Stilwell, "Migration from Vermont (1776–1860)," Vermont Historical Society *Proceedings*, 5 (1937), 109. Andrew N. Adams, *History of Fair Haven, Vermont* (Fair Haven, 1870), p. 183.

6. Pease and Niles, *Gazetteer*, p. 14. Dickinson, *Massachusetts*, p. 69.

19. Turnpikes, Canals, and Bridges

1. For specific information on the turnpike movement see Frederick J. Wood, *The Turnpikes of New England* (Boston: Marshall Jones, 1919). Dirk J. Struik, *Yankee Science in the Making* (Boston: Little, Brown, 1948), pp. 99–102.

2. Struik, *Yankee Science*, pp. 102–12, is excellent on bridge-building.

3. Leonard M. Ellis, *History of New Bedford and Its Vicinity, 1602–1872* (Syracuse, 1872), p. 170.

4. John Harriott, *Struggles through Life: Various Travels and Adventures in Europe, Asia, Africa, and America*, 3rd ed. (London, 1815), 2:171. Joseph T. Buckingham, *Personal Memoirs* (Boston, 1852), 1:12.

5. Henry S. Nourse, *History of the Town of Harvard* (Clinton, Mass., 1894), p. 40. John G. Holland, *History of Western Massachusetts* (Springfield, 1855), 1:480.

342 Notes for pages 143–152

6. Edward A. Kendall, *Travels Through the Northern Parts of the United States in 1807–1808* (New York, 1809), 1:136, 264, 266.

7. Quoted in Ulysses P. Hedrick, *History of Agriculture in the State of New York* (Albany: New York State Agricultural Society, 1933), p. 65.

8. John Drayton, *Letters Written during a Tour through the Northern and Eastern States of America* (Charleston, S.C., 1794), p. 64.

20. Combing the Back Country

1. Nathaniel and Thomas Allen, Pre-Revolutionary Account Books, American Antiquarian Society, Worcester, Massachusetts.

2. *Commerce of Rhode Island*, 2:111. J. E. A. Smith, *History of Pittsfield, Massachusetts, 1734–1800* (Boston, 1869), p. 47. Ellen D. Larned, *History of Windham County, Connecticut*, 2 vols. (Worcester, 1874), 2:47.

3. George W. Chase, *History of Haverhill* (Haverhill, 1861), pp. 451ff. George Sheldon, *History of Deerfield, Massachusetts* (Deerfield, 1895–96), pp. 919ff. Francis M. Thompson, *History of Greenfield, Massachusetts, 1682–1900* (Greenfield, 1904), 1:295. Martha M. Frizzell, *History of Walpole, New Hampshire* (Walpole, 1963), 1:24, 42.

4. Clarence W. Bowen, *Woodstock: An Historical Sketch* (New York, 1886), 1:213.

5. Augustine G. Hibbard, *History of the Town of Goshen, Connecticut* (Hartford, 1877), p. 365. Lewis M. Norton, *Goshen in 1812* (Hartford: Acorn Club of Connecticut, 1949). Jarvis M. Morse, *A Neglected Period of Connecticut History, 1818–1856* (New Haven: Yale University Press, 1933), p. 256.

6. John G. Holland, *History of Western Massachusetts*, 2 vols. (Springfield, 1855), 2:10. Jasper J. Stahl, *History of Old Broad Bay and Waldoboro*, 2 vols. (Portland, Me.: Bond Wheelwright, 1956), 2:10, 13. Federal Writers Project, *Massachusetts* (Cambridge: Riverside Press, 1937), p. 433.

7. Earle Newton, *The Vermont Story: A History of the People of the Green Mountain State, 1749–1949* (Montpelier: Vermont Historical Society, 1949), p. 120. Warren R. Cochrane and George K. Wood, *History of Francestown, New Hampshire, 1758–1891* (Nashua, 1895), p. 273.

8. Percy W. Bidwell, "The Agricultural Revolution in New England," *American Historical Review*, 26 (1921), 685.

9. Sidney Perley, *Historic Storms of New England* (Salem, 1891), pp. 187–213.

10. Lois K. Mathews, *The Expansion of New England, 1620–1865* (Boston, 1909), pp. 160, 183. Stuart H. Holbrook, *The Yankee Exodus: An Account of Migration from New England* (New York: Macmillan, 1950), p. 48.

21. Hay, Grain, and Livestock

1. Lord Gordon, quoted in Newton D. Mereness, ed., *Travels in the American Colonies* (New York: Macmillan, 1916), p. 413.

2. Edward Enfield, *Indian Corn: Its Value, Culture, and Uses* (New York, 1866), p. 60.

3. Arria S. Huntington, *Under a Colonial Roof-Tree . . . Diary of Elizabeth Porter Phelps of Hadley, Massachusetts, 1763–1812* (Boston, 1891), p. 41.

4. In discussing Justin Morgan, the trainer, and his horse "Figure," later known as "Justin Morgan," I have relied chiefly on Margaret Gardiner and Alexander Mackay–Smith, "The Great Justin Morgan Pedigree Controversy," *The Chronicle of the Horse*, 30 (1967), nos. 18:26–28; 19:20–22; 20:20–21; and 21:22. Among

other sources consulted are D. C. Linsley, *Morgan Horses: A Premium Essay on the Origin, History, and Characteristics of This Remarkable Breed of American Horses* (New York, 1857); Howard, Robert W., *The Horse in America* (New York: Fuller, 1965); review of Howard by Mackay–Smith, *Agricultural History*, 40 (1966), 312–13; Dorothy C. Fisher, *Vermont Tradition: The Biography of an Outlook on Life* (Boston: Little, Brown, 1953), pp. 211ff.; Samuel Swift, *Statistical and Historical Account of the County of Addison, Vermont* (Middlebury, 1859), pp. 103, 110; and Paul W. Gates, *Agriculture and the Civil War* (New York: Knopf, 1965), passim.

5. For more extended discussion I recommend Ellen M. Raynor and Emma L. Petitclerc, *History of the Town of Cheshire, Massachusetts* (Holyoke, 1885), pp. 86–88; and C. A. Browne, "Elder John Leland and the Mammoth Cheshire Cheese," *Agricultural History*, 19 (1944), 145–53.

6. Chester Dewey, *History of the County of Berkshire* (Pittsfield, Mass., 1829), pp. 90, 401.

7. Augustine G. Hibbard, *History of the Town of Goshen, Connecticut* (Hartford, 1877), pp. 365, 366. Federal Writers Project, *Connecticut* (Cambridge: Riverside Press, 1938), p. 470.

8. John B. Blake, *Public Health in the Town of Boston 1630–1822* (Cambridge: Harvard University Press, 1959), p. 208.

9. Grant Powers, *Sketches of . . . Coos County, 1754–1795* (Haverhill, N.H., 1847, reprint 1880), p. 225. John G. Curtis, *History of the Town of Brookline, Massachusetts* (Boston: Houghton Mifflin, 1933), p. 176. Rodolphus Dickinson, *A Geographical and Statistical View of Massachusetts Proper* (Greenfield, 1813), pp. 68, 73.

10. W. Winterbotham, *An Historical, Commercial, and Philosophical View of the United States of America* (New York, 1792), 2:87.

11. P. P. F. De Grand, *Boston Weekly Report of Public Sales and Arrivals*, for April 1, 1825. James Birket, *Some Cursory Remarks Made . . . in His Voyage to North America, 1750–51* (New Haven, 1896), p. 13. Benjamin F. Parker, *History of Wolfeborough* (Wolfeborough, N.H., 1901), p. 190.

12. Edward A. Kendall, *Travels through the Northern Parts of the United States in 1807–1808*, 3 vols. (New York, 1809), 1:88. Jane E. Johnson, ed., *Newtown's History and Historian* (Newtown, Conn., 1917), p. 181.

13. Thomas B. Hazard, *Nailer Tom's Diary of Kingstown, Rhode Island, 1778–1840* (Boston: Merrymount, 1930), p. 261.

14. Kendall, *Travels*, 1:309. Timothy Dwight, *Travels in New England and New York* (1796–1815), 4 vols. (New Haven, 1821–22), 3:134.

15. J. E. Wing, "Merino Sheep," in Liberty H. Bailey, *Cyclopedia of American Agriculture*, 5th ed., 4 vols. (New York: Macmillan, 1917), 3:619; also "Humphreys," *Dictionary of American Biography*. Albert E. Van Duzen, *Connecticut* (New York: Random House, 1961), p. 186.

16. Harold F. Wilson, "The Rise and Decline of the Sheep Industry in Northern New England," *Agricultural History*, 9 (1935), 25. Federal Writers Project, *Vermont* (Cambridge: Riverside Press, 1937), p. 166.

22. Growth of the Land: New Crops

1. Anonymous, Daily Journal, 1817–25 (Hampstead, N.H.), Old Sturbridge Village Library, Sturbridge, Mass. John Lincklaen, *Travels in the Years 1791 and 1792*

in Pennsylvania, New Jersey, and Vermont (New York, 1897), p. 93. Peter Whitney, *History of the County of Worcester* (Worcester: Isaiah Thomas, 1793), p. 155.

2. Fruit varieties and dates: I have distilled the facts from numerous sources, sometimes conflicting, including Ulysses P. Hedrick, *History of Horticulture in America to 1860* (New York: Oxford University Press, 1950); Worcester County Historical Society, *Fruit List of Old Varieties*, ed. S. Lothrop Davenport (Worcester, 1968); J. M. Stowe, *History of the Town of Hubbardston* (Hubbardston, Mass., 1881), p. 7; Robert Manning, *Book of Fruits* (Salem, 1838), p. 51; Edward H. Jenkins, *A History of Connecticut Agriculture* (New Haven, n.d.) p. 403; Marshall P. Wilder, *The Horticulture of Boston and Vicinity* (Boston, 1881), pp. 29, 31, 70; and *American Gardener's Magazine*, 1 (1835), 92.

3. Henry K. Rowe, *Tercentenary History of Newton* (Newton, Mass., 1930), p. 45. *Farmer's Monthly Visitor* (Concord, N.H., 1838), 1:170.

4. Hedrick, *Horticulture*, p. 310. Van Wyck Brooks, *The World of Washington Irving* (New York: Dutton, 1944), p. 93. MS letter in possession of John C. Willard, Wethersfield, Conn.

5. Stephen W. Fletcher, *The Strawberry in North America* (New York: Macmillan, 1917), pp. 12–20. John M. Weeks, *History of Salisbury, Vermont* (Middlebury, 1860), p. 84.

6. Charles F. Swift, *Cape Cod: The Right Arm of Massachusetts* (Yarmouth, 1897), p. 283. Albert E. Benson, *History of the Massachusetts Horticultural Society* (Boston, 1929), p. 469.

7. Jenkins, *Connecticut Agriculture*, p. 410. Malcolm Keir, "The March of Commerce," *Pageant of America Series* (New Haven: Yale University Press, 1925–29), 4:41. George L. Miner, "A Providence Packet Ship of 1812," Rhode Island Historical Society *Collections*, 26 (1933), 39.

8. Amos E. and Emily M. Jewett, *Rowley, Massachusetts: Mr. Ezechi Roger's Plantation, 1639–1850* (Rowley, 1946), pp. 285ff. Hempstead, *Journal*. P. P. F. De Grand, *Boston Weekly Report of Public Sales and Arrivals*, 1824–25.

9. Benjamin Goddard, "Daily Occurrences" (1812 diaries) at Brookline, Massachusetts Public Library. Timothy Dwight, *Travels in New England and New York (1796–1815)*, 4 vols. (New Haven, 1821–22), 1:21, 28. George L. Kittredge, *The Old Farmer and His Almanack* (Boston: Ware and Co., 1904), p. 84.

10. Hedrick, *Horticulture*, p. 204. John W. Barber, *Connecticut Historical Collections*, Improved Edition (New Haven, 1856), p. 85. Jenkins, *Connecticut Agriculture*, pp. 407, 408.

11. James L. Belden, *Seed List for 1821*, Wethersfield, Connecticut Historical Society. John C. Willard, of Wethersfield, MSS in the author's possession. William Downing, Hancock, Mass. *Seed List*, at Old Sturbridge Village Library, Sturbridge, Mass. Barber, *Connecticut*, p. 85. Massachusetts Horticultural Society, Boston, Collection of Seed Catalogues.

12. Dwight, *Travels*, 1:23. Bronson Alcott, *New Connecticut: An Autobiographical Poem* (Boston, 1881), p. 12n.

13. *Commerce of Rhode Island 1775–1800*, p. 269. Jenkins, *Connecticut Agriculture*, pp. 351, 417.

14. W. Winterbotham, *An Historical, Commercial, and Philosophical View of the United States of America* (New York, 1792), 2:85. Henry Wansey, *An Excursion to the United States of America in . . . 1794* (Salisbury, England, 1798), p. 48.

Victor S. Clark, *History of Manufactures in the United States, 1607–1860*, rev. ed. (Washington, 1870), 1:440. Edward Miller and Frederic P. Wells, *History of Ryegate, Vermont* (St. Johnsbury, 1913), p. 93.

15. Samuel Sewall, *History of Woburn* (Boston, 1868), p. 176. Dwight, *Travels*, 1:357. Percy W. Bidwell and John I. Falconer, *History of Agriculture in the Northern United States, 1620–1860* (New York: Peter Smith, 1941), p. 244.

16. Ethel S. Bolton, *Shirley Uplands and Intervales* (Boston, 1914), p. 29. *New England Farmer*, 8 (1856), 463. Federal Writers Project, *Massachusetts* (Cambridge: Riverside Press, 1937), p. 433.

17. Sylvester Judd, *History of Hadley, Massachusetts*, new ed. (Springfield, 1905), pp. 360, 361. John H. Martin, "Broom Corn, the Frontiersman's Cash Crop," *Economic Botany*, 7 (1953), 166.

18. Colman, *Fourth Report*, p. 30. Sherman A. Adams, revised by H. R. Stiles, *History of Ancient Weathersfield* (New York, 1904), p. 615. Herbert C. Parsons, *A Puritan Outpost: A History . . . of Northfield, Massachusetts* (New York: Macmillan, 1937), p. 260. Daniel W. Wells and Reuben Field, *History of Hatfield* (Springfield, Mass., 1910), p. 219. Massachusetts Board of Agriculture, *1882 Report*, p. 155.

19. John Harriott, *Struggles through Life: Various Travels and Adventures in Europe, Asia, Africa, and America*, 3rd ed. (London, 1815), 2:125.

20. *Commerce of Rhode Island*, 2:167. Miranda, *Travels*, p. 147. Alexander Harvey, "Journal," Vermont Historical Society *Proceedings* (1921).

21. This discussion is based largely on the following, plus pertinent local histories: George K. Holmes, "Some Features of Tobacco History," American Historical Society *Annual Report* (1919), 1:385–407; "Three Centuries of Tobacco," United States Department of Agriculture, *1919 Yearbook*, pp. 151–75; Jenkins, *Connecticut Agriculture*, p. 412; Elizabeth Ramsey, *The History of Tobacco Culture in the Connecticut Valley* (Northampton, 1930), pp. 119–28; Joseph C. Robert, *The Story of Tobacco in America* (New York: Knopf, 1952), pp. 57, 95, 102. W. W. Garner and E. G. Moss, "History and Status of Tobacco Culture, United States Department of Agriculture *1922 Yearbook*; Adrian F. McDonald, *History of Tobacco Production in Connecticut, 1742–1910* (New Haven: Yale University Press, 1936); and Edward A. Kendall, *Travels through the Northern Parts of the United States in 1807–1808*, 3 vols. (New York, 1809), 1:317.

22. Frederic G. Howes, *History of the Town of Ashfield, Massachusetts, 1742–1910* (Ashfield, 1910), p. 104. Chester Dewey, *History of the County of Berkshire* (Pittsfield, 1829), p. 86. N. K. Ellis, "Peppermint and Spearmint Production," *Economic Botany*, 14 (1960), 280–85.

23. "History of Silk in the United States," *Massachusetts Agricultural Repository and Journal*, 9 (1826), 128–30; 10 (1827), 145–54.

24. Wansey, *Excursion*, p. 48. Nelson Klose, "Sericulture in the United States," *Agricultural History*, 37 (1963), 226.

25. Lura W. Watkins, "When They Burned Peat in Middleton," *Old Time New England*, 52:75–80. John C. Pease and John M. Niles, *A Gazetteer of the States of Connecticut and Rhode Island* (Hartford, 1819), pp. 116, 198. Louise K. Brown, *Wilderness Town: The Story of Bedford, Massachusetts* (privately printed, 1968), p. 167.

26. *New Hampshire Agricultural Repository* (Concord, 1822), pp. 45, 50.

W. Storrs Lee, *The Yankees of Connecticut* (New York: Holt, Rinehart, 1957), p. 129. Amelia F. Emerson, *Early History of Naushon Island* (privately printed, 1939), p. 390.
27. Judd, *Hadley*, p. 378. Samuel Hopkins, *Historical Memoirs Relating to the Housatonnuck Indians* (Boston, 1753), pp. 25–27.
28. Chard P. Smith, *Housatonic, Puritan River* (New York: Holt, Rinehart, 1946), p. 236. Wansey, *Excursion*, p. 74.
29. Matthew Patten, *Diary 1754–1788* (Concord, N.H.: Rumford Press, 1903), p. 380. Lincklaen, *Travels*, p. 88. Samuel Williams, *The Natural and Civil History of Vermont* (Walpole, N.H., 1794), p. 314.
30. Leo Rogin, *The Introduction of Farm Machinery in Its Relation to the Productivity of Labor in the Agriculture of the United States* . . . (Berkeley: University of California Press, 1931), pp. 22–27. Bidwell and Falconer, *Northern Agriculture*, p. 208. Frank Gilbert, *Jethro Wood, Inventor of the Modern Plow* (Chicago, 1882). John G. Holland, *History of Western Massachusetts*, 2 vols. (Springfield, 1885), p. 397.
31. Dirk J. Struik, *Yankee Science in the Making* (Boston: Little, Brown, 1948), p. 101. Joseph C. G. Kennedy, *Agriculture of the United States in 1860* (Government Printing Office, 1864), pp. xxiii, xxv.
32. *Vermont History*, 23 (1955), p. 314. Lewis M. Norton, *Goshen in 1812* (Hartford: Acorn Club of Connecticut, 1949). Arthur W. Peach, ed., "As The Years Pass: The Diaries of Seth Shaler Arnold (1748–1871), Vermonter," Vermont Historical Society *Proceedings*, n.s. 7, no. 2 (1940), entries for 1835. Robert Frost, *Complete Poems* (New York, 1949), p. 47.
33. Harriott, *Struggles*, 2:386. John W. Hanson, *History of the Town of Danvers to 1840* (Danvers, Mass., 1848), p. 113. Pease and Niles, *Gazetteer*, pp. 172, 365.
34. Pease and Niles, *Gazetteer*, p. 98. Barber, *Connecticut*, p. 533. Kendall, *Travels*, 2:39, 148.
35. Massachusetts Historical Society *Collections*, 8 (1802), 156, 189. Daniel Ricketson, *History of New Bedford, Massachusetts, Including Westport, Dartmouth, and Fairhaven* (New Bedford, 1848), p. 269.
36. John B. Blake, *Public Health in the Town of Boston, 1630–1822* (Cambridge: Harvard University Press, 1959), pp. 156, 163. Colman, *Fourth Report*, p. 329.
37. Rodolphus Dickinson, *A Geographical and Statistical View of Massachusetts Proper* (Greenfield, 1813), p. 8. George Sheldon, *History of Deerfield, Massachusetts* (Deerfield, 1895–96), 2:919. Dwight, *Travels*, 1:315.

23. Comfort and Struggle

1. Benjamin Silliman, *Remarks Made on a Short Tour between Hartford and Quebec . . . 1819*, 2nd ed. (New Haven, 1824), p. 412. Edward Miller and Frederic P. Wells, *History of Ryegate, Vermont* (St. Johnsbury, 1913), p. 94.
2. A. N. Somers, *History of Lancaster* (Concord, N.H., 1899), p. 127. Edward A. Kendall, *Travels Through the Northern Parts of the United States in 1807–1808*, 3 vols. (New York, 1809), 2:35. John Lambert, *Travels through Canada and the United States . . . in the Years 1806, 1807, and 1808*, 3rd ed. (London, 1816), 2:307.
3. Frederick G. Howes, *History of the Town of Ashfield, Massachusetts, 1742–*

1910 (Ashfield, 1910), p. 147. Ellen M. Raynor and Emma L. Petitclerc, *History of the Town of Cheshire, Massachusetts* (Holyoke, 1885), p. 88. Simon G. Griffin, *History of the Town of Keene, 1742–1874* (Keene, N.H., 1904), p. 302. Dorothy C. Fisher, *Vermont Tradition: The Biography of an Outlook on Life* (Boston: Little, Brown, 1953), p. 60. Ellen D. Larned, *History of Windham County, Connecticut,* 2 vols. (Worcester, 1874), 2:413. Rodolphus Dickinson, *A Geographical and Statistical View of Massachusetts Proper* (Greenfield, 1813), p. 7.

4. Horace Greeley, *Recollections of a Busy Life* (New York, 1868), p. 50. Warren R. Cochrane and George K. Wood, *History of Francestown, New Hampshire, 1758–1871* (Nashua, 1895), p. 371.

5. Massachusetts Historical Society *Collections*, 8 (1802), 121, 151; 8 (1803), 121.

6. Lambert, *Travels,* 2:14.

7. Ernest L. Bogart, *Peacham: The Story of a Vermont Town* (Montpelier: Vermont Historical Society, 1948), p. 74n. Cochrane, *Francestown,* p. 37. Frances E. Blake, *History of the Town of Princeton* (Princeton, Mass., 1915), 1:303.

8. Massachusetts Historical Society *Collections,* 7:151. Vermont Historical Society *Proceedings,* 7:140.

9. Alice S. Blackwell, *Lucy Stone, Pioneer of Women's Rights* (Boston: Little, Brown, 1930), p. 12.

10. J. Farmer and J. B. Moore, eds., *Collections . . . Relating Principally to New Hampshire* (Concord, 1882), 1:14. Cobbett, quoted by Van Wyck Brooks, *The World of Washington Irving* (New York: Dutton, 1944), p. 22.

11. Timothy Dwight, *Travels in New England and New York (1796–1815),* 4 vols. (New Haven, 1821–22), 2:254. Samuel Orcutt, *History of the Towns of New Milford and Bridgewater, Connecticut* (Hartford, 1882), p. 448.

12. Levi H. Clarke, "Haddam in 1808," *Connecticut Towns* (Hartford: Acorn Club of Connecticut, 1949), p. 10.

PART IV. GOOD GROWING WEATHER, 1825–1860

24. Things to Come

1. Edward C. Kirkland, *Men, Cities, and Transportation: A Study in New England History 1820–1900,* 2 vols. (Cambridge: Harvard University Press, 1948), 1:89, 90. Lewis D. Stilwell, "Migration from Vermont," Vermont Historical Society *Proceedings,* 5 (1937), 134.

2. Percy W. Bidwell, "Rural Economy in New England at the Beginning of the Nineteenth Century," Connecticut Academy of Arts and Sciences *Transactions,* 20 (1916), 307ff. Ralph Hall Brown, *Historical Geography of the United States* (New York: Harcourt, Brace, 1948), p. 105. Stilwell, *Migration,* p. 105. Simon G. Griffin, *History of the Town of Keene, 1732–1874* (Keene, N.H., 1904), p. 382.

3. John Lambert, *Travels through Canada and the United States . . . in the Years 1806, 1807, and 1808,* 3rd ed. (London, 1816), 2:306. Augusta H. Worthen, *History of Sutton, New Hampshire* (Concord, 1830), p. 568.

4. P. P. F. De Grand, *Boston Weekly Report of Public Sales and Arrivals,* 1825. Kirkland, *Men, Cities,* 1:7.

5. John C. Pease and John M. Niles, *A Gazetteer of the States of Connecticut and Rhode Island* (Hartford, 1819), p. 324.

6. Richard B. Morris, *Encyclopedia of American History* (New York: Harper,

1953), p. 426. Sidney Withington, *The First Twenty Years of Railroading in Connecticut* (New Haven: Yale University Press, 1935), p. 29.

7. *Boston Cultivator*, Nov. 25, 1848. Henry D. Thoreau, *Writings*, ed. Bradford Torrey (Boston, 1906), 3:114.

8. Charles Russell, *Address Before the Hampden County Horticultural Society*, October 3, 1850, p. 19. Samuel Swift, *History of the Town of Middlebury, Vermont* (Middlebury, 1859), p. 111. T. N. Adams, *Prices Paid by Vermont Farmers, 1790–1940* (Burlington, Vt., 1944), p. 46.

9. Clarence A. Day, *A History of Maine Agriculture, 1604–1860*, University of Maine *Bulletin* 56 (1954), p. 156. Benjamin G. Willey, *History of the White Mountains*, new ed. (Cambridge, 1870), p. 58.

10. Charles W. Eldridge, "Journal of a Tour . . . in 1833," Vermont Historical Society *Proceedings*, 2 (1931), 54. John W. Barber, *Connecticut Historical Collections* (New Haven, 1836, 1856), p. 76.

11. Percy W. Bidwell and John I. Falconer, *History of Agriculture in the Northern United States, 1620–1860* (New York: Peter Smith, 1941), pp. 226, 340. E. Hasket Derby, *Boston: A Commercial Metropolis* (Boston, 1850). Carl N. Degler, *Out of Our Past: The Forces That Shaped Modern America* (New York: Harper and Row, 1959), p. 120.

12. John Hayward, *Gazetteer of Massachusetts* (Boston, 1846), p. 229.

13. Ellen D. Larned, *History of Windham County, Connecticut*, 2 vols. (Worcester, 1874), 2:400. Percy W. Bidwell, "The Agricultural Revolution in New England," *American Historical Review*, 26 (1921), 696. James F. W. Johnston, *Notes on North America, Agricultural, Economical, and Social*, 2 vols. (Boston, 1851), 2:422.

25. The Eager Young

1. Nathaniel Hawthorne, *Passages from the American Note-Books* (Boston, 1884), 1:162, 164. Frederick Marryat, *A Diary in America*, 3 vols. (Indiana University Press, 1960), p. 77. Ralph Waldo Emerson, *Essays*, revised ed., 2 vols. (Boston, 1888), 2:75. Henry Ward Beecher, *Pleasant Talks about Fruits, Flowers, and Farming* (New York, 1874), p. 99.

2. Ray Bearse, *Vermont Guide* (Boston: Houghton Mifflin, 1966), p. 281. John G. Holland, *History of Western Massachusetts*, 2 vols. (Springfield, 1855), 2:384. Clara Barton, *The Story of My Childhood* (New York, 1907). Alice S. Blackwell, *Lucy Stone, Pioneer of Women's Rights* (Boston: Little, Brown, 1930), p. 233. Daniel W. Wells and Reuben Field, *History of Hatfield* (Springfield, Mass., 1910), pp. 271, 352, 354.

3. Ethel S. Bolton, *Farm Life a Century Ago* (privately printed, 1909), p. 22. J. M. Stowe, *History of the Town of Hubbardston* (Hubbardston, Mass., 1881), p. 83.

4. Liberty H. Bailey, *Cyclopedia of American Agriculture*, 5th ed., 4 vols. (New York: Macmillan, 1917), 4:78. Clarence A. Day, *Farming in Maine 1860–1940* (Orono: University of Maine, 1963), pp. 12–16, 240. Oliver Bacon, *History of Natick, Massachusetts*, ed. James Savage (Boston, 1856), p. 105. Clarence H. Danhof, *Change in Agriculture in the Northern United States 1820–1870* (Cambridge: Harvard University Press, 1969), p. 57.

5. *New England Farmer*, 9:405. Horace Greeley, *Recollections of a Busy Life* (New York, 1868), pp. 56, 59. Cyrus Hamlin, *My Life and Times* (Boston, 1893), pp. 12, 41.

6. Bailey, *Cyclopedia*, 4:367–70. Dirk J. Struik, *Yankee Science in the Making* (Boston: Little, Brown, 1948), p. 357.

7. Bailey, *Cyclopedia*, 4:369, 404.

8. Elkanah Watson, *History of the Rise, Progress, and Existing State of the Berkshire County Agricultural Society* (Albany, 1819), p. 73. Bailey, *Cyclopedia*, 4:292.

9. Struik, *Yankee Science*, p. 188.

26. Sheep and Other Livestock

1. Joseph Joslin, *History of the Town of Poultney, Vermont* (Poultney, 1875), p. 81.

2. Harold F. Wilson, "The Rise and Decline of the Sheep Industry in Northern New England," *Agricultural History*, 9 (1935), 27. Kennedy, *Agriculture in the United States in 1860*, intro. Samuel Swift, *History of the Town of Middlebury, Vermont* (Middlebury, 1859), p. 104. Dorothy C. Fisher, *Vermont Tradition: The Biography of an Outlook on Life* (Boston: Little, Brown, 1953), p. 192.

3. Lewis D. Stilwell, "Migration from Vermont," *Vermont Historical Society Proceedings*, 5 (1937), 172, 173. C. Benton and S. F. Barry, *Statistical View of the Number of Sheep in . . . Maine, New Hampshire, Vermont, Massachusetts, Connecticut* (Cambridge, 1837), p. 33. John W. Weeks, *History of Salisbury, Vermont* (Middlebury, 1868), p. 81. John Hayward, *Gazetteer of New England*, 4th ed. (Boston, 1839).

4. Paul W. Gates, *The Farmer's Age: Agriculture 1815–1860* (New York: Holt, Rinehart, and Winston, 1960), p. 225.

5. Martha M. Frizzell, *A History of Walpole, New Hampshire* (Walpole, 1963), p. 549.

6. Edward H. Jenkins, *A History of Connecticut Agriculture* (New Haven, n.d.), p. 395. Chester Dewey, *History of the County of Berkshire* (Pittsfield, 1829), p. 401.

7. John G. Holland, *History of Western Massachusetts*, 2 vols. (Springfield, 1855), pp. 527, 575. A. N. Somers, *History of Lancaster, New Hampshire* (Concord, 1899), p. 228. Massachusetts Board of Agriculture, *1886 Report*, p. 34.

8. *Compendium, United States 10th Census*, revised edition, pt. 1, p. xxxiii.

9. Edward Wiest, *The Butter Industry in the United States* (New York: Columbia University Studies, 1916), p. 140.

10. Nathaniel C. Bradstreet, "Recollections of Bradstreet Hill," *Massachusetts Audubon Society Bulletin*, 35, no. 7 (October, 1951), 29.

11. Colman, *First Report*, p. 255.

12. Gates, *Farmer's Age*, p. 239.

13. Colman, *Fourth Report*, p. 252.

14. United States Department of Agriculture, Commissioner's *1870 Report*, p. 316.

15. Patrick Shirreff, *A Tour through North America . . .* (Edinburgh, 1835), p. 37.

16. *Boston Cultivator*, Sept. 23, 1848. Jenkins, *Connecticut Agriculture*, p. 392.

17. Colman, *Fourth Report*, p. 315.

18. *Agricultural Repository* 9:19, 10:211. James S. Grinnell, "Agriculture of Massachusetts," *Massachusetts Board of Agriculture 1881 Report*, p. 371. Albert S. Bolles, *Industrial History of the United States* (Norwich, Conn., 1879), p. 258.

19. Nathaniel Hawthorne, *Passages from the American Notebooks* (Boston,

1884), 1:200, 251. Eugene Graves, "A History of Maine's Nineteenth Century Beef Industry," M.A. thesis, University of Maine, Orono, 1967.

20. Percy W. Bidwell and John I. Falconer, *History of Agriculture in the Northern United States, 1620–1860* (New York: Peter Smith, 1941), p. 231.

21. Allen W. Thompson, *The Horses of Woodstock* (Cambridge: Riverside Press, 1881), p. 3.

22. Massachusetts Board of Agriculture *1882 Report*, p. 296.

23. Frizzell, *Walpole*, p. 552. *New England Farmer*, 9:73. Gates, *Farmer's Age*, p. 229. *Vermont History*, 23 (1955), 231.

24. Liberty H. Bailey, *Cyclopedia of American Agriculture*, 5th ed., 4 vols. (New York: Macmillan, 1917), 4:100. Clarence A. Day, *A History of Maine Agriculture, 1604–1860*, University of Maine Bulletin 56 (1954), pp. 195–200.

25. Thomas B. Hazard, *Nailer Tom's Diary, of Kingstown, Rhode Island, 1778–1840* (Boston: Merrymount, 1930), pp. 716ff.

26. *Boston Cultivator*, Nov. 10, 1849. John C. Bennett, *The Poultry Book: A Treatise on Breeding and General Management of Domestic Fowls* . . . (Boston, 1850), p. 286.

27. Henry D. Thoreau, *Writings*, ed. Bradford Torrey (Boston, 1906), 2:325.

28. Amos E. and Emily M. Jewett, *Rowley, Massachusetts: Mr. Ezechi Roger's Plantation, 1639–1850* (Rowley, 1946), p. 293. Graves, *Beef*, p. 79.

29. Arthur A. Brigham, "Notes on Rhode Island Reds," Rhode Island Agricultural Experiment Station, *Fourteenth Report*, part 2 (1901), pp. 324–28. "The Rhode Island Red," *New England Farm Finance News*, 9 (1954), 8.

27. Backbone Crops and New Departures

1. Massachusetts Board of Agriculture, *1855 Report*, p. 109.

2. *New England Farmer*, 9:395.

3. Frederick Freeman, *History of Cape Cod*, 2 vols. (Boston, 1860–62), 2:354.

4. Benjamin G. Willey, *History of the White Mountains*, new ed. (Cambridge, 1870), p. 58.

5. Vermont Historical Society *Proceedings*, n.s., 2 (1931), 115, January 18 entry.

6. Franklin McDuffie, *History of Rochester, New Hampshire* (Manchester, 1892), p. 328. Martha M. Frizzell, *A History of Walpole, New Hampshire* (Walpole, 1963). M. E. Goddard and Henry V. Partridge, *History of Norwich, Vermont* (Hanover, N.H.: Dartmouth Press, 1905), p. 183.

7. James C. Bonner, "Advancing Trends in Southern Agriculture," *Agricultural History*, 22 (1948) 255. Edward H. Jenkins, *A History of Connecticut Agriculture* (New Haven, Conn., n.d.), p. 410. John C. Pease and John M. Niles, *A Gazetteer of the States of Connecticut and Rhode Island* (Hartford, 1819), p. 342.

8. Clarence A. Day, *A History of Maine Agriculture, 1604–1860*, University of Maine *Bulletin* 56 (1954), pp. 163–65.

9. H. Blake, "Fifty Years of Farm Life in Northern Vermont," Vermont State Board of Agriculture *Fourth Report* (Montpelier, 1877), p. 93.

10. Edward W. Carpenter and Charles F. Morehouse, *History of the Town of Amherst, Massachusetts, 1731–1896* (Amherst, 1896), p. 285. Goddard and Partridge, *Norwich*, p. 133.

11. Alonzo and James R. Newhall, *History of Lynn* (Boston, 1865), pp. 416, 426, 432. Percy W. Bidwell, "The Agricultural Revolution in New England," *American*

Historical Review, 26 (1921), 693. Paul W. Gates, *The Farmer's Age: Agriculture 1815–1860* (New York: Holt, Rinehart, and Winston, 1960), pp. 264, 266.

12. Gates, *Farmer's Age*, p. 318.

13. Colman, *First Report*, p. 33. Day, *Maine Agriculture*, pp. 132, 167.

14. Harold M. Bailey, "Vermont in the Potato Lineage Book," *Vermont History*, 23 (1955), 120. Michel Oren and Janet Greene, "The Only Potato Fit to Eat," *Vermont Life*, 15 (1960), 54.

15. Day, *Maine Agriculture*, p. 208.

16. Gates, *Farmer's Age*, p. 261. Charles F. Adams, Jr., *The Town of Lincoln, 1754–1904* (Lincoln, Mass., 1905), p. 204.

17. Ulysses P. Hedrick, *History of Horticulture in America to 1860* (New York: Oxford University Press, 1950), pp. 437, 444.

18. Hedrick, *Horticulture*, p. 440. MSS Records (Belmont, Massachusetts Historical Society). Albert E. Benson, *History of the Massachusetts Horticultural Society* (Boston, 1929), p. 107.

19. "Cranberry Lore," *Food Marketing in New England* (November, 1954), p. 7.

20. Massachusetts Board of Agriculture *1863 Report*, pp. 103, 108. William B. Jordan, Jr., *A History of Cape Elizabeth, Maine* (Portland: House of Falmouth, 1965), p. 71.

21. Letter dated 11/27/1837 at Wethersfield, Conn., Historical Society. *New England Farmer*, 23 (1845), 381. *New England Farmer*, 2nd ser., 9 (1857), 326, 381, 474. George P. Jennings, *Green Farms, Connecticut: The Old West Parish of Fairfield* (Greens Farms: Modern Books, 1933), pp. 18, 131.

22. *Massachusetts Repository*, 7 : 41. Colman, *Fourth Report*, p. 219. Charles T. Jackson, *Report on the Geological and Agricultural Survey of the State of Rhode Island* (Providence, 1840), pp. 153–56.

23. "A Morning in a Market Garden," *New England Farmer*, 2nd ser., 7 (1855), 444. Colman, *Fourth Report*, p. 353. Isaac Hill, "Two Days in West Cambridge, Massachusetts," *Farmer's Monthly Visitor*, 1 (1839), 169–71.

24. Amos E. Brown, *Faneuil Hall and Faneuil Hall Market* (Boston, 1900), pp. 173–84. Henry Tudor, *Narrative of a Tour in North America* (London, 1834), 1 : 358.

25. *Boston Cultivator*, February 28, 1852.

26. Fearing Burr, *Field and Garden Vegetables of North America* (Boston, 1865), p. 203. James J. H. Gregory, *Squashes: How to Grow Them* (New York: Judd, 1867), p. 45. Benjamin Goddard, "Daily Occurrences," Diary, 1812, Brookline, Mass., Public Library. Walton C. Galinat, *The Evolution of Sweet Corn*, University of Masachusetts Agricultural Experiment Station *Bulletin* 591 (Amherst, 1971), p. 10.

27. Austin J. Coolidge and J. B. Mansfield, *A History and Description of New England, General and Local*, vol. 1, *Maine, New Hampshire, and Vermont* (Boston, 1859), p. 435. Hedrick, *Horticulture*, p. 285.

28. Hedrick, *Horticulture*, p. 251. Milford W. Atwood, "The Seed Catalogue," *New England Homestead* (January 10, 1959), 10. Communications from John C. Willard, Wethersfield, Connecticut (formerly of Comstock, Ferre & Co.): "Indian Corn," "Hybrid Corn," and "Seed Trade."

29. U.S. Census, *1890 Report of the Statistics of Agriculture of the United States at the Eleventh Census*, p. 575.

30. "Tobacco Culture," United States Department of Agriculture *1922 Year-book*, p. 408. Adrian F. McDonald, *History of Tobacco Production in Connecticut* (New Haven: Yale University Press, 1936), pp. 6–8. Jenkins, *Connecticut Agriculture*, p. 413. Massachusetts Board of Agriculture, *1892 Report*, pp. 140–58; *1893 Report*, p. 355.

31. T. M. Woodford, *Smith's 1855 Map of Hartford County, Connecticut* (Hartford, 1855).

32. Percy W. Bidwell and John I. Falconer, *History of Agriculture in the Northern United States, 1620–1860* (New York: Peter Smith, 1941), p. 246. United States Census, *1880 Report*, 3:244.

33. John H. Martin, "Broomcorn: The Frontiersman's Cash Crop," *Economic Botany*, 7 (1953), 166. Massachusetts Board of Agriculture, *1882 Report*, p. 155. Bidwell and Falconer, *Northern Agriculture*, p. 245.

34. Coolidge and Mansfield, *New England*, p. 420. *Food Marketing in New England*, 27 (1967), 31.

35. Sherman A. Adams, revised by H. R. Stiles, *History of Ancient Weathersfield* (New York, 1904), p. 617. Albert S. Bolles, *Industrial History of the United States* (Norwich, Conn., 1879), p. 438. John G. Holland, *History of Western Massachusetts*, 2 vols. (Springfield, 1855), 2:256. Nelson Klose, "Sericulture in the United States," *Agricultural History*, 37 (1963), 226.

36. Arthur W. Peach, ed., "As the Years Pass: The Diaries of Seth Shaler Arnold, Vermonter," Vermont Historical Society *Proceedings*, n.s., 8 (1940), 140.

37. Alpheus S. Packard, Jr., *Our Common Insects* (Boston, 1873), pp. 60, 61.

28. Marketing the Woods

1. *Boston Cultivator*, December 9, 1848. Edward C. Kirkland, *Men, Cities, and Transportation: A Study in New England History*, 2 vols. (Cambridge: Harvard University Press, 1948), p. 26. Colman, *First Report*, p. 13. Charles T. Jackson, *Report on the Geological and Agricultural Survey of the State of Rhode Island* (Providence, 1840), pp. 67, 144. Joseph B. Felt, *Annals of Salem*, 2 vols. (Salem, 1845), 1:257.

2. Francis DeWitt, ed., *Statistical Information Relating to Certain Branches of Industry in Massachusetts for Year Ending June 1, 1855* (Boston, 1856).

3. A. N. Somers, *History of Lancaster, New Hampshire* (Concord, 1899), p. 142. William H. Rowe, *The Maritime History of Maine* (New York: Norton, 1948), p. 120. Nathaniel C. Bradstreet, "Recollections of Bradstreet Hill," Massachusetts Audubon Society *Bulletin*, 35, no. 7 (1951), 292. Henry D. Thoreau, *Writings*, ed. Bradford Torrey (Boston, 1906), 4:431, 465.

4. Hugh M. Raup and Reynold E. Carlson, *The History of Land Use in the Harvard Forest* (Petersham, Mass., 1941), p. 25. John W. Barber, *Connecticut Historical Collections* (New Haven, 1836, 1856), p. 502. Bronson Alcott, *New Connecticut: An Autobiographical Poem* (Boston, 1881), p. 89.

5. Charles J. Latrobe, *The Rambler in North America* (London, 1835), 1:44.

6. Colman, *Second Report*, p. 80.

7. Colman, *First Report*, p. 327. *New England Farmer*, December 6, 1844.

8. *New England Farmer*, 24:197, 9:341. *Massachusetts Agricultural Journal*, 10 (1831), 276.

9. John C. Pease and John M. Niles, *A Gazetteer of the States of Connecticut*

and *Rhode Island* (Hartford, 1819), pp. 98, 172. Clarence H. Danhof, *Change in Agriculture in the Northern United States, 1620–1870* (Cambridge: Harvard University Press, 1969), p. 266. Charles Hudson, *History of Lexington, Massachusetts* (Boston, 1868), p. 414.

10. Edward S. Abdy, *Journal of a Residence and Tour of the United States 1833–34*, 3 vols. (London, 1835), 1:89. Henry Tudor, *Narrative of a Tour in North America* (London, 1834), 1:355, 376

11. Illuminating views on aspects of emigration are found not solely in Frederic Jackson Turner's well-known essay "The Frontier in American History," American Historical Association *Annual Report* (1893), 119–227, but also in Stuart H. Holbrook, *The Yankee Exodus: An Account of Migration from New England* (New York: Macmillan, 1950), especially pp. 73 and 108; Van Wyck Brooks, *Sketches in Criticism* (New York: Dutton, 1932): "The Tradition of Rootlessness" and especially "Thoughts on History"; Fulmer Mood, "A British Statistician of 1854 Analyzes the Westward Movement in the United States," *Agricultural History*, 19 (1945), 142–51. Lois K. Mathews, *Expansion of New England 1620–1865* (Boston, 1909); Lewis D. Stilwell, "Migration from Vermont," Vermont Historical Society *Proceedings*, 5 (1937), 63–245; and numerous other studies. The matter will receive further attention in a later chapter.

29. Yankee Inventors

1. Liberty H. Bailey, *Cyclopedia of American Agriculture*, 5th ed., 4 vols. (New York: Macmillan, 1917), 1:388, 4:63. Clarence H. Danhof, *Change in Agriculture in the Northern United States, 1620–1870* (Cambridge: Harvard University Press, 1969), pp. 182–241. Frank Gilbert, *Jethro Wood, Inventor of the Modern Plow* (Chicago, 1882), pp. 1off. John S. Barry, *A Historical Sketch of the Town of Hanover, Massachusetts* (Boston, 1853), pp. 148–50. Frank L. Remington, "When John Deere Engineered Efficiency into Tilling the Land," *Christian Science Monitor*, August 21, 1971.

2. F. L. Newton, "Notes on Old Plows," *Agricultural History*, 17 (1933), 9.

3. George P. Smith, "Evolution of Farm Machines," Massachusetts Board of Agriculture, *1899 Report*, p. 249. James Grinnell, "Agricultural Implements and Machines," *1882 Report*, p. 240. Charles G. Washburn, *Industrial Worcester* (Worcester: Davis, 1917), pp. 130–36.

4. C. L. Flint, "A Hundred Years' Progress of American Agriculture," Massachusetts Board of Agriculture, *1873 Report*, p. 28. Frances DeWitt, ed., *Statistical Information Relating to Certain Branches of Industry in Massachusetts for 1855* (Boston, 1856). Paul W. Gates, *Agriculture and Civil War* (New York: Knopf, 1965), p. 281.

5. Clarence A. Day, *A History of Maine Agriculture, 1604–1860*, University of Maine Bulletin 56 (1954), pp. 229, 282. Clarence A. Danhof, "Gathering the Grass," *Agricultural History*, 30 (1956), 170. Jesse Buel, *The Farmer's Companion* (Boston, 1839), p. 125.

6. Charles L. Flint, *Grasses and Forage Plants: A Practical Treatise*, 5th ed. (Boston, 1860), pp. 342, 345. George P. Smith, "The Evolution of Farm Machines," Massachusetts Board of Agriculture *1899 Report*, p. 255. Percy W. Bidwell and John I. Falconer, *History of Agriculture in the Northern United States, 1620–1860* (New York: Peter Smith, 1941), p. 296.

7. Day, *Maine Agriculture*, p. 220.

8. Kennedy, *Agriculture in the United States*, intro., p. xxv. *New England Farmer* (January, 1857), 39.

PART V. WAR AND READJUSTMENT, 1861 AND AFTER

30. For Better and Worse

1. Federal Writers Project, *Vermont* (Cambridge: Riverside Press, 1937), p. 33. Earle Newton, *The Vermont Story: A History of the People of the Green Mountain State, 1749–1949* (Montpelier: Vermont Historical Society, 1949), p. 182. Warren R. Cochrane and George K. Wood, *History of Francestown, New Hampshire, 1758–1891* (Nashua, 1895), p. 273. Elias Mason, *Gazetteer of the State of Massachusetts* (Boston, 1874), p. 57.

2. Moses T. Runnels, *History of Sanbornton, New Hampshire* (Boston, 1882), p. 331.

3. Paul W. Gates, *Agriculture and Civil War* (New York: Knopf, 1965), p. 219.

4. Joe B. Frantz, *Gail Borden, Dairyman to a Nation* (Norman, Okla., 1951), pp. 51, 229–37, 264.

5. International Tin Research and Development Council, *Historic Tinned Foods*, pub. 85, 2nd ed. (Middlesex, England, 1939), p. 9. William Underwood Company, Watertown, Massachusetts, *The Red Devil*, 1 (April, 1968), 2–3; 2 (August, 1969), 3–9. Clarence Francis, *A History of Food and Its Preservation* (Princeton: Princeton University Press, 1937), pp. 9–11. Clarence A. Day, *Farming in Maine, 1860–1940* (Orono: University of Maine, 1963), pp. 28–32, 157.

6. United States Department of Agriculture, *1870 Report*, p. 317. Dirk J. Struik, *Yankee Science in the Making* (Boston: Little, Brown, 1948), p. 236.

7. Liberty H. Bailey, *Cyclopedia of American Agriculture*, 5th ed., 4 vols. (New York: Macmillan, 1917), 3:365.

8. Gates, *Civil War*, p. 198.

9. Edward H. Jenkins, *A History of Connecticut Agriculture* (New Haven, Conn., n.d.), p. 411. Charlotte A. Lacey, *An Historical Study of Southport* (Fairfield, Conn., 1927), p. 44. *New England Farmer*, 9:326.

10. Day, *Farming in Maine*, p. 119. United States Department of Agriculture, *1870 Report*, p. 402.

11. Harold F. Wilson, "The Rise and Decline of the Sheep Industry in Northern New England," *Agricultural History*, 9 (1935), 28, 29. *Genesee Farmer*, 24 (1863), 333.

12. Massachusetts Board of Agriculture, *1850 Report*, p. 402.

13. Eugene Graves, "A History of Maine's Nineteenth Century Beef Industry," M.A. thesis, University of Maine, Orono, 1967, table II.

14. Adrian F. McDonald, *History of Tobacco Production in Connecticut* (New Haven: Yale University Press, 1936), pp. 12ff. United States Commissioner of Agriculture, *1870 Report*, p. 451. Gates, *Civil War*, pp. 143, 145. J. M. Smith, "Tobacco and Its Culture," Massachusetts Board of Agriculture *1882 Report*, p. 168.

15. Edward Enfield, *Indian Corn: Its Value, Culture and Uses* (New York, 1866), pp. 60–65. Charles L. Flint, *Grasses and Forage Plants: A Practical Treatise*, 5th ed. (Boston, 1860), p. 338. Edwin Sanborn, *History of New Hampshire* (Manchester, 1874), p. 358. *Vermont Life*, 23 (1955), 64. Dennis J. Donovan and Jacob C. Woodward, *History of the Town of Lyndeborough, New Hampshire* (Medford: Tufts University Press, 1906), p. 478.

16. Stephen W. Fletcher, *The Strawberry in North America* (New York: Macmillan, 1917), pp. 126–30. Massachusetts Board of Agriculture, *1881 Report*, p. 15. Gates, *Civil War*, p. 374.

31. Discouragement

1. Albert Van Duzen, *Connecticut* (New York: Random House, 1961), pp. 250–52. Lee Benson, "The Historical Background of Turner's Frontier Essay," *Agricultural History*, 25 (1951), 59–82, offers a helpful analysis of the period.

2. Rollin Lynde Hartt, "A New England Hill Town," *Atlantic* 83 (1899), 572. Fred A. Shannon, *The Farmer's Last Frontier: Agriculture 1860–1877* (New York: Farrar, Rinehart, 1945), p. 418.

3. Vermont Board of Agriculture, *1878 Report*, p. 141. Massachusetts Board of Agriculture, *1890 Report*, p. 121.

4. Charles H. Merchant and Merton S. Parsons, *Farm Property Taxation in Maine*, Maine Agricultural Experiment Station *Bulletin*, 366 (Orono, 1933), pp. 268, 269.

5. Albert Smith, *History of Peterboro . . . New Hampshire* (Boston, 1876), p. 211.

6. United States Commissioner of Agriculture, *1870 Report*, p. 260.

7. *Homestead* (April 29, 1871), p. 404.

8. *New England Farmer*, 8 (1856), 523. Massachusetts Board of Agriculture, *1889 Report*, p. xvii.

9. Lewis D. Stilwell, "Migration from Vermont," Vermont Historical Society *Proceedings*, 5 (1937), 65.

10. Lois K. Mathews, *The Expansion of New England, 1620–1865* (Boston, 1909), pp. 229–44. Frederic Jackson Turner, "The Frontier in American History," American Historical Association *Annual Report* (1893), p. 143. Luther Burbank with Wilbur Hall, *The Harvest of the Years* (Cambridge: Houghton, Mifflin, 1927), pp. 1–12.

11. George B. Loring, "New England Farming," Massachusetts Board of Agriculture, *1859 Report*, p. 51. G. W. Atherton, "Future of New England Agriculture," Massachusetts Board of Agriculture, *1896 Report*, p. 112.

12. Bernard C. Steiner, *History of the Plantation of Menunkatuck and of the Original Town of Guilford, Connecticut* (Baltimore, 1897), p. 139.

13. Percy W. Bidwell, "The Agricultural Revolution in New England," *American Historical Review*, 26 (1921), 701. Van Wyck Brooks, *Sketches in Criticism* (New York: Dutton, 1932), p. 119. Stuart H. Holbrook, *The Yankee Exodus: An Account of Migration from New England* (New York: Macmillan, 1950), p. 268. Page Smith, *As a City upon a Hill* (New York: Knopf, 1966), p. 53.

14. Harold F. Wilson, *The Hill Country of Northern New England* (New York: Columbia University Studies, 1936), p. 150.

15. George Hill, "Market Gardening," Massachusetts Board of Agriculture, *1883 Report*, p. 104.

16. John Black, *The Rural Economy of New England: A Regional Study* (Cambridge, Mass., 1950), p. 20.

32. Adapt or Perish

1. Massachusetts Board of Agriculture, *1881 Report*, pp. 7–9; *1884 Report*, p. 19. Frederick G. Howes, *History of the Town of Ashfield, Massachusetts, 1742–1910* (Ashfield, 1910), p. 121.

2. Oscar E. Anderson, *Refrigeration in America: A History of A New Technology and Its Impact* (Princeton: Princeton University Press, 1953), p. 82. Earle Newton, *The Vermont Story: A History of the People of the Green Mountain State, 1749–1949* (Montpelier: Vermont Historical Society, 1949), p. 194. Massachusetts Board of Agriculture, *1888 Report*, p. xiii. New Hampshire Board of Agriculture, *1891 Report*, p. 92.

3. T. N. Adams, *Prices Paid by Vermont Farmers 1790–1940* (Burlington, 1944), p. 132. Massachusetts Board of Agriculture, *1895 Report*, chart opposite p. 48.

4. *Vermont History*, 23 (1954), 147. Vermont Board of Agriculture, *1900–01 Report*, p. 124.

5. Massachusetts Board of Agriculture, *1880 Report*, p. 9. *1883 Report*, p. xiii.

6. Clarence A. Day, *Farming in Maine, 1860–1940* (Orono: University of Maine, 1963), p. 59. New Hampshire Board of Agriculture, *1881 Report*, p. 357. Vermont Board of Agriculture, *1869–70 Report*, p. 174. Massachusetts Board of Agriculture, *1887 Report*, p. 161. Rhode Island Board of Agriculture, *1887 Report*, p. 108.

7. Massachusetts Board of Agriculture, *1880 Report*, p. 190.

8. Edward L. Trudeau, *Autobiography* (New York: Doubleday, Page, 1916), p. 184.

9. Massachusetts Board of Agriculture, *1887 Report*, p. 228.

10. Day, *Farming in Maine*, p. 84.

11. Massachusetts Board of Agriculture, *1895 Report*, pp. xxv, 192, 509. Massachusetts Senate, *Document 5*, 1893. Rhode Island Board of Agriculture, *1892 Report*, p. 14.

12. United States Department of Agriculture, Bureau of Animal Industry, *Legislation [re] Bovine Tuberculosis* (Washington, 1901). *Relation of Bovine Tuberculosis to Public Health*, bulletin 33 (Washington, 1901). Massachusetts House, *Document 1341*, 1897. *Homestead* (August 19, 1897), 104.

13. Vermont Board of Agriculture, *1895 Report*, pp. 189, 240. Massachusetts Board of Agriculture, *1896 Report*, p. 512. Jasper J. Stahl, *History of Old Broad Bay and Waldoboro*, 2 vols. (Portland: Bond Wheelwright, 1956), 2:383.

14. *New England Farm Finance News*, August, 1954.

15. *Homestead* (February 25, 1894), 227.

16. Ibid. (April 29, 1899), 552.

17. Ibid. (August 13, 1898), 151.

18. *New England Farm Finance News* (August, 1954). United States Department of Agriculture, Bureau of Animal Industry, *American Breeds of Fowls: The Plymouth Rock* (Washington, 1901).

33. How the Garden Grew

1. Edward C. Kirkland, *Men, Cities, and Transportation: A Study in New England History*, 2 vols. (Cambridge: Harvard University Press, 1948), 1:492. Helen Hamlin, *Pines, Potatoes, and People: The Story of Aroostook* (New York: Norton, 1948), pp. 102, 144.

2. *Food Marketing*, 31, no. 1 (1971), 5. Harold M. Bailey, "Vermont in the Potato Lineage Book," *Vermont History*, 23 (1955), 120. Michel Oren and Janet Greene, "The Only Potato Fit to Eat," *Vermont Life*, 15 (Autumn 1960), 57.

3. Emily G. Balch, *Our Slavic Fellow Citizens* (New York: Charities Publishing Committee, 1910), p. 240.

4. Clarence A. Day, *Farming in Maine, 1860–1940* (Orono: University of Maine, 1963), pp. 30, 32. Vermont Board of Agriculture, *1900–01 Report*, p. 24.

5. *Homestead* (August 13, 1898), 147. Edward Jarvis, "Traditions and Reminiscences of Concord 1779–1878," MSS, Concord, Mass., Public Library.

6. Massachusetts Board of Agriculture, *1877 Report*.

7. J. B. Moore, "Market Gardening," Massachusetts Board of Agriculture, *1873 Report*, p. 87. Richard Hittinger, "Irrigation," *1897 Report*. W. W. Rawson, ibid., *1891 Report*, pp. 104–35; *1882 Report*, pp. 95, 98.

8. Thomas G. Fessenden, *New American Gardener* (Boston, 1828), p. 152. *Farmer's Monthly Visitor*, 1 (1839), 170.

9. *Homestead* (March 27, 1897), 396.

10. Charles F. Swift, *Cape Cod: The Right Arm of Massachusetts* (Yarmouth, 1897), p. 284. *Homestead* (August 27, 1898), 198.

11. Day, *Farming in Maine*, pp. 93–98. Massachusetts Board of Agriculture, *1880 Report*, p. 105; *1881 Report*, p. 95; *1896 Report*, p. 413. J. W. Clark, "Growing and Marketing Apples," Vermont Board of Agriculture, *1895 Report*, p. 102.

12. Theodore Gold, *Handbook of Connecticut Agriculture* (Hartford, 1901), pp. 64–67.

13. Elizabeth Ramsey, *The History of Tobacco Culture in the Connecticut Valley* (Northampton, 1930), pp. 149ff. Federal Writers Project, *Connecticut* (Cambridge: Riverside Press, 1938), p. 115.

14. Day, *Farming in Maine*, p. 167.

15. T. N. Adams, *Prices Paid by Vermont Farmers, 1790–1940* (Burlington, 1944), pp. 19, 36. Liberty H. Bailey, *Cyclopedia of American Agriculture*, 5th ed., 4 vols. (New York: Macmillan, 1917), 2:425.

16. Raup and Carlson, *Harvard Forest*, p. 25.

34. Any Way to Make a Dollar

1. Jenkins, Edward H., *A History of Connecticut Agriculture* (New Haven, n.d.), p. 395; Dewey, Chester, *History of the County of Berkshire*, (Pittsfield, 1829).

2. Alonzo J. Fogg, *Statistics and Gazetteer of New Hampshire* (Concord, 1875), pp. 87, 378. James D. Squires, *Mirror to America: A History of New London, New Hampshire, 1900–1950* (Concord: Evans, 1952), pp. 15, 146. New Hampshire Board of Agriculture, *1891 Report*, p. 205. J. Bailey Moore, *History of the Town of Candia, New Hampshire* (Manchester, 1893), p. 444.

3. New Hampshire Board of Agriculture, *1891 Report*, p. 203. Vermont Board of Agriculture, *1885–86 Report*, p. 81.

4. Julius A. Ward, "The Revival of our Country Towns," *New England Magazine* (November, 1889), 245.

35. Agriculture Organizes

1. Clarence A. Day, *Farming in Maine, 1860–1940* (Orono: University of Maine, 1963), pp. 205–10. Massachusetts Board of Agriculture, *1898 Report*, p. 170.

2. Liberty H. Bailey, *Cyclopedia of American Agriculture*, 5th ed., 4 vols. (New York: Macmillan, 1917), 4:422, 423. Edward H. Jenkins, *A History of Connecticut Agriculture* (New Haven, n.d.), pp. 378–82. Theodore Gold, *Handbook of Connecticut Agriculture* (Hartford, 1901), p. 25. Storrs School, 2nd annual *Report* (1889), pp. 11–51.

3. Bailey, *Cyclopedia*, 3:337, 357, 365. Massachusetts Board of Agriculture, *1865 Report*, "Guernsey Cattle in America." E. Parmelee Prentice, *American Dairy Cattle: Their Past and Future* (New York: Harper, 1942), pp. 144, 238, 374, 385. *Homestead* (November 12, 1955), 14.

4. Ernest L. Bogart, *Peacham: The Story of a Vermont Town* (Montpelier: Vermont Historical Society, 1948), p. 355. Day, *Farming in Maine*, pp. 48, 54. Massachusetts Board of Agriculture, *1899 Report*, p. vii.

5. T. N. Adams, *Prices Paid by Vermont Farmers, 1790–1940* (Burlington, 1944), p. 128. Earle Newton, *The Vermont Story: A History of the People of the Green Mountain State, 1749–1949* (Montpelier: Vermont Historical Society, 1949), p. 194. Quinebaug Historical Society *Leaflets*, 2 (1901), 69. New Hampshire Board of Agriculture, *1891 Report*, p. 203.

6. Jarvis M. Morse, *A Neglected Period of Connecticut History, 1818–1850* (New Haven: Yale University Press, 1933), p. 226. Day, *Farming in Maine*, p. 183. *Homestead* (December 24, 1898), 709.

7. Bailey, *Cyclopedia*, 4:294, 297.

8. Vermont Board of Agriculture, *1896 Report*, pp. 110, 203. Day, *Farming in Maine*, p. 191.

36. The Farm Wife

1. Vermont Board of Agriculture, *1895 Report*, p. 125. Rhode Island Board of Agriculture, *1886–87 Report*, p. 159.

2. Julius A. Ward, "The Revival of Our Country Towns," *New England Magazine* (November, 1889), 243. Vermont Board of Agriculture, *1896 Report*, p. 195.

3. Emily G. Balch, *Our Slavic Fellow Citizens* (New York: Charities Publishing Committee, 1910), pp. 240–42, 329–30. Ralph Harlow, "The Pole in the Land of the Puritan," *New England Magazine*, n.s., 29 (1933), 162–66.

4. Alvan F. Sanborn, "A Farming Community," *Atlantic*, 79 (1897), 588–98.

PART VI. A FOURTH CENTURY

37. Seven Million to be Fed

1. Edward H. Jenkins, *A History of Connecticut Agriculture* (New Haven, n.d.), pp. 378–82. Connecticut Agricultural Experiment Station, *1910 Report*, p. 75; *1900 Report*, p. 322; *1916 Report*, pp. xviii, 323; *1919 Report*, p. 4. Wayne D. Ramussen, "Scientific Agriculture," in Melvin Kranzberg and Carroll W. Purcell, Jr., eds., *Technology of Western Civilization* (London: Oxford University Press, 1967), 2:341.

2. Rhode Island Agricultural Experiment Station, *1908 Report, 1910 Report*.

3. Connecticut Agricultural Experiment Station, *1916 Report*, part 4, p. 185. United States Department of Agriculture, *1925 Yearbook*, p. 447. United States Department of Agriculture *Experiment Station Record* for the period.

4. Richard B. Morris, *Encyclopedia of American History* (New York: Harper, 1953), p. 715.

5. Rhode Island Board of Agriculture, *1905 Report*, p. 222. *Agriculture of Vermont* for 1913.

6. Earle Newton, *The Vermont Story: A History of the People of the Green Mountain State, 1749–1949* (Montpelier: Vermont Historical Society, 1949), p. 190. Clarence A. Day, *Farming in Maine, 1860–1940* (Orono: University of Maine, 1963), p. 263.

7. Newton, *Vermont Story*, p. 195.

8. Day, *Farming in Maine*, pp. 65, 70. *Agriculture of Vermont* (1913), p. 78.

9. Vermont Commission of Agriculture, *1920–22 Report*, "Dairymen," p. 13.

10. Hugh D. McLellan, *History of Gorham, Maine* (Portland, 1903), p. 252.

11. Theodore S. Gold, *Handbook of Connecticut Agriculture* (Hartford, 1901), pp. 64–67. *Food Marketing*, 5 (1946), 3.

12. *Homestead* (November 12, 1960). United States Department of Agriculture, *1925 Yearbook*, p. 260.

13. Wilfred Wheeler, "Cooperative Work in Grading and Marketing Fruits," Vermont Commission of Agriculture, *Horticulture Report* (1920–22), p. 21.

14. *Food Marketing*, 26 (1957), 6. Day, *Farming in Maine*, p. 161.

15. Albert Benson, *History of the Massachusetts Horticultural Society* (Boston, 1929), pp. 409, 483. United States Department of Agriculture, *1931 Report*, p. 174.

38. An Artful Adjustment

1. Clarence A. Day, *Farming in Maine, 1860–1940* (Orono: University of Maine, 1963), pp. 140–48, 222. Vermont Commission of Agriculture, *1920–22 Report*, p. 12.

2. Connecticut Experiment Station, *1900 Report*, pp. 322–29. Adrian F. McDonald, *History of Tobacco Production in Connecticut* (New Haven: Yale University Press, 1936), pp. 18ff. Meyer Jacobstein, *Tobacco Industry of the United States* (New York: Columbia University Studies 26, 1907), p. 60. Elizabeth Ramsey, *The History of Tobacco Culture in the Connecticut Valley* (Northampton, 1930), p. 169.

3. United States Department of Agriculture, *1925 Yearbook*, p. 907. Massachusetts Board of Agriculture, *1915 Report*, part 2, p. 257. Daniel W. Wells and Reuben Field, *History of Hatfield* (Springfield, Mass., 1910), p. 235.

4. Paul Fox, *The Poles in America* (New York: Doran, 1922), pp. 61, 73. Ralph Harlow, "The Pole in the Land of the Puritan," *New England Magazine*, n.s., 29 (1933), 162–66.

5. U.S. *12th Census*, vol. 6, pt. 2, p. 281.

6. Federal Writers Project, *Rhode Island* (Cambridge: Riverside Press, 1937), p. 352.

7. *Food Marketing*, 22, no. 1 (1961), 9; ibid., no. 3, 29. Massachusetts Department of Agriculture, *1921 Report*, p. 57.

8. John W. Winslow, "Canning Industry of Maine," *Homestead* (January 19, 1901), 94.

39. Close of the Third Century

1. Earle Newton, *The Vermont Story: A History of the People of the Green Mountain State, 1749–1949* (Montpelier: Vermont Historical Society, 1949), p. 192. *Homestead* (December 1, 1900), 540.

2. J. H. Putnam, "Poultry as a Cash Crop," Connecticut Board of Agriculture *1920–21 Report*, p. 42.

3. United States Department of Agriculture, *Chronology of American Agriculture 1790–1965*, revision of 1965.

4. New Hampshire Board of Agriculture, *1905–07 Report*, pp. xii–xv; *1918–20 Report*, p. 53; Vermont Commission of Agriculture, *1916–18 Report*, p. 7. *Homestead* (August 4, 1900), pp. 108, 116. Rhode Island Agricultural Experiment Station, *1899 Report*, p. 115.

Index

Lowell, Mass., 170, 185, 189, 193, 226, 234
Lunenburg, Mass., 112, 135, 164
Lyman, W. W., 240
Lyme, Conn., 117
Lynn, Mass., 66, 72, 89, 230; shoes, 64, 138–39
Lyon, Mary, 180, 196

Machias, Me., 284
Machines, farm, 235–41, 289
Macomber, John, 211
McSparran, James, 85
Madison, Conn., 161
Maine: agricultural experiment station, 282–83, 297; Agricultural Society, 199; apples, 255, 273, 303; berries, 255, 304; Board of Agriculture, 199, 281; canning, 248, 270; cattle, 27, 64, 202, 256, 265, 301; Central Railroad, 262; Civil War, 245; creamery, 284, 300; dairy associations, 249, 283; Department of Agriculture, 306; education, 129, 196, 197, 246; emigration, 148; extension service, 298; forests, 27, 28, 37, 170; grain, 190, 275; Grange, 286; hay, 212; hogs, 209; Horse Association, 209; immigration, 99, 100; Indians, 9; population, 131, 136, 245; potatoes, 162, 215–16, 269, 306–7; poultry, 210, 267, 285; railroads, 189; settled, 26, 27, 39, 120, 128, 135, 320; sheep, 201, 251; ships and shipping, 137, 170, 188, 228; silk, 226; State Jersey Cattle Club, 283; State Pomological Society, 285; summer business, 279; vegetables, 309
Maine Farmer, 197
Mainwaring, Captain, 76
Maize. See Corn
Malbone, Godfrey, 111
Malden, Mass., 93
Manchester, Conn., 227
Manchester, N.H., 142, 191, 193, 226, 234
Mann, Horace, 180, 194
Mansfield, Conn., 169, 227
Manual Labor School, 198
Maple products, 170–71, 275–76
Marblehead, Mass., 61, 66, 137, 222
Market gardens, 138, 163, 217–18, 220–22, 231, 253–54, 270–72, 309

Markets: colonial, 20, 35, 63; English, 33–34
Marlboro, Vt., 87
Marryat, Frederic, 195
Marsh, George P., 323
Marshfield, Mass., 272
Martha's Vineyard, Mass., 138, 216; sheep, 85, 157; shipping, 36, 61, 62, 72
Mason, John, 27
Massabesic Lake, N.H., 279
Massachusetts: Agricultural Journal, 229; Agricultural Repository and Journal, 130; Ploughman, 197, 211; Spy, 197
Massachusetts, Commonwealth of: Agricultural College, 282; agricultural experiment station, 275, 282, 296–97; Agricultural Society, 162, 199; apples, 255, 273, 303; Board of Agriculture, 199, 265, 281, 284; Board of Cattle Commissioners, 264, 266; broomcorn, 167, 224; cattle control board, 247; corn, 150, 303; cranberries, 304–5; Dairy Bureau, 281; dairying, 132, 248–49, 261–62, 263, 264; Department of Public Health, 249; education, 194, 246; Education Commission, 194; forests and forest products, 229–30, 321, 323; fruit, 255; Fruit Growers' Association, 285; Grange, 286; hops, 165; Horticultural Society, 199–200, 233, 304, 305; libraries, 196; maple products, 275; market gardens, 222, 254; onions, 308; population, 136, 245, 256–57; potatoes, 269; poultry, 267, 268; Revolution, 124, 125, 126; roads, 131; sheep, 202; shipping, 137; silk, 169, 226–27; Society for Promoting Agriculture, 130, 205, 238; strawberries, 254; tuberculosis control, 264–66; vegetables, 309
Massachusetts Bay Colony: conservation, 94; Court of Assistants, 63; crops, 20–25, 47, 48, 73, 77, 80; emigration, 26, 28–29, 100, 128; exports, 35; General Court, 20, 24, 26, 33, 34, 39, 40, 41, 42, 43, 44, 45, 124, 125; housing, 25; labor, 24–25, 111; land system, 39–43, 99; livestock, 18–20, 24, 49–50, 84; plant diseases, 68; Provincial Congress, 123; settlement, 13–17, 39, 112, 320; to-

376 Index

Russell, John B., 163
Russell, Mass., 234
Rust, 22, 23, 68
Rye: colonial, 22, 23, 29, 30, 52,
67–68; export, 58; post-Revolution,
151, 190, 213, 253, 275
Rye, N.H., 188
Ryegate, Vt., 165, 167

Saco River, Me., 11, 27
St. Albans, Vt., 262
St. Johnsbury, Vt., 286
Salem (Naumkeag), Mass.: bridge, 131;
cattle, 12, 18; crops, 22, 78, 79, 222;
emigration, 28–29; market, 46;
pests and diseases, 68, 90; regula-
tions, 94, 106; Revolution, 126; set-
tled, 11, 12, 112; trade, 36, 50, 59,
72, 137
Salem Village. See Danvers, Mass.
Salisbury, Conn., 100, 160, 161; iron-
works, 97, 127, 137, 169
Salisbury, Mass., 26
Salisbury, Vt., 100, 161, 202
Salmon, Daniel, 283
Salmon Falls, N.H., 95
Samoset (Hobomok), 7
Sanborn, Alvan F., 290–92
Sanborn, Edwin D., 91
Sanbornton, N.H., 226, 245
Sandisfield, Mass., 203, 278
Sandwich, Mass., 26, 46, 67, 94, 95,
158, 178
Sandy River, Me., 284
Saugus, Mass., 37
Sawmills, 27, 37, 96, 323
Saws, 101, 103
Saybrook, Conn., 29, 48, 78, 117
Scab, 90, 306
Scales, platform, 241
Scaticokes, 79. See also Indians
Scholfield, Arthur, 132
Scituate, Mass., 36, 59
Scituate, R.I., 129
Scythes, 103, 172; snaiths, 185, 237,
239–40
Seaweed. See Fertilizer
Seekonk, Mass., 28
Sewall, Samuel, 69, 95, 165
Sewing, 241, 288–89
Shakers, 163, 222, 323
Shaw, John, 132
Shawmut Peninsula (Boston), 11

Shays's Rebellion, 135
Sheep: Brighams, 202; decrease, 302;
diseases, 90; distribution, 10, 50, 52,
83–86, 147, 157–59, 200–201,
251–52; export, 57, 86; otter sheep,
158; raising, 83–84; Saxonys, 201;
Spanish Merinos, 158–59, 200, 251,
322. See also Wool and woolens
Sheffield, Mass., 100, 230
Shelburne, Vt., 178, 284
Shelburne Falls, Mass., 198, 239
Sheldon, Vt., 278
Shipbuilding, 33, 36–37, 64, 126,
137–38, 170, 181
Shirley, Mass., 165
Shirreff, Patrick, 205
Shoes and boots, 51, 64, 138–39, 261
Shoreham, Vt., 202
Shovels, 103, 172, 239
Shrewsbury, Mass., 64, 130, 144
Sickles, 103
Silk, 168–69, 225, 226–27
Silliman, Benjamin, 143, 177, 196
Silliman, Benjamin Jr., 198
Silos, 264, 302
Simmons, Amelia, 130
Simsbury, Conn., 95
Skiing, 279
Slater, Samuel, 132
Slavery. See Labor
Smith, Joseph, 180
Smith, Sophia, 196
Smith, Theobald, 283, 297
Smith, Thomas, 100
Smith College, 196
Smithfield, R.I., 215, 239
Smith-Hughes Act, 298
Smith-Lever Act, 298
Smiths, 25
Smouse, Captain, 145
Smut, 67
Snaiths. See Scythes
Society of American Florists, 285
Southampton, Mass., 143
South County, R.I., flax, 73; poultry,
210, 267; sheep, 85, 157
South Deerfield, Mass., 308
South Glastonbury, Conn., 274
South Hadley, Mass., 191
South Kingstown, R.I., 85, 111
South Manchester, Conn., 226
South Oxford, Mass., 139
Southport, Conn., 251, 269–70

LIBRARY OF CONGRESS CATALOGING IN PUBLICATION DATA

Russell, Howard S.
   A long, deep furrow.

   Includes index.
   1. Agriculture—Economic aspects—New England—History.
I. Lapping, Mark.   II. Title.
HD1773.A2R872   1982   338.1'0974   81-51605
ISBN 0-87451-214-X (pbk.)   AACR2